Worldwide Acclaim for S. Wordrow's

I Love Me, Vol. I

"Daft fad!" —Trafalgar rag *(La Fart)*

"Remarkable!" —Elba Kramer

"'Tis it! . . . Ohoho!" —Sam Xmas

"You buoy!" —*Eel Glee*

"Hat up!" —Utah

"Now I won!" / "Now I won!" —*Games* / —*E Mag.*

"Tao to a T!" —Hannah

"Toss it!" —Tissot

"Must sell at tallest sum!" —Proctor Trot Corp.

"Sit on! Ah pets!" —Stephan Otis

Elk City, Kansas: "A snaky tickle!"

"So patient a doctor to doctor a patient so!" —AMA

"We Jew!" —*Semite Times*

"Aha!" —Okinawa Niko

"O! Go to Togo!" —Ogopogo

"Retract it!" —Carter

"Not nil!" —Clinton

"Sun ever! A bare Venus!" —*Tunisia Raisinut*

"Igniting!" —I

"Nosegays so manic in a mossy age, son!" —Mom

"Har-har! Rah-rah!" —Lon Nol

"Put Eliot's toilet up!" —*Avon Nova*

"Rail on, O liar!" —Q. S. Egg, Esq.

"Too bad I hid a boot!" —U Nu

"Art lusts ultra!" —Zeus, Fox of Suez

"I moan!" —Naomi

Seville: "Babel lives!"

"Never a foot too far even!" —Skooby Books

"A bash!" —Saba

"Sit on a potato pan!" —Otis

"Call Ida! Call a Cadillac! . . . A gas!" —*Saga*

"Here so long! No loser, eh?" —*Rio Memoir*

"Star Comedy!" —Democrats

"Swap paws!" —*Tactile Lit. Cat.*

"A daffodil I doff!" —Ada

"Droll!" —Lord

"Slob my symbols!" —*Snafu Fans*

"Bah!" —Ahab

"Re peekaboo boob: A keeper!" —Yrella Gallery

"A!" —Walla Walla, WA

"Wow!" —Ida Y. Vuelta

"The Ultima Thule of Doubletalk!" —Qaanaaq

"Dogstar gnocchi! H. C. congrats!" —God

I Love Me, Vol. I

S. Wordrow's
Palindrome Encyclopedia

being a

magic mirror,

master key,

and treasure

map to some

well-defined

cracks and

hot spots

in reality

(all-round trips)

arranged

alphabetically

from aa to

zzz–zzz–zzz

I LOVE

ME, VOL. I

revealed and interpreted by Michael Donner

Algonquin Books

of Chapel Hill

1996

Copy(right!) 1996
Rennodleah
Cimabue de Ubá
(Michael Donner)

Manufactured in the
United States of America
and the Most Serene and
Fresh Gnomedom of
Barbaria.

Published by
Algonquin Books of Chapel Hill
Post Office Box 2225
Chapel Hill, North Carolina 27515-2225

a division of
Workman Publishing
708 Broadway
New York, New York 10003

For permission to reprint palindromes in this volume, grateful acknowledgment is made to the holders of copyright, publishers, or representa-
tives named on pages 407–8, which constitute an extension of the
copyright page.

Library of Congress Cataloging-in-Publication Data
Donner, Michael.
    I love me, vol. I : S. Wordrow's palindrome encyclopedia : being a
magic mirror, master key, and treasure map to some well-defined cracks
and hot spots in reality (all-round trips) arranged alphabetically from AA
to ZZZ-ZZZ-ZZZ / revealed and interpreted by Michael Donner.—1st ed.
      p.   cm.
    Title on t.p. is a palindrome.
    ISBN 1-56512-109-0
    1. Palindromes. I. Title.
PN6371.D65   1996
793.73—dc20   96-6145
                                             CIP

10 9 8 7 6 5 4 3 2 1
First Edition

To Gray Argot*

*Dedication NOITACIDED!
That is, **To Gray Argot** is an inoffensive
replacement dedication. The original,
Dedicated to Pot "Det. Acid" 'Ed,
was killed by censors at night in Rio.

Note: Get On

You have our permission to skip this introduction, **so crank on in, OK narcos?** Jump in anywhere you like. Eat in either direction. Dress optional.

As you must already realize, Dear Reader, this is not a regular book, even if it looks and feels and behaves like one. No, it's actually an exceptional and fantastic sort of beast, a literal AMPHISBAENA and a real prodigy, a being much more two-faced, fork-tongued, and cross-eyed than any regular book could possibly hope to be. So, in all honesty, we should call it by a different name, say, a **Kooblai al-Book,** if you would, to suggest that it is rather more something from out of a dream or far kingdom. For us at least, it has taken on the character of a Moby-book as well, a great white tome and extended meditation, if not a fanatic quest. . . .

"Ah! A Baha'i Ahab! Aha!" you say?

No, that's an understandable and even a clever guess on your part, but we're not really either a Baha'i or an Ahab in particular (no more than you're a narc or a narco, except possibly in the sense of "wordplay junkie"), nor are we even any more plural than you yourself are, save perhaps when going in both directions at once.

It has occurred to us, now that the question of religion has come up, that all beings are really one mind, one God, and that she's therefore indeed black, and sometimes he is white and often even read, and that she, too, no more than he or half again as much, sometimes speaks in both directions at once just to make it perfectly clear who's saying what.

Now *that* is where we think this book, or nonbook, begins and ends, and we'd have said so sooner if we hadn't felt it was a good idea to soften the kiss.

· · ·

But for anyone wanting a little more orientation in such an admittedly strange universe as the one we have begun to present, we can tell you that two-directional writing, which was a practical basis and preparation for palindromism if not yet the full-blown manifestation of it, developed early in the history of writing. Early writers and readers, notably (but not only) our Mediterranean forebears, were for a time very happy to go in either or both directions, as well as up and/or down. They usually did this by traversing their rock or tablet or papyrus in a pattern called BOUSTROPHEDON, or "as an ox turns while plowing a field," that is, naturally, alternating directions with each word row. This was surely plodding work, unless they somehow managed to get fluent at it, which we doubt because they dropped it rather abruptly around 500 B.C., presumably as soon as they realized how much easier and more fun it is to maintain a single direction of flow, and to get a pause at the end of every row for a bonus. This was the birth, or rebirth, of reader-friendly writing. From then on, writing and reading have been perforce almost exclusively a one-way street, albeit not always one heading in the same direction.

So there is evidently an innate if untutored ambidextrousness in human nature, a gift for going "both ways," as they say in baseball. And this ability or talent, which expresses itself as an impulse here and an inspiration there, will not be denied or restrained by prevailing norms. Indeed, somehow it erupts in many people—and rewards those who allow or ply it. You may want to think of PALINDROMIC outbursts as a sort of cultivated dyslexia. In any event, it is a historical certainty that by no later than about the third century B.C., those people who were not able to get enough of this very primitive form of two-part harmony found themselves, willy-nilly or deliberately, *composing* it. And ever since, though the PALINDROME has had its ups and downs, to turn a phrase, people have generally taken great pleasure in relating to its symmetry and grace, have often admired its verve, and have been endlessly entertained by its elfin wit. Now and again they have even discerned that the reason PALS are so special in all these ways (and more) is that they are not just sentences or phrases or poems but are also living thought forms—real gnomes at play, truly rare and golden probabilities in motion, the flesh become Word, the world **deified**.

The classical joker who traditionally gets all the credit for being the father of the palindrome, and who appears at least to have been the inventor or an early practitioner of the palindromic sentence and verse, is SOTADES OF MARONEIA (or third-century-B.C. Thrace). He was certainly the palindrome's first recorded major light, and though history remembers him as something of a barbarian, he wrote, we are told, in both Greek and Latin. These two languages were, fortunately for him, a lot easier to compose palindromes in than are most of today's languages. This built-in ease is owed partly to their generally more reversible letter patterns; partly to their peculiar rules of syntax, which permit a more flexible word order; partly to their almost total natural avoidance of anything so distracting as word spacing or punctuation or dual letter types; and (at least in Latin's case) to a high tolerance or carrying capacity for things abstract, open-ended, imaginative, and even illusory.

Anyway, as you might expect (and as we are actually only guessing), people admired and laughed at Sotades' scurrilous, often coarse, often satirical palindromes, and soon it must have become clear (if it wasn't from the start), first to Sotades himself and then to others, that there was indeed an unusual power in them. Eventually (we continue guessing), he somehow must have lost his touch with this power, gotten disconnected from his source, and let his thought flow unhappily and foolishly enough to attract the wrath of the local despot, Ptolemy II, Philadelphus. Sotades' reported

NOTE: GET ON

offense was a lampoon—whether palindromic or not we don't know—on the occasion of the monarch's marriage to his own sister. Ptolemy, and this is recorded history, had Sotades rounded up, sealed in a lead box, and thrown in the sea. The event is widely thought to have been the end of Sotades. Yet, as he must know, he is down there eternal as Davy Jones or Narcissus, and dry to boot. Palindromic verses, though not exactly rampant and though sometimes not allowed, have been written quietly and called Sotadics ever since.

We could tell you more right here about the history of palindromes, but history is just one person's version of what he partly saw or, more often, didn't see. Moreover, you will find that the artifactual highlights at least (that is, the goodly 'DROMES themselves), so far as we are acquainted and/or in love with them and believe we may rightfully honor them in this format, are all here in this our nonbook somewhere or other, usually in an appropriate place, for you to find when you desire. Here, too, are PALINDROMISTS, ancient and modern, as well as indefinite definitions and important hot spots of the world. In that sense it is an encyclopedia (though by its palindromic nature a CASUAL rather than a complete one), and not only of our self-love. Like any collection, it and we happily have somewhere to grow.

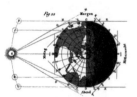

Ah, but where? Somewhere symmetrical, we're certain. For this nonbook is also a master key and treasure map to some cracks and hot spots in reality, well defined by cross-hairs (degrees of latitude and longitude, as in "X marks the spot"), to help us find them. The whereness of a palindromic name or place is vital to its identity, for it tells us where to go to dig for the promised or hoped-for treasure and how to continue our advance into the heart of symmetry (or into the cracks between the worlds). Palindromes not only issue from but generally exhibit and point or beckon toward any such place where we may expect additional outvasions from inner space to occur. So these points could be thought of as the gnomic navels or springs or acupressure points of the planet. And since palindromes are actually crosswords—words crossing in two directions—the geographic coordinates of palindromic places serve to "fix" them.

A more interesting topic for introduction is: Why indeed this preposterous nonbook at all, which perhaps really oughtn't to have existed? Well, to begin with, I—for again it is me here as well as we—wanted many happy returns. And I wanted to know the heart of symmetry. And I wanted to make a magic mirror and a master key and a treasure map, at least to such places as I myself had discovered or explored. And I wanted all-round trips. And I wanted something with a little reverse English on it. And most of all, really, I just wanted to make the world stop and laugh—to flood the joint with value—and I realized at a certain point that this manifest nonthing, the very one your eyeballs are by now possibly bulging at in disbelief, was my very best shot at fulfilling all the above desires because, as I have already thoroughly suggested, few things if any are as beguiling or charming or gracious as fine palindromes.

So, let the games begin, and on with the show—or, as we be jammin' in **Wordrow**, that peculiarly immersed and bubbly vernacular:

Nonwords, drown on!

Sotades Wordrow-Sedatos
(**HRH** Chameleon Rind, MD, I)
Royal Court of Barbaria
Twin Lakes Ct.
Twin Lakes, CT
6/9/96

I Love Me, Vol. I

aa (AH-ah). Geological term of Hawaiian origin, **aa** is a rough, cinderlike, generally dark form of volcanic lava resembling slag (refuse from the smelting of ores into metals). It has the distinction of being the premier palindrome alphabetically and creatively. Because it is produced by the expansion of trapped gases in volcanic sediment, **aa** looks as bubbly as it sounds and shouldn't be mistaken for the also-Hawaiian *pahoehoe* (puh-HOH-whee-*HOH*-whee *or* puh-HOY-hoy), a more flowing type of lava that has congealed into smooth, shiny, ropy forms. Not a flow so much as a lava splat or blop, **aa** is a small marvel—a hot spot caught turning inside out. Primal one.

a [. . .] a

Aa *also* **Aá.** From a Germanic word meaning water, akin to the French *eau,* and formerly the name of several rivers of the Celtic and Germanic lands. The modern **Aa,** a small coastal river of northern France flowing a mere fifty miles to the North Sea (via the town of Saint-Omer), 51°01'n/ 2°06'e, is the only river still bearing this once-generic name for river, and it is thus in literal translation the "River River," or "water in general" if you prefer. It survives in this form perhaps only because it is so inconspicuous, both in name and act, and yet it has somehow also gained the honors of being both the first place and the leading PALINDROMIC proper name alphabetically. Primal two.

Aa

AA through **AAAAAAA,** inclusive (designated "double *A,*" "triple *A,*" etc., presumably up to "septuple *A*"!). Here we have the full range of narrowest standard shoe widths, according to one now-forgotten and certainly somewhat dated source, which also offered **EE** through **EEEEEEE** inclusive to indicate in like manner the full range of widest standard widths. A contemporary reference source, also forgotten, still recognizes up to **AAAAA** and **EEEEE.** The more extravagant widths and narrownesses are perhaps in need of a reality check in a contemporary shoe store, for it seems peculiar today to run standard gauges out to such freakish, almost unimaginable extremes—though in being out there, whether formerly or still, they are not less well suited to this collection.

a.a. *or* **aa** *or* **A.A.** *or* **AA.** Once common pre-computer-age proofreader's ABBREVIATION for "author's alteration," especially as distinguished from a printer's error, "p.e." (or plain old typo). The two abbreviations were used, and are still used at times, in determining and indicating which of the two parties, author or printer, is responsible for and must bear the cost of making which revisions in a new draft or edition of a text (or other printed matter). Among several fairly common abbreviations of similar spellings but different meanings, this **a.a.** is perhaps the most signal one. (So fans of American Airlines and other **AA**s will seek and find their own meanings here.)

Aaa *or* **A'a'a.** Unofficial ABBREVIATION for Alaska. We like it because it is unofficial, and we figure that this is why Alaskans like it, too.

AAA. 1: ABBREVIATION for the American Automobile Association, among others. Usually called "Triple A." Light, streamlined, easy, comfortable, convenient. It bills itself as "the most trusted name in travel." We recommend the **AAA**'s annual *Road Atlas* for seeking out PALINDROMIC locations in North America, though the Gousha *Road Atlas*, for many years the best, is still a close second; using the two together will almost never fail you when you are out there in open country looking for PALINDROMES, though each of them should still be taken with a grain of salt. (See: **Salt an atlas.**) There is also the Rand McNally *Commercial Atlas and Marketing Guide*, a much more exhaustive, and much more ponderous, treasure-house. **2:** For nondrivers and/or non–North Americans, another noteworthy **AAA** is the airport code for Ararangúa, Brazil, alphabetically the world's first air destination.

Aa Junction. Whether of the road or railroad denomination we don't know, in Arkansas, given in both *Language on Vacation* and *Beyond Language* by Dmitri A. BORGMANN, who places it at the southern border of Johnson County (along the Arkansas River), south-southwest of Clarksville—but we can't find it on our maps, and he is the first to admit it was unpopulated as of 1965. Important? Well, it would be the leading PALINDROMIC place in the United States, if we could be sure it exists.

> **Aa** Junction.
> Leading palindromic place in the United States, if it exists.

aamusin : nisumaa. REVERSAL PAIR of Finnish words, which mean "in the morning" and "a wheatfield," respectively, according to BORGMANN, and which coalesce spontaneously in our mind, if not also in proper Finnish, to project an appealing scene from nature. For a fuller picture—a virtual haiku of proper Finnish growing out of this word-pair—see: **Nisumaa oli isasi ilo aamusin.**

a & a. ABBREVIATION (and not an ACRONYM) for "abbreviations and acronyms."

aba *or* **abba** (uh-BAH). **1:** Arabic: light, coarse, often striped fabric woven of camel or goat hair **2:** loose sleeveless garment made either from such fabric or from fine silk.

Aba. 1: city of Nigeria, 5°06'n/7°21'e **2:** town of China, 33°06'n/101°59'e **3:** town of Zaire, 3°52'n/30°14'e **4:** locality of Russia or Kazakhstan, it is not clear which, 51°18'n/ 83°47'e **5:** island in the White Nile, Sudan, 13°20'n/32°38'e **6:** arroyo on the island of Fernando Póo, Equatorial Guinea, 3°32'n/8°36'e **7:** beach of Guam, 13°15'n/144°40'e **8:** king of Hungary (1041–1044); **aka** Samuel. It appears **HRH Aba** has a clear title to being the alphabetically first PALINDROMIC personage and, though scarcely remembered by the dictionaries, is apparently unique among people in preceding even **Abba,** Father God Himself. (It also appears **Abba** may have punished **Aba** for this by taking his clothes—see: **A bared, nude . . . Aba.**)

A [. . .] A

ABA. ABBREVIATION for the American Bar Association, perhaps most notably, among many others. Pass the bar. For happiest returns apply at the Australian Boomerang Association. And for a copy of this volume, see a member of the American Booksellers Association.

ABA. Airport code for Addis **Ababa,** Ethiopia. We will be making our scheduled stop there shortly—all trays in the upright position—and we hope you will enjoy your stay in the greater **Ababa** area.

ababa (ah-BVAH-bvah). Spanish: red poppy.

ABABA. Common rhyming scheme for a five-line verse or stanza of poetry, in which the third and fifth lines rhyme with the first (these being symbolized *A*) while the fourth line rhymes with the second (these being symbolized *B*). **ABABA**'s recognition here raises the question of whether (and, if so, how) to acknowledge the possibly endless varieties of PALINDROMIC rhyme schemes. Perhaps it would be easy and interesting to select a good short poem to exemplify each common palindromic scheme. These poems could then serve as an area of contrast or transition with the rest of the book since they are only slightly and latently palindromic creations and easily distinguishable from *actual* ("hard") PALINDROMES—which, whether they are crafted or found objects, so obviously qualify as full-blown poems because they have sprung entire from the font of reversibility. (The objectives and possible benefits of comparing and contrasting the soft with the hard, the faint with the robust, or the minimal with the maximal palindromes—or poems— would be to scrutinize how various sorts of limitation produce divers expansions or excitations, to evaluate how little limitation is necessary for a desired growth, and thus finally to learn how to set a course for the freest, most enjoyable creation possible, the maximum gain without pain, fast-forward perpetual motion. Somebody should give us a grant.)

A [. . .] A

Ababa, Addis, *also* Adis **Abeba** (ABB-uh-buh). Capital of Ethiopia and, until the recent accession of Alma **Ata,** Kazakhstan, to the stature of independent-national capital, the only such capital containing a PALINDROME. (**Oruro** used to be the capital of Bolivia, and **Ava** of Burma.) An **Ababa** extra, a stage set for **Addis Ababa Sid, DA,** as also for MACARONIC exclamations of ¡**Adis Abeba Si! (Da!),** altitude 2438 m, 9°02'n/38°42'e.

a baba (uh BAH-buh). **1:** leavened rum or kirsch cake, usually made with raisins (sometimes called baba au rhum) **2:** the Polish or possibly Jewish granny (uh BUH-buh) first responsible for making this dessert (probably first formally identified as a PALINDROME in 1981 by Joaquin and Maura KUHN in *Rats live on no evil staЯ*, a delightful and probably unique collection of palindromes-only crossword puzzles!)

ABABA BABA. Title of a rum doggerel, reportedly by a Polish granny visiting Ethiopia (who was amazed to stumble upon one of her own baked goods in the market there).

> **ABABA BABA**
> **A baba, Sid,**
> **an item *I* did,**
> **I met in Adis Ababa!**
> **Ababa baba.**

It constitutes the alphabetically first PALINDROMIC poem and sentence we know of. In it are found a variant spelling of the Ethiopian capital and a feeble story line, but such things are easy to get away with if your grandson Sid, the very Sid you're telling it to, happens to be the public prosecutor there: **Addis Ababa Sid, DA.**

A bared, nude man named under Aba

Abababababa Press. See: KEBABIAN, Paul.

a bared, nude man named under Aba. And as for *why* he is so naked, possibly, see: **Aba.** The full phrase is attributed to Howard BERGERSON by Steven CHISM in *From A to Zotamorf: The Dictionary of Palindromes.* But we have checked

A [. . .] A

BERGERSON'S book, *Palindromes and Anagrams*, and can find in it no trace of this PALINDROME. Most likely CHISM alertly saw an opportunity to adapt the text from a similar yet distinct passage that occurs in a playlet by J. A. LINDON ("**In Eden, I**," which Bergerson does cite) and then proceeded to forget that not Lindon or Bergerson but he himself was its true author. It is, we realize, very easy to lose track of things like this, no matter how impeccable one's intent. And in the present case it was after all a gift rather than a theft that occurred.

À bas Saba. Thumbs down on the island in the Netherland Antilles. (Nah. We're not interested.)

Abash Saba. Humiliate the island. (Still no takers. Let's change the subject.)

A bash! Saba! At last! The island gets a good review. We go.

Abba (AH-buh *or* AH-baw). From the Aramaic or Hebrew word for father, both God the Father (as in Mark 14:36) and (often not cap) an honorific meaning father in eastern churches. Divine.

Abba. 1: town of Central African Republic, 5°20'n/15°11'e **2:** oil bore, a geological/geographical feature of Syria, 36°20'n/39°24'e.

AꟽBA (AHB-buh) (often spelled with the first *B* backward, to emphasize the symmetry). Name of the great Swedish **pop** group. Their hit record **"SOS"** has the distinction of being a PALINDROME by a palindrome or, one might say, a palindrome squared. (A second **ABBA** perhaps worthy of our fascination is the American Blind Bowling Association.)

"Abba dabba dabba dabba dabba dabba dabba" (Æ-buh DÆ-buh . . .), said the monkey to the chimp. Popular song lyrics, and possibly its title, c. 1950s. After an **abba-dabba**

this leads to an **abba-dabba** *that,* the two finally head off on an **abba-dabba** honeymoon. Strange but true. (We *would* kid you, but not about stuff like this.)

ABBREVIATION. Because even the best of abbreviations are by nature fragmentary and derivative, PALINDROMIC abbreviations are generally not so hot nor so obviously crazed as palindromic full words, names, phrases, sentences, or numbers, and so it is perhaps only natural that abbreviative PALINDROMES do not command the same degree of attention as do palindromes of integrity. The upshot of all this is that in this volume abbreviations may perhaps well be ignored entirely as second- or third-class citizens; or it may perhaps suffice, from any group of the same spelling or general character, to select a single most noteworthy or most valuable abbreviation to stand for the entire class; and/or it may be best to set abbreviations aside altogether as a special wilderness preserve for only the most fanatical of seekers. But in any and every case there is great leeway for personal choice and evaluation, for fancy and inspiration—and fortunately there's no arguing about taste.

Abeba, A(d)dis. Variants of Addis **Ababa,** the selfsame capital of Ethiopia; it is always a pleasure to get two or three PALINDROMES for the price of one.

ablata at alba (ahb-LAH-tah aht-AHL-bah). Latin for "banished but blameless" or "eclipsed but still white or bright." According to C. C. Bombaugh's *Gleanings for the Curious from the Harvest-Fields of Literature* (1890) (as reported by Tony AUGARDE in *The Oxford Book of Word Games*), this was the heraldic motto of a lady who was banished from the court of Queen Elizabeth "on suspicion of too great familiarity with a nobleman then high in favor." The lady's subtle remonstrance to her monarch, embellished as it was with an image of the moon covered by a cloud, may be the earliest recorded instance of an illustrated PALINDROME.

A [. . .] A

Able Melba. A peach we can toast; by BORGMANN.

Able was I ere I saw Elba. Sentiment, "attributable" to Napoleon Bonaparte (though probably never actually uttered by him, since his English was virtually nonexistent), that refers to the moment in 1814 when he reached Elba, the place of his disempowering exile. (Elba is the largest island in the Tuscan Archipelago and in the Tyrrhenian Sea, just off the west coast of Italy.) The "quotation" is a rare example of a perfectly good, indeed classic, English PALINDROME. (It is one of the three palindromes most often given as an example by the dictionaries, according to BORGMANN.) And its balanced perfection (see PERFECT PALINDROME) extends even down to the spacing between words and the alternation of capitalized and uncapitalized words. It is justifiably famous and, though some cognoscenti will fault it for being regular and thus primitive, it is in most eyes something of an ideal and a pillar of PALINDROMIA.

Able was I ere I saw Elba.

***ab ovo* BA.** Fantastic, indeed exceedingly whimsical honorary college degree awarded "from the egg"(!), that is, at or before conception. A good deal better than winning a mere full scholarship or even receiving an ordinary honorary degree, getting this diploma is the near equivalent (if not the literal accomplishment) of being born with a silver spoon in one's mouth. Naturally it makes a great gift certificate, and it has proved a surprising cash cow for an increasingly carefree **P.U. (Palindrome University). My! 'Tis "revinue"! (Mor' d'n *I* lap up!)**

Abstraction? : No, it carts BA. Seemingly a perfect encore or footnote to the prior entry, this unusual REVERSAL PAIR, comprising just a word that turns back, disintegrates, and then reintegrates before our eyes into a nicely clipped bit of dialogue, was, we believe, first observed and offered, though approximately and not in this exact form, by John POOL in *Lid Off a Daffodil.*

Abut a tuba. 1: useful PALINDROMIC euphemism: Be in or go to "an interesting place." **2:** first instruction for a new tuba student.

acá (ah-KAH). Spanish: (beckoning) here, hereabouts, hither, over here, to this general vicinity (where I am); softer than *aquí* (ah-KEE), which means to this very place where I am.

ACA. 1: truly inviting, enticing, beckoning (airport code of) Acapulco (see previous entry) **2:** ABBREVIATION of the American Carnivals Association (!), American Cat Association (!), etc. To these and many other curiosa and/or esoterica we were guided by Ralph DE SOLA's super *Abbreviation Dictionary.*

Acaca. Town of Somalia, 1°30'n/42°23'e.

acca (AHK-kah). Of Arabic origin: elegant medieval fabric of silk and gold, made mostly in Syria and taking its name from the Crusader city of Acre, now called Akko and situated in Israel.

Acca Larentia (AHK-kah lah-REN-tee-ah *or* lah-REN-chuh). Roman goddess of the fields and nurse of Romulus and Remus, the twin founders of Rome, often referred to solely by her first name. Her cognomen *Larentia* seems to connect her to the Lares, tutelary deities in nature and the hearth. But there is also a myth in which Romulus and Remus are nursed by a she-wolf. Is this then a different nurse, or an **Acca** transfigured into goddess-bitch? The meaning is obscure, but in either case the Roman sucklings, and all their posterity as well, have smacked loudly of both the feral and the majestic.

ACCA. ACRONYM for the American Correctional Chaplains Association. There is also **ACCCA,** acronym for the Association of California Community College Administrators, and so on, thanks again to Ralph DE SOLA's *Abbreviation Dictionary.*

A [. . .] A

Acrobats Stab Orca!

Acrobats Stab Orca! REVERSAL PAIR, originally a sentence by CHISM, that we think works best as shown here, that is, styled as a tabloid headline. (Knife-throwing high-wire artists blow stunt with killer whale at aquarium show. A minor mishap. All are well. The article snores. But it made for a grabby leader.)

ACRONYMIC PALINDROMES. The most famous of these, **radar** (for *ra*dio *d*etecting *a*nd *r*anging), is so memorable and effective because its palindromicity symbolizes the thing named itself, in action—that is, the letter sequence depicts the return of the bounced radio transmission to its starting position. Few if any other acronymic palindromes can claim such a devotion to duty, but palindromicity never fails to lend extra cachet or character, which is what acronymicity is also all about, so of course combining the two makes for more of the same and better. Other examples: **aha,** for "all have automobiles," and possibly also such relaxed things as **r 'n' r,** "rest and recreation."

Acro-Orca *or* **Acroörca.** High-breaching killer whale. See also: **Acrobats . . .** and **Namu had a human.**

Ada (EHY-duh). **1:** once-popular feminine given name, associated with Adela and Adelaide and possibly, though not definitely, derivative of the Hebrew *Adah*, meaning adornment or beauty. **Ada** is alphabetically the first (and yet is today becoming the rarest) of the many PALINDROMIC common names. She leads the in crowd, a cast of mostly familiar wonders such as **Hannah, Nan, Sis, Mom, Dad, Pop,** etc. But there is also an out crowd of perfectly neat couples such as **Noel** and **Leon** and odd couples like **Mike / Kim.** And there's even a far-out crowd where very strange folks and occurrences and comments such as **Al lets Della call Ed, Stella** are the rule. **2:** county of Idaho, whose seat is the state's capital and largest city (Boise), thus arguably the state's leading county, and thus perhaps the sort of place where one might actually hear the wistful mumbles **"O! Had I now won Idaho!"** but whose most natural and sustainable claim to greatness is as the only completely PALINDROMIC county in the United States—even if we do give the county of **Doña *Ana* a ñod** (or . . . **añ o.d.**) when in Las Cruces, New Mexico **3:** seat of Pontotoc County, Oklahoma; a small city, home of East Central State University, 34°46'n/96°40'w **4:** seat of Norman County, Minnesota, a small town in the middle of a smaller county, 47°18'n/96°31'w **5:** small town of Kent County, Michigan, 42°57'n/85°29'w **6:** small town of Hardin County, Ohio, 40°46'n/83°49'w **7:** hamlet of Conway County, Arkansas **8:** hamlet of Bienville Parish, Louisiana **9:** hamlet of Ottawa County, Kansas **10:** hamlet of Fillmore County, Nebraska **11:** hamlet of Lane County, Oregon **12:** hamlet of Mercer County, West Virginia **13:** small city of Serbia, 45°48'n/20°08'e **14:** small town of Ghana, 5°47'n/0°24'e **15:** small town of Okinawa, Japan, 26°44'n/128°19'e (right next to **Aha!** and not far from **Awa!**) **16:** lake of New Zealand **17: Ada,** Mount, on Baranof Island, Alaska, just south of (and likely visible from) **Sitka, AK ['T is?],** altitude 1380 m, 56°41'n/134°41'w . . . And herewith a salute to each and every **Ada** locality, as well as to the entire assembled sisterhood of sixteen or more **Ada** localities, for constituting the most numerous set of all PALINDROMIC place names: **A daffodil I doff, Ada.**

ADA. ABBREVIATION for **1:** the American Dental Association **2:** average daily attendance (often styled **ada**) **3:** airport code for Adana, Turkey. There are countless other versions and uses.

Ada: "Did Bob peep?" Bob: "Did Ada?" In which we meet a palindrome made up entirely of WORD PALINDROMES, and the John and Jane Doe of PALINDROMIA, **Ada** and **Bob,** who are algebraically interchangeable not only with each other but with any other PALINDROMIC names. See: FORMULAS.

Ada, Idaho.
Only completely palindromic county in the United States.

A [. . .] A

A daffodil I doff, Ada. (For a most plausible reason why, see **Ada.**) Credited to BERGERSON by CHISM, although we have found it only in J. A. LINDON's playlet, **"In Eden, I,"** quoted by Bergerson. Eloquent if daffy homage in any case.

Adam, I'm Ada. So Eve might well have ribbed Adam after his famous but stodgy intro line, **Madam, I'm Adam.** Yet it wasn't to be and so never was. Both BORGMANN and LINDON have incorporated this peculiar line into larger sketches. Compare Borgmann's **Sir, I'm Iris.** Same story all over again. But compare also—and this is evidently *why* the alternatives never happened—the much more convenient and simple **Eve!** as well as Borgmann's fully correct and reciprocal **Eve, man, am Eve!**

Adanac, Canada. A hamlet, **pop.** 17, near Unity, Saskatchewan.

A Dan acts Niagara War against Canada.

What *can't* happen in Palindromia?

A Dan acts Niagara War against Canada. Apparently a demonstration given by an ambitious master of the martial arts that harkens back to—or perhaps even reenacts!—a little-remembered campaign in the War of 1812. Alternatively, if even less scrutably, **Ragu's enacts Niagara War against cane sugar.** What *can't* happen in PALINDROMIA?

A dart's accordioned an adenoid, Roccastrada! Freak accident, as breathlessly reported to a Tuscan town. The use here of two eleven-letter words in a naturalistic syntactical arrangement is an accomplishment, even if we are left to wonder what it is, precisely, that has been accomplished by this dream poem.

Adaven, Denio Jct., etc., joined Nevada. For a sense of just how uncannily exact this dream sequence actually is, compare the previous few items for context and contrast, and then refer for hard facts to the following item and **Denio joined.** If you then have any doubt left (as our friend Neil and his school Eton once did) and are still inclined to bet against just how PALINDROMICally hot, nay radioactive, the entire state of Nevada is, see: **Eton, Caliente bet Neil a C-note.**

Adaven, Nevada (Æ-duh-v'n). Official name for what appears to be a cluster of miners' shacks (as indicated on the eponymous United States Geological Survey quad map) situated just below a picnic area in Humboldt National Forest, a few miles up Cherry Canyon from where it debouches into Garden Valley down around the Wadsworth Ranch mines, landing strip, and crossroads (population of all the above at or near zero, as best we can tell from here) in remotest Nye County. Yet this very possibly abandoned site constitutes the only locality-state REVERSAL PAIR we know of. (In today's upside-down and backward world, every state, indeed everywhere and everybody, could use one.) We look forward to driving Adaven's forty-two-mile dirt access road from State Highway 318, the closest paved road, at our earliest opportunity, in order to check out this candidate for U.S. PALINDROMIC capital. *Late flash:* After a ninety-mile tear on the dustiest of roads, a rock-punctured tire, summer heat, gadflies, thirst, refreshment, and fulfillment, we can now confirm the pronunciation and thriving existence of Adaven, at least in the form of "Canfield's Adaven Ranch, Adaven, Nevada," working Cherry Canyon on ghost Adaven's original townsite, which is still pointed at, as if it were a regular town, by publicly maintained road signs for more than forty miles in all directions.

adda. According to BORGMANN, an Egyptian lizard believed to have medicinal value. One odd **adda** is usually enough, though some say: **Add an even adda.**

Adda (AHD-dah). **1:** town of Kenya, 4°13's/39°05'e **2:** river of Italy from Lake Como to River Po via Lecco and Lodi, 45°08'n/9°53'e **3:** river of Sudan, via Angarbaka, a distant tributary of the Nile, 9°51'n/24°50'e.

A [. . .] A

ADDA. ACRONYM for the (*sesquipalindromic* would be overkill) Air Defense Defended Area.

Add an [even] adda. See: **adda.**

Addis Ababa Sid, DA

Addis Ababa Sid, DA (*or* **Abeba**). Fantastic Ethiopian federal prosecutor, possibly illegitimate issue of Sioux City Sue by Marcus Welby, MD, judging from stylistic evidence (and we know, for whatever it is worth, there is a Polish granny who visits him occasionally), and suspected comrade-in-arms ("PAL-in-'DROMES") of the if-possible-even-flimsier characters **Okinawa Niko, Lebanon Abel,** and that off-the-map and playful but forgettably bookish **Otter Bill Libretto.**

Adelberta : a trebled *A*. BORGMANN REVERSAL: a woman who's a natural soprano or **AAA** member.

Adelberta was I ere I saw a trebled *A*. A dizzy soprano loses her mind or name. It is difficult to let this one go so easily though, for she is the leading lady of BORGMANN's sestet of **Able . . . Elba** Echoes, which includes such other impressive voices as **Stressed was I ere I saw desserts.**

Adelbert : trebled *A*. Another BORGMANN REVERSAL: possibly a castrato, hopefully only a falsetto.

a detail of a foliated *A*. Say, a leafy serif, for example. From a central core and beginning place such as this, we can easily imagine things artistic and/or green developing in both directions, as in the following illustration spec for Simon's *Gold Leaf Made Simple* book: **Art: Si dips a detail of [a] foliated aspidistra.** (This particular example also readily reveals how central cores can sometimes be dropped out to good effect, built up, mixed, rematched, etc., thus: **Art: Si dips an aspidistra.** Or even: **Art: Si dips a detail of Ed's defoliated aspidistra.**)

Adida?! . . . If a shoe fits . . .

A dim or fond "No" from Ida? That is, exactly how ardently did she refuse? This PALINDROME, original so far as we know, was nevertheless actually cut and pasted back together from the ends of a sixteen-line poem we may not quote here but which is still, in our opinion, one of the finest PALINDROMIC poems ever written, the fairly X-rated "Ida Replies," by J. A. LINDON. (Nor is our almost complete truncation of the poem merely a mortified censor's abridgement; on the contrary.) Fortunately the text can be found in its entirety in BERGERSON's 1973 *Palindromes and Anagrams* (a book that, incidentally, is probably the world's greatest palindromic bargain, for it is still being sold at a 1970s price), and we are glad to be able at least to mark the poem's alphabetical place here and refer readers there.

adinida. A group of primitive protozoans lacking a transverse groove, according to BORGMANN.

¡Adis Abeba, Si!, Da! (*or* **Ababa**). Polyglot cry of rejoicing made by Soviet-Cuban forces entering the capital city of Ethiopia during their recent brief adventure in Africa, evidently styled after "¡Cuba, Si! ¡Yanqui, No!" and similar slogans. Some will object to or even disallow entirely the use of foreign words—and the MACARONIC blending here of Spanish, Russian, *and* Ethiopic will really get *their* goat—but others will see this and say only "Yes! Yes!—and let's go somewhere else for a change."

Adida?! . . .
If a shoe fits.

Admirable Del. Bar, I'm DA. Why this district attorney should be addressing himself to the First State's Bar Assn. in this peculiar way is a mystery until it is remembered that he is a member of it.

A DNA gun is in Uganda! Yoicks! (Life-*giving* gun makes debut there!) For some gratifying results, see: **Strafed amid . . . I made farts.**

Ad negates [a] set agenda. A commercial message cancels

A [. . .] A

a planned order of business. The KUHNS, so far as we know, were first to report this.

A dog! A panic in a pagoda! Likely by MERCER. Given by BORGMANN—and possibly BERGERSON, we are not sure—riddled by TERBAN, and illustrated in IRVINE, 1987, all according to CHISM. The text may refer to the **Asakasa** Pagoda of Tokyo and should be carefully distinguished from the next entry.

A dog, a pant, a panic in a Patna pagoda! By LINDON, according to BERGERSON. This PALINDROME is a masterful parody, and some may see in it a subtle critical evaluation as well, of MERCER's most celebrated gnomic utterance, **A man, a plan, a canal: Panama!** First, the original classic is almost referred to, flat out, as "a dog." And then there is the strong suggestion of much ado about so little, not only in the way the rhetorical cadences of the original are piled up, nor even in its blustery, spluttering alliterations, but most pointedly in the metrical imitation, or musical echo, of "a tempest in a (bleep-ity) teapot"—a phenomenon that the original may well have seemed in Lindon's ears to epitomize as it roared to its apotheosis in the public imagination. But we don't suppose there was anything mean or disgruntled about this jibe. Rather, it seems more a case of good-natured noblesse oblige, for Lindon clearly was top dog—and he will probably forever remain so. (Still, we are very excited to anticipate, and it will be extremely interesting to see and compare, Bergerson's forthcoming masterwork, more than twenty years in preparation.)

Adzam Mazda. A new-car dealership near Mt. Kisco, New York.

Aeaea (ee-EE-uh *or* ahy-AHY-uh). The island, believed to be modern Ustica, just north of Sicily, that was the legendary home of the sorceress Circe in the *Odyssey*. See also: **Aiaia.**

A dog! A panic in a pagoda!
Maybe the Asakasa Pagoda of Tokyo.

aenea (ah-EHY-neh-ah). Latin: **1:** an adjective meaning made of brass, copper, or bronze (in the neuter plural or feminine singular form) **2:** (as corresponding nouns) things brazen and even (if nonidiomatically) "a brazen woman"!

Aerate wet area. By the KUHNS: a natural, industrial-strength wall sign.

AeROKorea. With or without the *ROK*, this calls for a high-flying, pacific jet set.

Afa. Reportedly a "river of the South Pacific," at 17°29's/149°50'w, probably on Tahiti or a near neighbor.

AFFA. Unusual ACRONYMIC ABBREVIATION for **"Angels Forever, Forever Angels,"** WORD-PALINDROMIC slogan of the Hell's Angels motorcycle gang.

aga *or* agha (AH-guh). High official of the Ottoman Empire. Deriving from an Anatolian or early Turkish word meaning "grand" or "lord" (but possibly also from a related Hellenic word meaning "good" or "leader"), it is still used as an honorific in several Moslem countries. Among many important **aga**s through the ages are a hypothetical (Homeric) Agamemnon, Greek destroyer of Troy, who was perhaps originally a PALINDROMIC threesome, viz., **Aga Mem Non** ("Lord Woo Not," that is, Immovable, Resolute); and the **Aga** Khans, a hereditary line of religious leaders of the Shiite Moslems, of which **Aga** Khan III (**Aga** Sultan Sir Mahomed Shah, 1877–1957), upon whom much of the Ottoman Empire fell, is nevertheless best remembered by the dictionaries. **"Is it an aga saga?" "Na! 'Tis I!"**

Aga. 1: large town of the Nile Delta, Egypt, 30°55'n/31°10'e (*also* **Ajā**) **2:** small town of Norway, 60°18'n/6°36'e **3:** small town of Russia, 51°12'n/115°10'e **4:** small river of Russia, via **Aga** the town, a distant tributary of the Amur, 51°30'n/115°50'e **5:** island near Truk, South Pacific, 7°30'n/

A [. . .] A

151°44'e **6: Aga** Point, Guam, indeed the southernmost point of Guam, 13°15'n/144°43'e.

AGA. Airport code for Agadir, Morocco.

"Aga Gaga!" . . . **(A gag! A "gaga aga" gag!** . . . **Aga?** . . . **Aga gaga?):** Don't you get it, Highness?—Now we don't want to offend the Effendi, nor for that matter do we want to be insultin' the Sultan, so this one's "attributable" only to his former court jester, today seraglio eunuch.

"Aga Gag 'B'!" (A gab gag? . . . **Aga?):** Oh, no! Pasha doesn't get this one either!?—Attributable to the same, now mute, seraglio eunuch as the above.

aga raga. Musical accompaniment for an **aga saga.**

aga saga. All told (or tolled), the previous six entries, comprising at least a dozen distinct agas all together and amounting in Tandic-Icelurkish to the rough equivalent of one complete epic cycle. Compare also the Tinkish-Hurdu **aga raga.**

a gas saga. A possible appreciation of the foregoing item or items, this text originally served as the KUHNS' petrol epic, presumably an even longer story from 1973.

AGEE, Jon. Author and illustrator of *Go Hang a Salami! I'm a Lasagna Hog! and Other Palindromes* (New York: Farrar, Strauss, **1991**), and *So Many Dynamos! and Other Palindromes* (New York: Farrar, Strauss, 1994).

A Gloria air, Olga? Illustrated in IRVINE, 1992.

A global radar lab, Olga. By CHISM, in *From A to Zotamorf.* This must refer to the new weather satellite and the announcer at the Moscow Nightly News.

Aglow as Isis I saw Olga. By LINDON, according to BERGERSON in *Palindromes and Anagrams*. Atmospheric and mysterious, this item may actually be the herald or prophecy of the

A global radar lab, Olga.
The new weather satellite and the announcer at the Moscow Nightly News.

A ⌈ . . . ⌉ A

foregoing one! A comparison of the two styles of lightning bolt reveals that although both may be separated cleanly (namely, at matching word breaks) into a beginning, middle, and end segment, still the more-expert Lindon's apparently effortless and seamless continuity of flow stands in some contrast to CHISM's more rugged and modular, less articulate but still radiant semantic display. (And of course we mix apples and oranges to compare a perfectly literate sentence or poem with a perfectly clipped telegraphic note or phrase or perfectly epic epithet.)

A Goth saw Ada wash toga. Illustrated in IRVINE, 1992.

A goy did yoga. (He was a Hindu actually.)

A goy did yoga.

a goyin : niyoga. REVERSAL PAIR by BORGMANN, in which a Buddhist novice, not yet an ordained monk, is assigned . . . ultradenominationally . . . a task in Hindu law!

aha. Surprisingly clued "a sunk fence" by BORGMANN. Perhaps a version of the more standard *ha-ha*, a type of land-scaped moat or walled ditch familiar to Jane Austen readers.

aha! (ah-HAH). Exclamation of **1:** surprise **2:** triumph **3:** pleasure.

Aha. 1: Small town of Okinawa, Japan, 26°43'n/128°17'e (see **Aha-Ada-Awa**) **2:** mountains on Botswana-Namibia border, 19°45's/21°00'e. Borderlands generally being no-man's lands and cracks between worlds, what surprises, what triumphs, and what pleasures must lie in wait for us on our field trip to the remote **Aha** range! (**P.U., sir! A fast safari's up!**)

Aha-Ada-Awa Triangle. The Japanese town of **Aha** is right next to the town of **Ada** and not far from the town of **Awa,** which together form a tight PALINDROMIC town triangle only a few square miles in area—upon which a new sort of Great Pyramid may be imaginatively constructed with the weirdly

A ⌈ . . . ⌉ A

significant and appropriate letter *A* forming or occupying all the angles and the remaining letters of these towns, *H, D,* and *W,* denominating the edges that descend from the apex to each of the towns at the base. Such a surprising, triumphant, and pleasurable conception is a vast improvement upon existing pyramid and triangle mysteries, for here, instead of nasty mummies' curses and unnatural disappearances, we have only the thoroughly agreeable elfishness of the local tour guide, **Okinawa Niko,** to deal with.

aha. ABBREVIATION *and* a rare perfect ACRONYM for "All have automobiles."

Ahab! Aha! "Attributable" to Moby Dick. See: following entry, **Bah! Ahab!,** and **"Note: Get On,"** p. ix.

Ah! A Baha'i Ahab! Aha! For his miraculous conversion, see: **"Note: Get On,"** p. ix.

A Ham of Omaha

Ah! A Mayan on a Yamaha! Yucatan scene graciously contributed by CHISM.

A Ham of Omaha. Direct from the stockyards, a brand of distinction.

Ah, Aristides opposed it, sir, aha! BERGERSON credits MERCER as the probable composer, and we may guess that the Aristides referred to is Aristides the Just, Athenian military and political leader of the fifth century B.C., who is remembered for having opposed the Persian army at Marathon in 490, for having opposed his rival Themistocles, who banished him in **484,** for having opposed the Persians again under Xerxes at Salamis in 480 and Plataea in 479, and who indeed appears to have loved to oppose; but there are also Aristides of Thebes, a fourth-century-B.C. painter; Aristides of Miletus, a second-century-B.C. writer; Aristides of Athens, a second-century-A.D. philosopher; and Aristides of Mysia, a second-century-A.D. rhetorician to consider. So, among many plausible directions in which to seek a context and meaning for the full quotation, one good one anyway is: the full and somewhat formal response, initially self-assured and finally triumphant, of a well-prepared student responding to his schoolmaster's challenging examination question: "Please give the name of a Greek general who opposed the Persian army."

Ahem! It's time. Ha! By CHISM. (Yes, that last one was a bit long.)

Ah, me! O Poem! Ha! A triumph! Credited by CHISM to *WORD WAYS*.

Ah, Sasha! By CHISM—or *WORD WAYS*—though *which* is not clear; nor does it greatly matter.

Ah, Satan! : Natasha. REVERSAL PAIR, in which, as BORGMANN observes, a Russian "Christmas child" is, more or less, turned into its opposite. See also (or skip also) the following entry.

Ah, Satan . . . Natasha. Various items beginning and ending thus, *scratched*, of which the most likable, for being the least involved, was **Ah, Satan sees Natasha.** (This possibly by MERCER.) While omitting them from our collection, we still do take account of this relatively famous FAMILY of PALINDROMES whose meanings nevertheless are usually so ridiculous or of such questionable taste that only their place is marked here and only for purposes of developing contrast VALUE, promoting CASUALness, and precluding any possibility of endedness or exhaustiveness in this work, once and for all.

Ah, tag Agatha. Right. She may be more fun than Natasha and Sasha combined.

"Ah, Wyoming is a sign I'm 0."—YWHA. Note the rare zero, here pronounced "oh," as this text could only be sung to the tune of "Bloody Mary," and only by Jewish girls traveling cross-country to or from summer camp or college, in

A [. . .] A

celebration of the complete absence of the YWHA from this part of the world. (And YWHA therefore may be scanned "why-DUB yea-CHE.")

aia (AHY-uh). A Portuguese mammy and the mother of the Hindi **aya** (*or* ayah), the name for a native nurse or maid in British colonial India, all being descendants of a Latin (word for) granny, *avia.* This thin nurse is not to be confused, or is perhaps very much to be confused, with the fatter but also Portuguese, also Oriental, also PALINDROMIC, also three-lettered, also two-*a*ed, also wet-nurse **ama.**

aiaia. Variant of *aiaiai,* or roseate spoonbill, according to BORGMANN.

Aiaia. 1: river of the South Pacific, at 17°51's/149°15'w, coordinates that, for lack of a good chart, we would guess are probably on Tahiti or a nearby island **2:** (ahy-AHY-uh) transliteration into English of an originally Greek name for the more usually Latinized **Aeaea,** island home of the nymph Calypso in the *Iliad*—and thus by every reckoning a highly suitable haunt also for the similarly Westernized, Homeric nymph **Enone** (*also* Oenone, Oinone).

aibohphobia (AHY-boh-*FOH*-bee-uh). Irrational fear of PALINDROMES or other reversibilities, the faintest of hang-overs from Blake's "dread symmetry." This word is the *favorite* of several America Online users. Any fear of being over-whelmed or stressed by duality or symmetry may be set to rest by the realization that the two sides or "halves" of every-thing, right down to and including our physical selves, though so near to matching perfectly, are in both big and little ways wildly incommensurable. It is reassuring also to remember that we, like everything dual, rarely if ever actually fork completely in two but are held together, and moreover that we, and everything, are in reality proceeding very effectively and comfortably as *one*—no matter how it may seem.

A [. . .] A

Aid Acadia. Assist French Canada and/or Louisiana and/or that fantastic national park in Maine. The KUHNS have also made this appeal.

Aidia. Village of Papua New Guinea, 7°46's/144°08'e.

Aid, IA. See: **PRP.**

Aid nine men, India. But who and why and how, it will be hard to say—she has so many to choose from.

Aimed a cat at Academia. But it slept through the SAT (and may try again in the spring).

ainamania. 1: a love for those hairy, northern Japanese aborigines **2:** love of (having one's head up) one's bum **3:** love of having one's head up the crack between the worlds **4:** the word for PALINDROMANIA in Palindromese.

Aioia. Island, near Gambier Island, South Pacific, 23°06's/134°50'w.

Air-a-Bra, by Barbaria. A hot new fashion statement, a design house, or a state of mind. Barbaria can also be a country . . . a most serene and fresh gnomedom or kingdom, as it turns out, whose maharajah is the highflier met with just below.

Air Abraham (Maharbaria). Aka The Planes of Abraham, official airline of the above-mentioned Gnomedom of Barbaria (and the royal airline of its above-mentioned maharajah), serving the homeland (and the head) of the above state of mind and design house. A modern-day magic carpet known for high-altitude, high-speed flights with and to oracular seats.

Air an aria. Naturally. By CHISM.

air > aria. Change of tune, English to Italian, caught by the KUHNS.

Aibohphobia

A [. . .] A

Air IA. Another fanciful airline, say, one with commuter service from Des Moines to Chicago and Omaha.

Air of *UFOria*. Any of the several country-and-western songs (such as "I've Always Been Crazy but It's Kept Me from Going Insane" or "That's What Happens When Two Worlds Collide") from a Cindy Williams UFO comedy by this clever name.

Air IA.
Commuter service from Des Moines to Chicago and Omaha.

Airy Syria. By the KUHNS; a delightful travel slogan and poster title.

Aja. 1: village of Peru, 14°49's/74°57'w **2: Ajā** (or maybe **Aga**), large town of Nile Delta, Egypt, 30°57'n/31°17'e **3: Aja** Jabal, mountains of Saudi Arabia.

Aja. Album and song by 1970s rock-and-roll band Steely Dan.

AJA. 1: ABBREVIATION for the American Jail Association (!) **2:** airport code for Ajaccio, Corsica.

ajaja ajaja. According to BORGMANN, and via Funk & Wagnall's *Unabridged Dictionary*, one of a number of possible scientific names for the roseate spoonbill, a wading bird related to the ibis. Perhaps the name is an imitation of the bird's low croaking or clucking sound. For another take, see also: **aiaia.**

Ajja. Village of Jordan, 32°22'n/35°12'e.

Aka. 1: village of Togo, 7°49'n/0°40'e. **2:** river of Japan, into Sea of Japan via Tsuruoka, just north of lesser **Ara** River, 38°54'n/139°50'e **3:** river of Zaire (unconfirmed).

aka. ABBREVIATION for "also known as"; also known as American Kiteflyers' Association (when in uppercase).

Akaka Falls. Waterfalls and state park of Hawaii, located on the slopes of Mauna Kea, on the "Big Island," near Honomu, 19°52'n/155°09'w.

Akasaka (AH-kuh-SAH-kuh) *or, familiarly, **aka** just* **Aka** (AH-kuh). Tokyo nightlife district.

akirema : Amerika. Esperanto REVERSAL PAIR reported by BORGMANN, together suggesting "acquisitive America."

Akka. 1: small town of Morocco, 29°22'n/8°14'w **2:** locality of Mali, 15°24'n/4°11'w **3:** locality of Sudan (unconfirmed) **4: 'Akka,** an ancient site of Jordan, 32°15'n/35°53'e.

AK's Alaska. Must mean either the real Alaska (elusive) or else somewhere very far out or very far north, such as the North Slope, Coast, or Pole. Compare: **Aaa.**

ala (AH-luh). Biological term, from the Latin word for a bird's wing. An ala (plural *alae*) can wing it and become any winglike structure or part, such as an earlobe or the membranous border of some seeds (or the following flock or wing of entries all sharing this extremely common spelling).

Ala

Ala. 1: village of Chad, 9°42'n/19°03'e **2:** village of Italy, 45°45'n/11°00'e **3:** headland of Italy, 42°48'n/10°43'e **4:** islet of Celebes, 0°22'n/120°58'e **5:** river of China, 42°42'n/89°12'e **6:** river of Uganda **7: Ala** Kylä, the name of four different villages of Finland **8: Ala** Dag *or* Dagh, mountains of Turkey (there is understandably a good deal of confusion surrounding this entry, which appears to be the name of no fewer than five different mountains and two different mountain ranges) **9: Ala** Shan, mountain range and desert of Inner Mongolia **10: Alà,** Monti di, mountain range of Sardinia, Italy, 40°40'n/9°14'e **11:** a nearby village, **Alà** dei Sardi, 40°39'n/9°20'e **12: Ala** di Stura, small town of Italy, 45°19'n/7°19'e, situated on **13:** the Stura di **Ala** river. The last two together (**Ala di Stura on Stura di Ala**), however strange or convoluted their meaning may be (we don't know), do produce a neat reversal of words, or WORD PALINDROME (supported, in this case, by palindrome word pillars), and though of outlandish mien, this specimen is essentially just like the more domestic **all for one and one for all.**

à la *or* **a la** (AH-LAH). From the French (with *mode de* understood), "in the style or manner of," or "in accordance with."

Ala. ABBREVIATION for Alabama, arguably the nation's most PALINDROMIC state. (West Virginia, Texas, Nevada, and even Connecticut would have every right to disagree.) See also: **At Alabama, I am a balata; A Ma, Balaam: Ma Alabama!;** and **I am a Balaam's ass as "Ma Alabama, I ⌈the First⌉."**

ALA. **1:** ABBREVIATION for American Library Association. (CHISM and others have even been calling for an **ALA Gala.**) **2:** airport code for Alma-**Ata,** Kazakhstan.

ala-ala. BORGMANN clues this, more than a bit mysteriously, as "Memory: a gift to our language from the Philippines." Still, we may remember and graciously accept the gift in the style of Alabama and on behalf of the dozens of other *ala*s of all descriptions already given above.

Alagala. Village of New South Wales, Australia, 32°24's/ 147°42'e. This is where the **ALA Gala** should be held.

Al Ahram **: marhala.** REVERSAL PAIR by BORGMANN, in which a leading newspaper of Cairo fits or is fitted (actually retro-fitted) into an Arab measure equal to eight farsakhs. At least it seems to be fitting, in a very general sort of way.

alala. Thanks to BORGMANN we have: **1:** Hawaiian raven **2:** war-cry of the ancient Greeks **3:** type of Galician folksong **4: Alala,** primitive Babylonian deity.

¡A la meta, Ugo! ¡Guatemala! (ah-lah-MEHY-tah OO-go, GWAH-tehy-*MAH*-lah!). Spanish: "⌈Take it⌉ to the goal, Hugo! ⌈Hooray for⌉ Guatemala!" Cries heard at one of those frenzied Central American soccer championships.

A ⌈ . . . ⌉ A

Alan Alda stops racecar, spots ad: "Lana — L.A." Attribution unknown, reported by John JENSEN. Celebrity PALINDROMES were all the rage in the early nineties. This telegraphic example illustrates well how any small novelty (such as **Alan Alda . . . ad: "Lana — L.A."**) can be very nicely fleshed in or, one might say, wired, with the help of timeworn elements; and it also uses the modular style of construction, normally a somewhat limiting proposition, to very good effect.

Alan Alda stops racecar, spots ad: "Lana—L.A."

"Alcuin or a Camelback" OK cable macaroni!— UCLA. New talk show or sitcom, in which Charlemagne's great advisor rises again via a Phoenix channel, gets a favorable review on the Coast.

Alice, çà va ceci-là! French toast (Sissy-lah?): "Here goes this one there!"

Ali, name Manila. Why, soytainly. It'd be a thrilla.

Alla, Al. Mountain of Saudi Arabia, 15°03′n/45°52′e.

álla (AHL-luh). Italian: **1:** hall or alcove **2:** preposition equivalent to the dative feminine singular and meaning "to the," "by," "according to," or "in the style of."

allá (ah-YAH). Spanish: there, thither, to that place (where I am not). Compare: **acá**.

álla allá (AHL-uh ah-*YAH*). Italian-Spanish MACARONIC identical-twin REVERSAL PAIR and spontaneous semantic antic: "according to that place" . . . meaning styled with those crazy mix-and-match accent marks that they use only there with such flair, to exhibit the most exotic and marvelous of symmetries. A very far province of PALINDROMIA indeed.

Allah, lave Valhalla! CHISM credits BERGERSON, who credits John McClellan, who explains: "A pious Moslem speaks."

A [. . .] A

But, for us, it is the spirit of Islamic-Norse interdenominationalism that is especially likable here, and also the quaint demand within the prayer for a *clean-up of Heaven*!

Allah (Lawd!) eyed Walhalla. And He saw that this Plateau/Overlook on the North Rim of the Grand Canyon was good. So, too: **Allah lawded Walhalla.** Compare: **Allah, lave Valhalla.**

Allah notes a Seton Hall A.

Allah notes a Seton Hall A. Making the Dean's List at this Catholic College in New Jersey does not go unnoticed by God, whoever He is. Conversely, or perversely, this reminds us of the true case of someone's failure to be graduated from divinity school because their thesis was lost.

Allar munum ralla. Icelandic: "We shall all have a wild time." Attested to by BORGMANN.

Allegation? No, I tag Ella. Possibly by BORGMANN. Ella, my missing solicitor, will be coming up in a moment, and she will make the allegation. See also: **All erotic . . . Ella.**

Allen I. Gales : selaginella. REVERSAL PAIR by BORGMANN, in which a mysterious personage—seeming for all the world like a CIA type, but it's hard to be sure—jumps fully inflated from a sort of "resurrection plant."

Allen : Nella. REVERSAL PAIR of given names, by BORGMANN. Compare: **Leon Noel.**

All erotic, I lose ⌈lame female⌉ solicitor Ella. By LINDON, whom BERGERSON crowned Major Muse of the English PALINDROME. This surreal example is widely loved and recited. It is our guess that the following item, representing perhaps a bit of a syntactic refinement though probably not a semantic one, was derived from this slightly longer text rather than vice versa, and that **Allegation? No, I tag Ella** must have come first of all, and this by a long shot—and probably not really even in a line of descent! Under scrutiny, all three of these *all(/)e-* . . . *Ella* developments together reveal somewhat how palindromes, just like chess games and other living things, grow and evolve by all manner of surprising twists, fits, and starts. Here the leading element is probably *solicitor*, which virtually produces the pairing *erotic I lose* . . . *(-e) solicitor E-*. These two primary fragments, though both reversible and linkable in either direction, are nevertheless in the actual outcome supported and bridged by an additional or secondary element *(-e) lame femal(e)*. Finally, the grotesque but promising assemblage *erotic, I lose lame female solicitor E-* is closed and completed by a marriage of convenience into the *all(/)e-* . . . *Ella* family. The combinative sequences may vary, but usually they are all an outgrowth, or at least can be reviewed as a probable outgrowth, of the palindrome's longest single word, in this case *solicitor*. And yet, after all that, one can also see that the real genius of this development was just as likely none of the above but was instead the brilliant question: if *all erotic*, then what? Then *all erotic I lose* [or *lost*] *(-) solicitor Ella*, at least! That is the lightning, and the simple reclosure *lame female* then becomes a close, almost immediate thunderclap. (This analysis barely glimpses Lindon's magnificent double-barreled selectivity/creativity.)

All erotic, I lose my lyme solicitor, Ella. Probably by MERCER. (See also the previous item.) We take it that "lyme solicitor" is a Briticism whose exact meaning eludes us, but it feels well chosen in any case. (As to which came first, *my lyme* or *lame female*, we imagine the latter was the former, but both are at least by now stock items on the *-e* closure shelf, as are, say, *it*[,] *tie* and *babe* or *rare*.) Moreover the present is a good opportunity to report that the cause of the uncertainty in this and many other of our shaky attributions to Mercer lies perhaps partly, we are guessing, in his own modest indifference as a collector-composer; perhaps partly, too, in an intuitive apprehension that good short PALIN-

DROMES pop from their creators as free spirits in a free culture to become proverbial overnight, instant folklore (the more so today, what with cyberspace), their origin known only to a few cognoscenti, perhaps; and certainly also in BERGERSON's inability to pin down which items in Mercer's long inventory were actually his original creations. We assume, as did Bergerson when he published them in 1973, that the vast majority of the uncertain ones *are* by Mercer.

Al lets Della call Ed, Stella. Another neat one, probably by MERCER and very widely recited. Note that the speaker, unnamed, makes yet a fifth party to this swinging menagerie. Illustrated but with a key difference (no comma!) in IRVINE, 1987.

Al, let's go hog Stella. By POOL. Hard to imagine but not necessarily a bad idea. (Could be a rough translation into English of a dolphin mating-coalition song.)

Al lets no pets step on Stella. By CHISM. Good modular splice job, and she appreciates it, too.

All for one and one for all

all for one and one for all. A nice example of a WORD PALINDROME, with all seven words elegantly matched up in three-letter lengths. Also worthy of notice is the occurrence and interaction here of the peculiar set of elements "all-one-3-7." These echo mysteriously, or perhaps recapitulate, the already mystifying arithmetical combinations that occur in analyzing the principal NUMBERDROMES: $11 = 1 + 3 + 7$; $101 = 1 + (3 + 7)(3 + 7)$; $1001 = 1 \times 7 \times 11 \times 13$ (!); $10,001 = 73 \times 1 \times 137$ (!!); $100,001 = \ldots$ whereupon one may well hypothesize a riot of growth, an endless spiral of stunning coincidence, a place where the vibes are sympathetic and things feather together in an extravagantly obliging version of reality called, in shorthand, Universe 137. Hair-raising!

All I do pass is sapodilla. Comment, after Ozymandias, heard on a large chewing-gum plantation.

A ⌈ . . . ⌋ A

Allí trota la tortilla (ah-YEE T*R*OH-tah lah-to*r*-TEE-yah). Spanish: There goes [trots, runs, chases about] the tortilla or omelette. Some possible idiomatic translations are "That's the way the cookie crumbles," "That's how it goes," "There goes lunch," and "Here comes lunch," but these are merely guesses, for which no confirmation has been found. Authorship of the pure Spanish is credited by Willard ESPY to Anthony Bonner.

Allium : Muilla. BORGMANN's elegant REVERSAL PAIR of plant genuses, grafting the onion-garlic-leek-chive family onto a bulbous California herb of the lily family. As with so many of this all-seeing and all-recalling master's seemingly esoteric observations, this item proved on closer examination to be nothing but basic information as found in unabridged dictionaries, where we learned that the name reversal was an intentional act by a botanist who wanted to emphasize the similarity between the two genuses.

Allí ves a Sevilla (ah-YEE BVEYSS ah-sey-VEE-yah). Spanish: There you see Seville. Per ESPY and Anthony Bonner. *Bonita.* Spanish especially and probably all other Romance languages are much more conducive and obliging to PALINDROMIC composition than English is, yet we are unaware of any florescence of the forward-and-backward art anywhere, anytime, so great as the one we are currently enjoying in the English language. Our peculiarly advanced development probably owes a lot to the fact that our love of parlor and word games dating from early Victorian times has propelled us now well into a second century of continuous and intensive search and delight and growth.

"All or 0" Car: a Corolla. If anyone wants to redouble a **Toyota.**

A lob — a rap [as bat stabs] — a parabola! A slow pitch is belted out of the park, out of two different parks really, the bigger one by J. A. LINDON.

A [. . .] A

A lonely A. J. Foyt's not *It* on: "Sty of Jay Leno (LA)." We must have fallen asleep again while watching *The Tonight Show* and dreamt this *TV Guide* listing.

a Loyola. A saint or college, for example. By the KUHNS, after BORGMANN.

"Alu" Baths at Ashtabula. To keep even light metallic salts out of Lake Erie!

A lug I lack, Caligula. "Attributable" to his charioteer, who evidently forgot to check inside the lug wrench after changing a flat.

alula (AHL-yuh-luh, ÆL-yuh-luh). From the Latin diminutive for wing ("winglet"); scientifically speaking, the vestigial thumb at the base of a bird's wing, which on some birds takes the form of a special feather to prevent stalling during landing, just like a wing flap on an airplane.

Alùla. 1: small town of Somalia at its northernmost point, 11°50'n/50°45'e (*also* Caluula) 2: **Al-'ulā,** small town of Saudi Arabia, 26°37'n/37°52'e.

a lunula (uh LOON-yuh-luh). A little moon, by the KUHNS.

ama *or* amah (AH-muh, AH-mah). From Portuguese and Spanish, an Oriental maidservant attending to children, especially a wet nurse. See also: **aia**, **amma**, **aya**.

Ama. 1: riverfront community in St. Charles Parish, Louisiana, a burb of New Orleans 2: village of India, 26°53'n/82°38'e 3: village of Japan, 36°06'n/133°07'e 4: village of Peru, 11°29's/76°54'w 5: **Ama** Dablam, a mountain and glacier of Nepal, 27°52'n/86°52'e.

AMA. ABBREVIATION for the American Medical Association, wellness cartel. All in all, we'd rather be in **AMA**rillo. (That's airport code, for those who can dig it.)

Amaama. Town of Russia, 62°35'n/179°26'e.

ama-ama. Hawaiian name for the common mullet, according to BORGMANN.

A ma, Balaam: Ma Alabama! Not an ass, Balaam, **a ma!** But wait, because **I am a Balaam's ass as Ma Alabama, I . . .** is yet to come (also **At Alabama, I am a balata.**) In some minds the importance of finding or creating a PALIN-DROME for or within every state of the Union is great enough to excuse the sometimes dim creatures that result. The above three teratoids are especially gratuitous in light of the fact that Alabama already had **Semmes, Ala.** *and* **22** (rank of its admission to Union) with which to grace herself and was in no great need of PALINDROMIC enhancement. Indeed, many people probably already considered her our nation's leading and mother palindromic state.

A ma, Balaam: Ma Alabama!

a Madama (uh muh-DAH-muh). Evoking the lovely Butterfly lady; by the KUHNS.

A Maja plan a canal? Pajama! (MAH-hah). By the KUHNS. A delightful romp with that Goya girl (*desnuda? vestida?*— it doesn't matter), all over the place, and in the face of **A man . . . Panama.**

a Mali à la Dalai Lama. In the unlikely event Tibetan Buddhism ever takes hold on the far side of the Sahara. (Then the way would be open for even more far-sided things, such as **Spot saw a Mali à la Dalai Lama was tops.**)

a mama *or* **a Mama** (uh MAH-muh). A hot one by CHISM, one in a series, of a group. Compare: **a papa.**

A man—a Panama. By the KUHNS, a cleverly abridged and laid-back if less poignant form of **A man, a plan, a canal: Panama!**— now seemingly only about someone and his hat.

A man apart lusts *ultra* **Panama.** By the KUHNS. Balboa in 1513, we surmise, already at the Isthmus and completely iso-

A [. . .] A

lated from civilization, still desires to cross the beyond and discover the Pacific. (So he does.)

A man, a plan, a canal: Panama! By MERCER! This classic was described by BORGMANN as "one of the most felicitous palindromes ever written," and BERGERSON calls it "a universally admired gem—mined, cut and polished" by its creator. (This choice metaphor incidentally is very revealing of the actual stages of work involved in PALINDROME construction, as discussed for example under the **All erotic** entries.) Alastair Reid, in his book *Passwords*, has written (though mistakenly attributing the palindrome to James Thurber) that "it deserves to be enshrined on a monument, since, besides fulfilling its difficult technical requirements, it rings with true acclaim," and David Silverman (still according to Bergerson), has called it "the ultimate in palindromic engineering," and LINDON has done it the honor of palindromically parodying it—see: **A dog, a pant, a panic in a Patna pagoda.** As for the man (with the plan), well, historically Teddy Roosevelt or George W. Goethals could have been he, but so could many another man who has ever included a Panama canal in his plans (as in STUART's handsome illustration by Pamela Ford), and so if there is anyone who remains unconvinced of this palindrome's extreme venerability, they may be glad to have this saucy rejoinder to it: **No, it's a banana bastion.** We, for our part, prefer the admiration, allow the disallowance, and keep moving right along.

A man, a plan, a cat, a canal: Panama! Attributed to Jim Saxe, via the Internet.

A man, a plan, a cat, a ham, a yak, a yam, a hat, a canal: Panama! Attributed to Guy Jacobson, via the Internet. Similar but longer tours of force may be found in the same place, a probably man-made one of 49 words attributed to Guy Steele and a computer-generated one of 540 words claimed by Dan Hoey, who believes his PALINDROME could have been

A man, a plan, a canal: Panama!

stretched out ten times as long had a better word list and smarter program been used.

A mania plan: An anal pain? AMA! New nonmedical medical plan calls for high spirits generally and consultation with doctors only in the event of, or when seeking, a pain in the ass. See also: **"Victim,"** omit **"CIV."**

Amarillo Follirama (*or* **Jollirama;** *even* **Gollirama**). A thematic Texas Panhandle amusement, and/or amazement, park.

Amaryllis : Silly Rama. REVERSAL by BORGMANN, in which the shepherdess of classical poetry, or a bulbous plant named after her, engenders and encounters a strangely frivolous (one wonders why) Hindu deity.

a Mazama?? Why yes, there is a Mazama in Washington. (And many other near-palindromes of similar stripe may be correspondingly coaxed.)

Amen Enema. The purgative of choice in Purgatory.

AMERICA . . . America! Is any word spoken twice a PALIN-DROME? Yes, a very short WORD PALINDROME, and here we also have the start and finish of a magnificent twenty-seven-word (not the world's longest but possibly the best) WORD PALINDROME by LINDON, which we may not publish, though we can tell you the middle word is *but* and the other dozen (pairs) are, alphabetically, *a, from, intention, man, Mars, of, perhaps, ship, things, to, to,* and *tomorrow.* The format is not a sentence but evidently an article title cum source publication plus puckish comment. You may check your solution on page 109 of BERGERSON's book.

Am gin enigma. By POOL. Guzzler puzzler.

amiced : Decima. REVERSAL, giving, not too implausibly, a tenth Roman girl child dressed in a certain Christian liturgical vestment.

A [. . .] A

Amiced was I ere I saw Decima. By BORGMANN (who created it to make a point about how a FAMILY of PALINDROMES is developed).

Am I Kay? Yakima! Yes I am, and so it's off to town with **Analytic "City" Lana.**

a mild Lima. By the KUHNS, and the weather there will usually agree.

Am I loco? Lima?! What am I doing *here*? Or: **Am I loco, Lima?** (But it *is* crazy to talk to a city.)

amma (AHM-mah). Medieval Latin: mother; source of **ama.**

Amma (ÆM-muh). Hamlet of Roane County, West Virginia, 38°35'n/81°16'w; a misspelling of *Amie.*

Am ma. Short telegram, by POOL.

AMPHISBAENA

Amo la Paloma (AH-moh lah-pah-LOH-mah). Spanish: I love the Dove.

amoral aroma. "This perfume really works." The KUHNS.

AMPHISBAENA (ÆM-fihss-*BEE*-nuh). Mythological serpent having a head at each end of its body, and thus a fitting emblem for the idea of symmetry, or bipolarity, or PALINDROMICITY, or all three.

amunam : manuma. REVERSAL PAIR by BORGMANN, in which a Sri Lankan measure meets a bright-colored fruit pigeon of Fiji.

ana (ÆN-uh, AH-nuh). Collection of various materials such as facts, anecdotes, and pictures that reflect the character of a notable person or place, or an item in such a collection. The word is self-standing but is derived from the suffix **-ana,** as in *Americana.*

Ana (AH-nah, Æ-nuh). A female given name, especially in

A [. . .] A

Spanish countries, and part of the common surname Santa **Ana.**

Ana. 1: village of Afghanistan, 33°22'n/64°20'e **2:** village of New Guinea, 2°50's/141°39'e **3:** village of Togo, 7°44'n/1°12'e **4:** river of Chile, 53°40's/69°47'w **5:** river of Turkey **6: Aña,** village of Spain, 41°56'n/1°07'e **7: 'Ānā,** village of Lebanon, 33°41'n/35°45'e.

Ana, crass, amass arcana. Ignorant dear, accumulate profound secrets! Adapted from FITZPATRICK.

Anadarko's OK, rad Ana. See: **Okra . . . Anadarko.**

ANACYCLIC. Rare synonym for the words PALINDROME and PALINDROMIC, derived from the also rare French word *anacyclique* (according to BORGMANN), itself apparently derived from a Greek original meaning "revolve in a circle, turn or come round again," and therefore not really the perfect word for the linear to-and-fro kind of motion that a palindrome actually engenders.

ANACYCLIC. Synonym for palindrome, palindromic.

An admirer! I'm Dana! We're delighted to meet this CHISM character.

ANAGRAMS (ÆN-uh-græmz). Words or phrases formed by reordering the letters of other words or phrases (examples: the word *anagrams* itself and *ars magna*, Latin for "great art") by definition occurring in at least pairs but frequently in multiples—constituting a happy-returns-in-wordplay category of which all REVERSAL PAIRS and many but not all PALINDROMES are members. Some people prefer anagrams. Some prefer palindromes. Some prefer both. Measured objectively on a ten-scale of gnomic elfishness, a good anagram will score about a 12.34, while a good palindrome will sometimes reach and even exceed a 12.345. (Otherwise there is no comparing them.)—It is worth adding, to fully elaborate the mentioned scale, that a

A [. . .] A

good OMPHALOSKEPSIS may reach as far as the ultimate (12.34567890).

Ana, I'd nip Indiana. Just pass through a corner of it.

Ana, I'd nix Indiana. But how could you?

An alpaca cap, Lana? Or would you prefer a vicuña sweater?

Anal sex at noon taxes Lana. By LESSER.

Anal was I ere I saw Lana. By CHISM.

Analytic "City" Lana. An evocative and leading lady. BORGMANN'S.

anana (ah-nah-NAH). The pineapple often found in crosswords.

Ana, nab a banana. By POOL. Snatch it in the act.

an asana. A yogic position, and compare: **ANNA.**

Anastasia is at Sana. The missing Grand Duchess turns up in Yemen.

aneled : Delena. REVERSAL PAIR by BORGMANN forming the near-Homeric epithet **Aneled Delena,** in which an Oklahoma ghost town is duly immortalized for having received extreme unction (the dying or last rites of the historical Christian Church)!

"Anele Hts." was I ere I saw St. Helena. Of course, **Able . . . Elba** fairly demands this one additional investigation. *Anele* being the name for the last rites and oiling, and thus the heights of Anele, or "Anele Hts." being undoubtedly the "place" of all those widely reported, exquisitely delicious near-death experiences (partial resurrections, perhaps, or sublimations of life by virtue of the presence of death) associated with these rites and with dying in general, this second-degree mystery of the PALINDROMIC church indicates Napoleon knew he was already virtually dead meat, or shall

A [. . .] A

we say "history," before he ever set foot upon St. Helena, his equally illustrious but until now palindromologically forgotten island of exile. And if the game of all islands is called, whether Napoleon was stuck on them or not, the play grows still more wonderful. For **A buc was I ere I saw Cuba.** And **A nil at A.C.** [that is, no jock] . . . **ere** . . . **Catalina.** And **Sam[,] Ahab was I ere I saw Bahamas.** But in these waters Roger ANGELL probably won the cup hands down and forever as early as 1969 with **A dum["] reb was I ere I saw Bermuda.** Still, we keep coming, running up, and around, the world, with: **I? Anal was I ere I saw Lanai.** And **Yawdim** [viz., sort of seasick] **was I ere I saw Midway.** Once onto the mainland, if anyone is still listening, we're windier still with **No bag was I ere I saw Gabon,** and etc., but that is a still different story.

an era's arena. Any of the several incarnations of Madison Square Garden, and here a placemark, too, for a famous quatrain by MERCER we do not recite, "The Four Palindromes of the Apocalypse," appearing in BERGERSON's *Palindromes and Anagrams*, and possibly in one of BORGMANN's books as well. There is also, in a similar vein, **an error, Rena.**

A new order began, a more Roman age bred Rowena. Quite a beauty by BORGMANN, referring to the lady from *Ivanhoe*, we guess.

ANGELL, Roger, wrote "Ainmosni," an article about PALINDROMES and insomnia that first appeared in *The New Yorker* in 1969 and later in his book, *A Day in the Life of Roger Angell*, and later in John Pool's book, **Lid Off a Daffodil.**

Angola balogna. Phoney balogna! (Baloney. Bologna. Nice try.)

"An Ignatius Ejaculation!?" No! . . . (ital., u.c.:) . . . **"A JESUIT ANGINA!"** *or perhaps* **An Ignatius ejaculation's** . . . [no ital.! u.c.!] . . . **A JESUIT ANGINA!** Little tone poem/tableau in which Father Ignatius Loyola, founder of the Society of Jesus, **aka** the Jesuits, appears to have just been shaken by a monastic paroxysm and the monks back in the scriptorium also seem to be having a heck of a time spin-doctoring and steering his resultant brief, pious utterance into a seemly manuscript leader, all in proper typeface and size, if you see what we mean—in which case you may agree with us that this is certainly one of the weirdest and most squirrelish PALINDROMES ever contrived. (Still, it should probably be banned.) And consider also the various alternatives, more forced and so less successful: **An Ignatius ejaculates "Alas!," et al., (u.c.:) "A JESUIT ANGINA!"** (Or **"Air am I!," Marias.**) And see also: **Set, a Luca Jesuit "angina man," Ignatius, ejaculates.**

A nil or ace, Carolina!

That's the beauty of the pass-fail system, dear!

A nil or ace, Carolina! That's the beauty of the pass-fail system, dear! It's so nice and simple when you get the hang of it.

animal : lamina. REVERSAL, with a strong linkage possibility: **animal lamina,** a scalelike or platelike structure, as one of the thin layers of sensitive tissue in the hoof of a horse.

Animal loots foliated detail of stool lamina. Attribution unknown, reported by John JENSEN. It is a good example of the building-block school of construction that provides us with a child's illustration of a dog chewing off a portion of an elegant small furnishing.

animative : E vitamina. Ingenious REVERSAL PAIR by BORGMANN, in which a word for "inspiring" or "enlivening" joins with "the several recognized forms of vitamin E" in their supposed but unconfirmed plural form *if* expressed using the outdated variant of vitamin *vitamen* (which pluralizes into *vitamina*, at least in Latin)—now normally expressed as "E vitamins."

A [. . .] A

animativ : vitamin A. REVERSAL PAIR by BORGMANN that mates a reformed spelling of a word meaning "life-giving" with a life-giving substance—a marriage made in heaven certainly, which also inevitably and finally leads into the more natural spelling: **Animative vitamin A.**

Anina. 1: large town of Romania, 45°05'n/21°51'e **2:** town of Yugoslavia (unconfirmed).

Anita lava la tina (ah-NEE-tah LAH-bvah la-TEE-nah). Spanish: "Anita washes the bathtub." Credited to Anthony Bonner by ESPY.

anna (Æ-nuh). A former copper coin of India and Pakistan, equal to one sixteenth of a rupee, from a Sanskrit word meaning "small."

Anna (ÆN-uh *or* AHN-uh). **1:** small town of Union County, Illinois, 37°27'n/89°14'w **2:** small town of Shelby County, Ohio, 40°23'n/84°10'w **3:** small town of Collin County, Texas, 33°21'n/96°33'w **4:** hamlet of Bourbon County, Kansas **5:** large town of Russia, 51°29'n/40°25'e **6:** village of Nauru, South Pacific **7:** village of Portugal **8:** village of Spain **9:** bay of Australia **10:** creek of South Australia **11:** island in the Carolines **12:** plains of Western Australia **13:** point of Nauru, South Pacific **14:** Lake **Anna** and **15:** North and **16:** South **Anna** Rivers, Virginia, 38°04'n/77°45'w **17:** feminine name; originally **Hannah,** meaning "grace." The only two PALINDROMIC children of U.S. presidents were both Annas, one by William Henry Harrison (**Anna** Tuthill Harrison) and one by Franklin D. Roosevelt (**Anna** Eleanor Roosevelt); and three of our four palindromic first ladies were also named **Anna,** the wives of the above two (**Anna** Tuthill Symmes and **Anna** Eleanor Roosevelt) and of Calvin Coolidge (Grace **Anna** Goodhue). The non-**Anna** palindromic first lady was **Hannah** Hoes, wife of Martin Van Buren. So that represents something of a clean sweep of the White House for these two kindred palindromic names.

Anna.
Two palindromic children of U.S. presidents were both Annas.

A [. . .] A

ANNA. ACRONYM for Army-Navy-NASA–Air Force. We have to wonder why they didn't reverse the sequence, incorporate the full form of the already acronymic NASA, and produce the really interesting **ANASANA**—interesting even if one does not assume **an asana** (yogic position).

ANNA . . . First line of two WORD SQUARES by BORGMANN:

A	N	N	A		A	N	N	A
B	O	O	B		N	O	O	N
B	O	O	B		N	O	O	N
A	N	N	A		A	N	N	A

The first is a fancy "double word square," with different words horizontal and vertical. The second is a plain but still lovely PALINDROMIC word square with a simple, clear two-word message.

Anna deified Anna. Anyone or any thing with a PALINDROMIC name could do this to him/her/itself. The present text, however, is a good placemark for and super digest of a very witty PALINDROMIC poem of thirty-seven words, ten of them *deified*, five of them *sees*, four *and*, four *madam*, four *Edna*, and four name REVERSAL PAIRS, cocreated by MERCER and BORGMANN and recited by BERGERSON, page 95. You may wish to see if you can reconstruct the full PALINDROME from this information before referring there. We should probably tell you that the piece, actually a poem, is cast as a report to the chairwoman of a mutual deification society.

Anne, I see Sienna.

Annam manna. Central Vietnamese haute cuisine.

Anne, I see Sienna. Here begins a whirlwind tour across Italy and the Alps. The text is an almost basic PALINDROME, like an uninflected word stem in a strange language, out of whose central core other palindromes can emerge, and therefore it can serve also as the label for a file folder into which a variety of further developments may reasonably be grouped. See the following entries for examples.

A ⌈ . . . ⌉ A

Anne is not up-to-date, God! : Do get a dot put on "Sienna." A pair of REVERSAL SENTENCES by BORGMANN, not intended by him as a PALINDROME but conceivably functional as one—a disjointed ramble to be sure but understandable in light of the fact that in olden times (when all letters were what we now call capitals) the letter *I* was of course not dotted; yet it conveniently ignores the bigger fact that Sienna (*Sena* in those days) wasn't even spelled with an *I*.

Anne, I stay a day at Sienna. Probably by MERCER. (I'm stopping to get a dot put on it and update you.) It is not hard to fall back, or to jump over from the previous entry, into the basic **Anne, I see Sienna.** And it is easy to see how a change of venue from Sienna to Vienna or Ravenna could produce the strange turns of events in the following items.

Anne, I vote more cars race Rome-to-Vienna. Probably by MERCER. Yes, why not a *Really Grand Prix?* Note that the outer shell of this text is also variable, as for example by **Sage, vote more cars race Rome-to-Vegas.** And see also the previous several entries, and the following, for a variety of central developments. But unlike the delirious Vegas twist or Ravenna wrinkle (following), this Vienna PALINDROME's development is not at all forced; indeed it seems entirely classical and entirely inspired, as you might expect from Vienna.

Anne, varnish Tom's moths in Ravenna. A most peculiar entomological field assignment, but the task is almost forced upon her once Ravenna has been chosen for the destination. (CHISM credits *WORD WAYS.*)

Anona, Florida (south of Clearwater). Florida's only palindromic locality.

Anona. Named from the Spanish word for the custard apple, a local wild fruit, this locality of Florida is listed in the **AAA** index for that state and is keyed to its map grid at H-19 (in Pinellas County, south of Clearwater) but surprisingly is not shown there, nor is it found on any recent maps of Florida we have checked. Moreover it appears to be Florida's only

A [. . .] A

PALINDROMIC locality, if it does exist, and so by multiple default it becomes a unique palindromic ghost state-capital. Another *Anona,* built in 1867 and looking like a whaleboat, lifeboat, or similar craft, is depicted in miniature in the lobby of the Red Lobster in Torrington, Connecticut, and, for all we can guess, in Red Lobster lobbies everywhere.

anonanona. The Hawaiian word for *ant,* according to IR-VINE, 1987.

An Oz I ran in Arizona. "Attributable," if not to the governor of the state, then to the wizard and director of that funny Arcosanti closed-cycle biosphere bubble.

An oz. I rap, Arizona. For who raps so lightly there and why, and for an only slightly more forthcoming state PALINDROMIC capital, see: **Yell a V, Oro Valley!**

a null luna (uh NUHLL LOO-nuh). By CHISM, being a "no moon," and thus a newer than new moon.

[A] / nun / sees / eye / level, / huh? / Wow! Neat sentence, given by LESSER, in which every word is a PALINDROME.

Aoa. 1: island, or village upon it, of the South Pacific, 14°16's/170°35'w **2:** the adjacent bay, 14°15's/170°35'w.

A1A. Florida's Atlantic Coast Highway (compare U.S. **101** in California, Oregon, and Washington—the Pacific Coast Highway).

A-one[:] Genoa. A first-rate travel destination. But, "words" overheard on the train to the slaughterhouse there: **I'm, alas, A-one Genoa salami.**

AOXOMOXOA. Word (also a vertical MIRROR PALINDROME) occurring on a Grateful Dead album illustration, 1971; also, the title of that album.

Apa. 1: town of China, on eastern Tibetan Plateau, approximately 102°00'w/33°00'n **2:** tributary of the Rio Paraguay,

22°06's/58°00'w, that forms part of the Paraguay-Brazil border.

APA. 1: ABBREVIATION for the American Parapsychotic Association and American Palindromaniac Association (just joking, and checking to see if anyone is still awake—actually there's a whole slew of earnest psychobabble stuff almost of this ilk occurring at the same alphabetic location in DE SOLA's *Abbreviation Dictionary,* no fault of his) **2:** the airport code for Amapá, Brazil.

Apapa. Channel, point, and wharf of Lagos, Nigeria, 6°27'n/ 3°22'e.

a papa *or* **a Papa** (uh PAH-puh). Not necessarily a member of the Mamas and the Papas, but more likely of **A Mama & a Papa,** a hot new word group. See also: **St. Tes' . . . Massachusetts** and **Won't casts act now?**

APBPA. Association of Professional Ball Players of America, according to BORGMANN.

Apes: [U.S.] EPA. Animal riots activists or mimics clean up. Clean up what? **EPA tape** (the red variety). Also: **Ape sues a base U.S. EPA.**

A poem, a carol—or a cameo, Pa! By LINDON. Yuletide trick or treat. This one really is an exquisite little contraption. It is hard to imagine how it arose if not by the purest of wizardry. Note that it is entirely seamless (i.e., without any matching word breaks fore and aft of center), despite consisting of only short words. If the occurrence of any little PALINDROME at all, like, say, **"We sew,"** is already a one-in-a-million happenchance (and *it is*), how great a miracle, how many billions or trillions of bowls of alphabet soup would have to be drained before anything this lovely chanced to emerge!

Apollo, PA. This is a unique case of a special PALINDROME

A papa

A [. . .] A

Apollo, Pa

type: the name of a postal locality, complete with standard two-letter state abbreviation. It is approached but not equaled by the nonpostal township of **Linn, IL** (Woodford County) and the nonpostal hamlets of **Linn, IL** (Wabash County); **Lis, IL; Omaha, MO;** and **Roy, OR.** If **Apollo, PA,** has a true equal in the form of a going place with a real post office of the same name, it would have to be **a Walla Walla, WA,** sort of thing, or perhaps **Sitka, AK, 'tis,** but these are admittedly a reach if not a dance. Then, too, there is the intriguing, if inappropriate, **Adaven, Nevada. . . .** Finally, a separate matter but no less important than all the above, is **Apollo, PA**'s strangely perfect namesake: **Apollo, Pa,** that is, *father* Apollo, the god and patron of many things, the most pertinent to our subject being oracles—and also OMPHALOSKEPSIS, also called "navel-gazing," a splendid idea that not only produces a happy returning inward of the usual outward flow of thought but also suggests a sort of "symmetry in the round."

Apopa (ah-POH-pah). Village of El Salvador, 13°48'n/89°11'w; also the name of a baseball player—he was a pitcher, perhaps a Luis—too dimly recalled.

Ara. 1: small city of India, 25°34'n/84°40'e **2:** village of Ethiopia, 4°36'n/40°20'e **3:** village of Nigeria, 7°47'n/5°07'e **4:** village of Russia, 69°22'n/32°48'e **5:** locality of Japan, exact size and location unknown **6:** lake of Canada, 50°32'n/87°30'w **7:** river of Ireland, via Tipperary, 52°24'n/7°56'w **8:** river of Japan (greater), via Tokyo into Tokyo Bay, 35°39'n/139°51'e **9:** river of Japan (lesser), via Oguni into Sea of Japan, 38°09'n/139°25'e **10:** river of Spain, from the Pyrenees via Broto and Boltana into the Ebro, 42°25'n/0°09'e **11: 'Ara,** village of Israel, 32°30'n/35°05'e. Compare: **'Ar'ara. 12:** (EHY-ruh) constellation of the Southern Hemisphere (near the constellations Norma and Telescopium), which evidently impressed somebody, sometime, with its likeness

A [. . .] A

to an altar, for that is the meaning of the Latin word from which it was named **13:** (Æ-ruh) masculine name.

Araara. Island and pass of the South Pacific, 16°48's/ 150°58'w.

A raja lad au gratin, I tar Guadalajara. An all-orange-and-black Halloween costume is explained, or a bizarre dream is sung to a Gilbert and Sullivan tune ⌈scan: *GUAD'*-la JA-ra⌉, wherein an Indian prince, covered with cheese, does road work in Mexico.

Aramara. Town of Australia, 25°37's/152°19'e.

arañara (ah-*r*ah-nyah-*R*AH). Spanish: he, she, or it will scratch.

Arara. River of Brazil.

'Ar'ara. Village of Israel, 32°29'n/35°06'e. Compare **'Ara.**

Ararat : ta-ra-ra. REVERSAL PAIR with weak mutual attraction but for a hypothetical Noah's celebratory **Ta-ra-ra Ararat!**

Arbrå. Village of Sweden, 61°29'n/16°23'e.

arca sacra (AHR-kah SAHK-rah). Latin: Holy Ark, probably of the Covenant rather than the Flood and probably not the arc of the rainbow, which is rather *arcus sacer* or, when personified, the Goddess Iris (by special invocation, **Iri**), though all three (or four) are intriguingly interwoven in many traditions. Miraculous.

Ara.
Constellation of the Southern Hemisphere.

Arden : Nedra. REVERSAL PAIR of unusual given names, by BORGMANN.

AREA CODES. See: PHONE CODES.

Are ponies, Iona, a *noise* in opera? By LINDON. Not usually, but they may create a bit of a racket during the really big productions. Or perhaps the ponies referred to are the trots or librettos, in which case they probably are a noise. The text is another instance of Lindon's silky touch. An interest in opera may have led him to test *are po-* . . . *opera(?)*, which readily slides into *are poni-* . . . *in opera(?)*, and easily progresses to *are ponies* . . . *-se in opera(?)*, and again to *are ponies ion-* . . . *noise in opera(?)*, and finally meets with an opportunity to close the center, thanks to the emergence of the elegant *Iona.* Yet conceiving *noise* in italics may have been the real coup de grâce, whenever it occurred. Of course this reconstruction of the probable trudging does not quite explain how the lightning was produced, how it is that we feel ourselves actually present in a theater of the surreal, all in living déjà vu, but perhaps we may learn *that* by endeavoring to emulate, with alphabet blocks of our own, the master's accomplishment.

Are we not drawn onwards, we Jews, drawn onward to new era? Probably by MERCER, again (as always) according to BERGERSON's best guess. And a wondrous idea it is, to be led to forget the past—even overlook the present!—in contemplating a more beautiful future. The slight lurch from "onwards" to "onward" is almost imperceptible and can be eliminated by ESPY's finesse: **Are we not drawn onward, we few, drawn onward to new era?** Also successful but low-key is the basic **Are we not drawn onward to new era?** And, for an attempt to naturalize the telegraphic phrase "to new era," which slightly flaws all the above examples, see: **Degas . . . eras aged.** This entire FAMILY, you probably noticed, is heavily into modular construction.

Aria-gnus, Eva, have sung air "A." BORGMANN continues: "That may well be but how are they going to handle Air 'B,' with its coloratura trills and runs?" This shining exemplar of the totally wingo school of PALINDROME design, deemed worthy of publication and comment by its masterful composer, will be a comfort to novice constructors, most of

A [. . .] A

whose initial efforts may well resemble this one in degree of coherency and articulation. But no matter what the results, and especially if they do wax bizarre, there is likely to be great fun and therefore VALUE in the process of arriving at them, and often again in explaining them.

a rimless Elmira. Since eighties oracular seat blew its lid on Jane Roberts and Seth.

ark okra. Flood food, by the KUHNS.

Armagnac [:] can gam Ra! REVERSAL PAIR and a fact observed by Jane Capellaro: drinking the renowned brandy of this region of France can result in a visit with the Sun God or Supreme Being.

Ark okra

Arra. 1: mountains of Tipperary, Ireland **2:** river of Pakistan.

Artemis, I met Ra. By the KUHNS. I inform the Moon Goddess I have encountered the Sun God.

Art lusts ultra. The KUHNS' creativity desires the most. To the beyond!

Art: "Si dips an aspidistra." Similarly: **Art: Si dips a detail of [a] foliated aspidistra.** Likewise: **Art: Si dips a detail of Ed's defoliated aspidistra.** All these are discussed under: **a detail of a foliated *A*.**

Art's on a so-called "toot *della Cosa Nostra*." It's MACARONIC Sicilian party time.

***Art, USA* make *Kama Sutra*.** Magazines coproduce a premium book.

Arura. Town of Jordan, 32°02'n/35°10'e.

A rut: La Paz. I zap altura. Spanglish: Directly I solve my chronic altitude problem in Bolivia.

Asa (EHY-suh). **1:** hamlet of Quitman County, Mississippi **2:** small burb of Hiroshima, 34°33'n/132°26'e **3:** village of

A [. . .] A

Nigeria **4:** village of Sweden **5: Åsa,** village of Sweden, (distinct from plain **Asa**) **6: Aşa,** small city of Russia, 55°00'n/57°16'e **7:** river of Japan (greater), in western Tokyo Prefecture via Hachioji into Tama, 35°39'n/139°26'e **8:** river of Japan (lesser), via Mine and Sanyo, 34°01'n/131°09'e **9:** river of Venezuela, passing near La Paragua into the Paragua and Orinoco rivers, 6°50'n/63°18'w **10:** river of the Congo **11:** masculine name.

ASA. 1: standard ABBREVIATION for the austere American Standards Association, but likewise for the outgoing American Sightseeing Association *and* for the American Sunbathing Association, of all things. So one is naturally led to wonder what might not occur on their combined standard sunbathing and sightseeing tour to (where but) **2:** the Assab, Ethiopia, area airport.

A sacred admirer, I'm Dad E. R. Casa. Punny Valentine greeting seemingly from someone (Hispanic, perhaps) to his family (or else from God), meaning, with a helping hand from letter-talk ("Dad-E, R-Casa"): "I'm the doting and divine father here at our house."

Asakasa.
A picturesque Buddhist pagoda in Tokyo.

Asakasa (AH-sah-*KAH*-sah). Name of a picturesque Buddhist pagoda in Tokyo, according to BORGMANN.

A Santa's at NASA. By IRVINE, 1987, who predicted an increase in the space budget, according to William Safire.

As I was, I saw Isa. At her come-as-you-are party, that is. This is a lagniappe included not so much for its own sake as to mark the approximate spot of an unusual and widely quoted and admired *line*-palindrome poem, "As I Was Passing," by LINDON. Each line of the poem is repeated in reverse order, **ABCDDCBA,** with punctuation changes to fit the needs of each new moment, and the whole is rendered with a gloominess worthy of Edgar Allen Poe—which is one reason why, though we can hardly ignore it, we are not inter-

A [...] A

ested in quoting it here. (Actually though, in the end, all the dread foreboding evaporates into nothing but atmospherics.) For the complete text, see BERGERSON's *Palindromes and Anagrams*.

A slut nixes sex in Tulsa. Remarkable. Illustrated in IR-VINE, 1987.

A slut nixes sex in Tulsa.

A slut taxes sex at Tulsa. By CHISM. Business as usual—it's only remarkable if she nixes it.

A slut was I ere I saw Tulsa. By CHISM. I did a complete turnabout thanks to this fine city.—This PALINDROME strikes us as quite funny generally as well as being a special jest for palindromologists, a perfect "blue" note in any chorus of **Able was I ere I saw Elba** echoes.

Asosa. Town of Ethiopia, 10°03'n/34°32'e.

Assa. 1: small town of Kazakhstan, 43°02'n/71°10'e **2:** small town of Morocco, 28°34'n/9°27'w **3:** with *El,* a village of Libya **4:** river of Kazakhstan, 43°55'n/70°25'e **5:** river of Russia via or near Grozny, into the Caspian Sea, 43°13'n/45°25'e.

A surer—a radical pose, so placid—a rarer USA. CHISM credits publication of this jewel to *WORD WAYS: The Journal of Recreational Linguistics,* edited by Ross and Faith Eckler, who are apparently also responsible for having published his *From A to Zotamorf: The Dictionary of Palindromes.* It would be nice to ascertain and properly honor the author of this rare and delicate beauty. Some would not admit a PALINDROME to the **Hall of Follah** unless it is a full sentence with subject and verb, but we are glad to be able to nominate this "incomplete" specimen for the highest level of accolade: the coveted, elusive Great American Palindrome.

Ata. 1: village of Turkmenistan, 40°30'n/62°09'e **2:** a community in the nome of Attica, Greece **3:** islet of the Tonga

Islands near Tongatapu, 21°03's/175°00'w **4: 'Ata,** southernmost island of the Tonga Islands, 22°20's/176°12'w **5: Atâ,** village of Greenland, 69°48'n/51°00'w. See also: **Atta Atta.**

Ata, Alma, *or* Alma-**Ata** (AHL-muh-tuh). Capital city, metropolis, and political division of Kazakhstan, 43°15'n/76°57'e. A seemingly close relative of Addis **Ababa,** Ethiopian capital. Post-Soviet preferred spelling, however, appears to be *Almaty.*

Atai a gaiola, saloia gaiata! (uh-TAHY uh-gahy-OH-luh, suh-LAW-yuh gah-YAH-tuh). Portuguese: Tie the cage, naughty rustic girl. Given by BORGMANN. We're still trying to figure out what this one actually means, but for the time being we like it for its lilting cadence at least.

At Alabama, I am a balata (buh-LAH-tuh). A talking "bully tree" shows up at the university. Anything's possible in PALINDROMIA.

Atalata. Village of Principe Island, off West Africa, 1°37'n/7°27'e.

Atata. Island of the Tonga Islands near Tongatapu, 21°03's/175°15'w.

Ateleta. Village of Italy, 41°51'n/14°12'e.

A tin mug for a jar of gum, Nita? A bargain proposed by LINDON, seconded by many, and illustrated in TERBAN.

a Toyota. That **"All or 0" Car: a Corolla.** As distinct from a **Civic.**

Atta boy! (ÆD-uh). Expression of approval, commonly found in crossword puzzles.

Atta. Small burb of Delhi, India, 28°34'n/77°20'e.

Atta Atta. Reported according to BORGMANN by Ripley "as

being the name of a resident of **Ata,** a community in the nome of Attica, in Greece."

att ordidrotta. According to BORGMANN, "an excellent Swedish palindrome, meaning 'to contest with words.' It has the hallmarks of being a coined term, built up from the basic verb 'att idrotta,' which means 'to contest' or 'to go in for athletics.'" We like "to word-rassle."

Aua. 1: island just north of Papua New Guinea, 1°27's/143°04'e **2:** island of the South Pacific, 14°16's/170°40'w.

AUA. Airport code for Aruba, Netherlands Antilles.

AUGARDE, Tony. Author of *The Oxford Guide to Word Games* (New York: Oxford University Press, 1984), which includes a good chapter on PALINDROMES and a good bibliography. His citations herein were graciously permitted gratis.

auks : skua. REVERSAL PAIR, all arctic or antarctic sea birds, by BORGMANN.

Ava (EHY-vuh). Feminine name.

Ava. 1: town of Jackson County, Illinois, 37°53'n/89°29'w **2:** village of Kentucky, 36°44'n/83°25'w **3:** small town of Missouri, seat of Douglas County, 36°57'n/92°39'w **4:** historical capital of Burma, c. 1775, 21°49'n/95°57'e **5:** inlet of Canada, 63°50'n/71°57'w **6:** town of New York.

avaava. Small fish of the genus *Terapon,* according to BORGMANN.

ava-kava. Synonym for "kava-kava," a kind of pepper, according to BORGMANN.

"A Valdez" oozed lava. A crude mistake, yet not without its shred of truth, from the memoirs of the disoriented captain of Exxon's proud flagship, *Tanker A,* on the rocks but evidently fancying himself at the helm of . . . a volcano, both in the heat of the disaster and through the long firestorm that

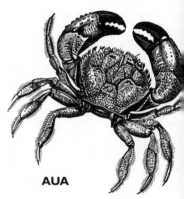

AUA

followed. Coincidentally, this text (if Valdez is pronounced "bvahl-DHEHSS" rather than "væl-DEEZ") is also the exact expression Colombian drug lords use when they wake up and smell the hot, black, thick stuff (they can't or won't say "Java" in Colombia) freshly squeezed by the real Exigente, Juan Valdez, or his burro "¡Así-no!" Valdez, high in the mountains.

avid [as a] diva. Wonderfully talented and spirited REVERSAL PAIR that grows naturally into a poignant simile and, chancing to be also the beginning and ending, and overall stage direction, of a brilliant Graham REYNOLDS drinking song, grows again for us into the perfect point of departure for a reference to BERGERSON's *Palindromes and Anagrams*, page 98, where the full performance may be enjoyed.

AVID OGLER GNOMES OPPOSE MONGREL GODIVA! This documentary text, in the style of a *Variety* headline, is seeming evidence that the zeal and discrimination of some dirty old dwarves were in fact to thank for the eventual casting selection—from among many and varied Godiva hopefuls—of just that high-bred and very real Lady who has been appreciated now for centuries in her role of scenic equestrienne. However, the text's authenticity, or at least its historiological interpretation—we are sure both are spurious—are busted by the cosmic fact that opposing an unwanted thing doesn't create or in any way promote a desirable one. (On the contrary.)

Avila's saliva. The miraculous dribble some claim to have seen issuing from the mouth of the swooning nun in Bernini's "Ecstasy of Saint Theresa."

Aviva. Given by CHISM as an English word, citing BORGMANN, without explanation. Elsewhere, from context it appears Borgmann takes this to be a feminine name, and the KUHNS, a Hebrew one.

A [. . .] A

Awa (AH-wuh). **1:** town of Okinawa, Japan, in the mysterious **Aha-Ada-Awa** Triangle, 26°36'n/127°56'e **2:** town of Shikoku, Japan, 34°04'n/134°12'e **3:** island of Japan in the Inland Sea near Takuma, 34°16'n/133°38'e **4:** island off Japan in the Sea of Japan near Murakami, 38°27'n/139°14'e.

a Walla Walla, WA. Actually, *the* Walla Walla, WA. See: **Apollo, PA.**

A war at Tarawa! (tuh-RAH-wuh *or* TAH-ruh-wuh). Probably by MERCER. The capital of the Gilbert and Ellice islands, an atoll of about eight square miles, and—fittingly we suppose, if a war is ever appropriate—the site of a major battle between the United States and Japan as recently as 1943. (Uh. Was that a war memorial? Uh. I dunno. Anyway let's build the next monument to frivolity.)

Awarawa Udjung. Headland of Java, 6°45's/111°58'e.

Aw, pull a yup, Puyallup, WA. And "just say yes" this once to the spellings **Pullallup** and **Puyayup,** of course in Spanish editions only.

axa (ÆKS-uh). Greek (and possibly English alternative) word for axes, that is, not the cutting tools but the plural of axon—in Greek meaning, in the singular, an axis of any sort, but coming in English to mean one sort of axis in particular, the core of a nerve fiber, also called a neuraxon.

AXA. Airport code for Anguilla, Leeward Islands.

Axixá (uh-shee-SHAH). Town of Brazil, 2°51's/44°04'w.

aya *or* ayah (AH-yuh). Hindu: native nursemaid (from the Portuguese **aia**).

Aya Thorgren. Model featured in the *Sports Illustrated* swimsuit issue, 1994 edition.

Aya. Island of Chad, 10°17'n/18°58'e.

Aya

AYA. 1: airport code for Ayapel, Colombia 2: ABBREVIATION for the American Yachtsmen's Association.

Ayaya. Village of Russia, 60°04'n/134°45'e.

Aza. 1: village of Chile, 19°18's/69°34'w 2: village of Japan, 26°14'n/127°41'e.

'Azaza. Village of Sudan, 14°10'n/35°31'e.

Aziza. Cosmetics brand name.

AZ Zip Pizza. Experimental express pizza delivery system by nine-digit zip code, now available anywhere in Arizona with proper shape postal box (summer only).

bab (BAHB). Persian and Arabic: gate. Hence, among many other things, the title of Ali Mohammed of Shiraz (1819–1850), the Persian founder of **Bab**ism, or Baha'i—who evidently must have thought of himself or his message as a gate for others or wanted others to think so—and the local name for the Mandeb Strait (namely, **Bab** el Mandeb), a very important seventeen-mile-wide neck of water between East Africa and South Arabia that links the Red Sea with the Gulf of Aden and is a gateway to the Suez Canal and the Mediterranean.

b [. . .] b

Bab (BÆB). **1:** nickname for Barbara **2:** pen name of the poet Child Gilbert.

BACK TALK *or* BACK SLANG. Playful, mostly British custom of calling things backward, a usually CASUAL but sometimes coy, sometimes enciphered form of word INVERSION that crops up in everyday chit-chat, wherein a bottle becomes an *elttob*; a button, a *nottub*; the police, *ecilop*; tobacco, *occabot*; etc. This according to BORGMANN in *Beyond Language*.

Bah! Ahab!

Bagdad Gab. Gossipy English-language Iraqi tabloid.

Bah! Ahab! Peculiar cry from Moby Dickens.

"Balderdash Teeth": Sad Red Lab. Off-color dog and his incredible tale.

Ban campus motto, "Bottoms up, MacNab." Probably by MERCER. Pretty. Yet here is a relatively rare case in which a little foreshortening does no harm, it seems to us, and possibly even makes for an improvement: **Campus motto: "Bottoms up, Mac!"** Perhaps best would be a debate between the two schools of thought.

B & B. Benedictine & brandy, and bed & breakfast—thus, **B & B & B & B.**

Bandits—avast!—I'd nab. All but pirated from LINDON's poem "Abduction." See also: **Bargees . . . grab.**

BARBARIA, the Most Serene and Fresh Gnomedom (or Kingdom) of. The no-man's-land in the crack between the worlds at the heart of symmetry, though for some just a far province of PALINDROMIA.

Barcarole's sum: a mussel or a crab. Gondolier's fee, conveniently payable from out of the catch made en route, inspired by a FITZPATRICK poem.

bar crab. The KUHNS' "exclude pincher"—a grabby form of pub life.

Bard[s] Drab. PALINDOMIA's or BARBARIA's exalted national poet[s], who, though shadowy, are often artistically assimilated with **Stratford's "Dr. Oft-Arts"** upon **Avon Nova.**

Bargees, I see, grab. Grabbed and adapted from a LINDON poem, "Abduction," which barges in with almost this very opening line and doesn't stop there. See **Bandits . . . nab,** and for the original, BERGERSON's *Palindromes and Anagrams.*

Basil is a b——! By LINDON, a clever type. Sprightly texts such as this always seem obvious with the advantage of hindsight, and it is true that novelties do abound, yet it takes a brilliant stroke to expose such an original jewel to the light.

BB (BEE-bee). **1:** standard size of lead shot 0.18 inches in diameter, hence a "bee-bee" **2:** (bee-BEE) Brigitte Bardot or Before Bach, and thus **BBBB.** We also wonder if it might have something to do with ball bearings.

BBB. 1: bed, breakfast, and bath (hence, **BBBBB:** same as **BBB,** but with Benedictine and brandy) **2:** Better Business Bureau.

"Bed stress," asserts Deb. Contributed by CHISM.

Beg, borrow, or rob.—*Geb.* Evidently a rare "signed PALINDROME" by either the Egyptian god of the earth or French writer Emile Gebhart, **aka** Geb. Sayings like this one can also turn right around with the help of a little repunctuation and say, say: **Beg, borrow, or rob Geb.**

Belle B. Bay of Newfoundland, arm of Fortune Bay, 47°36'n/ 55°18'w. Compare: **Bogo B.**

bel paese à pleb. In IRVINE, 1987. Evidently the plainest of West Point's several continental dining plans.

Bere B. A bay of Arctic Canada, 76°52'n/93°45'w.

BERGERSON, Howard. Author of *Palindromes and Anagrams* (New York: Dover Publications, 1973), one of our leading sources of inspiration, both for his own spectacular PALIN-DROMIC poetry, which he generally presents under the pen name Edwin FITZPATRICK, and also for his being the invalu-able major source of the indispensable but otherwise largely unavailable work of LINDON, MERCER, PHILLIPS, REYNOLDS, and others. For these reasons, any reader of this, our book, will likely appreciate reading his enormously more. Moreover, since he recently told us that all his major contributors are deceased, we imagine and believe that this leaves him far and away the world's greatest living PALINDROMIST (and we also believe that he should therefore be accorded the status of a most cherished individual). He also told us: "Though I work on a number of highly diverse projects simultaneously, the corpus of my own palindromic and other curiological poetry has grown steadily in quantity and improved steadily in quality. To bring to fruition this work, which will include Edwin Fitzpatrick's *Fifth Translation of the Rubaiyat,* his *Sotadic Sapphics,* his *Palindromic Leaves of Walt Whitman,* and much else, is one of my several consuming passions. When I attain to that plateau of accomplishment for which I am specifically aiming, I will seek a publisher for the successor of *Palin-dromes and Anagrams."* Staggering news. For our part, we are dizzy with delight to know that BERGERSON, at least, is still out there shooting the moon. And we fairly swoon to antic-

Bar crab

ipate such a blessed event in the annals of PALINDROMANIA as this forthcoming sequel of his, an event however that will have to wait and gather moment until he and the audience are ready (say, in our wildest but best guess, around the millenium, or **2002**)!

Beryl, nosy visionary Cyrano is Ivy's only reb. We don't know any Beryl and we don't know why we'd be telling her or him this even if we did, but it seems perfectly apt for a Cyrano to be both nosy and visionary, and it seems apt also, since the sixties, for the Ivy League to be virtually free of all rebelliousness—save perhaps for that of a single farsighted busybody. (Alternatively, we may prefer to have a nosy and visionary Rabbinic sort of reb, that is, a Reb, in which case we would be blown clear out of the Ivy League, for *it* most probably already boasts a very full complement of at least eight of these Rebs, and we would in that case be reduced simply to noting the religious preference, say, of someone named Ivy, who, it should be said in all fairness, would then still be free under this interpretation to attend any Ivy League school. But whatever the ultimate reading, the combination and interaction of these three or four very peculiar proper names is highly bizarre in every case.)

Beware venom! Music I summon, ever a web! By LINDON, who knows and says what he doesn't want *and* then proceeds directly to what he desires in an admirable demonstration of gnomic virtuosity. How does so potent a poem emerge? Well, Lindon was, we gather from this text (and from many other references in his works to music, orchestras, opera, etc.), quite a music lover, as well as an appreciator, evidently, of the VALUE of contrast. Inevitably musing upon the word music, he must have seen early and often the self-standing *music I sum*, and may well have paused there with some satisfaction, for often well enough is partly done. Yet how far behind could the question have trailed: if we spell it all the way out to *music I summon*, then what? Then

Beware venom!
Music I summon,
ever a web!

B [...] B

-nom[.] music I summon, which virtually forces the promising . . . *venom[.] music I summon[,] ev-,* a possible but not very convincing closure itself as *venom music I summon, Ev,* ("says the snake charmer to his assistant"), which directly elicits the additional yet still not entirely satisfactory closure *re venom: music I summon ever* ("says the short yet very telling letter of explanation dictated by the snake charmer"). And yet from these arguably mediocre possible conclusions, which we are not aware he ever laid claim to, it was still owing perhaps only to Lindon's great genius that he even persevered to glimpse for the first time what is now to us the all-so-obvious fourth closure and crowning touch, nay apotheosis, of this proverb-league, inside-the-park four-bagger (or "gnome run"). Alternatively, even simultaneously, he may also have hatched this thought "from the outsides in" and via a "West Indian folk-truth" stepping-stone: **Beware venom, mon, ever a web.** Such a two-directional approach to composition, when it can be observed or surmised at all, is the mark of an expert and a master. (Though Lindon's PALINDROMES are so characteristically fine and delicate as to seem traceable and attributable to him on stylistic grounds alone, still, for this and most of our other attributions to Lindon, we rely on BERGERSON.)

beweb (bee-WEBB). To enclose in a web.

BHB. Airport code for Bar Harbor, ME.

bib (BIBB). **1:** to indulge in drinking; to tipple **2:** protective cloth worn under the chin or over the chest **3:** European cod, according to BORGMANN.

Bib. **1:** biblical **2:** (usually **bib.**) many other ABBREVIATIONS pertaining to books.

BIFRONTAL. Very nice synonym for the word *PALINDROME,* analogous to *bifronte,* the Italian word for *palindrome,* according to BORGMANN.

B [. . .] B

Bilge be glib.

Bilge be glib. Jack be nimble, Jack be quick . . . Johnny B. Good . . . and luck be a lady tonight.

Birdie I'd rib. Just funning, of course. See, too: **Sevareid ribs [as] Birdie raves.**

bird rib. Breast part, or an instance of giving someone the bird in jest.

Birds drib. Archaic formulation of cosmic law, generally mistranslated today as "Shit happens." (It is not really that shit happens so much as that love makes the world go round and birds of a feather flock together.)

Birth. Girl. Lass all right. Rib. Witty and concise yet charmingly redundant baby announcement, credited by CHISM to *WORD WAYS*. First rate.

Bishop made lame female damp? Oh, Sib! By LINDON. Outrageous. He spilled the wine, no doubt. We have seen a lame female before (**All erotic . . . Ella**), perhaps the same one, and though she is not ubiquitous or even cliché, it is interesting to observe how she and similar choice phrases such as "made damp," conveniently appearing here as well, may occasionally be inserted into the very middle of things to bring under control, or weird out entirely, a work in progress. *Bishop made damp, oh sib* alone is clearly nowhere near as good. And *bishop, oh sib* is hardly worth mentioning as anything at all. Yet in the hands of a master these few widgets twist together just so and, voilà, we are treated to a rich outburst of the surreal.

Bismarck's a task. Cram, sib. Brother, you better read that entire assignment on the Iron Chancellor before the exam tomorrow.

Bison, O sib! Brotherhood of the Buffalo slogan.

Blake [Dana] De Kalb. Another distinguished offspring of BORGMANN'S.

BNB. ABBREVIATION for the former British North Borneo (now Sabah).

bob (BAHB). To move (up and down) a variety of things in a variety of ways.

bob (BAHB). **1:** knoblike pendant (also called a plumb bob) **2:** a float **3:** jerk **4:** tap **5:** haircut type **6:** hair lock **7:** horse tail **8:** sled type **9:** skate type **10:** shilling.

Bob (BAHB). **1:** masculine name, usually a nickname for Robert **2:** lake of Ontario, 44°55'n/78°47'w.

BOB. Airport code for Bora Bora.

bog : gob. Gritty REVERSAL PAIR that is the beginning and ending of many oft-quoted PALINDROMES, and though some people dig this sort of stuff (and **putrid dirt up**), we are not looking to make too much of a mess.

Bishop made lame female damp? Oh, Sib! He spilled the wine, no doubt.

Bogo B. (as in Bay; BOH-goh), Philippines. Between Cebu and Leyte, 11°05'n/124°01'e. Compare: **Belle B.**

Bombard a drab mob. High-gloss confetti distributor's catchy slogan. Illustrated in IRVINE, 1987, and last seen on the Internet.

Bonaparte we trap, a nob. Say the Russians as he enters Moscow.

Bonk! One Mac. Newton sees not wen came (no knob). Attribution unknown, reported via the Internet by John JENSEN. Sir Isaac's famous Apple proves to be a Macintosh, but the rest of the story takes an even stranger turn in cyber-space.

boob (BOOB). The fool *or* the breast, not necessarily with it. It is astounding that there are so many PALINDROMIC alter-natives, namely: **bub, dud, pap, teet,** and **tit.** (And yet per-haps this is not so staggering in itself, but just as a natural development or artistic outgrowth of the already astonish-

ing palindromic set **aia, ama, amma, aya, mom,** and **mum**—
if indeed not also **pup** and all **lap pal** critters generally.)

borgmann, Dmitri A. The logologists' logologist, author of
Language on Vacation: An Olio of Orthographical Oddities (New
York: Scribner's, 1965) and *Beyond Language: Adventures in
Word and Thought* (New York: Scribner's, 1967). Borgmann
combined—in these books and generally—an adventure-
some, playful, ingenious originality with an apparently total
ability to recall in detail everything he ever encountered. He
should be designated an international treasure. We are
delighted to be able to present in this our collection a great
many of the gems he originally discovered or mined.

Borodin I do rob. The kuhns confess but are not guilty.

Bosnia Gains Ob! Headline summarizing latest peace agreement humors Bosnia (and hurts a governor) by extending
its territory across half of the former Soviet Union, that is,
clear to this short-named but far-flung Siberian river's
Arctic mouth and nearly Mongolian source, probably all
due to a tiny typographical error. If the correct reading
proves to be **O'B.,** as is perhaps more likely, this would refer
to an Irish civil warrior and therefore still indicate good
luck.

Bosses sob. Illustrated in stuart and terban. ("What do
owners of a company do when business goes bad?")

Boss is S.O.B.! Perhaps, but the center should be strongest,
as the "sun" of a "be" is.

Boston, O do not sob! The kuhns. (The Sox will play another day.)

Boswell, Lew, S.O.B. Marine drill sergeant Lewis Boswell
in best clipped form.

Bottomless Atlas, solo, casts a colossal tassel. (Motto B).
The most impressive complete survivor from the ancient let-

tered motto series. "Motto A" has become lost without a trace, and we cannot dignify with individual alphabetical entries the probably fragmentary, or speculative or unauthenticated others: **Cot tomato, hot A! (Motto C); Dot to my dits, Morse's Rom tidy (Motto D); Got to me! (Motto G); Hot tomalley, Ella! (Motto H); Jotto! (Motto J); Lotto! (Motto L);** [??—Text completely missing . . .] **(Motto M); Not to me, babe! (Motto N); O Otto! (Motto O); Pot-to-Manna! (Motto P); Rot to mottos, Otto! (Motto R); Sotto motto (Motto S);** and possibly but not plausibly a **Giotto Motto (IG)** and **Blotto Motto (LB).**

Boss is S.O.B.!

BOUSTROPHEDON (BOO-struh-*FEED*-'n *or* BOO-struh-*FEE*-dahn *or, much more delightfully,* booss-TRAW-fehy-*DAWN, as the original Greek adverb*). How an ox turns while plowing a field: one row out and the next row back, etc. Included here for its beauty even more than its relevancy, it is still today an approximately good picture of the mental back-and-forth sweeping motion commonly used for seeing and seeking PALINDROMES, but it was formerly the very quaint way some very ancient Greeks actually wrote and read—thereby virtually provoking the birth or discovery of PALINDROMY. In mental gym you can develop an exhilarating fluency for ambidextrous ox turns (booss-TRAW-fehy- . . .), then, in a flash (and how does the trudging produce the lightning?) will come an even more exhilarating -*dawn* (wow! right between the brains!) when you find yourself reading, and therefore seeing and moving, both ways at once!

Bruce none curb. Happily the guy is irrepressible.

BSB. Airport code for Brasilia.

btb. ABBREVIATION for "bus tiebreaker," according to DE SOLA, who does not explain it. Though a strange concept, it is certainly beguiling enough to catch our fancy and lead us to muse about playing in some way with buses, as, for example, by racing them, stacking them, jumping over them, stuffing them with people, etc. Neat! (But it might be even neater to know *who's* talking and what game they *are* playing.)

bub (BUBB). Fellow, bubble, or **boob.**

Buckle no parts, nor, Pa, pop apron strap on elk cub. By POOL. Another choice pet PAL.

Buckley's on a nosy elk cub *or* **Buckleys sag on no gassy elk cub** *or, conversely,* **Buckleys sag, level gassy elk cub.** It's all bull at the Elks Club when Conservatives risk a ride on the wild side.

Bucks are paper! Ask, cub! Flush parent bears present money.

BUILT-UP REVERSALS. The following are by BORGMANN:

    Elbert : treble
   Delbert : trebled
  Adelbert : trebled *A*
 Adelberta : a trebled *A*

BURIED CITIES

Bulgaria! Air! [. . . A glub.] Nonwords drown on. "Attributable" to Sotades.

BURIED CITIES. By BORGMANN: "It is a queer fact that there are 15 French and Italian cities buried in the word PALINDROMES; 7 French cities and 8 Italian cities. The French cities: Paris, Le Mans, Amiens, Orléans, Laon, Sedan, and Prades. The Italian cities: Rome or Roma, Milan or Milano, Naples or Napoli, Palermo, Pisa, Salerno, Siena, and San Remo."

Burl Ives Evil Rub! (trademarked as **Mt. Burl Ives Evil Rub**™). Whimsical "folk" remedy, a wellness restorative, sort of like Ben-Gay, only milder—to soothe the savage soul. (Indeed it doesn't actually rub against evil at all but works instead by allowing and mounting good.)

Bush saw Sununu swash sub. Attribution unknown, reported by John JENSEN. Well and cleverly constructed, this item is without context if it doesn't refer to their navy days or, if they didn't have any together, to an incident involving an undersecretary.

Bush: Sub! *also* **Bush: Ah, sub!** *and* **Bush: Oh, sub!** This is playing upon his role as understudy to and ultimately substitute for Reagan, and all Bush League as PALINDROMES. **Bush H-Sub** would be a good name for a nuclear submarine (but no reason to start a new one), and so we are left without a good Bush item in hand while seeming only to give him the bird. Perhaps the preceding entry will serve to fill the position until a better (and preferably a solo) one can be found.

But sad Eva saved a stub. See: **Cigar? Toss it in a can, it is so tragic.** Good slapstick cartoon sequence with a wide following.

BxB. Bishop takes bishop, in chess notation. PALINDROME lovers are likely chess lovers because PALINDROMY is a cross between chess and poetry.

But sad Eva saved a stub. Good slapstick cartoon sequence.

C [. . .] C

ca. I Dozen (or one "Zodiac"). Substandard but fairly recognizable signs of a round twelve.

cainamaniac. A great fan either of numbing agents such as novacaine and cocaine, or, usually capitalized, of envious, fratricidal sorts, or else of either or both of these and/or either or both varieties of **ainamania**.

Cain, a Monomaniac. Shingle for a single-minded person of one name. By the KUHNS.

Caliente bet Neil a C. (This is actually a C-note, $100, as will eventually be clarified at **Eton, Caliente bet Neil a C-note.** There is also an almost equally good variant, as will also be seen from the evidence presented below: **S.E. Caliente bet Neil aces.**) As for what the wager was about, we can tell you that the (southeast) Nevada town of Caliente, though not a PALINDROME itself, was understandably hot to trot, wishing fervently to become recognized as the official PALINDROMIC hot spot of an already radioactively hot palindromic state (see **Adaven : Nevada;** also **Denio . . . joined** and **Reno oner**), and the town evidently went so far as to bet $100 that no one could find a hotter one than itself. After all, its official current (1990 census) population stands at an amazing **1,111,** four aces, its current *AAA Road Atlas* coordinates are K-11 (which translates, alphanumerically, also to **11-11,** four more aces!), and its name even means "h-o-t-t-hot"! (If some of these indications seem arbitrary and/or ephemeral, it should be noted that an earlier census gave Caliente a rare ROTATOR PALINDROME **pop.** of **916,** and also that **AAA** is unlikely to be supplanted or to change its successful format any time soon.) Nevertheless, our crazy friend Neil, as the texts indicate, actually took the bet, thinking to win with **Otto** (New York), which, at **pop. 777,** does make a good run for the money—at least until its **AAA** coordinates, J-38, and other weaknesses reveal it for what it is: a relative bust at nothing more than two pair plus three of a kind against Caliente's eight aces in joker-wild Nevada. Neil of course had to pay, and he then wisely returned to palindrome school for an **Eton . . . C-note.**

Callac (kah-LÆK). Small village of France near Guingamp in Côtes-du-Nord, 48°24'n/3°26'w.

Call a spade an Ædapsallac. Yes, and see what happens. This sort of thing should not be encouraged, however. For a sample of what could result, consult: **Copywriters . . . sretirwypoc,** or **Drowatonsi . . . not a word,** or **Not Gnirrabta . . . Barrington.**

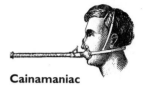

Cainamaniac

Call Ida! Call a Cadillac! Call anyone! . . . Or quite the contrary.

Calvert : Trevlac. REVERSAL PAIR of modern communities, in Texas and Indiana, respectively.

Camper's rep, Mac. Man of that rare calling and breed, the Scotch-Irish squatter's agent.

Campus motto: Bottoms up, Mac. Should be inscribed somewhere. See also the teetotaling **Ban campus motto, "Bottoms up, MacNab."**

Camus sees sumac. Illustrated in IRVINE, 1987.

CANCRINE VERSES (KÆNG-kreen). A Latinistic term (from *versus cancrinus*) for PALINDROMIC verses, associating and emblazoning them with *cancer*—the crab, the summer solstice, the sun, the south—and *heat,* and, via the Greek cognate word *karkinos,* all of the above images plus *pincers,* or "tweezers."

Can go! Cognac! It's a launch! The good stuff has arrived!

Capac. Hamlet of St. Clair County, Michigan, 43°00'n/ 82°55'w. In a far fetch, this could be a relative of, or the same as, Manco **Capac,** son of the sun in Inca myth.

C [. . .] C

carac. A galleon or large cargo ship, according to BORGMANN.

CARCINOI (KAHR-sih-noy). From χαρχινοι, the Greek word for "crabs," a word meaning PALINDROMES. For an explanation, see: CANCRINE VERSES.

case > sac. Metamorphic container belonging to the KUHNS.

Castaneda [sees a] den at SAC! The Strategic Air Command turns out to be run by a bunch of Don Juan freaks.

Casual Lausac. Name of a very laid-back mix-and-match clothing salesman covering a vast territory, we would guess, from Lausanne (Switzerland) all the way to Cransac or Callac (France).

CASUAL. Casualness is an important element in palindromognomy, this occurring-by-chance, unpremeditated, not planned, informal, relaxed, without specific purpose, aimless, unconcerned creativity. And we make a point of being casual not merely for the considerable VALUE of letting one's hair or clothing or limbs *chance to fall,* which must account for some of its etymology, but especially because it means "just happening or *chancing to fall,* like out of a clear blue sky," which is how PALINDROMES, especially very good palindromes, do seem to matriculate. They are marvels of happenchance and happy return, hot spots burning in reality. You can feel this heat as well as the accompanying sense of déjà vu that for some reason especially riddles the best of palindromes. And their centers of symmetry, the very hearts from which they sometimes seem to issue and return, are of course always situated at the crack between the worlds of left and right—an interesting place to be and to orient if, as we surmise, our two brains, left and right, are not so much about the widely credited split between Intuitive and Rational, or English and Math, or Art and Science, as they are about the almost completely overlooked interrelationship between Outer and Inner, Physical and Nonphysical, Temporary and Perma-

c [. . .] c

nent. (How could the left-right axis ever be confused with the in-out, the up-down, or the fore-aft? the pragmatist in us wonders. And the dreamer in us marvels back, How could all the axes *not* be equal and synonymous as they whirl about one another in the integral dance of life!)

CC. 1: airline code for Crown Aviation **2:** cubic centimeter **3:** carbon copy.

CCC. Civilian Conservation Corps, among others.

CCCC. ABBREVIATION for Cape Cod Community College.

CDC. Airport code for Cedar City, Utah.

CEC. Airport code for Crescent City, California.

CFC. Chlorofluorocarbon.

CGC. Airport code for Cape Gloucester, New Britain.

CHC. Airport code for Christchurch, New Zealand.

Cherokees seek ore, H.C. Holy Cheez! Communion *and* hard money?! It's as if they'd become White Men!

CHIASMUS (kahy-ÆZ-muss). Quasi-palindromic sort of rhetorical balancing device in which the second pair of two paired structures is in some sense made into a reversal of the first pair, as in Coleridge's "Flowers are lovely, love is flowerlike" or Pope's "Works without show, and without pomp presides." The mirror-image character of the AB:BA pattern exhibited by the four terms of a chiasmus taken together reminded Greek academicians of the four-directional shape of the letter *X*, in those days called *chi*, and that is how chiasmi got their name.

CHISM, Stephen J. Author of ***From A to Zotamorf: The Dictionary of Palindromes*** (Word Ways Press, 1992), probably the most numerous collection of PALINDROMES and PALIN-DROMIC words and phrases we will ever see (yet, like the pres-

Χαρχινοι

C ⌈ . . . ⌉ C

Cibohphobic

ent book, still not fully inclusive of BERGERSON's and BORG-MANN's entire collections). CHISM observes: "Every small, lackluster palindrome represents a victory over incredible odds. The ones that crystallize a thought or create a provocative image are absolute miracles!" Many of his fine creations in this, our book, were written after 1992 and graciously contributed by him upon request.

Christ, Sir H.C. *Mister* Holy Communion, a Catholic pal. Also: **Christ, [is it,] Sir? (H.C.?)** and/or **Christ [is It]! "Sir H.C."!**, etc.

cibohphobic. Having an irrational fear of PALINDROMES. Compare: **aibohphobia, ainamania, ebohphobe, cainamaniac, ciloholic,** etc.

ciborian : Nairobic. A BORGMANN double-mint REVERSAL (both words coined by him but on his own always-impeccable recognizance), probably best reversed to form the spiritual **Nairobic Ciborian,** a design style, we would say, typical of the Eucharistic-wafer boxes found in Metropolitan Kenya. An accomplishment.

CIC. 1: airport code for Chico, CA **2:** Roman numerals for 199 **3:** Marcus Tullius Cicero, abbreviated.

Cigar? Toss it in a can, it is so tragic. By LINDON, who continues: **But sad Eva saved a stub.** A nice sequence of one-liners, oft recited and so well loved, we think, because it is such a fine spoof of all moralistic propaganda and all pushing against.

cilic (SILL-ikk). Referring to cilia, the microscopic hairlike processes extending from a cell surface and often capable of rhythmical motion, or to eyelashes.

ciloholic. One who is addicted to PALINDROMES. Compare: **aibohphobia, ainamania.**

CIMABUE DE UBÁ, Rennodleah (RENN-uhd-*LEH*-yuh CHEE-mah-*BOO*-ehy JEE-oo-*BAH*). A fantastic Brazilian artist of Florentine and Celtic extraction who is a probable companion or counterpart of Michael Donner. Her name appears mysteriously as an alias on his driver's license application.

Cinci packs K.C. a picnic. Bengals have Chiefs for lunch, their way.

Cine got . . . (?) . . . Oh! Photogenic! That face-lift sure did wonders for the old movie house.

cinic (SINN-ikk). Doglike, a reformed spelling, according to BORGMANN.

citamatic (SAHY-duh-*MÆ*-dick). Advanced word-processing software that automatically cites, records, and files all references, footnotes, and bibliographical materials and requests and secures permission to quote whenever necessary (without which this book would not have been impossible).

Cite operas as are poetic. Good policy, possibly first enunciated by BERGERSON or FITZPATRICK, we are not sure which, yet the text is seemingly prerequisite and certainly akin to LINDON's possibly senior brilliancy **Cite opera? We fail, Eli. A few are poetic.** Hence we may speculate that both PALINDROMES originated with LINDON. And with fragments as potent and major as these, many minors will inevitably arise, such as **Cite opera, fare poetic** and **Cite opera, rare, poetic.**

Ciloholic.
One who is addicted to palindromes.

citotic (sahy-TAH-dick). Marked by a psychotic compulsion for citing original sources by chapter and verse.

civic (SIVV-ikk). **1:** pertaining to public affairs or to a city **2:** (capitalized) type of compact Honda.

CoC. ABBREVIATION for Chamber of Commerce.

C [. . .] C

Cod doc

cod doc (CAHD DAHK). Illustrated in TERBAN, who clues it "cold water fish physician."

CoDoC. Artistic ABBREVIATION for Cooperation in Documentation and Communication.

COEN, Gary. Author of *The Poetics of the Palindrome*, (master's thesis, University of Texas at Dallas, 1978), cited by CHISM.

Colbert : Trebloc. REVERSAL PAIR of living communities, by BORGMANN, in Oklahoma and Michigan, respectively.

Colby, Kansas, is a snaky bloc. None of the usual elephants and donkeys in this real-world political hub and seat of Thomas County. Also **Colby, Kansas is a snaky bloc** (that is, without the comma after Kansas) may become a CIA whisper.

Collard : Dralloc. REVERSAL PAIR by BORGMANN linking John Collard, British author, 1769–1810, with his own pseudonym or anonym.

COLORADO. Mentioned honorably here, and perhaps challengingly, as one of the few PALINDROME-free states, that is, containing not a single palindrome (at least among the names of its major localities—though some people may be interested to know that Dotsero, a place in Eagle County, was formerly retrorsed, according to BORGMANN, by a neighboring REVERSAL twin town, Orestod) and never, so far as we know, successfully palindromized itself. (We have been toying with **Oir o dar, o loco Colorado—Río,** "[To] hear or give, O crazy Red—the River, that it," but this is fragmentary if not delirious.)

Colvin : Nivloc. REVERSAL PAIR of ghost towns, in Alabama and Nevada, respectively. By BORGMANN.

COMPOUND PALINDROME. Single word or longer assemblage composed of a series of PALINDROMES, such as *reverses* (**rever** plus **ses**), *papooses* (**pap** plus **oo** plus **ses**), *Agamemnon* (**Aga** plus **mem** plus **non**), **Report it, Roper! / Pull a "Gallup"!**, or even **Egad! An adage / was a saw!**

Copywriters should learn to convey their ideas clearly and incisively without using gobbledygook that sounds like ekil sdnuos taht koogydelbbog gnisu tuohtiw ylevisicni dna ylraelc saedi rieht yevnoc ot nrael dluohs sretirwypoc. Quoted by IRVINE, 1987, who says John Ciardi once received it from a reader of his column in *Saturday Review.*

Cora sees a roc. By LINDON. Fabulous. This text may seem, like all short PALINDROMIC sentences, inevitable, but catching sight of this powerful, legendary bird required a keen eye and perhaps also an extra sensitivity for language and for the surreal. Does this mean that **Camus sees sumac** and **Dora sees a rod** and **Don did nod** are less good? Yes, the more fanciful or far out, the better, we think.

Cornwall lawn roc. A huge, powerful, happily fabulous bird of prey for the front yard, not to be confused with the domestic Rock Cornish hen.

Count No 'Count. Local nickname, a WORD PALINDROME, for novelist William Faulkner in his hometown of Oxford, Mississippi.

CQC. ABBREVIATION for "Citizens for a Quiet City," though *which* city is naturally a well-kept secret.

CRACK BETWEEN THE WORLDS, THE. A term borrowed from Don Juan Matus via Carlos Castaneda, and possibly intended by them in a different sense, it is for PALINDROMOLOGISTS the usually invisible center of symmetry or blending point between the right and the left, or between the outer and the inner, or—and here Don Juan would probably agree—between the manifested and the nonmanifested worlds. The crack between the worlds is emblematic of, and is perhaps the clearest imaginable physical representation of,

C [. . .] C

the access point and route to inner space (though ompha-loskeptics may claim, with some reason, to have gone so far as to square or cube even this degree of near perfection, that is, if, as seems likely, the crack actually proves to be a two-headed spiral).

CT, etc. ("Connecticut, et cetera.") PALINDROMIC nickname for a new kind of recirculating play state that typically begins triple-talking with Kinetic-Connecticut-Etiquette, breaks irregularly for Chic-Kentucky-Fried or Fried-Chicken-Tucky, eventually could even get down to Cloak-Calforna-Cajun, etc.

Cuba Buc. Pirate of the Indies.

Cub v. Buc. Words for the marquee at Three Rivers or Wrigley Field.

Cuc. River of Brazil (and possibly a bit of French Guiana), into the Amazon, 1°22'n/53°33'w.

CXC. Roman numerals for 190.

cyc. ABBREVIATION both for *cycles* and for "curb your curios-ity" (this latter meaning is probably from military and/or security lingo).

c ⌞ . . . ⌟ c

Dabale arroz a la zorra el abad (DHAH-bvah-leh a*R*OHSS ah-lah-SOH*R*-*r*ah el-ah-BVAHDH). Spanish: The abbot gave rice to the fox (vixen, strumpet). Quoted by Alastair Reid. Intriguing.

Dad. Father or **Pop**, or **a papa**, even **Abba**, that is, **ole-man name (lo!)**—world's possibly most PALINDROMIC individual!

d [. . .] d

Dad (Gab!), Ma, etc.?: "Team" Bagdad. For an explanation, see: "**MADD Astartes" set "Rat Saddam."**

Daedalus: Nine . . . Peninsula: Dead. One of the strangest line scores, illustrated in IRVINE, 1987, and last seen surfing the net.

daft fad. The KUHNS' madcap mania, and a perfectly good cover for PALINDROMANIA.

Dad

Daft, I meet Señorita Edna, gorge grog and eat iron, esteem it fad. By LINDON. Frolicsome daft. And long. It is possible here, in this mostly modular construction, to catch a glimpse or glimmer of the master PALINDROMIST's art, for since we see that cuts may be made that still leave a sensible result, though not as sensibly surreal a result (specifically *gorge grog* first and then, too, *Edna . . . and*), we may surmise that the semantic and comedic peak was reached by mounting these same steps. Only a great deal of experience and wit, trial and error, and, perhaps most important, desire could produce such a stroke of genius.

Dailies use *Iliad.* Evidently in serialized installments. Compare: **Yes, Syd, on *Odyssey.***

dairy myriad. Lots and lots of milk cows, strictly speaking ten thousand of them; at least partially illustrated in IRVINE, 1987.

Dalad Qi. Small town of China, 40°28'n/110°02'e (*Qi* seems to mean "town").

Dallas is all ad. Nicely illustrated in IRVINE, 1992.

Dallas : sallad. REVERSAL PAIR by BORGMANN, in which a nineteenth-century salad goes to Texas.

Dame Russia is sure mad! She thought democracy and free markets would be easier to learn than *this*. Credited by CHISM to *WORD WAYS*.

Damn! I, Agassi, miss again! Mad! Attribution unknown; reported by John JENSEN.

Damon was I ere I saw Nomad. By Gordon W. Grossman, reported in William Safire's "On Language" column in *The New York Times Magazine* in early 1989, where we learn that an investment firm named Nomad Partners LP had just bought the stock of the Damon Corporation, a chemical laboratory company, in a hostile takeover.

Damosel, a poem? A carol? Or a cameo pale? (So mad!) Possibly by MERCER. A grand infatuation. To see very clearly how one good PALINDROME idea may lead to another, compare LINDON's probably earlier **A poem, a carol—or a cameo, Pa!**

Damsels in a deep stress assert, "Speed! An isle's mad!" Virgins tense again (St. Croix or St. Thomas from the look of it), and a call goes out for prompt assistance, so we are writing in an instant happy outcome and return to paradise.

d & d. Deaf & dumb, drunk & disorderly, and dungeons & dragons, all together of course suggesting a rousing round of **d & d d & d d & d**—but probably not a very good idea after all.

DATES. The foreshortened ten-year interval between PALINDROMIC years, or special period of balancing, occurs only at milleniums and would appear to present special opportunities. (Between nonmillenial centuries the interval is much longer, 109 years, as was the case recently, and will be soon again, between **1881–1991** and then **2002–2112**, and in such long oblivion, generations may come and go without ever awakening to a PALINDROMIC year. On the other hand, the interval at the turn of the first millenium shrank to only one year, resulting in the continuous triennial millenium **999–1000–1001** and quite a rush we should think, but this phenomenon will not repeat until the end of the tenth millenium.) The present period of balancing, **1991–2002,** a dozen years enclosing a decade embracing a millenium, like all such periods has its point of greatest balance not at the actual millenium point but at its own midpoint, which turns out in this case to be the moment of New Year's 1997. Let others argue whether the real millenium occurs in 2000 or 2001 and at what time of year. (They will.) Our palindromic millenium is already upon us, will last a full dozen years and will halve itself for us conveniently, like a carton of eggs, in a fleeting and precise moment of maximum balance, 1996 becoming 1997, prefiguring yet actualizing the millenial transition at least three years before most people will realize that anything millenial could possibly have yet happened. (This early celebration of the millenium has the added bonus and virtue of being in complete agreement with the traditional birthyear of Creation, **4004** B.C., since **4004** + 1996 = 6000, and of being within a week of complete agreement with the traditional birthday of Christ, on December 25, 4 B.C., insomuch as 4 + 1996 = 2000. For all these reasons, the holiday season of 12/25/96 through 1/1/97—better yet, make that Thanksgiving, or even Halloween, 1996 right on through to Ground Hog Day 1997 inclusive—ought to be an unusually interesting season for partying. See also: **999** and **4004.**)

Dame Russia is sure mad!

Following are signal PALINDROMIC years, with selected historical events found in them.

> **4004** B.C. The year of Creation, the exact date being October 23, as first reckoned from various biblical and other information by James Ussher in A.D.

D [. . .] D

1650. A similar or possibly the same scheme traditionally places the moment of Christ's birth (presumably on December 25) in the year 4 B.C. The peculiar and exact four and four-thousand relationship between these two widely-believed-in, symbolically foursquare years seems almost a bald incitation to millenialism and cabalistic numerology if not outright palindromism and quadratic OMPHALOSKEPSIS. See also: **999.**

2002 B.C. Last days of XIth Dynasty and rule of Upper Egypt.

1991 B.C. The pharaoh Amenemhet I (XII Dynasty) now rules from Lower Egypt.

777 B.C. Uzziah is king of Judah.

767 B.C. Uzziah is still king of Judah.

747 B.C. Beginning of Babylonian Chronicle, with Nabonassar.

727 B.C. Shalmaneser V of Assyria besieges Samaria.

696 B.C. Twenty-third Olympiad. Boxing is added.

626 B.C. Chaldean general Nabopolassar seizes Babylonian throne and breaks away from Assyria. Assyria's King Ashurbanipal dies.

565 B.C. Taoism is founded.

555 B.C. Nabonidus overthrows Chaldean dynasty in Babylon. (See: **626.**)

545 B.C. Amasis rules Egypt (XXVIth Dynasty), and Nabonidus and Belshazzar rule Babylon.

525 B.C. Cambyses conquers Egypt, and Egypt remains under Persian kings until **404.**

474 B.C. Pindar moves to Thebes, writes *Odes.*

424 B.C. Upon the death of Xerxes II, Darius II becomes ruler of Persia.

323 B.C. Alexander the Great dies, and Euclid is born.

272 B.C. Antigonus defeats invasion of Pyrrhus of Epirus.

11. Augustus Caesar was emperor of Rome in both **11** B.C. and A.D. **11.**

D [. . .] D

111. Trajan was emperor of Rome.

161. Marcus Aurelius becomes emperor of Rome.

232. Alexander Severus is emperor of Rome.

242. Gordian III is emperor of Rome.

252. Gallus is emperor of Rome.

262. Gallianus is emperor of Rome.

282. Carus becomes emperor of Rome.

292. Maximian is emperor of Rome.

333. Constantine the Great is emperor of Rome.

343. The Roman emperor Constans is replaced by Constantius II.

373. Valentinian I is Western Roman emperor and Valens Eastern.

383. Roman legions begin to withdraw from Britain under Emperor Magnus Maximus.

393. Theodosius the Great is Roman emperor in East and West for a brief period.

434. Valentinian III is Western Roman emperor, and Theodosius II is Eastern.

444. Valentinian III is still Western Roman emperor, and Theodosius II is still Eastern.

454. Valentinian III is still Western Roman emperor, but Marcian is now Eastern.

484. Aristides banished. (See: **Ah . . . Aha.**)

636. Arabs win Persia at the battle of Cadesia.

646. Arabs recapture Alexandria.

656. Clotaire III becomes king of the Franks.

686. Conon becomes pope.

737. Childeric III becomes king of the Franks.

757. Paul I becomes pope.

797. Irene is Empress of Byzantium.

818. Louis I, the Pious, is Holy Roman Emperor.

828. Egbert of Wessex is recognized as overlord of other English kings, the first king of England.

838. Egbert is still king of England, and Louis I, the Pious, is still Holy Roman Emperor.

D ⌈ . . . ⌉ D

848. Gottschalk, a Benedictine monk, advocates predestination. Ethelwulf is king of England.

858. Ethelbald, eldest son of Ethelwulf, becomes king of England. Louis II is Holy Roman Emperor.

868. Ethelred I is king of England. Louis II is still Holy Roman Emperor.

878. Syracuse taken by the Arabs. Alfred defeats the Danes at Edington, and Danelaw begins.

888. Odo becomes count of Paris. Alfred the Great is king of England.

898. Edward the Elder is king of England. Lambert and Arnulf are co-Holy Roman Emperors.

909. Cluny founded.

919. Henry I becomes king of Germany.

929. Athelstan is king of England. Stephen VII becomes pope. Henry I is Holy Roman Emperor.

939. Edmund becomes king of England, and Stephen VIII becomes pope. Civil War in Japan.

949. Edred is king of England.

959. Edgar the Peaceful becomes king of England. St. Dunstan tries to enforce clerical celibacy.

969. Fourth PALINDROMIC year in the reign of **Otto** I, the Great, of the Holy Roman Empire.

979. Ethelred Unræd ("the Unready's") first of four palindromic years on the throne of England.

989. Vladimir the Great adopts Christianity in Russia. Hugh Capet is king of France.

999. In this year Sylvester II becomes pope, Bagauda becomes the first king of Kano, in northern Nigeria, and the Poles conquer Silesia. And, toward year's end, all across Europe and the Byzantine, monasteries and churches are thronged with faithful believers bearing gifts of land deeds, jewels, valuable manuscripts, and wagonloads of possessions in hopes of favorable Judgment. As church bells ring continuously on December 31, nobility kneel with peasants, and many are amazed when the world does not come to an end at midnight. For background, see also: **4004** B.C.

1001. Arab explorer Mahmud of Ghazni makes the first of his seventeen expeditions to India, while Ethelred II ("the Unready") celebrates his fourth palindromic year as king of England, **Otto** III his third as Holy Roman Emperor, and Robert II (the Pious) his second as king of France.

1111. Henry V of the Holy Roman Empire compels Pope Paschal II to renounce the right of investiture (namely, to acknowledge the independent power of the emperor), while Louis VI (the Fat) rules France, and Henry I, England.

1221. Genghis Khan overthrows Khorasmian empire and Robert becomes emperor of the Eastern Empire. Henry III, Alexander II, Philip II Augustus, and Frederick II are on the thrones of England, Scotland, France, and the Holy Roman Empire respectively.

DATES: **1221**

1331. Japanese emperor Godaigo renews his efforts to regain power from the Hojo regent. Civil war begins.

1441. African slave trade begins, in Lisbon. University of Bordeaux is founded. Jan van Eyck dies at Bruges.

1551. Saxony and France make peace, but Turkey and Hungary go to war. Archbishop Cranmer publishes forty-two articles of religion. Edward VI is king of England, Mary is the Queen of Scots, and Charles VII is king of France.

1661. The first evening school is established (in New York), and the first bible in an Indian language (Algonquian) is published (by John Eliot in Cambridge, Massachusetts). Louis XIV becomes absolute monarch of France, Mazarin dies, the English acquire Bombay, and the Chinese, Formosa.

D [. . .] D

The Treaty of Kardis between Russia and Sweden restores all conquests to each other.

1771. The first equestrian and dwarf exhibitions take place (in Boston), Carl Scheele discovers oxygen, and Russia conquers the Crimea. First edition of the *Encyclopædia Britannica* appears. Gustavus III becomes king of Sweden. George III and Louis XV already rule England and France.

1881. The only year in the presidency of James Garfield (who is the first presidential candidate to campaign in a foreign language and whose mother is the first First Mother to live in the White House) and the first year in that of his successor, Chester A. Arthur, and just a year among many in the reign of Victoria. The American Red Cross, the American Federation of Labor, and the first business school (Wharton) are founded. The first successful dynamo, cream separator, photographic film, player piano, and electrical lighting system are developed, J. H. Logan introduces the loganberry, and the first international phone conversation and national lawn tennis championship take place. Peace breaks out, between New Zealand settlers and Maori aborigines and in South Africa following the Boer War. Alexander III becomes czar of Russia. Work begins on the Panama Canal. Sitting Bull surrenders, but the Mahdi appears in the Sudan. Kingdom of Roumania begins.

DATES: **1961.**
Rotator year, a
bonus (nonnormal)
palindrome.

1961. **Rotator** year, a bonus (nonnormal) PALINDROME.

1991. The normal palindromic year of the twentieth century, though if you had missed it you would only have had to wait until **2002** for another — less of a wait than usual. George Bush is president, and Elizabeth II is queen.

2002. The PALINDROMIC year to come, completing the

D [. . .] D

current twelve-year period of balancing (**1991–2002**) and the PALINDROMIC millenium. See also: **1991.**

Day came—not one Macy ad. By Joaquin KUHN.

daylily ad. Ephemeral but beautiful garden flower commercial, by the KUHNS.

DD. 1: airline code for Command Airways 2: due date 3: dutch door 4: "He gave to God" (*Deo Dedit*) 5: Doctor of Divinity.

ddd. Deadline delivery date.

Dear cameras are "MacRaed." Gordon won't endorse or perform for cheap.

decider : rediced. REVERSAL, converging in: **Decider rediced.** (Decision-maker gambled again.)

Deb abed *or* **deb abed** (DEB uh-*BED*). Could be a decent story here, as LINDON's little poem, "Away with That Table Game!" in BERGERSON's *Palindromes and Anagrams*, shows.

Debbed

Debase wedlock, cold ewes abed! This line, according to BERGERSON—who suggests that a familiarity with the opera would be a help in interpreting it—is an outtake from Edwin FITZPATRICK's otherwise inscrutable PALINDROMIC opera, "Fling Thong." We look forward to seeing this text in its full context, hopefully in his forthcoming book, for it is a fine example of sophisticated, seamless construction, and its drollery is evident even without a libretto.

debbed (DEBBD). Made a debut, as a deb(utante).

Debed. River, in Armenia and Georgia, into the Caspian Sea via Alaverdi, 41°22'n/44°58'e.

DE BISSCHOP, Jani. Published a sixty-line Latin PALINDROMIC poem in the year 1700, according to BORGMANN.

D [. . .] D

Deb nixes sex in bed.

Deb nixed Dex in bed. Natch. It's no place for pep pills!

Deb nixes sex in bed. Now she's just being different.

Decadent Ned aced. Illustrated in IRVINE, 1992.

decils : sliced. REVERSAL, without great synergy: the positions of two planets, 36° apart . . . are halved.

de-deeded. Given by CHISM as an English word, citing *WORD WAYS*, without explanation. It feels natural enough as a nonce compound (though the hyphenation seems avoidable). Since "to deed" means "to transfer by means of a deed," "to *dedeed*" might mean "to undo, remove, or deprive of a deed" or even "to deprive of a deed as well as the property covered by the deed."

Dedicated Det. Acid 'Ed *also* **Dedicated to Pot Det. Acid 'Ed.** (*or* **to Idiot**); *and see our dedication* **to Gray Argot.** All together, quite a collection of paths and characters built along lines played by Stacy Keach in Cheech and Chong's *Nice Dreams* and leading in the end to Committed Investigative Psychedelic Education. And there is always Ed's sidekick sleuth to back him up, with a similarly open-ended outlook: **Det. I. Milton's not limited.**

Dedication NOITACIDED! (*NAWYT*-uh-SAHY-did). If there were such a word, it would mean *censored*, killed by night (or, in lower case, killed the whole night), usually in Rio, Lisbon, or Provincetown, in the advanced Portuguenglish spoken in such cosmoplaces. (See our deadication page.)

dedivided. The KUHNS' "separation outcome" and yet, in one probability, happily returned to *unity*.

deed (DEED). The action or the document.

DEED. Behold the first line of the following WORD SQUARE, by BORGMANN:

```
D  E  E  D
E  C  C  E
E  C  C  E
D  E  E  D
```

deedeed (DEE DEED). Euphemistic substitute for the word *damned*, according to BORGMANN.

Deem if I meed. See: **Deer Maddam reed.**

Deeps : speed. The most intense or extreme parts fly by.

Deer body do breed. By POOL. More explicit and playful but not more natural than **Deer breed**, by LINDON (a truism, or possibly an animal movie).

"Deer cedar, let sap erupt pure pastel," Ra decreed. This Stephen CHISM dream in living technicolor stands, in our estimation, on a very high level and reminds us how delighted we are that he is one of our leading cocreators.

Deer feral are freed. The tame ones are kept.

"Deer flee freedom in Oregon." / "No, Geronimo—deer feel freed." REVERSAL PAIR of sentences by BORGMANN, evidently not intended by him as a PALINDROME but certainly amounting to an excellent parody of one, wherein a logical fallacy offered up by a perfectly wooden Indian is confounded by an even more illogical rebuttal from a patronizing interlocutor. The chat has a lovely surreal air about it.

Deer frisk, sir, freed. An echo or summation of either or both of the previous two items, possibly by MERCER.

Deer Maddam reed : Deem if I meed. John Taylor's PALINDROME pair, published in 1614, which was dedicated to **"Anna"** Queen of Great Britain, presumably Anne of Denmark, wife of James I.

Deft fellow at New York, Roy, went AWOL, left Fed. Clever escape artist made it over the wall at the big house.

D [. . .] D

degaraged (DEE-guh-*RAHJD*). Automotive exposure, according to the KUHNS. The word seems an odd and yet impeccable way to describe something (presumably though not necessarily a vehicle) that has been taken out of a garage, or lost its garage, for whatever reason or time period. Indeed it is odd that it seems odd when one considers that just about every vehicle has probably at some time, or even often, been **degaraged**!

Degas aged. It was inevitable.

Degas, are we not drawn onward, we freer few, drawn onward to new eras aged? Given by AUGARDE, who comments: "As palindromes get longer, sense tends to be left behind." This one is sensible enough and even exudes a charming, idealistic sentimentality—assuming only that it is "we" (the unidentified speaker and the artist, and perhaps some others) who are "aged," which would be only natural as new eras accumulate and which was the case with Degas toward the end of his life (1917), when he was in his eighties. BERGERSON and BORGMANN both guess it is by MERCER.

Degenerative? : Evita reneged. REVERSAL SENTENCE in a word. Evita cancelled her part, for she wanted no part of this falling apart. And no matter, for BORGMANN gives even more spectacular examples of the form—see: **retroposition** . . . and **retroperitoneal** . . .

degged. "Sprinkled" or "dampened," primarily oral, and used only in parts of England, according to BORGMANN.

deified (DEE-uh-fahyd). Made into (a) God; apotheosized; divinized.

Deified? Mistress asserts I'm deified. Yes, it seems an odd idea at first, but she's right. By CHISM.

deifier : reified. REVERSAL PAIR, and probably a match made in Heaven for such rarefied metaphysical concepts (if only we could understand them).

Dei fingis: **signified** (Latin and English, respectively). "It is of [or from, or out of] God that you fashion [or invent, or form, or imagine] (anything)," for some reason a twist of mind suggesting those big old index fingers that meet on the Sistine ceiling.

Deirdre wets altar of St. Simon's—no mists, for at last ewer dried. By LINDON. IRVINE, 1987, considers it inspired. It is sublimely wacky, and much to be emulated, we think.

Deity sat scenic in ecstasy tied. God on his throne was bound to be the very picture of exalted delight.

deivied. Neologism by the KUHNS, who clue it interestingly "Harvard, out of its league"; but the idea of almost anything getting stripped of its ivy is natural enough.

Degas aged.

DÉJÀ VU: We never met a PALINDROME that wasn't riddled with this mystic essence, echoing and reechoing as they do.

deka-naked. Gymnastic descriptive of the quorum that occurs whenever ten or more nudists foregather.

dekayaked. Coined by the KUHNS ("flipped from a small cold boat"), in a clear analogy with words such as *debarked, deplaned,* and *detrained.*

De la Plata, Catalpa Led. Argentine horse-racing result.

Delaware Vera waled. Though why she found it necessary to whip that river, we may never know.

Delbert and Edna trebled. By BORGMANN. Meaning they had triplets, conceivably even quadruplets, and/or sang the highest part.

Delbert-trebled. BORGMANN's coined adjective from a RE-VERSAL PAIR, which he defined as "tripled by someone named

Delbert." If this impresses you, skip directly to **Delessert-nontresseled.**

deled (DEE-leed). Taken out or deleted or marked with a "dele," the proofreader's squiggle that indicates a deletion is to be performed on the portion of text circled or crossed out. Compare: **stets.**

De Leon Noëled. Ponce went caroling.

Delessert-[non]tresseled. BORGMANN's twin monster coinages requiring a hypothetical Frenchman named Delessert and a variant (one might almost say a totally transcendent) participial modifier also require half a page of preparation and explanation. Take our word for it or, for an extreme ride, find his out-of-print book, *Language on Vacation.* The two words, both the "simple" **Delessert-tresseled** and the perhaps overwrought **Delessert-nontresseled,** if allowed (we do!), take the word-length honors by a longshot, and then they win twice again for ingenuity, and finally again for chutzpah.

Delevan : naveled. REVERSAL PAIR, spontaneously combining into **Naveled Delevan,** an almost-Homeric epithet, giving a strong indication of the presence of an oracular seat in this town of Cattaraugus County, in western New York, 42°28'n/78°28'e.

DELIA, *The Complete Story of a Girl's Own Adventure.* As related by a number of sources:

> **Delia ailed.** She got better eventually, though, so read on. It's an inspiring story.
> **Delia and Edna ailed.** (Possibly by MERCER.) Misery & Co., a chain of pain and no help yet, but . . .
> **Delia bailed.** Good idea to empty the bilge for a start, just to pump up the field.
> **Delia failed.** Ah, but she can try again. This is a story of persistence and determination.

Delia hailed. Waved for help, no doubt. Another good idea.

Delia mailed. Requesting more assistance. Even better.

Delia nailed. Good idea to have something to do, and the boat needed the work.

Delia railed. That was no help.

Delia sailed. At last a truly great idea. You can tell because it feels easy and pleasant.

Delia ailed.

Delia sailed as sad Elias ailed. (Possibly by MERCER.) Elias was no help. Best to just ignore him.

Delia sailed, Eva waved, Elias ailed. Eva was a great help. (Possibly by MERCER, illustrated in TERBAN. This is a neat example of a PALINDROME sandwich.)

Delia sits a petite. Past I sailed. LINDON breezes right by, elegantly as usual. This really helped. Notice how the entire mood is brightened by his magic touch.

Delia tailed. Lightly into the breeze, in LINDON's wake. Yes, she's getting the idea!

Delia wailed. Magnificently on her trumpet in a flight of inspiration, and now she's fine.

"Deliver desserts," demanded Nemesis, "emended, named, stressed, reviled." She'll have them anyway. Any which way. Possibly by MERCER. BORGMANN observes: "This is one of the longest palindromes that avoids the use of short words. With the exception of one 5-letter word, each word in it consists of 7 or of 8 letters. A remarkable accomplishment!"

Deliver no evil, avid diva . . . live on reviled. Beginning and ending of a thirty-five-line palindrome poem by BERGERSON admirable for its length but short on coherency. Entitled "Edna Waterfall," it cascades to well over a thousand characters, which must be some sort of a record, though no claim is made by the author—other than that it is a dramatic poem that at least *seems* to have a plot, climax, sustained mood, and continuity of thought. It includes such

D ⌈ . . . ⌉ D

niceties of vocabulary as *erotogenic, nonassimilative*, and *prognosticate*, and one finally has to wonder what is the point of marshaling such virtuosity upon such a thin illusion—which is probably the point.

Deliver no evil; live on reviled. BERGERSON makes a great deal of this REVERSAL-PAIR sentence, seeing about it a preternaturally luminous aura, and his lengthy divinatory study of it in *Palindromes and Anagrams*, pp. 15–16, makes interesting reading and food for thought.

deliver : reviled. REVERSAL PAIR but not a likely PALINDROME.

Deliver nun [un]reviled. Crisp telegraphic messages that still hardly make sense.

Della called. Noted by CHISM, who tactfully ignored that she balled and palled.

Dellums mulled. Democratic congressman from California, Ronald, deliberated (whether or not to cocreate still more laws, no doubt).

DeMaillat : *Talliamed*. REVERSAL claimed but, amazingly, misspelled (as "DeMaillet") in BORGMANN's *Language on Vacation*, possibly his only mistake ever, and probably not his fault, which pairs the surname of a French author with the title of a well-known work by him, deliberately so named.

Demi-timed

demi-aimed (DEH-mee-ehymd). Attributed by CHISM to BERGERSON without explanation and seeming to mean "aimed not precisely but only generally or approximately."

demi-rimed (DEH-mee-rahymd). Attributed by CHISM to *WORD WAYS*, without explanation, and seeming to mean "not fully hoarfrosted" or "rhyming only every other line."

demi-timed (DEH-mee-tahymd). Attributed by CHISM to *WORD WAYS*, without explanation, and seeming to mean either "partly timed" or "timed approximately."

Deng is said to lag a lot; Di assigned. The old leader is reported to be slowing down still further, if that is possible, and so the young princess is called upon to speed him up. Alternatively: **Deng is said to bore robot; Di assigned.** And as a last resort: **Deng is sated, a cadet assigned** (to replace him, we presume).

denier : reined. REVERSAL PAIR, with a medium to strong connection: **Denier reined.** (And Affirmer drove, naturally.)

denies : seined. REVERSAL PAIR of weak natural attraction. But: **He denies I seined, eh?**

Denigration? : No, I tar gin, Ed! REVERSAL SENTENCE, in a word. Observed by BORGMANN. Combining the two halves into a repartee does seem like a good idea, even if the meaning is vague or dark.

Denim Axes Examined. "Blue jeans cartels under investigation," by the KUHNS.

Denio Jct., etc., joined. In the high desert of northwestern Nevada, the tiny localities of Denio, Denio Junction, and Denio Summit (or Pass), with a total population of possibly zero, are all within about a dozen road-miles of one another and, though also virtually adjoined by the Crescent Sand Dunes and the Oregon state line, are indeed surrounded by little else for many miles around. Thus all these otherwise isolated cartographic features, including all three Denios, out of sheer loneliness may very well have joined, as the text claims, something or other, at least themselves, and they certainly have been joined now in our mind. Moreover, if there is any desire for them to have joined Nevada, probably the only sensible object available, then we would have achieved **Adaven, Denio Jct., etc., joined Nevada.** In such a case "etc." would logically stand not only for either or both the other Denios but also for any or all the other places in the state as well.

Denned

denned (DEHND). Lived or hid in a den, hibernated, had cubs.

Dennis and Edna sinned. By LINDON, and probably many others. Illustrated in STUART. BORGMANN observes that this is a member of a whole FAMILY of PALINDROMES, with such relatives as: **Pat and Edna tap. / Enid and Edna dine. / Delia and Edna ailed. / Elbert and Edna treble. / Delbert and Edna trebled.**

Dennis, Nell, Edna, Leon, Nedra, Anita, Rolf, Nora, Alice, Carol, Leo, Jane, Reed, Dena, Dale, Basil, Rae, Penny, Lana, Dave, Denny, Lena, Ida, Bernadette, Ben, Ray, Lila, Nina, Jo, Ira, Mara, Sara, Mario, Jan, Ina, Lily, Arne, Bette, Dan, Reba, Diane, Lynn, Ed, Eva, Dana, Lynne, Pearl, Isabel, Ada, Ned, Dee, Rena, Joel, Lora, Cecil, Aaron, Flora, Tina, Arden, Noel, and Ellen sinned! BORGMANN's 263-letter solution to the "problem of the long PALINDROME." It takes off from the previous entry (**Dennis and Edna sinned**) and lengthens it "by transposing the two center words and then adding the names of many other individuals who are also purported to have sinned. One possible result [the one given] includes 61 first names, some masculine and some feminine," all taken from *Merriam-Webster's Seventh.* "By using a longer list of given names, it would be possible to pour more names into the midpoint of the palindrome (the *S* in *Sara*), and to increase the length to 500, or to 1,000, or to 2,000 letters. For instance, 'Sabba' is a feminine first name. Inserted just before 'Sara,' it keeps the palindrome intact and raises the letter count to 268." Not that we want to encourage sin, nor even understand what it means for that matter, so perhaps a more wholesome orgy would have begun **Enid, Nell, Edna . . . and Ellen dine.**

Dennis sinned. Plain if obscure talk from a strong REVERSAL PAIR.

Denoon : nooned. REVERSAL PAIR by BORGMANN, in which an old community no longer to be found on the map of Waukesha County, Wisconsin, has, naturally, already risen to its zenith.

"Dens? Do casinos reward? Mine don't. Ned, I've still (it's evident) no denim drawers on," Isa cods Ned. By LINDON. A wonderfully comedic sketch artfully concocted of mostly unusual ingredients. It has our extra esteem for being extra long and extra clear at the same time. The really amazing thing about LINDON is how he manages so gracefully to create a mood and even a personality while giving almost no hint that his own hands are securely tied behind his back by the PALINDROMIC requirement. This uncanny ability of his must be a result of great experience and good taste as well as inspiration.

Dentist: "Sit, Ned." Offered by CHISM for the present collection and observed by Mark Saltveit in *WORD WAYS* at about the same time. This neat little sleeper is strangely all that Ned can recall of what he believes was a wonderful visit, most probably all owing to the nitrous.

Depardieu, go razz a rogue I draped. Attribution unknown, reported by John JENSEN. Seemingly an outtake from *My Father, My Hero*.

Depilatory? Rot a lip, Ed. Observed by Mark Saltveit in *WORD WAYS*.

depots : stoped. Storehouses or stations, mined in a particularly steep way; a weak REVERSAL PAIR.

derats : stared. REVERSAL PAIR, with no linkage evident.

Derby bred. Churchill Downs quality, by the KUHNS.

Desiderata : At a red is Ed. Wishing the lights would change.

Designation? : No, I tan GI's, Ed. REVERSAL SENTENCE, in a word. Observed by BORGMANN. Combining the segments makes for a mixup at a military checkpoint.

DE SOLA, Ralph. Lexicographer of the *Abbreviations Dictionary* (New York: Elsevier, 1974), an intriguing compendium and the source of many of the most arcane PALINDROMIC ABBRE-VIATIONS we have listed in this book—and of many besides, which we have not listed. The existence of so vast a reserve of PALINDROMIC gold under his sole stewardship makes him potentially a very rich man if he can figure out a way to exploit the mineral rights by the time all regular PALIN-DROMES have been used up.

Desserts I desire not, so long no lost one rise distressed. Probably by MERCER. A ridiculous sentimentality is wonder-fully delineated even as poetic license must be invoked to help out a shaky syntax. The text appears to have unfolded inward from *desserts . . . stressed* via *distressed* and then through *desserts I desire not . . . [-t] one rise distressed*, but the seamless whole does not break down easily, leaving us to wonder what a stroke of genius must have been necessary to close the peculiar center. See also: **Here so long? No loser, eh?** and the following entries.

Desserts I Stressed. A pastry-chef's autobiography, by the KUHNS.

desserts : stressed. A natural phrase, and even a telegraphic sort of sentence, with a variety of meanings (such as: an epi-taph for a heavyweight; words found on the résumé of the above pastry chef) making use of an emphatically delicious REVERSAL PAIR of words, probably the longest and best of its type in English.

Dessert's stressed. Pages and pages are devoted to it on the menu.

dessert-stressed. Overcome by the pleasure of it all.

Dessert's stressed.

D ⌈ . . . ⌉ D

dessert : tressed. Weak REVERSAL PAIR, unless it evokes a **tressed dessert.**

desuffused (dee-suh-FYOOZD). Word possibly invented by POOL—descriptive (and here we are only guessing) of the peculiar effect seen when a video being played in reverse shows a liquid, color, or light *leaving* a medium throughout which it had actually, or previously, spread or suffused.

"Detail a Tercel," Alec retaliated. Vindictive assignment at a car wash.

"Detail a termite," Tim retaliated. Pert rejoinder to the above, or else a vindictive assignment at an entomology lab.

Detail if fast's affiliated. Give particulars of the hunger strike's auspices.

Detail lapse's palliated. A trivial slip is excused.

Detail lapse's palliated.
A trivial
slip is excused.

detainal : laniated. REVERSAL PAIR by BORGMANN, in which we can see the practice or act (or perhaps the writ, the *detainer*) of detention or custody torn to pieces before our very eyes. We are free.

detannated (dee-TÆN-ehy-d'd). Attributed by CHISM to *WORD WAYS* without explanation, seeming to carry a scientific meaning of "separated from or free of tannin (tannic acid, an important tanning and clarifying agent)." See also: **detartrated**.

detartrated (dee-TAHR-trehy-d'd). AUGARDE cautions that this "may not qualify, as there is doubt if it is really used in science." But we don't care if it isn't. And BORGMANN, in *Language on Vacation*, says of it:

Judging by appearances, this is a coined word. It means "separated from, or free of, tartaric acid." However, *tartrated* is a dictionary word and *de-* is an extremely common prefix in chemistry. It seems highly probable, therefore, that the word can be found in print somewhere: in a

D [. . .] D

chemical, medical, or technical dictionary; in a pharmacopoeia or other drug manual; or in some periodical devoted to the physical sciences. The problem is merely to locate its source.

Even though the unquestionably existing printed source of our palindrome has not yet been pinpointed, **detartrated,** written as a solid, unhyphenated word and consisting entirely of common, mutually compatible Indo-European (Latin) elements, must be honored as the finest English PALINDROME, a champion among champions. Major dictionaries teem with chemistry terms such as *dehydrated*, *denitrated*, and *desulphurized*. It is only a matter of time until they admit **detartrated** to their ranks, for it is the palindrome of the future!

detartrater : retartrated. REVERSAL PAIR by BORGMANN, seemingly telling us that a certain remover of tartaric acid (by trade) made so bold as to restore the tartaric acid—in at least one particular case. On a scale of 1 to 10, it scores a remarkable **11.**

Devil never even lived.

Det. I. Milton's not limited *or* **Det. I. Milton, not limited.** And see his partner: **Dedicated Det. Acid 'Ed.**

Deva[s] saved. It came as a surprise to us, but it certainly appears from the text that the ancient Hindu God[s] used to do "Salvation" exactly as in the subsequent Christian soteriology.

deviler : relived. REVERSAL PAIR, medium: tormentor had it all to do over again.

Devil never even lived. CHISM says a mouthful: the Devil is at most a man-made thought form, not a primordial being.

dewed (DOOD *or* DYOOD). Moistened with droplets of condensation, usually said of flat surfaces, usually happening overnight.

D [. . .] D

Deweys, ye wed. We so pronounced you man and wife, Mr. and Mrs. Dewey.

De Zima! Da camera [and Edna] are macadamized! Houston chamber ensemble visiting Lincoln Center [wid dat nice lady] run afoul of a too-spirited pothole repair crew.

Diagnose Song Aid. By the KUHNS. It helped remind us that "We Are the World."

Dial aid. Call for help, by the KUHNS.

Diameter (Cnossos's on Crete), maid? (*or* **Di, a meter**). It appears a new kind of professional, a diameter maid (or possibly just a regular meter maid named Di), or some young lady, no matter who, perhaps Ariadne herself, is asked by someone (perhaps an overzealous Greek customs official filling in a declaration form) to reveal the true size of the fabulous capital city (or parking meter) of King Minos. But unexpected new events may also lead a different maid to **Reveal one diameter . . . ever.**

Diamond-eyed no-maid! Relative of a gold digger, perhaps. By LINDON, who has Adam calling Eve this as they trade insults at the conclusion of his rather raucous and disjointed sixty-odd-line PALINDROME playlet, **"In Eden, I."**

Diana saw Dr. Awkward was an aid. By LINDON. Characteristically madcap. And it is encouraging to see again that this master builder neither disdains the primitive, modular style of construction nor avoids commonplace materials if he can bring about an interesting effect by their use. See also the following entry.

Diana saw I was an aid. A help at the palace, on Olympus, or just anywhere, by Jane Capellaro. As can be seen from this and the previous example, **Diana saw [any PALINDROMIC name, noun, or noun phrase you may like] was an aid.** Discovering or experimenting with pat FORMULAS such as this, just like picking up the idioms of a new language, can be a big boost toward building PALINDROMIC fluency and confidence.

Dian, I am reviled, I turn, I dump Martin Gardner, I rend rag 'n' I tramp mud in rut, I deliver main aid. By LINDON. What a kidder! For this must have been at least a good-natured joke, perhaps a response to a challenge of some sort, and likely a kind of tribute and appreciation. (GARDNER has recited more than one of LINDON's poems in his "Mathematical Games" department in *Scientific American*.)

diaper : repaid. Weak REVERSAL PAIR: far-fetched for a diaper to repay or be repaid.

did. Performed or completed or created or made or . . .

Did Ada say as Ada did? Ada or any other PALINDROMIC name, that is.

Did I do, O God, did I as I said I'd do? Good, I did! Probably by MERCER. An apparent amnesiac speaks, fitfully, in fifteen words, using only six different letters, with none of the words more than four letters long. It would be easy to underestimate the difficulty of constructing with such peculiar little building blocks. Analysis is certainly difficult. The starting point may have been a just-off-center *as I said*, which gives the not-yet-promising *-d[ ]I as I said* but leads with a little effort to *did I as I said I'd* and perhaps quickly thereafter to *-od, did I as I said I'd do?*, but not obviously thence to *God, did I as I said I'd do? g-*, and still there is no end in sight. On the other hand, the starting point may just as easily have been the formulaic *did I . . . ? I did!* or the self-standing *do, O God, do good* or their also-self-standing combination *did I do, O God, do good? I did!*, yet again the outcome is far from obvious. Perhaps it was only as a result of playing both ends against the middle and vice versa, a technique requiring both concentration and knowledge, and

D [. . .] D

probably a lot of trial and error, that the unexpectedly charming result emerged.

Di heard art—Strad. (Rae hid!) By LINDON. Two cartoon characters make for a sweet-and-sour contrast within half a line. It is beautiful to see the six quick words flow forth seamlessly, like a series of deft brush strokes by a master calligrapher or painter. Though the text is relatively short and may appear to issue from the *Strad* quite CASUALly and without too much coaxing, we believe there is still little likelihood that another mind at another time could ever compose or discover this artfully inflected score.

Dike kid

dike kid. Hans Brinker, according to the KUHNS. Or perhaps the little Dutch boy who plugged the leak.

Di, Mary, Ptah at Pyramid. (Photo caption continues:) He told them the pyramids were and are simply physical depictions of the primary, nonphysical universe, in which a gamut of vibrational levels or intensities unify in and emanate from the Top; the consignment of God-King individuals to the pyramids symbolized eternal life but was never meant to guarantee an eternal life since, as they all well understood, life is eternal; the religious and architectural organizations were (and still are today) just a means of controlling people. . . . *The Illustrated Encyclopedia of Crossword Words*, by Nort Bramesco (New York: Workman, 1982), identifies Ptah as the architect of the universe and sire of gods and mortals, a craftsman and therefore the patron of artisans and workers.

Dim Rodney repardoned ungarbed deb, rag-nude, no drapery, end or mid! This is LINDON, of course, on another seamless tear, working from whole cloth (the open center fold at *ungarbed deb* and the pair of *dim / mid* folds or openings notwithstanding), and he is here typically, wonderfully, totally off the wall while still totally in control.

D [. . .] D

dioramas : samaroid. Picturesque REVERSAL PAIR by BORG-MANN, in which scenic tableaus of or about samaras or "key fruits" (those winged, paired, usually one-seeded fruits that can be stuck on the tip of one's nose, as of the ash or maple) seem to dance into a whirlwind of action in **samaroid dioramas.**

Dior droid. Designer robot, illustrated in IRVINE, 1987.

Disgorge grog, Sid. By POOL. At Sid's place, known as **Gorge Grog,** this is how to *order* a drink.

DNA: "la-la land." An original conception and assessment, contributed by CHISM.

D'nali Land. Vicin'ty Mt. M'Kinley, or p'r'aps all **A'a'a.** Compare: **I laned Denali.**

Doc, note, I dissent. A fast never prevents a fatness. I diet on cod. Weight watcher discredits physician and opts for seafood. Credited by ESPY to Penelope Gilliatt. According to BERGERSON, it was told to James Michie by a mathematician in 1944 who did not make it up either. According to GARDNER, Michie won a prize for it in a *New Statesman* PALINDROME contest in 1967. So much for pinning down its authorship. Moreover, since the text is so greatly and widely loved, it is a good proof of the proposition that success has many fathers (while failure is a bastard).

Dog doo! Good God!

"*Do* cotton on." "No, not to cod." Adapted from LINDON. A dinner invitation and refusal.

Dod Ballapur. Small city of India, 13°18'n/77°32'e.

Dog doo! Good God! By CHISM. A natural! Probably has been acted out just so lots of times.

Doges use God. By POOL. Those Italian magistrates would do anything to keep the people under control.

dog god. By TERBAN, who gives "canine deity" as a clue.

Perhaps an Anubis, or his less famous littermate, **Sib Un-Anubis.**

Dog hoopla: Alpo. Oh, God! By CHISM. You know: ad shows hungry dogs tearing in from all directions.

Dogma: I am God. Meaning I'm free to think whatever I may wish. (This dogma's a bitch!)

Dogma I deliver. Reviled I am, God. Well, then cut it out. Adapted from FITZPATRICK.

Do gnosis on God. By the KUHNS. Intuitively apprehend the Godself.

Dog o' God. "The Dog of God," the name given by Lapplanders to the bear, which "has the strength of ten men and the wit of twelve," as per BORGMANN.

Dogon! O, no! God! These incredible West African people seriously maintain they migrated here from the doggone Dogstar, which they continue to orient on, commune with, and adore!

Dog pinnacled on a Toyota (no Del.) can nip God. By High Priestess Jane Capellaro, who will explain it on request. See also, however, fully explained, the dogless, dogmaless, karmaless, carless, yet still shaggy **Pinnacled Del can nip.**

Dog sit in a lap, pal, an' it is God. By POOL. Strange and powerful.

"Dogstar gnocchi! H.C. congrats!"—God. Miraculous telegram, indicating "What a stellar Holy Communion dinner, folks, and let there be more serious fun." The text is also stylistic evidence that God is a Roman Catholic.

Do I rep as Ivanoff? On a Visa? *Period*? (*or* **as Ivanov?** *or* **as Ivan?**). Whose, and which, credit card should I use to entertain clients, and are *all* expenses covered? This also

"Dogstar gnocchi! H.C. congrats!"—God. Miraculous telegram.

D [. . .] D

works, though maybe less well, as a single unbroken question.

"Do nine men interpret?" "Nine men," I nod. Probably by MERCER, referring, we may guess, to the Supreme Court of his day—that is, before it had women on it—and possibly even hinting broadly about its lack of them, especially if the second *men* is italicized. We are not aware of anyone ever actually making effective use of PALINDROMES for activist or political purposes, but come to think of it, they would make a refreshing addition to the existing dialogues and slogans.

Do nod. Agree to take a nap. See also: **Don't nod.**

Do not refer to Nod. You know, the land east of Eden where Cain lived after Abel? Well, don't mention it, and don't even think of it. However, the uncannily fluid positive/negative/positive text may be nothing worse than a lovely conundrum, and, like a blue rose, it is freighted with a heavy suggestion of hip gnosis, in which case refer to it all you like and swoon with eternal DÉJÀ VU. (See also: **Zzz-zzz-zzz.**)

Do not start at rats to nod. Probably by MERCER, brilliantly pairing and activating, like a two-part epoxy cement, a couple of otherwise unimpressive components. This text appears to be a poetic graffito or a surrealistic warning-sign-cum-blinking-light (say, to keep students from falling asleep in psychology lab or drivers from falling asleep in a long tunnel), or else it could be the Pied Piper's secret tip for counteracting hypnotic suggestion and maintaining his famous and all-important control over the situation.

Don't abrogate tag or bat nod. A tongue-tied or funny-talking BARBARIA's only political principle: Don't annul someone's selection or object to their approval.

Don't nod. Beg to differ and stay awake. See also: **Do nod.**

Do offer a ref food. By POOL. Good halftime advice. Money's too tacky.

"Do orbits all last?" I brood. An astrophysicist ponders entropy. We answer: Contrary to many popular beliefs and theories, everything is permanently in a groove and getting better. Life and growth do not run down or fizzle out but are endless. So, yes, orbits do all last, and moreover there's no reason to brood or VALUE in doing so.

Dopey? Yep, O.D. Our **dedicated Det. Acid 'Ed** reporting in for Off Duty, not to the emergency room.

Dormin : Nimrod. REVERSAL PAIR by BORGMANN, giving a sleeping pill hunter dreams of the chase.

Dorset abates rod. English county lessens corporal punishment. By the KUHNS.

Do sod. By all means, plant grass. By the KUHNS.

Do stop. Pot sod. Do Stop is also a locality in Kentucky.

Dotsero : Orestod. REVERSAL PAIR of localities, by BORGMANN, the former still shown on maps today but the latter forgotten. Both are located in Eagle County, Colorado. . . . Subsequent research reveals **Dotsero-Orestod** to have been a rather delicious case of palindromy and poetry in motion, for, according to George R. Stewart, who has written several interesting books about the origins of place-names, the pair were graphically situated at the opposite ends of a railroad spur, and moreover the name Dotsero was probably the railroadese (we think Chicano-Morse) format of the conventional "(Milepost Zero-) Dot-Zero" (0.0), formal starting point of the spur that (we think) was probably not only used to ship Orestod **Ores to Dotsero** and beyond but was evidently also ended, or actually arrested, at Orestod. Cf. the obverse: **Point No Point** (.0.).

DOUBLETALK. Arguably any palindrome or palindromes,

Do offer a ref food.

though especially if glossed by a riff of punning or other wordplay, as for example in our **Pulitzer . . .** prize.

Drab as a fool, as aloof as a bard. Probably by MERCER. This mysterious pair of similes has a certain charm, evoking perhaps a dull jester, perhaps a laid-back minstrel, and certainly someone having some sort of an identity crisis. Compare it to the slight but complete transformation that occurs in the following items.

Drab Moll Lombard. Dull, Northern Mafiosa type, even dressed up (**O, Drab Moll Lombardo**).

Drab Reg, no longer bard. Possibly by MERCER, but we are doubtful. He's usually so entertaining. This one from BERGERSON's long "Probably Mercer" list may well prove to be no longer bard Mercer speaking at all but, as signed, Drab Reg.

Dracula Valu-Card. New credit card with parasitically-to-predatorially high interest rates.

Drakard, John. English newspaper proprietor (1775–1854), per BORGMANN.

Drat Saddam: a mad dastard. William Safire credits IRVINE, 1987. An unusually felicitous and mild execration, as execrations go.

Drat! Such custard. By the KUHNS.

Drat! Suck custard! By POOL.

Draught nine men in th' guard. By John McClellan, according to BERGERSON. Ingenious. Some will object to the unusual shortening of the definite article, but it's not unnatural in this fairly Elizabethan setting, and we are generally in favor of invoking poetic license and looking for all manner of new, or old, ways to expand the PALINDROMIC universe and our collection.

Draw eels leeward. Getting them out of the wind is good advice, from POOL.

drawer : reward. REVERSAL PAIR, with a strong attraction—
See: **reward drawer.**

Drawers at uppity-bred salons: Nola's derby tip put as reward. An only slightly wild and crazy idea, compared to the much longer and much stranger creation of FITZPATRICK from which it is reconstituted. For the whole and original picture, see BERGERSON's *Palindromes and Anagrams.*

Dr. Awkward. Clumsy but eminent brain surgeon.

drawn Aegeanward. Pulled poetically to the sea of the Cyclades by the KUHNS.

Draw, Neva, havenward. By the KUHNS, who clue it: "Russian river boatman's prayer as he nears St. Petersburg."

drawn inward. A nice phrase, at least, and highly omphaloskeptic.

Draw no dray a yard onward. Possibly by MERCER, who listed it for BERGERSON, or by BORGMANN, who also recited it, but it is such a simple and basic construction that it could be much older, perhaps a picket sign or slogan from an early Teamsters' action. Compare the more contemporary twist in the following entry.

Draw no llama a mall onward. The llamas stop here, shoppers. It's contrived and slapstick, but what the heck. First given in *Games,* around 1980, by someone from **Glen Elg,** Maryland, whose name we forget.

drawn onward. A nice phrase, and characteristic of PALINDROMISTS.

Draw not onward. Stay where you are, say the KUHNS.

Draw, O Caesar, erase a coward. Probably by MERCER. We

Dr. Awkward

D ⌈ . . . ⌋ D

have no idea if this catchy and oft-quoted line has any basis in historical fact, that is, whether any Caesar was ever actually challenged to a duel. But historical accuracy is of less consequence in a PALINDROME than dramatic force, which this item certainly has.

Draw, O coward! Memorable and very basic text that appears in many books and is even illustrated in IRVINE's, 1987.

Draw, O Howard! Title and digest of a *rhyming* PALINDROMIC poem by LINDON.

dray yard. Credited by CHISM to *WORD WAYS*. Evidently a parking lot for low, open wagons.

Dreier, D. (Dave). Name of Republican congressman from California, as formatted for an alphabetical voting record or roll call.

Dr. I. E. Weird. Partner of **Dr. Awkward** and perhaps **Dr. Enid I. Nerd.** (And yes, I. E. stands for "that is.")

Dr. Mad, Oxoboxo Dam Rd. See: **Oxoboxo.**

Dr. No was, I saw, on Rd. That was Route **700, 007.**

Droll! I'd accept Peccadillo Rd.! At worst it's paved with whimsical intentions, and it looks as if it could lead to a totally no-fault reality.

Droll, Lord? (Are you kidding? It was a cosmic joke.)

'DROME. Short for PALINDROME when British wordsmiths speak or write informally (according to BORGMANN). We like it because it rhymes with and suggests GNOME.

"Drowatonsi" is not a word. Offered by **Walter Fretlaw** or David Jennings Morice, it is not clear which, under the title "Cheater's Palindromes," in *WORD WAYS*.

Drown word. Leisurely, poetic way to say "Can it!"

Dr. I. E. Weird

drowsy baby's word. All the harder to make it out, therefore. By LINDON, we think, but we haven't been able to pin it down. Perhaps it will be found among his juvenilia.

Dr Pepper Prep (Pep Rd.). School for future bottlers. See: **Pep.**

Dru's basis is absurd. He's all right, but just don't take him seriously.

Dry ebb at _Abbey Rd._ The new wave, really a flood tide, that had been the Beatles went all the way out with this their final album. For the curious, slightly earlier sign of their breakup, see: _Let It Be_: **"Eb' Titel"?!**

Duane [Rollo] Renaud. BORGMANN's mysterious personage, perhaps a detective.

dud. Any disappointingly ineffectual thing, such as a firecracker that doesn't.

Dumbo, lob mud. Trainer's command for a flying elephant.

du sud. French: of or from the south.

dxd. ABBREVIATION and a neat sort of mnemonic device or mimic gimmick for "discontinued."

D [. . .] D

e [. . .] e

Ebb, be. Lay back, live and let live; also, without the comma, apparently a poetic way of saying that the tide is going out, for it serves as the otherwise unintelligible first and last lines of a tall, thin PALINDROMIC poem of twenty-nine similarly terse lines: "Shipwreck," by Graham REYNOLDS, given by BERGERSON in *Palindromes and Anagrams.*

ebohphobe. One who is afraid of his own shadow, or of symmetry in general. See also: **aibohphobia** and **cibohphobic.**

E. Borgnine drags Dad's gardening robe. Attribution unknown, reported by John JENSEN. This is a precious find, rich in whimsy. We would guess it was a winner in an early nineties magazine contest. It is interesting to see how *Borgnine* almost forces a *gardening robe* into being, which in turn dictates precisely that *E. Borgnine drag[s]* it, but then the choice of *Dad's* from among the many available PALINDROMIC possibilities for finessing a syntactical closure was a stroke of genius and good taste. (Indeed the text well illustrates how a good closure, though it nails things neatly down, still actually opens up more than it closes, for the completed PALINDROME may then echo and reecho and grow on us through time.)

Ebro e Otel, ma Amleto e orbe! Italian classic: "Othello is drunk, but Hamlet is blind!"

Ebullient Neil, lube! Observed by Mark Saltveit in *WORD WAYS.*

ecce (EHK-kehy). Latin: behold! lo! look! look at! as in *Ecce Homo* ("Behold the man!"), words used by Pontius Pilate to present Christ crowned with thorns to his accusers in John 19:5, and, as a result, the general name applied to any picture of Christ wearing the crown of thorns.

eciton : notice. REVERSAL PAIR, wanting perhaps to be a message to (or about) the foraging or army ant(s).

Ed. A general. A renegade. Epitaph for a failed coup leader.

Ed, a General Delivery levitator, rotatively reviled La Renegade. Our protagonist, a drifter with no permanent address or visible means of support, seems to have periodically denounced an individualistic traitoress. (We can't imagine why.) If the second comma is omitted from the text, the result is an extra player to do the dirty work, but no problem—though in such cases less is generally more. (And still we have no idea why.) But if it's *La Renegade* (in italics), she becomes, more fittingly—and perhaps just fittingly enough for the indicated periodical denunciation—a periodical. Nice word lengths and good variety show, despite or not despite the modest semantic strength.

Eda Nomel's Lemonade. Coming soon to Madison Avenue. Attribution unknown; reported by John JENSEN.

Ede. 1: large town and commune of the Netherlands, 52°03'n/ 5°40'e **2:** city of Nigeria, 7°44'n/4°27'e.

'E dialed Adelaide?! / 'E did, did 'e? Actually he touchtoned country code 61 plus city code 8.

edicide (EDD-ih-sahyd). The act of getting rid of one's editor.

Edicide

'E did, did 'e? A Cockney **deed.**

Ed, I saw Harpo Marx ram Oprah W. aside. An outrageous and excellent linkage of at least one and a half personalities, this text is a rare achievement. Attribution unknown; reported by John JENSEN.

Edith, cold-eyed, eyed loch tide. By LINDON. Had Nessie done a water slide? In any case, this vivid and statuesque construction gives us a clue about how beauty arises from an artist's resourceful probing of palindromically potent bits and pieces. The mid-start *-d=eyed* (doubly propitious since it may be redoubled at any juncture, if desired, to form

E [. . .] E

−d=eyed, eyed) may lead to *cold-eyed* and *cold-eyed loc-* and *cold-eyed loch* and *−h, cold-eyed, eyed loch* before *Edith* is even thought of. *Or*, vice versa, by thinking of *Edith . . . -h tide* first, LINDON may have reached inward toward *Edith, col- . . . loch tide* and *Edith, cold . . . -d loch tide* before he'd eyed *eyed*. *Or*, again, with vast experience, one may work alternately by intuition and trial and error, and in both directions at once, until something hot like this coalesces, as if spontaneously.

Edit "Pirates Set a Rip Tide." Work assignment at R.L.S.'s publisher.

Edit, Sir Aristide. Put a good spin on the American occupation, Mr. President. The text is from *WORD WAYS*.

E. Divide. We know of no such place in reality, but it will probably eventually emerge somewhere just east of the Continental Divide like, say, Atlantic City, Wyoming, near South Pass. West Divide, if there is any interest in one, would then have to be sought just to the west of the Divide thereabouts: say, at the head of Pacific Creek.

Ed I woo! Tim, Allan, Eden all—am I too wide? A truly great line from a rhyming PALINDROME poem by LINDON entitled "Nonsense!" Each of the poem's four lines is a palindrome, the others being generally less intelligible than and nowhere near as outrageous as this line, the last. (We have taken the liberty of removing a comma after Ed.) Here a good test-start at *too wide* gives *Ed I woo (T-)*, and we may want to stop at **Ed I woo, Tim. Am I too wide?** or **Ed, I woo Tim. Am I too wide?** But we may also surmise that Lindon alertly saw at this point his opportunity to enlarge the import and humorous impact of the word "wide" by simply reopening the center and expanding the population. He might even have continued along the lines of the following item, but we would agree that adding bulk in this case does not increase wit.

Ed, losing, I sign, Isolde. Irish princess closes letter to her friend Ed about her hopeless love affair. But we can cheer her up with a shopping spree at **Mart Sir Tristram.**

Edna "Lala" Tina Ardis Marva Adela Diane Lynne Pearl Ora Cecile Fanny Laverne Eliadia Rasia Mary Meta Kassia Radella Anne Norah Sela Gaia Mable Mina Rae Barba Mairi Manon Nell Essa Lee Lass Ellen Nona Miriam Abra Bea Rani Melba Maia Gale Sharon Enna Alleda Raissa Kate Myra Mai Saraid Aileen Reva Lynna Felice Carol Rae Penny Lena Ida Leda Avram Sidra Anita Lalande. Extended reverie by BORGMANN in exactly three hundred letters, a take-off on the real name of *Marquis Marie Joseph Paul Yves Roch Gilbert du Motier de Lafayette,* with help from *What to Name the Baby* and H. L. Mencken (but that is a long story). He considered the second Rae an imperfection but we see no reason why one repeated name should be frowned upon. Take **Ford Madox Ford** or Boutros Boutros-Ghali for example. And just mentally unifying Mina Rae would fix it all anyway.

Edna! Mel! Lana did an allemande! She's a great dancer.

Edom à la mode. The ancient kingdom with a scoop on top.

Ed or Les sent Nesselrode. It has to have been one or the other.

Ed undid nude.

Ed undid nude. By Joaquin KUHN.

ee. Scottish eye.

EE. 1: airline code for Eagle Commuter Airlines **2:** ABBREVIATION for Electrical Engineer.

EE through **EEEEEEE** inclusive. Shoes sizes, real or imaginary. See: **AA** through **AAAAAAA.**

eel glee. Electric merriment, by the KUHNS.

E ⌈ . . . ⌉ E

eel, urbane hen à brûlée. From a strange menu in IRVINE, 1987.

Egad! A base tone denotes a bad age. By composer Henry Purcell (1659?–1695).

Egad! A base tone denotes a bad age.

Egad! An adage! Illustrated in IRVINE, 1987.

Egad! An adage / was a saw! COMPOUND PALINDROME (that is, really not one, but two in succession) by BORGMANN, who hails it, or them, as "singularly apt," for an adage *is* a saw, and we would add singularly apt again in the use of that rare and lovely archaic verb tense, the *gnomic aorist* (a past tense typically used in adages and saws to indicate their indefinite time, as in "curiosity *killed* the cat" or "a stitch in time *saved* nine"). Egad! Overwhelmed by gnomes!

Egad! Loretta has Adams as mad as a hatter. Old age! By Hercules McPherrin. Quite a tale. BORGMANN considers it remarkably long. And it is remarkably good.

Egad! No bag! A voodoo vagabondage! It's hard to believe how those Haitian boat people manage to travel so light, but there is a simple explanation for it.

E.g., Dole-Lodge. Exemplary ticket.

Egad! No bondage! Illustrated in IRVINE.

Ege. Hamlet of Noble County, Indiana (an outer burb of Fort Wayne).

Egge. Mountain range of Germany, 51°40'n/8°55'e.

Egnar : range. A locality, and its locale, in Colorado.

ego loge. 1: exclusive small compartment or box in a theater, or sometimes the front rows of the mezzanine, reserved for only the most selfish of people **2:** the "upper deck" of the psyche where the sense of self resides. Other things to consider are: **Ego led Isa Ott to a side loge** and **Ego-led, I sat at a side loge.**

Egremont's a fast "No Merge." Traffic in this Berkshire town of lovely two-lane roads moves right along without bottlenecks, thanks to their locally developed traffic signal, really no signal at all, called the **Egremont "No Merge."** See also: **Was it no merger? . . . Oz or Egremont I saw?**

Eh, ça va, la vache? (EHY sah-VAH lah-VAHSH?). Quoted by Alastair Reid. French: Ah, does the cow go by here?

Eh? Cuomo? Mouche. But so what if the Quebeckers make him out to be a lightweight—Mario could still fly.

EIGHTY-EIGHT *or* **88.** Hamlet of Barren County, Kentucky. A local postmaster chose the name because it was easy to "spell."

Eine treue familie bei Lima feuerte nie. German: A loyal family near Lima never fired a shot. According to BORGMANN.

Eivets Rednow. Not a PALINDROME but a REVERSAL REVERSAL or *mixed reversal* occurring on the cover of a Stevie Wonder album. For more on this format, see: **Wolley Segap.**

Ekalaka Lake! Actual geographical body of water situated at the west end of the real but remote town of Ekalaka (EEK-uh-*LÆKK*-uh) in the high, dry plains of eastern Montana (Carter County). Also an astounding, probably unique spiraling PALINDROME poem, or semantic eddy:

> **Ekalaka Lake!**
> **aka: Lake Ekalaka**
> **(/Ekalaka Lake)!**

Indeed, we recall having visited the town (and its nearby, also-otherworldly hot spot, Medicine Rocks) many years before the poem ever came to us, though we are sure we didn't think then to look out for a lake and of course can't now recall having seen one. (Still, we'll be sure to go back there for a new look, and a listen, as soon as possible.) At all events, the 1979 USGS map of the Ekalaka Quadrangle does show at least a sizeable reservoir or catch basin partly

Ekalaka Lake.
Eastern Montana
(Carter County).

115

Elba, I'm amiable.

within Ekalaka's town limits (itself a perfect mile square and square mile), and though the map does not specifically give a name for this, Ekalaka's only body of water and the biggest for miles around, the map still does very suggestively position the Ekalaka name so right up against the lake and so far from downtown Ekalaka as to almost audibly ask: "Let's get this perfectly square: Is Ekalaka the town or the lake, or both, and is the lake **Ekalaka Lake** or Lake Ekalaka, or both?" Having said this, and feeling very pleased with ourselves for it, we could not resist telephoning the town of Ekalaka to ask what the people there *actually* call this body of water, and perhaps recite our PALINDROMIC good news to them, and at the post office we were summarily enlightened: "Oh, *that*! That's the sewage lagoon!" At which we could but marvel, "Eek, a lack o' lake!" But, fortunately, we couldn't bear to let the matter rest in such a condition, and we felt compelled to revisit Ekalaka and to verify firsthand the lake's actual disposition. What a relief to learn that the postlady was wrong or just goofing on us! For big as day, just behind the rodeo grounds and at least a quarter of a mile above the sewage lagoon, there shone the lake, a large man-made catchment basin watering numerous cattle and wild ducks. The lady who runs the Wagon Wheel Cafe downtown said this lake has never had a name and also said she had never heard of any **Ekalaka Lake** or Lake Ekalaka anywhere, and allowed as she had never realized the reversibility of the name **Ekalaka Lake,** whatever it may or may not mean. We of course were ecstatic to be able to officially name this body of water on the spot to suit ourselves, that is, by both the short form and the full three-line texts given above. (How often does one find some place that still needs a name nowadays *and* just happen to have not just one but a whole bouquet of perfect names available?) And we trust that in time other people, too, will begin to love and refer to this perfectly unique body of water as we do.

E [. . .] E

Ekal : Lake. The name of a locality and its county in Florida.

eke (EEK). **1:** (with prep. *out*) to make or complete with great difficulty **2:** postscript or appendix, according to BORGMANN **3:** Middle English: also; likewise.

Elba cover, rising up mid ill I'd impugn, is irrevocable! The idea of prominently displaying the predictable **Able was I ere I saw Elba** palindrome on some book's cover (certainly not this one's), for reasons of high recognizability and mass-marketing promotional benefit, has grown, thanks to the author's implicit negativity and opposition toward it, into an irreversibility.

El Baerga's agréable. Indians' flexible second-baseman Carlos here seems as well disposed as we are toward a North American Free Talk Agreement. (Very peligreuse!)

Elba frets no malign gila monster fable. By the KUHNS. Not a poisonous reptile on the island!

Elba, I'm amiable. By the KUHNS. Napoleon, to the island of his exile.

Elba rap a parable. A biblical stature and high accolade for the well-known saying, **Able was I ere I saw Elba.** But the KUHNS understand it to mean, "All this talk of Napoleon is mere allegory."

Elba—Rome: My! A day memorable! And yet only 130 miles as the crow flies.

Elbert and Edna treble. By BORGMANN. It's their habit to triple everything.

Elbert : treble. REVERSAL PAIR of medium strength. See also: **Treble Elbert.**

El Chevrolet?? . . . **Oh! (Hotel or veh'cle?)** Words that must have been overheard on a street in Miami or somewhere.

eld daw twaddle. Old crow talk, by the KUHNS.

eld dire riddle. By the KUHNS, calamitous conundrum of yore, as of the Sphinx.

Eleele (EH-leh-*EH*-leh). Small village on the south coast of Kauai, Hawaii, 21°55'n/159°35'w.

Elele. Village of Nigeria, 5°07'n/6°48'e.

ELEVEN. See: NUMBERDROMES or NUMERICAL PALINDROMES.

Elk City, Kansas, is a snaky tickle! Easily the most hilarious and therefore best real town plus state name in the country as well as in the annals of PALINDROMY. Recent on-site investigation revealed that today's Elk City is a shadow of its former self. Its two-block downtown, like that of many small towns in the middle west, is in an advanced state of dilapidation, there being now only a small post office, a small bank branch, and two nameless saloons still working. As if prophetically, the filling station on the bypass had only high-test available the day we visited. We saw no snakes. The folks were nice. We are still waiting for the tickle. Perhaps there is one in eternity.

Ella Sal Lasalle. A BORGMANN gal.

elle (ELL). **1:** French: she **2: Elle,** fashion magazine.

Ellemelle. Listed by CHISM as an English word, citing *WORD WAYS* without explanation. It certainly is a handsome one! Wonder what it means.

Ellen, all I've noted: a cadet, one villanelle. By LINDON. Enigmatic and intriguing, to say the least. Perhaps a confidante writes a confidante, or a private detective writes a client-friend. As you may know, a villanelle is a nineteen-line poem of fixed form consisting of five tercets (three-line stanzas) and a final quatrain (four-line stanza) on two rhymes, the first and third lines of the first tercet being repeated alternately as a refrain closing the succeeding stanzas and joined as the final couplet of the quatrain. (That is, AbC deA fgC hiA jkC lmAC.) From an old rustic Italian song, the *villanella*, transplanted to France.

Elsie Isle. By the KUHNS. Most likely Jersey or Guernsey.

El tot, Sir Aristotle. From a future edition of *What to Name the Baby.*

Embargo! : O, grab me! REVERSAL PAIR, with strong natural affinity, by BORGMANN.

Embargos so grab me. "Attributable" to Fidel Castro.

Embargos so grab me.

Emil asleep, Hannah peels a lime. Possibly by MERCER. At last, it's refreshment time for the baby-sitter. With enough limes to peel, many other PALINDROMIC names may drop in as well.

Emil, asleep, peels a lime. Dreams he's peeling! By LESSER, who calls it Dali-esque.

Emil, a sleepy baby, peels a lime. And, since he is now experienced thanks to his previous lime, he manages to peel this, his next lime, while still, albeit just barely, awake! Precocious when groggy, baby Emil! It is no mere coincidence that he peels a lime in this improbable condition but fully a coincidence, a *prodigy*, a token of his mastery and perfection.

Emit Emir Prime Time. Televise, or broadcast or publish or transmit in any way, the Nielsen leader.

Emme. River of Switzerland, via Burgdorf, 47°13'n/7°34'e.

En af dem der tit red med fane. Danish: "One of those often rode with a banner," according to BORGMANN.

enamor : romane. REVERSAL PAIR with an uncannily strong mutual attraction: to inspire with love, charm, captivate ro-

E [. . .] E

mantically—with a literary "romance" in a romantic Romance language, namely French.

Ene (EH-neh). River of Peru, via Quimpetirique into the Tambo-Ucayali-Amazon, 11°09's/74°19'w.

ENE. East-northeast.

En gamel, rah, Charlemagne! A marginal-at-best and certainly fractured French Foreign Legion sound bite, a cheer or toast perhaps, in which it is unclear whether Charlemagne is the Gallicized rider or the Arabized camel.

En giro torte sol ciclos et rotor igne. Latin: "Lo! I, the Sun, whirlingly wheel 'round my circles and revolve with fire." Given by BORGMANN. Blazing sky wheelies! A paragon of ANACYCLIC virtuosity.

Enid and Nadine.

Another nice couple.

Enid and Edna dine. Possibly by BORGMANN. Illustrated in IRVINE, 1987, and TERBAN.

Enid and Nadine. Another nice couple.

Enid, did I tap? / Pat, I *did* dine! REVERSAL SENTENCES by BORGMANN: a pair that can dance and dine separately or together.

Enid : dine. The Oklahoma city is believed to have been so named because it was a good dinner halt on the early trails.

ENIGMA. Official organ of the National Puzzler's League, it has been an occasional source of palindromes for over a century.

Enné Ouadi (enn-*NEHY* WAH-dee). Wadi (often-dry stream) of Chad, via Biltine, 14°24'n/18°45'e.

Enola : alone. According to George R. Stewart in *American Place-Names* (Oxford University Press, 1970), Enola Hill, Oregon, is a lone hill, and Enola, Pennsylvania, was named from a fictional character, probably also a loner. Enola,

South Carolina, was first actually named Alone and was only later reversed. Enola, Nebraska, alone came not from Alone but from someone named Malone who lost either his head or his tail depending on how you look at it (and who suggests to us the progeny **Enola Malone**).

Enola Bay Abalone?? Say "ah, baloney" if you must, yet almost Gay and wanting so well to be gay, this mother-of-pearl harbors, effectively, an "A" balm. So let's all feel great once again and forget it.

E Pacific ape

Enone (ee-NOH-nee). The modernized Œnone, a nymph, beloved of Paris but newly a PALINDROME.

Enon None. A notorious group of defendants who all got away between Dayton and Springfield, Ohio. Compare: **Net Ten** and **Nevele Eleven.**

Enosis is One. The KUHNS' statement of unity.

enrober : reborne. REVERSAL PAIR of medium strength: one who invests with a robe is carried again.

E Pacific ape. The late-developing New World anthropoid genus that includes all the talented species of **SE Pacific apes,** famous for their amazing west-to-east island-hopping migrations from the East to the West over thousands of miles of open ocean in flimsy canoes. See: **No worse, Pacific apes row on.**

Epe. 1: small town of Germany, 52°11'n/7°02'e **2:** large town of the Netherlands, 52°21'n/6°00'e **3:** small city of Nigeria, 6°37'n/3°59'e.

"'Epocsi' reparations?" "No, I tar a periscope." Here in our theater of the bizarre, a submarine waterproofer is at first mistaken for an ornery Krazy Gluer.

epode dope. 1: semantic glue used by a lyric poet such as Archilochus or Horace when composing couplets of dactyl-

E [. . .] E

lic hexameter over pentameter, that is, pasting a long line above a shorter one **2**: the poet himself or his drug of choice.

"Eracide"? Medicare! Puts an end to an era.

Eran i modi di dominare. Italian: "These were the ways of dominating." Sounds like it could be the last line of Machiavelli's *The Prince,* but it's BORGMANN.

Erdre (EHRDr). Small river of France into the Loire at Nantes.

ere (EHR). Aforetimes, aforetimes.

Ere we were here, we were.

Ere hypocrisies or poses are in, my hymn I erase. So prose I, Sir, copy here. Probably by MERCER. An extremely nice, long, and poetic hymn, if we may say so. *Hypocrisies* straightway gives *-se I, Sir, copy h-,* and it is relatively (or perhaps only seemingly) easy to close the ends by *ere hypocrisies . . . -se I, Sir, copy here.* Then, at least with the advantage of hindsight, *prose* comes fairly readily to mind, and so: *ere hypocrisies or p- . . . prose I, Sir, copy here.* But we are still a long way from closing the center. It is true that *poses are* is almost suggested outright by *ere hypocrisies or p-* and therefore that *erase[.] so prose I, Sir, copy here* is forced, and everything is looking very neat-edged and promising at this point, but in reality we still are facing only a disjointed pair of long chains, and we still cannot imagine the mental gymnastic that must have been necessary to visualize and catch the perfect completion with the modular core *in, my hymn I.* Perhaps it came as a result of first completing the subordinate clause in the shortest possible order, with *ere hypocrisies or poses are in[,]* and then working backward from *-n I erase[.] so prose I, Sir, copy here.* Or the very capable constructor may well have had the advantage of being familiar with the entire four-word central modular fragment in advance—and may even have been working toward it, consciously or subliminally—but *we* might not have thought of it in a million years. Nor can we imagine the overall persistence and determination that must have been necessary to produce the whole full-length and entirely coherent movie.

Ere verses, I rises revere. Before poems, I venerate small hills. A natural bucolic, by the KUHNS.

Ere we were here, we were. "Statement of our firm belief in a previous existence," by the KUHNS.

Ere we were heroes, a base ore here we were. Also by the KUHNS. It evidently takes the alchemical view of refining the coarse into the fine, which is fine. It's good to remember, though, that we are not "here" to prove ourselves worthy of anything. We're already fine and always were.

***Erewhon* : nowhere.** Poetically licensed near-REVERSAL (that is, not spelled *Erehwon*, as would be proper, but with the *w* and *h* oddly rereversed, as if in the Old or Middle English spelling) by Samuel Butler, the title of his Utopian novel.

Ere wise, "Ma *Games*" I were. This seems to mean, but actually does not mean, that in a previous life or episode, before I had much smarts, I was the Mother of *Games*. Strictly speaking, the subjunctive verb forces a meaning of "I would sooner be the Mother of *Games* than wise," seemingly a foolish preference. (Still, I have all of eternity to get wise, and though many may claim to be the father, none can deny the mother.)

Ergotism? Sit, ogre. By POOL. An exorcism on LSD that enfolds the attractive REVERSAL PAIR **ergo : ogre.**

Er . . . I fondle her as late petals are held—no fire. Still, stunning. By LINDON. It is really fascinating to watch this text open out, word by word, gracefully, seamlessly, and without much hesitation, from the central core idea of *late petals* to *as late petals* to *as late petals are* to *her as late petals are* to *her as late petals are held* to *fondle her as late petals are* *held*—*no f-* to the surprising and original start-finish/culmination.

eroded ore. Yet a high assay; contributed by CHISM.

Eros, Ore. See: **PRP.**

Eros saw Aviva was sore. By BORGMANN. Actually any PALINDROMIC name could replace the exotic Aviva in this FORMULA-type PALINDROME, but she was bizarre enough to pose for the picture.

Eros? Sidney, my end is sore.

Eros? Sidney, my end is sore. Illustrated in IRVINE, 1987.

"Erudition?" "No. I 'tidure.'" (TEECH'r). Evidently a leading edge caterer.

ESE. East-southeast.

espagnolette-long apse. A gleaning from the mysterious BORGMANN—what could it mean? An espagnolette is a window latch. Along similar but slightly more scrutable lines, John McClellan has devised the also lovely sentence **Espagnola solos along apse. Solos** is one of those handy core verbs, like **sees** and **did.**

ESPY, Willard R. Author of *An Almanac of Words at Play* (New York: Clarkson N. Potter, 1975), *Another Almanac of Words at Play* (New York: Clarkson N. Potter, 1981), and other wordplay books rich in PALINDROMES.

esse (ESS-seh). Latin: **1:** to be **2:** being (noun) **3:** in Scholastic philosophy, actual being, or existence.

Esse (ESS-eh). River of Italy, into the Arno, 43°16'n/11°54'e.

Essé (ess-SEHY). Village of Cameroun, 4°05'n/11°53'e.

Essen I finesse. I handle the German steel city with a deceptive strategy. By the KUHNS.

esssse. Given by BORGMANN as "one of the clever ways in which our obviously intelligent 14th-century predecessors used to spell the word 'ashes.'" Yes, we can see that.

et alibis : sibilate. REVERSAL PAIR by BORGMANN that can lead to a scholarly reverie in which *et alibi* footnote references (meaning "and elsewhere") audibly *hiss*, certainly a wild and phantasmic turn of events, since these Latin words actually contain no hissable sounds. See also: **Sibilate pet alibis.**

E.T. arises, irate. This unlikely scene contributed by CHISM seems to depict that funny-looking little guy waking up on the wrong side of the . . . er, universe.

État *I* capacitate. "The state is not only mine, it is *me* (and is empowered by me)," Barbaria's optional pledge of allegiance—though having one's own sovereignty, and even one's own divinity, is almost unavoidable here. Curiously, nay hauntingly, similar words of the Great Inca god-king, Manco **Capac,** are: **État I, Capac, capacitate.** (For clarification: **état = state** in French, both in Barbaria and Peru.)

Etats derussify my fissured state. "Attributable" to Mikhail Gorbachev. Former Soviet republics crack apart and send the Russians packing.

état, state. Altered state, French to English, by the KUHNS.

états : state. REVERSAL PAIR of state(s), French and English, by BORGMANN.

été (ehy-TEHY). French: **1:** summer **2:** been.

étêté (ehy-teh-TEHY). Headless, in heraldry.

E.T. is opposite. *UFO Magazine* photo caption.

Et la marine va, Papa, venir à Malte. French: And the navy, Daddy, is going to come to Malte. By BORGMANN.

E [. . .] E

***Etna* di Dante** *or* **Etna, do Dante.** Wherein a volcano seems to have been divinely/comedically mistaken for a regular *Inferno*.

Eton, Caliente bet Neil a C-note. Our friend Neil—returning to his prestigious and palindromically potent prep school (preparatory to PU, that is) after a hot summer of gambling in Nevada—reports on, or is reported for, his illustrious but unsuccessful PALINDROME wager, as described above under **Caliente bet Neil a C.**

E tu, malamute?
Brutish sled-dog turns
on Italian musher.

E tu, malamute? Brutish sled-dog turns on Italian musher.

Eureka! Fake rue! Words spoken upon synthesizing an "herb of grace" medicine.

Euston saw I was not Sue. Possibly by MERCER. Also: **Denton saw Bob was not Ned, / Gorton saw Lil was not Rog,** etc.

Eva, can I pose as Aesop in a cave? Probably by MERCER. Such imposture may be a bit outré but is understandable. Two simple modules, *pose as Aesop* and *Eva[,] can [I . . .] in a cave[?]*, each essentially self-standing, are here combined to jack up the whimsy level. An alternative in the same style, also probably by MERCER, is **Eva, can I stab bats in a cave?** But if we don't really like or want to **stab bats,** we still have many other things available to test in this context, such as **stack cats** or **stir grits.** Such trial and error is clearly a good way to proceed, and beginners or anyone would do well to gather and experimentally assemble any similar, or totally original, bits and pieces. For a more elaborate, advanced development that takes off from the same starting place, compare the following entry.

Eva can, I see, bone no bees in a cave. By LINDON. Delightfully absurd. This text would have been the structural equivalent (though not the artistic equal) of the two previous items by MERCER **(Pose as Aesop** and **Stab Bats)** if

LINDON had simply quit at **Eva, can I see bees in a cave?** But with the expansion in the center resulting from the alert attempt *Eva can, I see, . . . -ees in a cave,* a more fanciful and sophisticated direction emerged, as first the *bees* and then *no bees* and finally the novel *bone no bees* filled in like an inside straight in poker. It is fascinating to observe in this example *how* the gnomes pay a dividend or reward for a constructor's resourcefulness.

Evade Dave. He's *It!*

Evade me, Dave. I'm *It!* Possibly by MERCER. Illustrated by AGEE in **So Many Dynamos.**

Eva gave. At home and, being a PALINDROME, again at the office.

¡Eva, lave! (EHY-bvah, LAH-bveh). Spanish: "Wash, Eva!" from Anthony Bonner via ESPY.

eve (EEV). **1:** night before **2:** period preceding **3:** to become moist or damp, according to BORGMANN.

Eve (EEV). Feminine name, wife of Adam, and a sufficient if simple response to **Madam, I'm Adam.**

Ève (ehv). Small town of France, 49°05'n/2°42'e.

Eve is a sieve. By LINDON. She's so forgetful. ("Now *what* was it that was forbidden? . . . And *which* fruit was that about?") Like Lindon's similar little pearls, **Basil is a b—,** **Cora sees a roc,** and **Deer breed,** this item shows that a very selective simplicity *is* a kind of sophistication. Are these obvious? Perhaps, but so are the scores of less interesting short ones not associated with Lindon's name.

Eve, **mad Adam,** *Eve!* This bizarre BORGMANN version of Eve's response to **Madam, I'm Adam** assumes poor hearing in Adam or poor acoustics in Paradise. In this version of the story, the dialogue does not stop here but continues, appro-

Eve

E [. . .] E

priately and with a very strange echo, **Mad? Am I, madam?** Another Borgmann offering is **Eve, man, am Eve!** And of course, there is just the eloquently simple **Eve!** All three are ingenious, but top laurels for this occasion are won hands down by the creations of LINDON's that follow.

Eve, maiden name. Both sad in Eden? I dash to be manned. I am Eve. By LINDON. In this version, Eve wastes no time answering Adam's famous opening line, **Madam, I'm Adam.** The following item, also by Lindon, wastes even less: **"Eve" mine. My hero! More hymen! I'm Eve!** For here she's faster still, if that were possible, while inventing in the same snappy process a new genre: X-rated, slapstick, Bible-movie palindromes. Both items were, we believe, gifts of the gnomes to Lindon for his simply deigning to test the most natural of responses, *I am Eve* and *I'm Eve.* (*Sir, I'm Eve* doesn't admit of such treatment.) One can see, without our even troubling over the analysis, how both texts must have miraculously unfolded: first backward from their predetermined endings and then forward from the resultant forced starts, thence zig-zagging by alternating stages from both ends to their amazingly satisfactory central closures.

Even Eve.
Adam was odd
until he met her.

Even Eve. Near-Homeric epithet by the KUHNS, who say Adam was odd until he met her.

Eve? No gig on Eve! It's no discredit to, or blot upon, her wonderful self that she got into the wrong produce. Indeed our whole idea of sin is a mistake. At the very most and best, it could only mean "missing the mark," that is, flowing less in the direction of what is desired than in the direction of the lack or absence of what is desired. So what is the big deal but an extravagance of miscomprehension? Moreover, to subtract insult from injury, **Devil never even lived!** (The *gig* text is actually just a throwaway to mark the approximate alphabetical location of a fantastic little rhymed palindrome quatrain by LINDON entitled "Without Rites in the Garden," the first line of which, comprising three additional syllables, is an expansion upon the center of our more basic and, by contrast, threadbare text. See BERGERSON's *Palindromes and Anagrams* for the full poem.)

. . . Ever, Yr. Eve. By John McClellan. Good, tight close for our drastically abbreviated **Eve** section, which really could have gone on forever, seeing as how the Garden of Eden's main characters, and for some reason **Eve** most especially, have been milked and squeezed (and not to exhaustion) for every ounce of PALINDROMY they might yield.

Évian : naïve. Anglo-French REVERSAL PAIR for water made without sophistication.

Evil I did dwell; lewd did I live. See: **Lewd . . . dwel.**

E. Village[:] LSD's legal! Live! Remarkable. See under **Yosemite . . . times! Oy!**

Ev, is Australian snail art suasive? Yes, it's slow but compelling.

Evita, General Lull Are Negative (*or . . .* **General and NAL Are . . .**) *also* **Evita, General Flare Negative** (*or* **Blare** *or* **Glare**). Various political signals and/or headlines from a favorite Latin American dictatorship. The NAL must be the opposition, probably something like National Alliance of Labor.

evitative (*EHV*-uh-TEHY-duhv). Avoidant. According to BORGMANN:

> Dictionaries, bless their perverted little souls, record such nouns as *meditation* and *levitation*, and also the corresponding adjectives, *meditative* and *levitative*. Such is not, unfortunately, always the case. Take, for instance, the rare noun *evitation*, defined as "an avoiding or shunning." For this noun, no dictionary condescends to show the corresponding adjective. To the LOGOLOGIST, who has trained

E [. . .] E

himself to be an expert in reasoning by analogy, this omission presents no problem. He knows, beyond any shadow of a doubt, that the adjective corresponding to *evitation* is **evitative**. This adjective, **evitative**, is a major triumph for the logologist, since it is [PALINDROMIC].

By applying analogical and related talents diligently, the word expert is able to evolve words such as **evitative,** not found in any dictionary but every bit as real and as legitimate as the finest dictionary words, possessing the virtue of exhibiting some desired form of verbal beauty.

Evolve, Bev: Love!

evitator : rotative. REVERSAL PAIR by BORGMANN, suggesting an avoider, revolving, begging to be a **rotative evitator,** like, say, a whirling dervish, or a planet.

Ev! O, love! *also* **Rev, O lover!** And so on.

Evolve, Bev: Love! (*or* **Ev, Lev,** etc.). By CHISM. Must have been a sixties thing.

Evolve. Rev love. / Evolvers rev love. Good bumper stickers.

ewe (YOO). **1:** female sheep (sing.) **2:** also owed, according to BORGMANN.

Ewe (EHY-vehy *or* EHY-wehy). **1:** West African ethnic group (of modern Togo, Ghana, and Dahomey) and their language **2: Ewe** (YOO), loch, a fjord or bay of Scotland, 57°48'n/5°40'w.

Exe (EKKSS). River of England (Devon), via Exeter and Exmouth into Lyme Bay of the English Channel, 50°37'n/ 7°25'w.

Exult [at] luxe. Rejoice greatly in being elegantly sumptuous.

eye (AHY). Organ of vision, and a word with figurative meanings that radiate out in all directions. Interestingly, the Spanish equivalent, **ojo,** acts the same way.

E [. . .] E

Eye. **1:** village of Cambridgeshire, England, 52°35'n/0°10'w **2:** village of Suffolk, England, 52°19'n/1°09'e **3:** peninsula on easternmost Isle of Lewis, Scotland, 58°13'n/6°13'w.

eye-peep : peepeye. REVERSAL PAIR by BORGMANN that, though of little combinative strength (yielding only a redundant or reciprocal form of peekaboo) still commands our attention for being a unique case of a reversal of COMPOUND PALIN-DROMES. Thus, though a PALINDROME by nature cannot be a reversal (of anything but itself), we do encounter in this pair alone a sort of "PALINDROMIC reversal twins."

Èze (EZZ). Exquisite medieval cliffside village overlooking the French Riviera near Monte Carlo.

Eze. ABBREVIATION for the Old Testament book of Ezekiel.

ezylyze (*EZZ*-ih-LAHYZ). Word created for the occasion, meaning, as a transitive verb, to create a PALINDROME spon-taneously and, intransitively, to become a palindrome before one's very eyes.

Eye.
Village of
Cambridgeshire,
England.

E [. . .] E

f [. . .] f

Face decaf! By CHISM. Said on mornings when real coffee is not available.

faf. "Flyaway factory," one of DE SOLA's inscrutable ABBREVIATIONS; perhaps a military term or business phenomenon of the postindustrial era.

FAMILY. Dmitri BORGMANN showed that it's possible to produce an entire series or family of PALINDROMES by changing only the first and last words of the **Able . . . Elba** classic. Compare variously: **Sore . . . eros, Live . . . evil, Sire . . . Eris, Stressed . . . desserts,** and **Adelberta . . . a trebled *A*.**)

FDF. Airport code for Fort de France, Martinique.

ff. 1: musical ABBREVIATION for *fortissimo*, "very strong," meaning "to be played very loud" **2:** nonmusical abbreviation for *fecerunt* ("they've made," though not what some might think).

ff. Publishing ABBREVIATION for *folios*, "leaves," meaning lots of different things having to do with sheets of paper and their pagination; especially, whenever **ff.** follows a page number cited in a reference or footnote, "and the pages that follow" (for example: "pp. 77ff.," meaning page 77 and, at least, pages 78 and 79 as well).

FF. 1: fast form of Air Link **2:** brothers (*fratres*).

fff. 1: fat, forty, and female, according to DE SOLA's *Abbreviation Dictionary*, though we might want to play that one down **2:** *forte fortissimo*, very, *very LOUD*, indeed as loud as possible; but see: **ffff.**

ffff. Very, *very, VERY LOUD!*—or just read the following pages very loudly.

fffffffff. This and the following pages are to be played very, *very, VERY LOUD* by a fat, fortyish female.

F fit no Pontiff. Simple but effective grading system at the College of Cardinals.

Fiery lyre *IF*. First line of PALINDROMIC poem: "An If And Or Abut":

> **Fiery lyre *IF***
> **DNA *AND***
> **Romeo poem *OR***
> **tuba *ABUT*!**
> —Eponymous

finif. Underworld slang for a five-year prison sentence, according to BORGMANN.

finnif (FINN-iff). A five-dollar bill or a five-pound note in slang, per BORGMANN.

FITZPATRICK, Edwin. A mysterious fictional poet and PALIN-DROMIST, seemingly of a Victorian sensibility, the creation and perhaps the alter ego of contemporary master palindromist Howard W. BERGERSON.

Finnif

Fleecing niggard notables, Nita's a tinsel, baton-dragging, nice elf. Elaborate and curious character blending the natures of a Robin Hood, a trickster, and a Tiny Tim, and perhaps a Santa's-helper type; after BERGERSON. (See also: **Flee to me, remote elf.**) The adaptor's debt to the original composer is enormous in cases of such lengthy and unabashed borrowing—and purely modular rearrangement —as the present text represents, and yet a comparison of the immensely better original in Bergerson's *Palindromes and Anagrams* will make it clear that a respectable and newly original, if extremely modest, creation has nevertheless been born here. (That is to say: If we could see far in this case, it was because we were standing on the shoulders of a giant.)

Flee, elf! Ah, but from what? Elves are never in any danger.

Flee to me, remote elf. Start and end of BERGERSON's eighteen-line PALINDROME nonsense poem, "The Faded Bloomers' Rhapsody," cited by ESPY but too long and too bedazzling to quote, even here. The sentence is illustrated, besides, in STUART.

flesh self. The conscious physical temporary being, distinguishable but inseparable from, and really an outgrowth of, the nonphysical, permanent, inner being, or soul, or Godself. The **flesh self** is one of the two sides or directions of the two-way person, or *anthropalindrome*, that is a completely blended being. The linear (unidimensional), right-left polarity of a typical PALINDROME symbolizes in a sketchy way the multidimensional, in-out polarity of the anthropalindrome. See also: CASUAL.

Florida dad, I Rolf. Intense new contestant on *Jeopardy* introduces self.

Ford Madox Ford

Flow, alas, solo cosmic. I'm so colossal a wolf. Great sinew pair torn (and reconstituted) from an otherwise indigestible FITZPATRICK poem, now seeming to be a line from Hermann Hesse's *Steppenwolf.*

Ford Madox Ford. A rare WORD-PALINDROME personal name, the pen name of novelist and critic Ford Madox Heuffer.

FORMULAS. There is a fairly long list of a sort similar to **Ada: "Did Bob peep?" Bob: "Did Ada?"** with the formula "A: Did B peep? B: Did A?" Although an enormous number of "new" PALINDROMIC sentences could easily be generated by combining and permutating (that is, "multiplying out") the full set of syntactical tricks with the assembled rosters and vocabularies, it is our guess that few if any of the results would have much new interest or merit. (Nevertheless, many excellent new creations do result from the *inspired* juxtaposition and recombination of time-worn elements.) An extra thing to like about this particular formula is that each word of it is itself a PALINDROME. See: COMPOUND PALINDROME.

Foster : Retsof. REVERSAL PAIR of small but still-extant places, in Rhode Island and New York, respectively, pinpointed by BORGMANN.

From A to Zotamorf. Ingenious subtitle, really a super title, of Stephen J. CHISM's *The Dictionary of Palindromes.* For the meaning of *zotamorf,* a wondrous invention in itself that the inventor never gets around to explaining, we propose: "any verbal vagary or ingrowth, such as *From A to Zotamorf itself* or, say, **Hall of Follah** or **Call a spade an Ædapsallac,** that begins with a recognizable word or phrase and then trails off into the realm and language of fantasy to create an original PALINDROMIC evocation." For the opposite, or really the same thing but executed in reverse (that is, *from* rather than *to* a happily returning endpoint), see: **cainamaniac, ciloholic,** and **ezylyze.**

fromato-zotamorf (froh-MAH-duh-*ZOH*-duh-mawrf). Any zotamorf, looking like it wants to be a strange new pasta shape, that has been prepared with cheese and tomato. For another recipe, see: *From A to Zotamorf.*

Frustrate Lee? (*or* **Lana, Lulu,** etc.). **Let Art surf!** Almost anyone's favorite beach boy.

FTF. Being *"face to face"* (in the magic mirror) with the airport code for Ft. Flatters, Algeria (an old French Foreign Legion outpost), evidently *becomes one.* It is also of possible interest that, having previously only offended her, now this fort flatters Algeria.

Foster : Retsof.
Two small but
still-extant places,
in Rhode Island and
New York, respectively.

F [. . .] F

g [· · ·] g

gab bag (GÆB BÆG). Illustrated in TERBAN, who clues it "a gossipy paper container." Hmm.

gag (GÆG). Prevent utterance or choke—but surely a joke!

GAG. First line of easy-to-swallow WORD SQUARE by BORGMANN:

G A G
A D A
G A G

gala lag. A form of jet-set fête lag or party fatigue, by the KUHNS.

Galápagos so gap a lag! Charles Darwin enthusiastically explains, in perfect GALAPALDYGOOK, why he chose the Galápagos for seeking missing links in the origins of species: for some reason just these and no other islands so foreshorten and exaggerate any shortcoming in fitness for survival (viz., so gap a lag!) that they provide the ideal (that is, the most abrupt and accelerated) laboratory/observatory conditions for examining and evaluating evolution in process. . . . And, believe it or not, only a few months after unearthing the text, we actually saw some field researchers on Public Television testing this very proposition (and achieving an acceleration in evolution there far beyond even their fondest imaginings) with the help of the thirteen species of Darwin's finches that have evolved on the various Galápagos, along with Mr. Darwin's theories and his recorded observations of these very birds—not to mention God.

GALAPALDYGOOK (guh-*LAH*-p'l-dee-GOUK, *also GLAH*-b'l-dee-GOUK; after *gobbledygook*). A very far but precise dialect of **ESE Wordrowese.** See previous entry.

gallag. Defined by *WORD WAYS*, in a correction, as a little bitch, not bird.

Game [s] / *E* **Mag.** A pair of (actually make that three) real magazines, good bedfellows for playfully resolving the world's environmental puzzles. And, moreover:

Games **(a case!) Mag.** That peculiar publication is an example. Of what? A medical disorder? A legal affair? Something rather more like a beverage order, we should think.

Games **(I rise!) Mag.** Same book now clearly gets respect and appreciation!

Games: **N.E.'s Nonsense Mag.** Published in New York, it is the entire Northeast region's most extravagant act of foolishness and frivolity!

Games **(on nose!) Mag.** It wouldn't be the first time it took a dive. . . .

Games **(or *A Rose*) Mag.** . . . and arose smelling like a rose . . . for many another game.

gamey eye mag. Illustrated in IRVINE, 1992.

Garbage Gab Rag. "The Magazine for Talking Trash." Also recycles as *Garb Age Gab Rag,* a trade publication for clothing manufacturers and/or rag pickers.

**Games: N.E.'s
Nonsense Mag**

Garbage Man **(Name Gab Rag).** The distinguished professional newsletter (were it not for the added tag line, so easily mistaken for an action comic), and the rear guard of our strange little magazine department.

garbage megabrag. Say, "We can make more and better (from) garbage than anyone." (Please note that this and the previous entries do not refer to the real but unrelated and very nice magazine named *Garbage.*)

Garden one drag. The fall before the fall: A lackful or disparaging thought banishes paradise awareness.

GARDNER, Martin. Writing about mathematical games, Gardner presented in *Scientific American* (August 1970) a broad summary of number and word PALINDROMES, acknowledging the "deep, half-conscious aesthetic pleasure" that people take "in the kind of symmetry palindromes possess."

Gargantua tag: a wag, a taut nag rag. New dimensions of Rabelaisian sport, whose meaning we can scarcely deign to imagine. (Moreover, the *wag* may give way to a *bag*, a **gag,** a *hag*, a *sag*, or even, if least plausibly, a *fag*.) With slight changes in punctuation, many different kinds of sentences are possible here.

gateman : name tag. REVERSAL PAIR, of strong attraction: **gateman's name tag** or **Name tag: "Gateman."** It was possibly MERCER who first stretched this correspondence out into the witty but still somewhat ragged conception **Gateman sees name, garage-man sees name-tag.**

GBG. Airport code for Galesburg, Illinois.

GEG. Airport code for Spokane, Washington.

Gelatin knit a leg.

Gelatin knit a leg. By the KUHNS. A remarkable recovery and a medical discovery.

Gemini, Meg. Signed ID. For Zodiacal reference, see also: **Leo, Joel,** and **So G. Rivera's tots are Virgos.**

GEORGIA. Mentioned honorably here, and perhaps challengingly, as one of the few PALINDROME-free states, that is, containing not a single palindrome (at least among the names of its major localities) and never successfully palindromized itself, except perhaps along the lines of the following, rather free-form fantasy:

> **Georgia: I gro', eg'!** (*comma optional; also* **Georgi** *or* **Georgianna**). I'm bigger and better and pregnant again, old girl.

Gg. Thanks to BORGMANN and the New York Public Library card catalog,we have this pseudonym of the translator into French of a Russian work on history, a translator known only by another strange pseudonym, "Nicolas-on."

GG. Airline code for Gem State Airlines.

Ggg. *Gorilla gorilla gorilla*, Linnaean taxonomic classification for the lowland gorilla.

GGG. **1:** airport code for Gladewater-Kilgore-Longview, Texas **2:** trademark of a men's clothing manufacturer.

Gibe big. Heckle loudly.

Giddier ore I'd dig. By Joaquin KUHN, who contributed it to this book at the last minute after seeing some of our work in preparation. We are thrilled to have this true poem and guiding light in our collection, and very grateful to count the KUHNS among our leading cocreators.

Gig (GIGG). **1:** masculine name **2:** joke **3:** demerit **4:** whim **5:** (usually paid) musical performance.

Gig Harbor. Village of Pierce County, Washington, 47°19'n/ 122°34'w.

Giles "Selig." See: HALES.

Girl, bathing on Bikini, eyeing boy, finds boy eyeing bikini on bathing girl. WORD PALINDROME by LINDON, widely recited and admired.

Girl, I owe nabob a new oil rig. Illustrated, if you can imagine that, in POOL.

Girlless, agnostic, I, Tsongas, sell rig. Presidential hopeful Paul, being apparently unattractive to women and looking uncertain, capitulates and appears to cash in by disposing of his political machinery.

girl rig. Useful phrase with a variety of possible meanings for various tastes and wishes. By POOL.

Glen Elg (glenn-ELG). **1:** village of Australia, 34°59's/ 138°31'e, a burb of Adelaide and a popular resort **2:** hamlet of Howard County, Maryland (*also* **Glenelg**) **3:** locality of

Scotland, 57°13'n/5°38'w 4: river of Australia, Victoria, from Rocklands Reservoir to Discovery Bay of Southern Ocean via Casterton and Dartmoor, 38°03's/141°00'e.

Gliding . . . gliding. Start and finish of a magnificent twenty-seven-word (not the world's longest but among the best) WORD PALINDROME by LINDON, about which, though we may not publish it, we can still tell you that its middle word is *see* and the other dozen (pairs) it comprises are, alphabetically, *certainly, ethereal, is, jumping, near, see, see, something, unearthly, we, you,* and again *you.* The format is a complete statement plus a comically disjointed response to it in two additional complete sentences, and you will find the correct solution on page 109 in BERGERSON's book.

GNAT. First line of buggy WORD SQUARE, by BORGMANN:

G N A T
N O V A
A V O N
T A N G

Gnostic illicit song.

It goes "I don't know ..."

Gnipping. Listed by CHISM as an English word, who cites *WORD WAYS* without explanation. It certainly is a beauty. We would guess it is the name of a lake in Canada or perhaps some kind of a Welsh participle.

gnostic illicit song. It goes "I don't know . . ." and isn't allowed.

gnu dung. Illustrated (!) in IRVINE's *Madam I'm Adam.*

God! A dog! Amazing creature.

God! A red nugget! A fat egg under a dog! Possibly MERCER. Illustrated in IRVINE.

God, a slap! Paris, sir, appals a dog. By LINDON. Anything might happen. Even a dog talks. This absolute stroke of genius is unexplainable if not as an outgrowth of *Paris,* *sir, ap-,* in which case the eventual arrival of the deus ex machina resolution via *God* and *dog* must have seemed a veritable epiphany.

Goddesses so pay a possessed dog. We wonder how so. And BERGERSON, in amazement, wonders who is responsible for this one, though he places it in his "Possibly MERCER" inventory. *Goddess* and *goddesses* were a natural line to want to test in view of the well-established potency of the **God : Dog** REVERSAL. *Possessed dog* was inevitable then, and *goddesses so pa-* . . . *a possessed dog* could not have been far behind. Finally choosing *pay* over *pat* or *pad* or *pall* was probably not difficult from a poetic point of view even if the meaning is somewhat illusionistic. Thus we have here a rare case of a nearly NATURAL—or inevitable—PALINDROME, and so it seems fitting that its parentage, like that of all true folklore, remains obscure.

God! Nate bit a Tibetan dog! BORGMANN continues: "Hmmmm . . . What does Nate know about Tibetan dogs that we don't? Was it a Tibetan prayer dog, a Tibetan spaniel?"

God : Dog. REVERSAL PAIR (with strongly ironic attraction) that has been much remarked upon over the years.

Go droop, stop, onward draw no pots, poor dog. Words to a costermonger's dying dog, 1867.

Gods ridicule lucid IRS dog. Illustrated in IRVINE, 1992.

Gods send a madness: D.O.G. A novel and clever appreciation by the KUHNS.

God, to have Eva. Hot dog! Attributed by LESSER to Herbert Harvey.

Go, fatal cello-doll! *Éclat?* **A fog!** By LINDON. More off-key orchestral humor, this one a unique three-panel cartoon in

God, to have Eva. Hot dog!

so few as six or seven words. We surmise Lindon must have come upon *cello-doll ec-* while routinely testing various musical instruments. From there *-tal cello-doll eclat* could not have been far behind, and similarly *fatal cello-doll eclat a f-*. The real breakthrough must have occurred not in the chain-linking so much as in the discovery of a novel punctuation or staging opportunity.

Gog (GAHG). Along with Magog, stands seemingly for all the heathen nations, in Revelation 20:7–8.

Go hang a salami! I'm a lasagna hog! *and Other Palindromes.* Title of book by Jon AGEE (New York: Farrar, Straus, 1991).

"going and coming or coming and going." WORD PALINDROME. See: VUELTA.

Golconda had no clog. Things went along smoothly in this ancient Indian city known for its riches, or in this Ohio River town of Illinois, or in any of the several famous mines bearing this name.

Golf? No, sir, prefer prison-flog.

goldenrod-adorned log. A decorative but idle idyl idol. Compare the following entry.

Goldenrod a silly ram ate, wan on a wet, amaryllis-adorned log. Languid and silly indeed not to go for the amaryllis, though the wetness of the log may have discouraged him from this; a reconstituted morsel browsed entirely from "The Faded Bloomers' Rhapsody," by BERGERSON (see: **Flee to me, remote elf**).

Golf? No, sir, prefer prison-flog. Possibly by MERCER. Strange kidder, if so. This item, notwithstanding its tastelessness, has a great many admirers and reciters, a fact probably owing more to golf's popularity and intensity than to the poor judgment of the masses.

Gorge grog. Perhaps originally by REYNOLDS. See: **avid [as a] diva** and **Disgorge grog, Sid.**

Gorgon—no grog! By POOL. Medusa's an incredible sight, even when we haven't been drinking.

Gramm! Arg! Political slogan.

Grenada had an erg. It used to be a low-energy state.

GRG. Airport code for Georgetown, Guyana.

Grubs knife Finksburg. The tale of how cutworms divide a Maryland hamlet.

Grub went Newburg. "Plain eats improved by fancy sauce." The KUHNS.

Grub Staatsburg. Upper Hudson Valley eatery.

Grub St. tips as Pittsburg. See: **Pittsburgh . . . tip.**

Gubug. Town of Java, Indonesia, 7°03's/110°40'e.

gug (GUGG). English dialect: an inclined plane in a coal mine, down which cars move by their own weight, according to BORGMANN.

Gulp a slab o' balsa plug. Ad for an improbable chaw in IRVINE, 1992, nicely illustrated by Steven Guarnaccia.

Gulp tub, but plug. Inspired by a REYNOLDS drinking song, this is good advice for anyone who wants to drink a significant amount of bathtub gin.

gum mug. By POOL, and also TERBAN, who clues it "a heavy cup to hold chewing sticks."

Gurdjieff am I, Maffei. . . . (J-drug?) In eternity, George Gurdjieff, the shadowy, Rasputin-like Armenian Greek mystic (1880?–1948) with some wild "esoteric" ideas and a quiet but intense following in most major cities even today introduces himself to the Italian tragedian Scipio (Marquis) de Maffei (1675–1755) . . . and passes him the joint.

Gustav Klimt milk vats—ug! Illustrated in IRVINE, 1987.

Gramm! Arg!
Political slogan.

gut tug. By POOL, a visceral drama, say, like a heartthrob or tear jerk, only different.

Gwallawg. Welsh: **1:** hawk **2:** stammerer. According to BORGMANN in *Beyond Language*, who cites an obscure 1863 naming dictionary for his source, **Gwallag** ap Lleenawg was a mid-sixth-century champion remembered in old Welsh poems for having fought King Ida of Bernicia, a North Sea kingdom.

hah (HAH *or* HAHH). Exclamation of surprise, wonder, triumph, puzzlement, or pique.

Ha! I rush to my lion oily moths, Uriah! Probably by MER-CER. A voice from beyond the pale. This is an eruption of what typically occurs when you just intend fun and allow anything at all to happen along. Here quite a beautiful raving lunatic cartoon pops out, there an unexpected tropical paradise, etc.

h [. . .] h

Haiti, ah! By the KUHNS. Surprise, delight, satisfaction in western Hispaniola!

Ha! Jar a ham! : Maharajah! REVERSAL SENTENCE in a word, observed by BORGMANN. Combining the segments simply tells His Highness it's time to preserve meat or jolt an amateur radio operator.

Hajjah. Another name for, or a place within, one of the Yemens.

Hakeem Olajuwon's now UJA! Lo! Meek! Ah! It's doubly surprising to imagine "The Dream" traded to the United Jewish Appeal and to also dream him, one of the NBA's strongest players, submissive. When will he stop showing us yet another move?

Ha! I rush to my lion oily moths, Uriah!

Halah. Biblical place in Mesopotamia to which the king of Assyria sent captives from Samaria, according to BORGMANN.

HALES . . . BORGMANN'S WORD SQUARE, poetically surpassing Arepo himself (see: **Sator . . . Rotas**) in delivering a fully comprehensible sentence—here a report of a ritual performance by Hawaiian missionaries:

```
H A L E S
A N E L E
L E V E L
E L E N A
S E L A H
```

HALES, Giles "Selig." According to AUGARDE, man who claimed in 1980 to have written "the world's longest palindrome," comprising 58,795 letters.

hallah. Variant of challah (KHAHL-luh), a loaf of yeast-leavened, white egg bread, usually braided, traditionally eaten by Jews on the Sabbath, holidays, and ceremonial occasions.

Hallah, Allah! (KHAH-luh UH-luh). "Give us this day our daily egg bread" (see above) in a prosperous, postmodern, ecumenical Israel-Palestine. Consider also: **Hew hay, Yahweh.**

Hall of Follah (*or* **Ollah**) ([F]AH-lah *or* [F]AH-luh *and especially* fah-LAH *and* 'LL-uh). PALINDROMIC Hall of Fame or Heaven.

Hamah. 1: city of Syria, 35°08'n/36°45'e **2:** Syrian political division, 35°10'n/37°00'e.

Hanah (KHAH-nah). Hebrew: be gracious; the root of such names as **Hannah, Anna,** and **Ana.**

Hannah (HÆN-uh). **1:** village of Cavalier County, North Dakota, a port of entry on the Canadian border, 48°58'n/98°41'w **2:** hamlet of Centre County, Pennsylvania **3:** **Hannah** Bay, Ontario, 51°05'n/79°45'w, the southernmost reach of James Bay, itself the southernmost reach of Hudson Bay **4:** hamlet of Grand Traverse County, Michigan, consisting basically of St. Mary's Church and School and a few residences **5:** the mother of Samuel, a judge and prophet of Israel (Samuel 1:20). When she was having difficulty becoming pregnant, **Hannah** vowed to the Lord that if he gave her a son she would "give him to the Lord all the days of his life (and no razor shall touch his head)." It worked. The original meaning of this recently rare but now popular name was "graciousness" or "grace." See, too: **Hanah, Ana,** and **Anna. 6:** last name of film star Daryl and major-league baseball catcher Truck.

<aside>

Hallah, Allah!
"Give us this day our daily egg bread."

</aside>

hannah, Ophiophagus. Scientific name for the king cobra.

¿Hanna, vas a Savannah? A perfectly good question, Mark, in Spanish South Georgia.

"Ha! On, on, O Noah!" The title of a humorous rhyming quatrain by LINDON composed entirely of one-line PALIN-DROMES, recited by ESPY and, with a difference, by BERGERSON earlier.

Harass selfless Sarah. Probably by MERCER. To help her find herself? We doubt it. The ridiculousness of a line like this is of considerable VALUE, however, just for the chuckles. Compare with this the following (equally stupid) oft-repeated idea.

Harass sensuousness, Sarah. Probably by MERCER. Get down on physical fun? Not likely! This item and the previous highlight effectively a beautiful pair of near-PALINDROMES, *selfless* and *sensuousness*, though one still wishes to give them a more tasteful wrap than **Harass Sarah.** *Toss* and *boss* only produce conclusions in *sot* or *s.o.b.*, which are no help. There is of course **Ma is as selfless as I am.** But this idea won't go with *sensuousness*. Perhaps someday someone will find a solution, or forget the problem.

har-har : rah-rah. REVERSAL PAIR of medium synergy: "Har-har! Rah-rah!" (great joke!). For another angle, see: **Rah-rah har-har.**

Ha! Robed Selim smiles, Deborah! Probably by MERCER. Our PALINDROMIC camera captures a historic and fleeting moment of truth from the early post-Byzantine period, as the mysterious Deborah, a dark lady perhaps somewhere off behind a curtain, is informed by an excited and even more mysterious companion (perhaps a fellow intriguer) who is also behind the curtain but is peering out, that the Ottoman Sultan Himself can be seen from there in normal attire expressing his pleasure about something.

"Har-har! Rah-rah!"

H $\begin{bmatrix} \ldots \end{bmatrix}$ H

Harpoon no Oprah.

Harpoon no Oprah. Television syndicate policy prohibits preempting its biggest fish.

Harpo : Oprah. Entertaining REVERSAL. To watch them come alive together, see: **Ed, I saw Harpo Marx ram Oprah W. aside.** Also, Oprah's production company is named Harpo, probably after the fact.

Harrah (HÆR-uh). **1:** small eastern burb of Oklahoma City, Oklahoma County, Oklahoma **2:** Ḥarrah, village of Yemen, 14°57'n/50°91'e, on Gulf of Aden **3:** al-Ḥârrah, small town of Syria, 33°03'n/36°00'e, next to **4:** Jabal al-Ḥârrah, mountain of Syria's Golan Heights, 33°04'n/35°59'e **5:** al-Ḥârrah, a lava flow of Saudi Arabia and the Syrian Desert, 31°00'n/38°30'e. **6:** village in the Yakima Indian Reservation, Washington.

Harrah (HÆR-uh), Toby. Major-league baseball infielder.

Harrisburg grub, sirrah! Negligible, perhaps equally so as the following entry.

Harrisons? No, sirrah! Unsuccessful campaign slogan and button denouncing the candidacies, and later the presidential administrations, of both William Henry and Benjamin.

Harris : sirrah. REVERSAL PAIR of medium combinative strength, but only if we are inclined to address him contemptuously, which we aren't.

Ḥaṣāh, al-. Wadi of Jordan, 30°38'n/37°09'e.

Hattah-Kulkyne. National Park of Australia (Victoria), 34°40's/142°30'e.

Hat up, Utah! Greeting or weather forecast in the Beehive State.

Hat, Utah. See: **PRP.**

Hav', O Hejaz, a Jehovah. This partially unearthed Dead See Scrawl is quite evidently a nearly complete transcription of the original divine pronouncement by which *Jehovah* let there be the oracular seat at the Kaaba in Mecca, situated near the southern edge of Saudi Arabia's *Hejaz* region. The slightly ragged but still earth-shaking text, given the issue, proves and proclaims once and for all—visibly, audibly, even musically (to a catchy Latin beat)—that there is but one God.

HCH. ABBREVIATION for Herbert Clark Hoover, thirty-first president, and the only fully PALINDROMIC presidential monogram until **RWR.** (Calvin Coolidge and Woodrow Wilson were actually JCC and TWW.)

HEART OF SYMMETRY. This trompe l'oeil and paradox—for the heart is neither exactly centered between the right and left sides of the body nor symmetrical in shape itself—is the perfect image for reminding oneself that the great majority of PALINDROMES are actually not symmetrical at all but are only figurative approximations of symmetry, say, as it might be seen aberrating in a fun-house mirror. As such, they may perhaps be considered nothing more objectively real than a strange literary convention, but they would even in that case still be electromagnetically charged thought-forms, still **so many dynamos.**

He denies I seined, eh? Sound bite from a fishermen's controversy.

He Goddam[n] mad dog, eh? Cussed fellow in vernacular, credited by ESPY to James Thurber. This item in one form or the other gets a lot of play.

heh. 1: to laugh or snicker **2:** various exclamations and sounds of laughter. (Also **heh-heh** and other variants such as **heh heh, heheheh,** and **heh-heh-heh.**)

HEH. Her (or His) Exalted Highness.

H [. . .] H

He laminated a cadet animal, eh? Made plywood that looked like an Army mule, did he?

Hell! A spacecraft farce caps all, eh? Probably by MERCER. Here *we* have NASA's greatest fear in a nutshell, but the text was most likely reached long before outer space was ever penetrated, and its reference point was probably a black-and-white science fiction movie or Orson Welles's *War of the Worlds* radio invasion. It is neat to observe how the *spacecraft* immediately produces and joins up with *farce caps*, and then stimulates the quasi-idiomatic growth into *all*, which steers matters, via *-ll a*, almost directly into the simply perfect outside closure, *Hell! A . . . all, eh?*

Helleh. River of Iran, into Persian Gulf via Fars and Bushehr, 29°10'n/50°40'e.

Help, Max! Example H? (Sorry, Min, but I couldn't get that one either.)

Hem, eh? A fine if short stitch. See also: **We sew.**

He or I act at Cairo, eh? Yes, either of you. It makes no difference, as you suppose.

Here is Buffalo Olaf! (Fubsier, eh?) Enter a Viking version of Buffalo Bill, horns and all, only somewhat fatter and squatter. The cause of his relatively greater fubsiness must be assumed to be the buffalo but has nothing to do with their number: **Olaf: Fubsier! (As are/is buffalo).**

Here so long? No loser, eh? Probably by MERCER. A casino marvel. This is a deceptive little construction, easy to dismiss as either obvious or vague yet not truly either. Analysis of it yields not a crack nor even really much of a handle to get hold of anywhere, except for an idiomatic and promising start at *so long* (plus a potent continuation through *no los-*, which in another probability gives **Desserts I desire not so long no lost one rise distressed**). And the unusual

Helleh.

River of Iran.

double query breaks through quietly but surely into a range of sophistication and vividness that perhaps few creators could have caught or managed to imagine.

Here no orchestral arts, eh, crooner, eh? By LINDON. Virtuoso chat. The musician in him must have been intrigued to find that *orchestra[l?]* may continue into *arts, eh, cro-*, and *croon* could not have been long in coming, hence *no* and then essentially the same convenient closure as in the preceding example. The central *l* is a big enhancement, if possibly an afterthought. The double *eh* is all the more artful for seeming deliberate, but we suspect it was a windfall.

He set up side disputes, eh? Contributed by CHISM.

He spots one last sale. No stops, eh? By CHISM. Dramatic tension and uncertainty.

He stole lots, eh? By CHISM. A great embezzler is fondly remembered.

He stressed desserts, eh? Emphasized sweets, he did.

He toped at a depot, eh? Never made it home, eh? Well, what do you know?

He traded art, eh? Bartered by CHISM for a copy of this book.

Hew hay, Yahweh.

He traps part, eh? And lets the rest get away.

Hew hay, Yahweh. While the Sun/God shines . . . the Jolly Reaper.

HfH. Habitat for Humanity.

HH. 1: His (or Her) Highness or Holiness **2:** airline code for Somali Airlines.

hhh. Triple-hard pencil lead.

H ⌈ . . . ⌋ H

HHH. Hubert Horatio Humphrey, whose 1968 presidential campaign gave us a widely distributed PALINDROMIC bumper sticker.

HIGHWAYS. (U.S. federal only)

11. U.S. Route **11,** the leading PALINDROME of the old, preinterstate federal highway system both in point of numerical priority and extant length (U.S. **66** was once longer but has been mostly obliterated), used to be the very important Evangeline Highway, or Acadia Road, the main drag between French Canada and French Louisiana, and it is still completely intact between the Canadian border at Rouses Point, New York, and New Orleans, a distance of about 1600 miles, but it has been largely supplanted by a succession of interstates (north to south): 81, 75, 24, 59, and 10.

22. Old U.S. Route **22** joins Newark, New Jersey, with Cincinnati, Ohio, a distance of nearly 700 miles, and though it still wends its own way, it has been largely replaced by Interstates (east to west) 78, 81, 76, 70, and 71.

33. Old U.S. Route **33** today begins just north of Niles, Michigan, and travels pretty much southeast for about 600 miles, through South Bend, Fort Wayne, and Columbus, all the way to Richmond.

44. I-**44,** the nation's first (lowest-numbered) PALINDROMIC interstate highway, begins heading west (actually west-southwest) within sight of the Gateway Arch and the Mississippi River in downtown St. Louis; follows the ghost of the legendary Route **66,** highway to adventure and kicks, for most of its own length but for only a leg of the ghost's; goes into the twilight zone itself for 3 miles in Oklahoma City owing to a confusion of mileage markers; and then drifts off to the south-southwest across the

HIGHWAYS: **44.**
I-44, the nation's first palindromic interstate.

Red River Valley to end in Texas at the Falls of the Wichita, having covered 630 miles (of which 260 are turnpike and 370 freeway)—the third longest of our nineteen palindromic interstates.

44. Old U.S. Route 44 begins a stone's throw from Plymouth Rock and travels 240 miles due west— through Providence, Hartford, some of the nicest country imaginable, and Poughkeepsie—to Kerhonkson, New York, gateway to the Borscht Belt.

55. I-55, the nation's longest PALINDROMIC interstate highway, running roughly north-south for 950 completely toll-free miles between downtown Chicago and the westernmost outskirts of New Orleans, is, however, not the best route between its own two ends, because nearly 50 miles of driving can be saved if Interstate 57 is used instead between Chicago and southern Missouri (to avoid a strong westerly drift through St. Louis)—yet even if the unnecessary extra miles could be deducted from its total, it would still remain the nation's longest palindromic interstate by far, nor do we take anything away from it on account of its indirection.

66. Interstate 66 (as an interstate, an anomaly, since it is entirely situated in the single state of Virginia), heading east, ends dramatically in Arlington on the approach to the Theodore Roosevelt Bridge over the Potomac into Washington, D.C., *facing* right up the Mall, past the Lincoln Memorial and the Washington Monument, to the Capitol; yet it begins conventionally at an I-81 interchange 79 miles to the west, just beyond Front Royal and the beginning of the Skyline Drive. (We hope our use of reverse gear didn't create a problem for you.) I-66 shouldn't be confused with the legendary and mostly defunct (U.S.) Route 66, which used to run more than 2,000 miles from Chicago to Los Angeles but appears to

HIGHWAYS: **66**

H $\begin{bmatrix} \cdots \end{bmatrix}$ H

have been much more extensively obliterated than any other old U.S. route (perhaps because Interstates **55, 44,** and 40 have in most places been built right on top of it), so that today there are only a few sections in Arizona, Missouri, Kansas, and Oklahoma left, and these have all been downgraded from "U.S." to "state" Route **66.**

77. I-**77** runs north-south about 650 miles from downtown Cleveland, via a highly scenic crossing of the Appalachians, to the southernmost reach of the Columbia, South Carolina, Beltway, though about the last thirty of these miles are indicated as temporary, and it is anyone's guess what their final status will be and whether I-**77** will be able to maintain its rank as the second-longest PALINDROMIC interstate after all is said and done. Old U.S. Route **77** comes up from the Rio Grande at Brownsville, through Dallas, Oklahoma City, and Lincoln, and it may at one time have reached for the Canadian border, but it has been repeatedly decapitated until today it now quits at the Missouri River near Sioux City after less than 1300 miles.

88. I-**88** is a unique example of a discontinuous PALINDROMIC interstate, with a 140-mile, mostly turnpike western segment in Illinois, which links the Quad Cities area with the Chicago area, and a 120-mile entirely free and highly scenic eastern segment in New York, which links the Binghamton area and the Southern Tier with the Capitol District (Albany area). Both segments run generally east-west.

99. Old U.S. Route **99** is a ghost that used to run the full length of the West Coast east of the Coastal Range but was pretty much replaced by I-5 and now survives, but only as State Route **99,** only in California's Central Valley, in Oregon, and in the Seattle area.

H ⌊ . . . ⌋ H

101. U.S. Route **101** is the major Pacific Coast highway, though mostly out of sight of the sea in its southerly reach, from the Santa Ana Freeway in downtown Los Angeles, through San Francisco and over the Golden Gate Bridge, and then very much up the *coast* from Eureka to and around the Olympic Peninsula; at 1550 miles, it is a close second to U.S. **11**.

121. Perhaps the most interesting of the old U.S. routes, U.S. **121** is a complete ghost 480 miles long and still fully maintained as State Route **121** from end to end; that is, from Rock Hill, South Carolina, south through Augusta, Georgia, to Lebanon Station, Florida.

HIGHWAYS: **121**

131. U.S. Route **131** travels 267 miles in Michigan and 1 mile in Indiana, south from Petoskey, through Grand Rapids and Kalamazoo, to the Indiana Toll Road north of Middlebury.

141. U.S. Route **141** is a quiet 150-mile stretch north of Green Bay through Iron Mountain in the Upper Peninsula of Michigan, trailing off into the middle of the woods.

151. U.S. Route **151** travels 310 miles southwest from Manitowoc, Wisconsin, through Fond du Lac and Madison, then through Dubuque and Cedar Rapids, Iowa, to a final junction with I-80 west of Iowa City.

171. U.S. Route **171** runs north-south 180 miles from Lake Charles to Shreveport, Louisiana, slipping between Natchitoches to the east and Nacogdoches to the west.

181. I-**181** is a short spur off of I-81 between Johnson City and Kingsport, Tennessee, about 20 miles long and oriented northwest-southeast at right angles to I-81. U.S. Route **181** connects San Antonio and Corpus Christi in less than 150 miles, but I-37 has improved that ride slightly.

H [. . .] H

191. U.S. Route **191** quietly covers almost 1300 miles traveling generally south from Malta, Montana, through Yellowstone and Grand Teton National Parks and Navajo Country, to Chambers, Arizona.

202. U.S. Route **202**, the old Northeast Bypass, slides 640 miles southwesterly along the Atlantic Seaboard (but *behind* [west of] the major coastal cities) from Bangor, Maine, to Wilmington, Delaware. It is mostly suburban now and fairly well congested all the way.

212. U.S. Route **212** begins as the Beartooth Scenic Highway at the northeast entrance to Yellowstone National Park, then heads east across sparsely populated areas of Montana, Wyoming, and South Dakota to Shakopee, Minnesota, nearly 930 miles later.

222. U.S. Route **222** runs about 110 miles southwest from Allentown, Pennsylvania, to Perryville, Maryland, at the mouth of the Susquehanna.

464. I-**464** is a 7-mile-long southerly spoke within the I-64/664 ring or beltway that surrounds much of the inner Norfolk and Hampton Roads area and in this case projects into Chesapeake, Virginia.

474. I-**474** is the 15-mile-long southwesterly bypass around Peoria, Illinois, avoiding at the cost of a couple of extra miles a more congested portion of I-74 that runs straight through that city's downtown area and serves as the central freeway there even as it proceeds along its own way between Cincinnati and the Quad Cities.

494. I-**494** is the southern and western half plus a bit of the eastern quarter of the Minneapolis-St. Paul area's nearly rectangular beltway, accounting for 42.6 miles, or 55.1 percent of its 77.3 total miles.

505. Interstate **505** is a 33-mile-long north-south corner-cut along the western Sacramento Valley triangu-

lating the northern reaches of I-5 with perpendicular I-80 to San Francisco.

535. **I-535,** 3.4 miles in length, is one of the two shortest PALINDROMIC interstates, linking Superior, Wisconsin, with Duluth, Minnesota, by taking a southeasterly turn across St. Louis Bay near the north end of I-35.

565. **I-565** is a short spur about 18 miles long, extending east-northeast off of I-65 between Huntsville and Decatur, Alabama.

575. **I-575** is a 26-mile-long northeasterly spur off of I-75 between Pickens County and Marietta, Georgia, leading out to Atlanta's northernmost suburbs.

585. **I-585,** at 3.4 miles in length one of the two shortest PALINDROMIC interstates, is a southeasterly spur off of I-85 into the center of Spartanburg, South Carolina.

HIGHWAYS: **585**

595. **I-595** is a short east-west spur off of I-95, linking Fort Lauderdale with I-75 and Alligator Alley and the Gulf Coast beyond, itself only about 14 miles long.

666. U.S. Route **666** travels about 610 miles generally north-south from the Mexican border at Douglass, Arizona, along the Coronado Trail, through New Mexico and Colorado, to Monticello, Utah.

676. **I-676** is a 10-mile easterly spur off of I-76 near its end in Philadelphia, forming with it a beltway around that city and adjacent Camden, New Jersey, and then extending south as far as I-295.

696. **I-696** is an east-west spur running 28 miles off of I-96 and skirting the north side of Detroit.

787. **I-787,** the highest-numbered PALINDROMIC interstate, is a 9-mile-long northeasterly spur off of I-87 running through downtown Albany, New York, and along the Hudson River as far as Troy.

H [. . .] H

HIH. His or Her Imperial Highness.

HMHMH. His Majesty's Household Master of the Horse, according to BORGMANN.

Hoh. 1: river of Washington, with a watershed that includes most of Mt. Olympus, that flows into the Pacific at 47°45'n/124°29'w **2: Hoh** Head, cape of northwest Olympic Peninsula of Washington, 47°46'n/124°29'w **3:** the **Hoh** Indian Reservation, a few miles south of **Hoh** Head and north of the mouth of the **Hoh** River. See also: **Westward Hoh! Draw + sew.**

H.O. Horrifics: No Race Car on Sci-Fi R.R. (Oh! Oh!) It's hard to imagine what all the excitement's about, though we suppose a science fiction model-railroading story could be conjured up to fit. We don't remember where we first saw this.

**Homeopath ...
(A poem.) (Oh.)**

Homeopath . . . (A poem.) (Oh.). Actually four poems.
  Homeopath Gin Night: (A poem.) (Oh.). First they cut and shake and cuss the deck again and again.
  Homeopath Gift Fight: (A poem.) (Oh.). Then they have this thing like a food fight, but the neat part is they get to keep whatever's thrown at them.
  Homeopath Gill Light: (A poem.) (Oh.). Usually found among the thrown gifts, this is a thing they use for measuring small doses, or for fishing, at night.
  Homeopath, Git Tight: (A poem.) (Oh.). Finally the drinking song (for Gin Night or anytime). All four are normally recited together, like a Hippocratic oath or pledge of allegiance, at every such convention.

Hoopoe, O pooh! By the KUHNS. Could easily be a line from Rumi's *Conference of the Birds.*

"Hose Riot repercussion: A hot pap to Hanoi's 'Suc' Repertoires.'" "Oh." (*or* **A hot poop**). A civil disturbance in Vietnam over stockings (and/or minor enough to be quelled by a fire company) is, in the sequel, so typically turned to

H 〔 . . . 〕 H

advantage for sucking up foreign aid dollars that it arouses no particular reaction when reported on the evening news. Use of contracted spelling and any other nonstandard speech sounds or spelling, such as *Suc'* for *Suck* in this example, may be justified if the results can be easily read and enjoyed. Or they could be used to imitate Tom Brokaw's peculiar speech or smile. Also, in PALINDROMES where longer words occur, especially ones that might otherwise never be successfully palindromized, greater extremes of poetic license are accordingly in order. Here, if anyone needs to hear it, the sucking sound is clearly evinced by the presence of the **pap,** if not the hose as well. Still, maybe the **poop** makes a more appropriate center, given the total context and situation.

Hosni's **accompany** *my* **nap moccasins??** . . . **Oh!** I awaken with a lurch from an incredible sleepwalk in which the nap moccasins of Egyptian president Mubarak show up alongside my own bedroom slippers, though the details are, as is usual in cases like this, a little soft. . . . Given the word *moccasins*, or the word *accompany*, the text is virtually forced.

HRH. His (or Her) Royal Highness.

H: (Sarcastic . . .) "It's a crash." Credited by CHISM to *WORD WAYS*. Clever device, perfectly vague.

HSH. Her (or His) Serene Highness.

huh (HUH?!). Interrogative exclamation of surprise.

HRH.
His (or Her) Royal Highness.

H ⌈ . . . ⌉ H

i [. . .] i

I (AHY). Asks BORGMANN: "A one-letter palindrome? Well, there are numerous alphabetic letters doubling as full-fledged words. Common one-letter words include 'a,' 'I,' and 'O.' An examination of any large, unabridged dictionary reveals that each of the 26 letters of the alphabet possesses meanings other than that of simply being a letter. All one-letter words are automatically palindromes, for they cannot help but read the same from the back as from the front; either way, it's the same letter." We understand and like this sharply rational, logological view but see it just the other way round *as well.* For it's clear that one-letter words (and one-digit numbers) do not visibly flip-flop. They don't fla-grantly wend their course in reverse. They don't make us marvel and cross our eyes the way PALINDROMES with mov-able parts do. For the simple truth is the one-letter jobbies, with the possible exception of **I,** are just not that hot. They're just not intrinsically crazed. They just don't vibrate like real palindromes. And though this is a CASUAL view, it is also strictly etymological, for "one-letter palindromes" (in quotation marks for good reason) obviously *don't* "run back" the way they're supposed to (in the original Greek) but just sit there in a blob on the page. Another reason one-letter palindromes aren't considered palindromes in this book is: we already have plenty of blatant palindromes to deal with and enjoy without adding extra, latent ones. And as we are frankly not always totally infatuated even with all the two-letter and three-letter palindromes we meet, we can't get very excited about embracing three dozen new one-character characters that won't do much for the overall collection. We admit they're special, especially **I,** and—let's decide it once and for all—except for **I,** they are optional.

I administer Retsin. I'm Dai. Magician Vernon announces he is giving out some of that funny-tasting gum and then, as if by afterthought, he introduces himself. A hush falls over the audience.

I am a Balaam's ass as "Ma Alabama, I." If states were personages and could talk, Mother Alabama, or **Ma Alabama,** would perhaps then appropriately become "I," or "the First," in name (while continuing to reign alphabetically first and, thanks to her abbreviated form, **Ala.,** uniquely PALINDROMIC). But it is not clear yet who Mother Alabama the First is, nor what makes her a Balaam's and not just any regular or horse's ass. Perhaps someone can elucidate this.

i & i. Believe it or not, "intercourse and intoxication"; these are, according to DE SOLA, "aspects of **r & r.**"

ibi (IBB-ee). Latin: "then" and "there," but never "then and there."

Ibi. 1: town of Nigeria, 8°12'n/9°45'e **2:** river of Japan, into the Ise-wan via Kuwana, 35°03'n/136°42'e.

ici (ee-SEE). French: here.

Idi (EE-dee) Amin. Former ruler of Uganda.

Idi. Village of Sumatra, Indonesia, 4°57'n/97°46'e.

I did, did I? Yes, *you did* this one, Mr. CHISM, as far as we can tell.

Idodi. Village of Tanzania, 7°47's/35°11'e, in Ruaha National Park.

I, Ed, sung an *Agnus Dei.* It was a bit awkward, Ed, but inspiring nonetheless. Perhaps an improvement is: **I, Ed, sung a gnostic illicit song:** *Agnus Dei.*

If I had a hi-fi . . . I'd play it in the mo-orning. (Turned up loud by IRVINE, 1987, in the title of one of his illustrated palindrome books, and played also, we believe slightly earlier and so more quietly, in an illustration caption by AGEE.)

Iggi. Listed by CHISM as an English word, citing BORGMANN without explanation. We suspect a misprint.

I, Ed, sung an
Agnus Dei.

I ⌈ . . . ⌉ I

Igigi. All the gods of heaven, in the ancient Babylonian religion, according to BORGMANN.

Igniting I. Fiery ego, by the KUHNS. This one lights us up, too.

ii. An illegal immigrant.

Ii. Village of Finland, 65°19'n/25°22'e, found in a map index but unconfirmed on the map; its coordinates fall at mouth of *Ii*joki River.

II. Roman numerals for *two*.

II. Airline code for Imperial Airlines.

III. Roman numerals for *three*.

IIII. Sometimes Roman numerals for *four*.

I? *I Love Me, Vol. II.* See: *I Love Me, Vol. I.*

Ijaji. Village of Ethiopia, 8°59'n/37°13'e, on the road between Addis **Ababa** and **Asosa**.

Ikazaki (EE-kah-*ZAH*-kee). Village of Shikoku, Japan, 33°32'n/132°39'e.

Iki (EE-kee). Island of Japan, 33°47'n/129°43'e, off Kyushu in the Eastern Channel of the Korea Strait.

I Laned Denali. Memoir of an Alaska Highway Department worker.

Ili (EE-lee). River of Kazakhstan, into Lake Balkhash via Kapcagaj, 45°24'n/74°02'e.

illi (EEL-lee). Latin third-person demonstrative pronoun: "they (masculine)," namely "those men," when used as a plural subject; when singular, an indirect object of any gender, namely, "(to or for) that (man, woman, or thing)."

Illi, Ba. **1:** river of Chad, 10°44'n/15°21'e **2:** town of Chad, 10°30'n/16°34'e.

"Il Licitto" by Botticilli [sic]. (Some, with probably better reason, say **"Illicitto."**) A good but obviously not good enough (and therefore especially poignant) painting of "The Legal Child" (more likely "The Bastard Child"), an adoration scene centered on the artist's own infant-self portrait, by Sandro Botticelli's illegitimate and unidentical twin brother. This mostly forgotten, unschooled, and probably shaggy yet still wonderful wildlife evidently also claimed the Botticelli family name, and thus had to eat the nickname: **Ipe ("Pili-fied on air am I") di Mariano dei Filipepi.** And from so perfectly shadowy a personality comes the impressive stop-per for his more-illustrious sibling's well-known parlor game (also called Botticelli), if indeed such a silly body does not by virtue of his very existence alone break too many of the rules: **Now, it is illicit to be Botticilli. Sit. I won.**

I love Evoli. With *love* indicated by red heart, PALIN-DROMISTS' coy bumper sticker.

I Love Me, Vol. I. An excellent book title and focus, if we may say so, which evolved naturally enough out of a some-what less narcissistic project entitled, simply, *I Love Vol. I*—after a brief intermediate phase as *I Lov' Me 'Dromes (Use Mor' Dem!): Vol. I.* Sequels could be titled *I? I Love Me, Vol. II* and *I? I! I Love Me, Vol. III,* not to mention *Vi, Love Me! (Vol. IV)*, *V-Love (Vol. V)*, *I.V.—Love (Vol. VI)*, etc. (A commemorative A.D. **2002** reedition of vol. I is planned, and if there is enough demand, perhaps a **'99** model could be spun into play. Vols. II et al. will be about whatever we are having fun with at the time.) The present title/focus, which might be summed up with the word *self-appreciation*, was finally decided upon in preference to many another title/focus not only because it satisfies the requirement of being PALINDROMIC and therefore ingrown, but even more point-edly because "as participants within the universe, as those who add unto the universe by virtue of that which we are, there is nothing in all of the universe that is of greater

I ♥ Evoli.
Palindromists' bumper sticker.

163

I [. . .] I

importance than the way we are feeling about ourselves, because as we see ourselves we attract, as we see ourselves we ooze, as we ooze or radiate we influence all that is." The quote is from a Texas oracle named Abraham, as clear and as hot a source as we have met. On another hand, from the similarly wonderful Hudson River School of the oracle Emmanuel: "At the golden moment when you are ready, you understand that your quest has really always been the search for *Self* and for the lighted way Home."

I Love Vol. I. For which see: *I Love Me, Vol. I.*

I Lov' Me 'Dromes (Use Mor' Dem!): Vol. I. Wherein 'DROMES is standard British jargon for PALINDROMES, and the rest is admittedly quasi-literate—but elvishly in character.

I'm a boob, am I?

I'm a boob, am I? (*or* **a pup, a dud**, etc.). Just one selected from a veritable plethora of umbrages I might take. There is no reason for offense, though, and the tone could be softened just by choosing a better subject, say, **a dad,** or **an Amoco man.**

I made kangaroo tutu! Too rag-naked am I! "Attributable" to an aborigine in a shrunken or jumpy loincloth. And possibly better without *tutu.*

I, man, am regal; a German am I. Probably by MERCER. Nice composition. The length of *German* identifies it as the probable starting point. This would not only determine *[-n] am reg-* but would also point up the need for an *I* to go with the *am*, all of which could only, it seems, sort itself out into the arrangement: *I . . . -n am reg- . . . German . . . [-]I.* As soon as the composer recognizes the necessity for the final *I* to have its own *am*, the gaps are then perhaps very easily closed.

I, Marian, I too fall; a foot-in-air am I. Probably by MERCER. Robin Hood, or anyone, for that matter, in love. *Marian* seems to be the ruler. Producing *-n air am*, she forces at least a pair of *I*'s fore and aft: *I, Marian . . . -n air am I*. (Compare the previous item.) Things could then grind quickly to a halt with a mediocre *I, Marian, in air am I*. But keeping options open in the center and looking for a more leisurely closure was, we are guessing, the sensible decision that led to the very fine result. Then, having persevered to reach *a foot-in-air*, the composer still had to find one last trick, the all-important semicolon that prevents the headlong and wrong reading of *I too fall a foot*, and what a beautifully romantic effect unfolds from this pragmatic little intervention!

I'm atop Op.—Pi hippopotami. Fast new zoo director announces at first staff meeting that she has taken charge of the operation and immediately orders an increase in the number of hippos, from seven to roughly twenty-two.

Imi. Village of Ethiopia, 6°28'n/42°18'e.

I moan, Naomi. Irresistibly attracted REVERSAL PAIR, observed by ESPY.

I'm Otaw, atop a Potawatomi. Evidently a misconception, historical variant, or renegade of the Otoe or Ottawa tribes, though we can't say which or what he's doing up there.

I'm runnin'.—Nurmi. The attribution is unknown for this little brilliancy "attributable" to Paavo Nurmi, the Finnish Olympic miler. It was reported by John JENSEN.

In a regal age ran I. Possibly by MERCER. "Attributable" to Ronald Reagan.

Indul a pap aludni. Hungarian: "The person is going to sleep." From BORGMANN.

"In Eden, I." PALINDROMIC playlet by LINDON. See: **Diamond-eyed no maid!**

Infidels led Ifni. The infidels here were of course the Span-

I [. . .] I

ish, for Ifni, situated on the far southwest coast of Morocco, used to be an overseas province of Spain. Now an integral part of Morocco, it has had Islamic leaders only since 1969.

Ini. River of Nigeria, via Nigurore into the Benue and Niger rivers, 9°30'n/12°30'e.

Inini (INN-inn-*EE*). Formerly interior French Guiana in general, which comprised the great majority of its land area but only a small fraction of its population. Today only a river of that region of French Guiana, via Saül, and into the Moroni at the Surinam border, 3°39'n/54°00'w.

In Italy, Latin I! Classic foreign-study ad for the perfect place to begin learning the Roman language.

In it ram a martini. By POOL. Compare: **Martini: in it ram,** by REYNOLDS, from his drinking song, **"Avid as a diva . . ."** found in BERGERSON's *Palindromes and Anagrams*.

Innostunut sonni? Finnish: An excited bull? By BORGMANN.

Inoni. Village of Congo, north of Brazzaville, 3°04's/ 15°39'e.

In it ram a martini.

INTERIOR PALINDROME. PALINDROME occurring within a word, such as *footstool* or *possessor*.

Interpret Ni. Explain this chemical symbol, by the KUHNS. Well, it is of course the symbol for nickel, a silvery, hard, ductile, ferromagnetic metallic element. It's used in alloys, in corrosion-resistant surfaces and batteries, and for electro-plating. Its atomic number is 28, atomic weight 58.71, melting point 1453 degrees centigrade. Moreover, fans of the film *Monty Python and the Holy Grail* may recall the possibly irrelevant medieval Kingdom of Ni and its knights, whom (though we can't be sure of the spelling) we do remember wanting "a shrubbery" in appeasement for something or other and as being rather plantlike themselves and among the best parts in a very funny movie. (But of course you had

to be there.) Well, that's the best we can do. Perhaps someone else can interpret it better.

INTERNATIONAL PALINDROME CLUB. Based in Barcelona, according to IRVINE, 1987.

INVERSION. Practice, common in many times and places, of
spelling things backward either to conceal them or to feature them specially. This procedure produces a primitive
sort of happy return but not yet a full-blown PALINDROME.
"Parsnip" makes *pinsrap,* "trowsers" can be *sreswort,* and "palindromes" quite naturally, though still not PALINDROMICally,
gives *semordnilap* in Victorian English. Among North American place-names, the remnants of many such inversions can
still be found, from which the original names are just waiting to pop back into focus at any second glance: such names
as Nivloc, Remlap, Retlaw, Retsil, Retsof, Trebloc, and Trevlac, scattered all over the United States and Canada, bear
eloquent witness to this practice and need only be read
backward afresh to reveal their origins.

IOU quoi? *or* **IOU Q.: quoi?** Either way, it is a question of
what IOU?

Ipe ("Pilified on air am I") di Mariano dei Filipepi. See:
"Il Licitto" by Botticilli.

I pot cod, nag, and octopi. TV chef explains as he prepares
an exotic chowder (or distinctive surf and turf) recipe.

I pot *coy* octopi. This Detroit Redwings fan's potshots are
thrown onto the ice only after *opponents'* goals (cleverly since
a cleanup delay cools the hotter team).

IQ-arid Iraqi. Expression meaning "a dry wit and no
dummy." This may refer to Mother Saddam himself as well
as to any **Mad[d]am** or **"Smad[d]ams"** (if Shiite, then
"She[s]mad[d]am[s]ehs"), that is, any madder or smarter
version of Saddam (likewise stronger, handsomer, etc., hence

I [. . .] I

most probably a She-Saddam or, when usually indistinguishably plural, She-Saddams), or just any and every Sade dame, or doe, whether mass-kissed like him or not. (And if this be Saddamy, then make the most of it, too.) For a whole bevy of 's madams, see: **"M.A.D.D. Astartes"** . . .

I.Q. arises Iraqi! Yes, it turns out that the whole idea of intelligence quotients and testing goes back to an ancient Mesopotamian practice, a sort of S.A.T. taken in cuneiform, used for purposes of labor intensification on public works. See also: **Re lucid Iraqi's IQ: a ridiculer** and **To Iraqi test set, IQ a riot.**

I, Rasputin, knit up sari. Attribution unknown, reported by John JENSEN. This slight treatment of the great Rasputin was perhaps inevitable.

I revive, RI! See: RHODE ISLAND.

iri (EE-ree). Latin helping verb form, from the verb *ire* ("go"), normally used to form the future infinitive of other verbs. There is no simple English equivalent. "To be about to [verb]" or "to be going to [verb]" is about the best we can do. Moreover, when capitalized (by modern convention only, since the Romans "capitalized" everything), **Iri** becomes the especially lovely form of the invocation to the rainbow, really to the Rainbow Goddess, Iris.

Iri. Small city of South Korea, 35°56'n/126°57'e.

Iriri. 1: major river of Brazil, tributary of the Xingu and Amazon, 3°52's/52°37'w **2:** smaller river of Brazil, into Baia de Guanabara, north of Rio de Janeiro **3:** Novo **Iriri,** yet another river of Brazil, tributary of the larger **Iriri** and, like it, flowing from Mato Grosso into Para, 8°46's/53°22'w.

IRVINE, William. Author of ***Madam, I'm Adam*** and *Other Palindromes*, illustrated by Steven Guarnaccia (New York: Scribner's, 1987); of ***Senile Felines*** *1991 Desk Calendar* (New

York: Harcourt, 1991); and of *If I Had a Hi-Fi . . . and Other Palindromes* (New York: Dell, 1992). We believe that our author-autographed copy of the original edition of the last-mentioned of these works is already a collectors' item. In its introduction, Irvine says, "There is an irreproachable splendor about a good palindrome that is music to the eyes of an eager student of wordplay, something that compels us to spend countless hours thumbing through dictionaries as if they were steamy bodice rippers."

Isasi. Village of Nigeria, 6°40'n/3°23'e, on the Ogun River.

I saw elf fur. Tall in a vanilla truffle was I. "Laced with what?" we wonder. This line appeared mysteriously on our computer screen, its source unknown.

Is Don Adams mad? (A nod) Si! Attribution unknown; reported by John JENSEN.

Is Elk City, Kansas, a snaky tickle, Si? A variation of **Elk City, Kansas, is a snaky tickle,** arguably less good than the original because it is a pointless complication and a blurring of the original's sharper focus. (We reserve the right to change this opinion if someone named Si were to actually turn up among Elk City's 334 souls.) This example is given because it is good to be able to tell when well enough is perfect. PALINDROMES do not necessarily improve with length. But for a rather more judicious deployment of the same handy "Is . . . Si?" device, see: **Is Laertes' set real, Si?**

Is ex-rex Xerxes I? He or I may be the First. The speaker seems slightly confused, as is often the case with former kings. Also, back at the harem: **I sex Rex Xerxes I.** This latter ("attributable" to any of his concubines and not necessarily his favorite or fastest one) is a reworking of the same letter sequence as in the primary text above and produces now both I and the First. The alternation between or among different readings of an essentially single PALINDROMIC se-

Iriri

I ⌈ . . . ⌋ I

quence produces, just like a common pun or charade but more so, an extra twinkling or shimmering in the semantic empyrean.

I, sir? Is Osiris I? Sister's apposite riposte to a brother who says inscrutable things such as *Sí sí,* **sis! Isis is I, sis! Isis!**

Is Isis I? Is my "I"—am I—the source of fertility, wellness, and culture? You bet.

Isis is I! A minor revelation when compared to *Sí sí,* **sis! Isis is I, sis! Isis!**

Is Laertes' set real, Si?

Is it an aga saga?—Na! 'Tis I! For an explanation, and even an example, see: **aga.**

Is Laertes' set real, Si? Pure and simple, Simon is asked a question—probably about Ulysses' father's teeth.

Is not "Tube-Tumefaction" Eban OFF on a Benoît Café mute button? (Si!) (Also *ON* in place of *OFF.*) Expecting and getting a positive response, a group of blissed-out French troubadours entertaining at a club where an ensemble of silent TVs also plays in the background improvise a lay, incorporating an original heroic epithet, about retired Israeli diplomatic divine **Abba** Eban, who has just chanced to come on screen and, though of course inaudible, seems in all his dignity to make the TVs loom larger and larger, and so to nearly eclipse the troubadours themselves . . . until they honor him (and distinguish themselves and the house) with this true chanson, so long in length, coordination of elements, culture clutter, and dreamworthiness. (Take your time laughing at such as this. If you are extremely lucky, or unlucky, you may find yourself composing them.)

iso rikas sika sokosakissa kirosi. Finnish: a fat, rich pig cursed in a poker gang. Possibly by Heikki T. Suopanki; reported on the Internet. It looks so easy to compose PALIN-

DROMES in a language one doesn't understand, but judging from the relative abundance of Finnish citations in so many of the places we have explored, we would guess either that Finnish is a highly palindrome-conducive language or that the Finns are a highly palindrome-conscious nation, or both.

Is sensuousness I? Another good question by the KUHNS, which they paraphrase "Am I pure feeling?" Answer: yes, in both cases, and more.

Is so bad a boss I? By Joaquin KUHN.

Itatí (ee-tah-TEE). Small town of Argentina on the Rio Paraná, 27°16's/58°15'w.

I tip away a wapiti. A choice line from LINDON's poem **"Ha! On, On, O Noah!"** impressive for the effortless mastery it exudes.

I told Edna how to get a mate: "Go two-handed."—Loti. Probably by MERCER. Loti may be Pierre Loti (Julien Viaud), the French writer and painter (1850–1923). Among his books is *Le Mariage de Loti*, on which the present advice may perhaps be based, judging from the book's title. The ruler is likely *two-handed*, which gives *-d Edna how t-* and fills out quickly into *how to* and eventually, under the guidance of a masterful composer, into *how to get a mate: go*. The start and signature finish then just fall into line, as if they were waiting in the wings.

I? Truman, H., Sir Krishnamurti. That's a typically modest Harry Truman barely presenting himself to the eminent Indian philosopher-teacher Jiddu Krishnamurti, who early in his long career dissociated himself from an ardent following of Theosophists, who had reared him and were proclaiming him the new Messiah.

It's Asti. That's a sparkling Italian wine, from the KUHNS.

It's Asti.
That's a sparkling Italian wine.

I ⌈ . . . ⌉ I

It's at serene rest: Asti. It's so peaceful, but bubbly, too, in this northern Italian wine district.

IUPUI. Indiana University–Purdue University at Indianapolis, site of 1992 U.S. Olympic swimming trials.

I, zany Nazi. Illustrated in IRVINE, 1987.

Jaj-man. One who engages a Brahman to perform religious ceremonies on his behalf, according to BORGMANN. Though hypenated and so evidently not a self-standing PALINDROME, it's still too nice a word to ignore, particularly in view of the scarcity of *j*-palindromes.

j [. . .] j

Jalapeña Jane, pal, a J? A request for her hot, friendly, and comprehensively anticipatory catering service. Also, without a question, "a *J*" may easily become the alphanumeric equivalent of "a Ten" on a ten-scale, running in reverse of the more usual, more scholarly (and only half as precise) scale "*A-B-C-D-F*."

Janâj. Village of Egypt, near the Rosetta Branch of the Nile, 31°00'n/30°46'e.

Jar a tonga, nag not a raj. By LINDON. Appreciated by IRVINE, 1987. A fundamental principle of nineteenth-century British colonial policy.

Jar a tonga, nag not a raj.

JENSEN, John. In 1992 Jensen posted an electronic request for PALINDROMES, indicating a return address at the Department of Political Science, Carleton University, Ottawa. He received a great many via the Internet and the mail, and later posted a 480-line summary of them, which we found on the Net. Not surprisingly, most of the ones he received and posted had been previously published, but there were a couple of dozen unsigned original gems among them, mostly involving celebrity names, which we have sourced to him for lack of any known authors. For these we surmise a single source, perhaps the assembled winners of a magazine contest.

Jessej. Town of Russia, on a lake in Siberia, 68°29'n/ 102°10'e.

JJ. 1: masculine nickname, usually derived from initials, or a version of "Junior" **2:** airline code for Coddair Air East.

JMJ. Monogram of Jesus, Mary, and Joseph.

JONSON, Ben. Said by the *Oxford English Dictionary* to have written, c. 1629, "had I weav'd fifty tomes of Logogriphes, or curious Palindromes," a palling condition whose conclusion is not given and is indeed hard to imagine.

JPJ. Initialed by John Paul Jones.

JUJ. Airport code for Jujuy, Argentina.

kaiak. See: **kayak.**

kakkak. Small bittern, a wading bird, of Guam, named in imitation of its cry, according to BORGMANN in *Beyond Language*.

Kanak (KAH-nahk) *or* Kanaka. South Pacific Islander, especially of New Caledonia.

Kanakanak. According to the *AAA Road Atlas*, a small community a short drive from Dillingham, Alaska. Probably the world's longest inhabited one-word PALINDROME.

Kaput: Strabo, so Bart Stupak. Meaning it's a busted idea that two people linked palindromically (such as Harpo and Oprah, or in the present case, Strabo, the Greek geographer contemporaneous with Christ, and a still-functional Democratic congressman from Michigan) are probable coincarnations of each other, for it can't be proved. Yet, we caution, it can't be disproved either, and the Tibetans at least, to mention only the most respected contemporary group, center their entire socio-politico-religious life on similarly rarefied and arbitrary "evidence" of reincarnation. (Yet again, if the idea of PALINDROMIC coincarnation is *not* kaput, then the meaning of the text *is*, making of it a completely circular, self-canceling event, a snake eating its own tail and leaving behind only a hot spot in reality.)

Kanakanak.
Town in Alaska; probably the world's longest inhabited palindrome.

Karak. 1: town of Malaysia, 3°24'n/102°02'e, near Kuala Lumpur **2: Karak** *or* al-**Karak,** a town and political division of Jordan, 31°11'n/35°42'e.

Kassak (KAHSS-ahk). Caucasian Cossack, according to BORGMANN.

Katak. Town of Iran.

Kavak. Three towns of Turkey: **1:** near Elazig, 38°24'n/39°26'e **2:** near Samsun, 41°05'n/36°03'e **3:** near Sivas, 39°18'n/37°30'e.

Kawak. 1: name of a butte in Oregon 2: Chinook: to fly.

Kaws ⌈deified⌉ SWAK. The custom of sealing (letters) with a kiss was possibly elevated to its present capital importance by these Plains Indians.

kayak *or* **kaiak** (KAHY-æk). Watertight Eskimo canoe of skins on a wood frame, or a canvas or plastic version of same used for sport.

Kayak

Kayak (KAH-yæk). Island of Alaska, in Gulf of Alaska, south of Katalla, 59°52'n/144°30'w.

Kayak salad—Alaska yak. Illustrated in IRVINE, 1987.

Kay, a red nude, peeped under a yak. By LINDON. Oft quoted and widely loved. Last seen on the Internet.

Kay dated a cadet, a Dyak. By LINDON. A Borneo tribesman at the military academy, and probably the same Kay as above in another episode of her wild and notorious life.

Kazak (KAH-zahk). Variant spelling of the Kazakh nationality, as in Kazakhstan. One might find a **Kazak** living along the **Ili** River.

Kazak, Eddie. Major league baseball infielder.

KBK. Airport code for Kirkjubaejar, Iceland.

K.C. Attack. Chiefs' Offense.

K.C.: It's a stick! By CHISM. We're not really sure what it means, but it has a nice heft to it.

KCK. Airport code for Kansas City, Kansas.

KEBABIAN, PAUL. Author of *Lettersquare Palindromes* (Scarsdale, NY: **Abababababa** Press, 1978). Cited by CHISM.

Keep on "No-peek." Don't look yet. Don't look yet.

KEEP OUT! TU! 0-PEEK! "No trespassing! That means

you! And no peeping either!" in advanced standard (or MAC-
ARONIC Latinese) letterspeak.

Keep warm or from raw peek. Two divergent ways of not
chilling out. Contributed by Joaquin KUHN.

Kekek. River of Quebec, flowing into—it's hard to tell—
Lake Megiscane, or, more likely, Lake Pascagama, 48°24'n/
75°48'w.

kelek. A float of reeds used for crossing rivers in Asia
Minor, according to BORGMANN.

Kent T'ne'k, referring not to Superman in loose wear but
to our loose-spelling and tight-with-the-nitrous Super dentist George Hetson, who miraculously came all the way from
Teaneck to practice in Kent. (Such things happen in reality,
too.)

Kentucky **by K. Cutnek.** Seemingly a soap or thieves' or
horse opera.

KHK. Airport code for Khark Island, Iran.

Kiik. Village of Kazakhstan, 47°31'n/72°55'e.

KIK. Airport code for Kirkuk, Iraq.

Killik (KILL-ikk). River of Alaska that drains from North
Slope (of Brooks Range) in Gates of the Arctic National
Park into the Colville River and Arctic Ocean, 69°00'n/
153°58'w.

King, are you glad you are king? Justly famous WORD PAL-
INDROME by LINDON.

Kinik. Village of Turkey, 39°05'n/27°23'e.

kinnikinnik *or* **kinnik-kinnik,** *or countless other spellings*
(*KINN*-nikk-uh-NIKK). Any of a variety of American Indian
smoking mixtures including especially the bearberry, presenting probably the longest English NATURAL PALINDROME.

**Keep warm or
from raw peek.**
Two divergent ways of
not chilling out.

K [. . .] K

Kivik. Village of Sweden, 55°41'n/14°15'e, on the Baltic Sea.

KKK. *Kataas-taasan Kagalang-galan-gang Katipuna* (Pilipino: Mightiest Warriors Fighting for Freedom) and *Kinder, Kirche, Küche* (German: Children, Church, Kitchen, the traditional three *K*s of Teutonic womanhood), not to mention the American version, striking out the side.

KKKK. 1: Kansai (or Kawasaki) Kisen Kabushiki Kaisha (but never all five together [**KKKKK**]), the names of two Japanese steamship lines **2:** Koenhavns Kul og Koks Kompagne, meaning the **CCCC** or Copenhagen Coal & Coke Company!

KMK. Airport code for Makabana, Congo.

Knock conk

Knock conk. By POOL. Play paddleball with the universe using your head as the paddle. For good results, we recommend a *soft* beachball, little or no wind or sun, and one or more conks — not conchs. See *how many* consecutive knocks on the conk you (and any collaborators) can manage before the ball hits the ground, and you've played Headway; surpass your previous record and you've *made* headway. One of the beauties of the game is that it contrasts and ultimately confounds the usual idea of "making headway" (being successful in relation to some preconceived format) with the many immediate rewards of dizziness, punchiness, exhilaration, the joys of physical abandonment and control, and communion of self or selves with everything. So in reality you make tremendous headway, creating VALUE in many senses, whether or not you make headway in increasing the number of happy returns — that is, the times you **knock conk.**

Know a wonk *also* **known wonk.** Not sure what a wonk is but once saw a magazine article, possibly in *The New Yorker*, about C-SPAN founder and talking head Brian Lamb that referred to him as one (a "media wonk," perhaps) in its title.

Knudsen added, "Danes dunk." Not an inter-Scandinavian

racial remark but just a comment over Danish or donuts, or hoops, somewhere around Copenhagen.

Kodok. Village of Sudan, on White Nile, 9°53'n/32°07'e; also called Fashoda.

Kok. River of Thailand (Hkok in Burma, hence, together: **Kok/Hkok**), a tributary of the Mekong, 20°14'n/100°09'e.

KOK. Airport code for Kokkola, Finland.

Kolok. River of Thailand (called Golok in Malaysia) on Thai-Malaysian border, flowing into the South China Sea at Tak Bai, 6°15'n/102°05'e.

Kooblai al-Book. The Kublai's royal book of Xanadoo, perhaps. See: p. ix.

kook (KOOK). An odd or eccentric person.

Kramer : remark. REVERSAL PAIR with strong attraction: **Kramer remark: Remark Kramer** (He says to observe him).

Krk Otok (meaning island). Island of Croatia, in the Adriatic Sea, 45°05'n/14°35'e.

KRK. Airport code for Cracow, Poland.

Küçük. 1: Küçük, Agri Dagi, a mountain of Turkey next to—or really a shoulder of—Mt. Ararat (Agri Dagi), near the Iranian border (see: **Ta-ra-ra Ararat** for some local history) **2: Kucuk,** a river of Turkey, probably actually accented as above.

KUHN, Joaquin and Maura (collectively, the KUHNS). Authors of *Rats live on no evil staﬂ: The BackWords Puzzle Book* (New York and Toronto: Everest House, 1981), a delightfully bizarre collection of PALINDROME crossword puzzles, of which the only copies known to us to exist are in the Free Library of Philadelphia and the Atlantic County Public

Kolok.
River of Thailand
(*Golok* in Malaysia).

Library, surely for some strange reason. . . . Of esthetic impulses, Joaquin Kuhn recently wrote to us from the English Department at St. Michael's College, Toronto:

> I have a very strong preference for palindrome sentences, whole ideas that incorporate a subject and a predicate, however wacky the complete utterance may be. One of my reasons for this is that in human language, it is the sentence, the communication of a whole idea, that everything else exists for. Not words in themselves, but words put together in meaningful patterns. A palindrome that contains the grammatical pattern of a sentence but somehow floats free of ordinary logical sense is to me a special form of nonsense creation. It invites closer and closer scrutiny, in hope of its yielding some sense, like a charm or oracular utterance in need of solution. A palindrome sentence is created following two rigorous laws: it has basic grammatical structure, and the sequence of letters reverses in the middle (no exceptions!). When such a rigorously composed group of words makes sense of any kind, it carries a kind of mystic appeal, as though when character sequences were turned back on themselves, they revealed extraordinary truths like Jungian shadows or subconscious doubles—mirror images of language of hermetic significance. A palindromically uttered truth (bizarre though its content may be) seems doubly true.

A PALINDROMIST after our own heart, Mr. Kuhn also observed: "Sometimes the [PALINDROMIC] utterance is so enigmatic that a prose paraphrase is helpful to focus the scanner's attention. This allows a skillful ironist to suggest a line of inquiry, a kind of definition of the idea."

Kuk. River of Alaska.

Kujdjuk. A beauty from *WORD WAYS*, though no definition was given.

Kuk. 1: mountain of Slovenia, 46°16'n/13°45'e **2:** river of Alaska, draining from North Slope (of Brooks Range) into the Arctic Ocean at Wainwright, 70°36'n/160°00'w.

K [. . .] K

KUK. Kollege of Universal Knowledge, cited without further explanation by DE SOLA, but it looks good from our house; in fact it seems to belong in Palindrome U. on principle.

KvK. Not *Kramer vs. Kramer* but "Kill van Kull," an arm of Upper New York Bay pointing, or really aiming, more or less directly from the Statue of Liberty and New York City's Battery Point southwest to Shooters Island and through it to Elizabeth, New Jersey. This body of water sounds as ominous as "Kill the Ump" or "Moider de Bum," but not to worry, there's still no reason to kill or shoot or even point at anyone since the old Dutchman van Kull is long since history; "kill" is just the local word for creek in those parts (surviving also in adjacent Arthur Kill and throughout the Catskills) and, as of the present reckoning, approximately if not exactly **111,111** people still think Elizabeth-on-**KvK** a good place to live and let live.

KvK

Kyzyk. Believed but not confirmed to be something somewhere in Kazakhstan.

K ⌈ . . . ⌉ K

I

1 ⌈. . .⌋ 1

Lager, sir, is regal.

La Cal (lah-KAHL). River of Bolivia, into the Curiche Grande at the Brazilian border, and then into the Paraguai, 17°27's/58°15'w.

⌈La⌉ Dolce Vita man: an amative clod, ⌈Al⌉. Reassembly from a FITZPATRICK poem.

Lager, sir, is regal. By LINDON. High compliment. Illustrated in IRVINE, 1987.

La Gogo Gal. Seventies club.

Lago Nogal. This is Walnut Lake in Spanish, whether or not one exists.

Lago Poopó gal. Andean woman.

laid rock cordial. New bar drink by POOL served over ice cubes.

LAL. Airport code for Lakeland, Florida.

Lal Lal. Reservoir of Australia (Victoria), 37°40's/144°04'e, draining into the Moorabool River.

Laminated E.T. animal. Illustrated in IRVINE, 1987.

Laminate pet animal. An ad for a new taxidermy technology.

l & l. Leave and liberty. Compare **r & r** and **i & i.**

Lan, my hymn: "Odessa Gideon, a Motel Bible to Man" (*OED*: "I Gassed on My Hymnal."). In a dream (was it of Texas? the Ukraine? Delaware?) I request the organist Lan (or it may have been the Chilean airline LAN — I'm not certain of that either) to play my favorite inspirational music, and I make sure to specify that I want the arrangement of it given under a different title in the authoritative *Oxford English Dictionary.*

Lap a pal. By POOL. Compact seating plan.

La Paz yam[s] may zap[,] Al. Four roughly equal variations on Bolivian cuisine.

lap-lap : palpal. A picturesque REVERSAL PAIR by BORGMANN in which the sound of lapping waves can be heard or felt . . . aptly, by crustacean antennae. Perhaps **palpal lap-lap** is a better order.

La Plata natal pal. A very early childhood friend, perhaps even a long-lost twin, from Argentina or Colorado.

lap pal. "Snuggly friend," illustrated in TERBAN.

La renegade led a general. Female revolutionary took charge.

La Ruta Nadir. (Ol' Florida Natural.) "The Bottom Road" or lowest (and traditional) route to the Lower Keys (namely rum or some other local hooch) and also a great brand name for such.

La Sal (luh-SÆL). Town of San Juan County, Utah, 38°18'n/ 109°14'w, in the **La Sal** Mountains, and near **La Sal** Junction.

La Sal.
Town of San Juan County, Utah.

Las Animas [, CO, docs]: am I nasal? I ask this Colorado town, seat of Bent County, [or its attending physicians] if my nose seems stuffed up. But the correct answer is no, for if it really had been, I'd have said, **Las Adibas, ab I dasal?**

Lattimer : remittal. REVERSAL PAIR, in which a somewhat rare surname and the cancellation of a penalty strongly converge into **Lattimer asks a remittal** (this latter is possibly by FITZPATRICK).

Laval (lah-VAHL). **1:** town of France, 48°04'n/0°46'w, in Mayenne on the Mayenne River **2:** city of Quebec, Canada, near Montreal, 45°35'n/73°45'w.

Laval, Pierre (lah-VAHL). Quisling premier of France, according to ESPY.

Lay a wallaby baby ball away, Al. Possibly by MERCER. Illustrated in IRVINE, 1987, but still hard to grok.

Lay orb royal. Bet the coronation regalia. By the KUHNS.

LBL. Airport code for Liberal, Kansas.

Lear's in Israel. That crazy old geezer's alive and well in the Middle East, thanks to POOL.

Lebanon Abel. An associate of **Okinawa Niko, Addis Ababa Sid, DA,** and company.

Le Bon **Nobel.** The good *prix* of conscience, Franco-Swedish style.

Ledyard Draydel. **1:** Connecticut-Jewish/Mashantucket-Pequot seasonal casino at the Foxwoods Resort **2:** the game of chance played in it; a cross between craps and roulette, with personality endorsements by such as Mel Brooks.

leel (LEE-uhl). Faithful, loyal, true, in Scotland, according to BORGMANN.

Leer at a reel.

leer at a reel. View a probably X-rated movie.

Leeward raw eel (LEE-wuhrd *or sometimes* LOORD). Antillean fishmonger's cry, especially at Anguilla, a Lee-ward Island whose name meant eel in the original, "raw" Spanish (ahn-GHEE-ah, before the English ever had a chance to cook it into æn-GWILL-uh). For landing there, see: **AXA.**

le falafel. Not in our French dictionary and not likely to be admissible in either gender, yet falafel, the originally Levantine and now world-famous garbanzo- and fava-bean staple, will be hard for the French Academy to snub forever in view of its growing worldwide popularity and of the French historical and cultural connection with Lebanon and Syria —and it may as well be masculine.

Legal Age: L. Evidently the Latin legal age, fifty (!), expressed naturally enough as a Roman numeral.

Leg in, Nigel. By POOL. No ride.

Leg, Nan, as an angel! Instruction at a school of sacred dance.

Leg, net oiler Eliot Engel. A Democratic congressman from New York is named for political payoffs and encouraged to run.

Leibniz in Biel! The German philosopher and mathematician (1646–1716) turns up just across the border, alive and well we presume, in the manufacturing city and railroad junction of northwestern Switzerland.

Leila Mag Gamaliel. A fancy full, by BORGMANN.

lemel. Metal filings, according to BORGMANN.

Leo, Joel, *and* **Leo[n], Noel.** Etc. Intro bits. Or "signed" IDs. See also: **Gemini, Meg.**

Leona [Nona] Noel. A vision for the ninth day of Christmas, from BORGMANN.

Leon Noel. A French judge, according to LESSER.

Leon sees Noel. He survives until Christmas! Actually he sees here just a convenient, pat formula for joining REVERSAL PAIRS.

Lepel'. Town of Belarus, 54°53'n/28°42'e.

Les denatured an "Omelette-Lemonade Rut." (An Edsel!) This of course refers to our friend Les's wildly unsuccessful nonalcoholic adaptation of the not-to-be-trifled-with Jack Iron Cocktail sometimes drunk continuously in the lower Grenadines. The real article is made by pouring a shot of tonka-bean-flavored 180-proof rum over a raw turtle egg, all of which is then gulped together with or chased by a squirt

Leon Noel.
A French judge.

L [. . .] L

of local lime, hence our peculiar nickname, above. Moreover, this shaggy-dog kind of PALINDROME has itself been widely rejected as an Edsel of its kind, although the effort to gang long words, whatever the eventual meaning, is in itself an esthetic high for some.

LESSER, Eugene. Author of the neat little book *A Palindrome Is a Pal Indeed* (Pt. Reyes Sta.: Floating Island Publications, 1991). He says, "What especially fascinates me about palindromes is that they have always been there, dormant in the language, like the unformed image within the marble slab, awaiting the sculptor to chip away all else and give it life."

Let It Be: **"Eb' Titel"?!** For the Beatles, their tidal wave of nearly a decade was already starting to run out (and certainly they and their spell could be seen to be breaking up) when they recorded this their penultimate album. Yet see, after all: **Dry ebb at** *Abbey Rd.*

Let O'Hara gain an inn in a Niagara hotel. Attribution unknown, reported by John JENSEN.

Lettergram : Margrettel. Ten-letter (count 'em) REVERSAL PAIR by BORGMANN, or rather as told to him by the "Wondrous Wizard of Wordplay," but with the usual persuasive documentation. One can hear, even picture Margrettel being called as the lettergram arrives, her excitement, etc. And what wonderful news it must hold! Compare: **Telegram : Margelet.**

LETTERKREEFTDICHT. Dutch: PALINDROME, according to BORGMANN.

Levant navel (luh-VÆNT NEHY-v'l). A focal point in Eastern Mediterranean belly dancing and the object of many a nonretroflective but still enjoyable OMPHALOSKEPSIS.

level (LEH-v'l). Noun, adjective, and verb, all having a variety of things to do with rank, position, evenness, and flatness.

LETTERKREEFTDICHT.
Dutch for
palindrome.

L ⌈ . . . ⌉ L

Level. 1: Level (leh-BVEHL), island of Southern Chile, 44°29's/74°23'w, in Archipelago de los Chonos **2: Levél,** village of Hungary, 47°54'n/17°12'w.

leveler : relevel. REVERSAL PAIR with strong affinity: the one whose job is to level is bidden to do so again.

LEVINE, Lawrence. Author of *Dr. Awkward & Olson in Oslo: A PALINDROMIC Novel* (St. Augustine, Florida: self-published, 1980). Cited by CHISM.

Levins snivel. Special apocalyptic lightning display ending not with a bang but a whimper. Also a REVERSAL PAIR.

Levitativel. Listed by CHISM as an English word, credited to *WORD WAYS* without explanation. We certainly hope it's a word.

Lewd did I live & evil I did dwel. By John Taylor, 1614. This is the earliest traceable PALINDROME in the English language, according to AUGARDE, and the first one ever composed in English, period, according to BORGMANN. It depends on an ampersand (which some would cavil at), an old English spelling of the word *dwell*, and an archaic use of the word *evil* as an adverb (meaning "evilly"), and it's tasteless but still precious. Augarde adds that nowadays it would be better written as **Evil I did dwell; lewd did I live.** BORGMANN offers **Lewd did I live; evil I did dwel.** Plus the clever and reasonable **llewd did I live & evil I did dwell.** (In the early days of printing, capital letters were sometimes represented by doubling the corresponding lowercase letter.) Plus the roisterous PALINDROMIC in-joke: **Lewd did I live and, Edna, evil I did dwel.** Plus five additional rearrangements, plus the hint of whole families of palindromes yet to issue from them. But we would prefer to change the subject.

Lew, Otto has a hot towel. Possibly by MERCER. Overheard at the spa or barber's. Illustrated in TERBAN.

Lewd did I live & evil I did dwel.

Lia Fáil. "The stone of Fál," circa 500–250 B.C., which cried out when any legitimate king of Ireland stood on it. When the High King, Conn of the Hundred Battles, stepped onto it, it uttered a number of shrieks. These were interpreted by the Druids as representing the number of Conn's descendants who would be kings of Ireland. Various other sacred stones were used at these inaugurations, testifying to the widespread Celtic belief in the supernatural powers of certain stones.

Librar' Bil'. We owe and pay these foreshortened but real thanks to all the helpful people at two of the nicest and oldest public libraries in the United States, the Scoville Memorial in Salisbury, Connecticut, and the Free Philadelphia, as well as to those at the private but exceedingly generous Edsel Ford Memorial Library of the Hotchkiss School, also in Salisbury; the mysterious Atlantic County Public Library, of New Jersey we think; the truly wondrous Connecticut interlibrary loan network; and the still more staggering national interlibrary system of which it is a member.

Lib regrets bologna, mango, lobster, gerbil. Illustrated in IRVINE, 1992.

Lib regrets: no malign gila monster, gerbil. Apologizes for her extravagant misapprehension, even if the gerbil does seem preferable.

Lid off a daffodil. From a FITZPATRICK poem. See also: POOL.

Lid off a daffodil. I doff a daffodil. Adapted from a FITZPATRICK poem. See also: **A daffodil I doff, Ada.**

Lil (LILL). Feminine nickname, from Lillian or Lily, but not really a diminutive—despite the fact that **Lil** (and **Li'l**) *can* mean little and sometimes even Lilliputian.

LINDON, J. A. Fairly assessed by BERGERSON as the "Major Muse of the English Palindrome," Lindon has nevertheless

Lid off a daffodil. I doff a daffodil.

had little to say outside of his PALINDROMIC utterances. He did reveal in the November 1966 *Worm Runner's Digest* how the composition of even comparatively short PALINDROMES is so very much like a game of chess. He explained that just as it takes two to make a game of chess, and just as one player may well resolve beforehand to play a favorite opening but nevertheless soon, with a scattering of uncoordinated pieces, find himself, willy-nilly, embroiled in the complexities of an entirely different continuation, so the PALINDROMIST may decide that his next offering is going to be a perfectly constructed sentence, containing nothing unnatural, but, since every word he uses must also be used in reverse, he must be prepared to watch all manner of irrelevancies creep in. He drove the point home by reminding us that in real life, unlike real PALINDROMIA, a cigar is not necessarily tragic, nor do dairymen necessarily arrive in myriads. The entire corpus of Lindon's work, or at least the portion given by Bergerson, which is the best available collection, is truly staggering— not merely for its quantity but (especially) for its sublime quality, a perceptible level of excellence that is perhaps occasionally approached by others such as MERCER and Bergerson but never really equaled. It appears Lindon was no less at home composing long poems as one-liners. His genius will likely forever light up the palindromic sky, much like that of a Gary Kasparov or a Babe Ruth or a Michael Jordan in their respective fields.

Linn, IL. 1: township of Woodford County **2:** hamlet of Wabash County. See: **Apollo, PA.**

Lion Oil. Illustrated by AGEE, formerly a real trade name.

LIPOGRAMMATIC OPTICAL TRICKS. See: MIRROR PALINDROMES.

Lisa Bonet ate no basil. Attribution unknown, reported by John JENSEN. Almost, but not quite, a rare natural REVERSAL SENTENCE in a real name.

Lis, IL. Hamlet of Jasper County. See: **Apollo, PA.**

Lister : Retsil. International REVERSAL PAIR of ghost towns, in British Columbia and Washington, respectively. By BORG-MANN.

LITERATIM (liht-uh-REHY-tihm *or* liht-uh-RAH-tihm). Adverb meaning "letter for letter," "letter by letter," "one letter at a time," and with regard only to the letters and not to the punctuation or the spaces between them, if any—the prevailing custom or canon for reading and writing PALINDROMES.

Live not on evil. Probably ancient. See also the following two entries.

Live not on evil deed, live not on evil. Possibly by MERCER. This and the following item well illustrate how a simple PALINDROME may on occasion redouble itself (perhaps even multiply repeatedly) and may then enclose like a sandwich an additional palindrome or palindromes. This is modular construction at its simplest.

Live not on evil, madam, live not on evil. Probably by MERCER. See also the previous two entries.

Lladd dafad ddall.

Live on evasions? No, I save no evil. A snappy one given by LESSER, who says he is blown away by its devastating truth.

LL. *or* **ll.** ABBREVIATION for "lines."

Lladd dafad ddall. Welsh: "Kill a blind sheep," according to BORGMANN.

Llama Mall. Illustrated by AGEE and in STUART.

lll. Left lower limb.

llll. Left lower lung lobe.

Llul sagas lull. By John McClellan. Ramon Llul was a medieval philosopher.

LNL. Airport code for Land O' Lakes, Wisconsin.

Loco Torpedo rode Protocol. Probably a Cuban national known by this nickname or code name who worked as an attaché at the U.S. Embassy in Havana. Similarly and variously with **code, mode, ode,** etc. And cf. **Loco torpor, O Protocol!**

Loco torpor, O Protocol! By CHISM. Sensitive observation.

Lodi, add an Adda idol. Italian hero worship, evidently of Napoleon once again, begins where he defeated the Austrians in 1796. But his image is ultimately thrown into the river there, like others before it.

LOGOLOGIST (loh-*GAHL*-uh-JIST). One who studies, enjoys, or coins words, often for their own sake, often with a view to finding unusual uses or meanings for them.

LOGOLOGIST.
One who studies,
enjoys, or coins words.

logologol (loh-GAH-luh-gawl). Thought to be the real go-power in **Can-Go Cognac** and **Nigeria-Zaire Gin,** the beverages of choice of LOGOLOGISTS—when choosing to speak easily about speech.

LOGOLOGY. The study or enjoyment of words, literally "speaking of speech," another happy return.

Lol. 1: village of Sudan, 6°26'n/29°37'e **2:** an unrelated, distant river of Sudan, 9°13'n/28°59'e, flowing into the Bahr al Ghazal and Nile.

lol. 1: little old lady **2:** Internet ABBREVIATION for "laughing out loud."

Lon Nol (LAHN NOHL). Former premier of Cambodia.

loopy pool. Any extreme gathering of secretaries, vehicles, or lovers of massé shots. See also: **pool loop.**

Lord, Signora's sarong is drol'! CHISM credits *WORD WAYS* and does not address the question of what to do with lame spellings. We would say: If it can be understood, and this one certainly can, it works.

Lor, tepid! Ah, had I petrol! CHISM credits *WORD WAYS* for this rare and lusty gem, in which "Lor" appears to be a Loretta.

Low at New York, Roy went AWOL. No wonder he left.

LPL. Airport code for Liverpool, England.

Luft, Sir Tristful. Hey **Nat (Sir Tristan),** take a heavy song and make it airier, or if in doubt go shopping at **Mart Sir Tristram.**

LUL. Airport code for Laurel, Massachusetts.

luna nul (LOO-nuh NULL). No moon—and therefore a new moon. This is also the beginning and ending of Graham REYNOLDS's "Hymn to the Moon," given in full by BERGERSON in *Palindromes and Anagrams.*

Lyrebirds sass Dr. I. Beryl. These Australian beauties don't normally talk back to the vet.

Ma'am (MÆM). Contraction of **Madam,** usually as a term of respectful address.

MACARONIC. Blending different languages, a common occurrence in PALINDROMY, which tends to exploit and appropriate all imaginable resources of meaning. The *American Heritage Dictionary* suggests that this blending gets its name "perhaps from the way macaroni is heaped on a plate and mixed with sauce."

m [. . .] m

Madam (MÆD-uhm). Title of courtesy for a woman who manages a brothel.

Madam Anna M. Adam. BORGMANN matron of honor.

Madame, not one man is selfless; I name not one, Madam. Certainly not myself. Possibly MERCER. Compare the probably prior and more natural though logically defective **Ma is as selfless as I am.** The text, despite its own incongruencies, may have been offered as an improvement upon the earlier and simpler try.

Madam, I'm Adam. Putatively the first PALINDROME. Illustrated in STUART and also in IRVINE, 1987, who uses it for his title. BORGMANN identifies it as one of the three palindromes most often cited by the dictionaries.

Madam, I'm Adam.

Mad? Am I, madam? Evidently by BORGMANN; illustrated in TERBAN.

Madam, in Eden I'm Adam. Possibly by MERCER or BORGMANN. Excellent clarification.

mad dam. By TERBAN, who clues it "very angry water barrier."

MADDAM. ACRONYM for macromodule and digital differential analyzer machine, per BORGMANN, who believes it the longest such in existence.

"MADD Astartes" set "Rat Saddam." The Mothers Against Drunk Driving Phoenecian Goddesses of Love and Fertility

Softball Team, or MADD Astartes for short, defeat an also foreshortened, also essentially mad, also essentially women's club (its rodent mascot/captain notwithstanding) that normally goes by the longer-winded name **Dad (Gab!), Ma, etc.?: "Team" Bagdad!** For more on this one-bag dad and associated Pollybaggers (veiled mothers, possibly even doubleheaders, of super-low blows and extra-base hits), see: **IQ-arid Iraqi.**

Mad R. Dam. The name of an Army Corps of Engineers project just west of Winsted, Connecticut, protecting this vulnerable city from the ravages of the well-named Mad River. Curiously there is no dam on the Mad River itself but rather a series or cluster of dams on all of its major tributaries.

Mad? Stop at a Potsdam! A city of Germany and a town of New York that share a name illustrious for peaceful talks, harmoniousness, rest, recreation, refreshment, etc., sensibly copromote tourism to a most peculiar niche audience. Also, styled as **Potsdam['s] Mad Stop,** a wildly convenient store there, and as **Potsdam's mad. (Stop.),** a telegram advising us (to quit joking) about this place/these places. Finally, for those wanting a single, full sentence, **Mad stops sass Potsdam.** (Making crazy braking maneuvers is seen as a form of impudent back talk to this place, in Germany or New York.)

Mae, not a peep at one A.M.! See: **Max . . . A.M.**

magni-lingam. Any large phallus worshipped, especially in ancient Rome, as a symbol of the Hindu god Shiva.

Maham. Town of India, 28°59'n/76°18'e, near Delhi.

Ma handed Edna ham. By LINDON. Homespun. Illustrated in TERBAN.

Mahayana? Nay, a ham. A ridiculous performer is at first mistaken for some kind of a representative of the "greater vehicle" of Buddhism (its mostly central and east Asian expression, as distinct from the "lesser vehicle," or Hinayana, its mostly South Asian form—which however is called Theravada by those not wanting to belittle it).

Ma, I am. A PALINDROME fit for a newborn.

Ma, I am a ma, I am. By POOL. A PALINDROME fit for a new generation.

Ma, I am Ron. I'm a minor, Ma. I am. By CHISM. Baby Ron's precious first words.

Maiden woos, so owned I am. Great chunk, recast, from a FITZPATRICK poem.

Ma, in a Brussels less urban I am. Made it from downtown to the suburbs and called home.

Maine Ben I am. Meaning "I'm not a Jersey Joe or a Tennessee Ernie." (Also **Ken, Len, Zazen,** and company.)

Maine hen I am. Not a Rhode Island Red.

Maine pen I am. E. B. White or a Thoreau, for examples.

Maine Sen. I am. "Attributable" to George Mitchell and others.

Maine pen I am.

Maine, *Veniam*! In the quest for the elusive PALINDROMIC state capital of Maine, this prophetic voice, a blend of Caesar, Teddy Roosevelt, and MacArthur perhaps, tells that state, and in Latin no less (*veniam*: "I shall come"), to expect a fully qualified place to turn up in it some day, perhaps unlike some of the other dozen or so palindromically empty states for which no such encouragement exists in any language.

Ma is a nun, as I am. Nice one (probably by MERCER), nicely pictured in IRVINE, 1987. Of course any single-word PALINDROME would do to replace the **nun** at the core, but perhaps none would do so well.

Ma is as selfless as I am. Possibly by MERCER again, though this one has a way of issuing so naturally and effortlessly from the key word *selfless* via *-s selfless* via *as selfless a-* via *-s as selfless as* via *is as selfless as I* (and is so close to the above *Ma is a . . . as I am*) that it could have been a repeated invention. It is a gem in any case, despite or perhaps especially because of its wry illogicality.

"Ma"—Jerome raps pot top—"spare more jam!" Probably by MERCER. A dramatic development from a subtly woven construction. The central **pot top** is not strictly necessary today, but it was a good finishing touch before the days of Rap.

Majority tiro jam. A rare filibuster by freshmen of the leading party.

Majors nab an SRO jam. It'd be a miraculous catch following such a foul strike. (But the Indians-Braves Series made a good bid for one.)

major SRO jam. A lot more crowded than an ordinary standing-room-only crowd.

malam (MAH-lahm). Latin: I shall prefer.

Malayalam (MÆL-uh-*YAH*-luhm). A Dravidian language related to Tamil and spoken on the Malabar coast of southwestern India. It has given English the words "copra" and "teak," and it is believed to be (PALINDROMICally) unique among languages but for the **Ooloopooloo** dialect of the aboriginal Australians. BORGMANN identifies it as the longest English PALINDROME common or important enough to make the collegiate dictionaries as of 1965.

Malcontents avast! Net no clam! Be happy or you won't get paid.

Maligning, I lam. As I slander, I also thrash (and/or run). Better to lay back.

Malo malo malo malo. Latin WORD PALINDROME sentence: "I'd rather be in an apple tree than an evil man in adversity" (*Oxford English Dictionary*). ESPY says: "I suspect Lester E. Rothstein is right when he says in *Enigma*: 'Even with the addition of prepositions plus the word *quam* ("than"), the phrase is so ambiguous it would have been Greek to any classical Roman.'" But Rothstein and Espy, we believe, may have missed here the three (admittedly rare but perfectly Latin) self-standing (nonprepositional, nonconjunctive) ablative constructions of (1) "place where" (or locative), (2) "comparison," and (3) "attendant circumstances," which all together parse this sentence swimmingly *as is*. Moreover, Latin was actually more hospitable than Greek ever was to all manner of syntactical combinations and subtleties, so it is probably incorrect to say that this sentence would have been Greek to a Roman. On the contrary, it would probably have been as understandable, provocative, and amusing to a Roman as its charming translation is to us, and it would probably only be Greek to someone unused to both Latin and Greek.

Ma is as selfless as I am.

Manam. Island off the north coast of Papua New Guinea, 4°05's/145°05'e.

Ma, nap on no Pan-Am. Contributed by CHISM for the present occasion.

Manet tastes sap assets at ten A.M. Triple-talk about the artist's prodigal enjoyment of late breakfasts with maple syrup or someone's weakness for morning art auctions. **Manet, ten A.M.** is thanks to Will Shortz on National Public Radio.

Man, Eve let an irate tar in at eleven A.M. By LINDON. It was a riot, but you don't want to hear about it. Nevertheless, this at least was the shorter and sweeter version. Don't bother to compare the following elaboration.

Man, Eve let an idiot—a retromastoid idiot, Sam, or teratoid—in at eleven A.M. By LINDON, evidently continuing the story anyway. ("Well, all right, just a detail or two.") Monstrously funny. This and the previous entry are a good pair to show the contrast between a quick and a leisurely central closure. Once *idiot* was tested, one *-toid idiot* presumably led to another. Nevertheless it is at least equally possible that both texts were outcomes—first the longer and then the shorter, via an afterthought/simplification—of a prior test of *retromastoid*.

Man, Eve stays sassy at seven A.M. See: **Max . . . A.M.**

Man, I rush Surinam (MAHN . . . *SOOR*-uh-NAHM). In like manner as Matilda used to run Venezuela. Moreover, you **Rep Paramaribo job: "I ram a rapper."**

manitu : *utinam*. REVERSAL PAIR strongly linking the Algonquian nature spirit with the Latin adverb indicating a wish or desire ("would that . . . !" or "oh that . . . !") in an interdenominational sort of "God willing."

Man, Oprah's sharp on AM. Attribution unknown, reported by John JENSEN. Must be AM radio—we have never seen her on in the morning.

Mao bore, jaded, a Jeroboam. The chairman was still carrying, though he looked surfeited, a very big wine bottle. Or perhaps it was the jug that was green.

Ma! Ow! Two A.M.! See: **Max . . . A.M.**

Maram. Village of Manipur province, India, 25°25'n/ 94°06'e.

Marc, scram. Thus was Antony so easily exiled.

Marge, let's "went." I await news telegram. Probably by MERCER. This clever novelty presents us with a good object lesson: while testing and trying and probing, never rule

M [. . .] M

anything out until you're sure it's a bust, for the gnomes are highly inventive and original at every turn. We have added the apostrophe, probably an inadvertent omission by BER-GERSON. See also the following entry.

Margelet : telegram. Strong REVERSAL PAIR: British diminutive of Margaret, this telegram's for you. Rings a bell. The pair can also be parlayed as in the previous entry or, more naturalistically, via *Marge let[s] . . . telegram*, into various directions, such as **Marge let a moody baby doom a telegram** or **Marge lets Norah see Sharon's telegram,** both probably invented by MERCER. And see also: **Lettergram : Margrettel.**

Marg, I pen an epigram. By POOL. Precisely.

Marc, scram.

Margo M. Mammogram. A strange CHISM character.

Mark Kram. A former writer for *Sports Illustrated*, according to LESSER.

marram (MÆR-uhm). Australian beach grass, *Amophila arenaria*, often planted to stabilize shifting dunes.

Mars' ram. Ares' Aries, by the KUHNS.

Martensdale lads net ram. This from the town in Iowa, **pop.** 491. They clear livestock, or a Dodge truck if **Ram.**

Martini [:] in it ram. Blurry but potent REVERSAL PAIR and "sentence" occurring in a Graham REYNOLDS drinking song, which POOL turns into **In it ram a martini.**

Mart Sir Tristram. A medieval shopping mall or convenience store.

Marty bogs. (Go by tram.) Carpool message.

Mary [Belle] Byram. One of BORGMANN's sprites.

Ma set a date, Sam. By CHISM. In fact she's got the whole wedding planned already.

Mask OK, Sam? Yes, but to reveal rather than conceal.

Matam. Village of Senegal, on Senegal River and Mauritania border, 15°40'n/13°15'w.

Matinees? Seen it (A.M.). Observed by Mark Saltveit in WORD WAYS.

Max, I stay away at six A.M. Possibly by MERCER. There's probably a good story here. Compare: **Man, Eve let an irate tar in at eleven A.M.** or **Manet tastes sap assets at ten A.M.** And there's always ready-made stuff like **Mae, not a peep at one A.M.!** Or **Ma! Ow! Two A.M.!** And **Man, Eve stays sassy at seven A.M.**

May a banana nab a yam? By POOL. Unlikely.

May a moody baby doom a yam? Possibly by MERCER. Illustrated in IRVINE, 1987. BORGMANN adds: "Some infants simply have it in for certain types of foods. We knew one tot who became wild at the sight of a pomegranate, ripping it apart with his tiny fingers." We have seen the central *a moody baby doom a* previously combine with *Marge let . . . telegram.* Does that make it a cliché? No, rather a convenience. Similarly, **Emil, a sleepy baby, peels a lime.**

May Eva, Hume's emu, have yam? By CHISM. Certainly, if there is any left from the baby and banana; now is no time to object to a walk on the wild side.

MCM. Airport code for Monte Carlo, Monaco.

megagem. The KUHNS' large jewel. And any especially fine PALINDROME.

Megan, I finish sin if I nag 'em. By LINDON. (Well, then nag 'em when they've finished.) It is wonderful to see such an outrageous result ensue so quickly from the simple start *finish sin if* and the obvious continuation *I finish sin if I.* What is far from obvious is the brilliant closure with *Megan . . . nag 'em.*

megatart's stratagem. A nice example of how a word may project a REVERSAL partner into existence and become with it a joke or a phrase or a poem.

"Megaton"'s not a gem. As words go, we agree. And to think that redefining this word as a single ton less, or a single ton more, than its well-established meaning (of exactly one million tons of **TNT**), thus producing an explosive VALUE equal to either **999,999** or **1,000,001** tons of the blasted stuff, would have made it a **megagem!** But what's a ton of **TNT** more or less between friends?

Megawatt Ottawa Gem. A shocking and capital nugget of Canadian-mined power, by the KUHNS.

MEM. Airport code for Memphis, Tennessee.

MERCER, Leigh. A shadowy but first-rate British creator and collector of PALINDROMES, many of whose excellent one-liners and longer works adorn the books of BERGERSON and BORGMANN, and a few of which are repeated on these pages, but who has not published any of his works himself, so far as we know. It would be wonderful to verify the many attributions that have been tentatively made to him.

mesem. South African herb, also known as a fig marigold; as per BORGMANN.

Met System. All the minor-league franchises, collectively, of the New York Mets.

Me walleye 'll awe 'm! A PALINDROMOLOGIST, cross-eyed, blithering, ingrown after long years of practice, is still expecting to make a big impression on people.

MGM. 1: Metro-Goldwyn-Mayer, maker of movies 2: airport code for Montgomery, Alabama.

millim. Original name for millimeter, or one-thousandth of a meter, proposed by George J. Stoney, the Irish mathematician and physicist; as per BORGMANN.

Megatart's stratagem

M $\left[\,.\,.\,.\,\right]$ M

Mim. Village of Ghana, 6°54'n/2°34'w.

MIM. Roman numerals for 1999. And see the following rare footage of it.

Mi minimo: Donna Shalala H.S., Anno Domini MIM. This determined graffito and ultimatum from the Latin-American/ American-Latin dreams of a mixed-up but harmless (probably utopian) activist translates into waking reality quite readily as: "My rock-bottom demand and last-ditch position is that a high school be named for Clinton's Health and Human Services Secretary before the millenium—or else."

Minim.

A half note in music.

minim (MIHN-ihm). **1:** half note (in music) **2:** tiny unit of fluid measure **3:** any insignificantly small portion of a thing.

Minnesota to Sen. Nim! Election results.

Mirim (mee-HEENG), Lagoa. Lake of southernmost Brazil and, as Laguna Marin, easternmost Uruguay, 32°45's/ 52°50'w.

MIRROR PALINDROMES. Indicated here as plural because two or perhaps three types of these misnomers exist, which may be called vertical and horizontal mirror palindromes, respectively, depending on whether they are written vertically (down the page) or horizontally (across it in the normal fashion), or, in a few cases, both. (None of these are really PALINDROMES at all but happy returns of a different stripe: LIPOGRAMMATIC OPTICAL TRICKS.) The vertical type takes advantage of the vertical symmetry that occurs naturally in only eleven letters: A H I M O T U V W X Y (uppercase only). Thus any words written vertically with these and only these letters will be readable in a mirror placed alongside them, as for example:

A	H	I	M	O	T	U	V	W	X	Y
T	O	O	U	H	H	T	A	A	X	W
O	O	T	T	I	A	A	U	X	X	H
M	T	A	T	O	T	H	X	Y	X	A

M ⌈ . . . ⌉ M

BORGMANN gives HOITY-TOITY as a ten- or even eleven-character vertical mirror palindrome (eleven counting the hyphen, and though hyphens rather fall apart in this format, we'll still call it an eleven on a ten-scale, it's so nice).

The second type of mirror palindrome, the horizontal variety, takes advantage of the horizontal symmetry that occurs naturally in only nine letters: B C D E H I K O X. Thus any words written horizontally with these letters will be readable in a mirror placed above or below them, for example: CHOICE, COOKIE, HOOKED, ICEBOX, CHECK-BOOK. A third class of mirror palindromes, those that meet the requirements of both the vertical and the horizontal varieties, may use only four letters—H I O X—and will yield few words, but two such, for whatever they might be worth, are OX and OHIO.

Mirth, sir, a gay asset? No, don't essay a garish trim. Probably by MERCER. Merrymaker bent on fun meets with (and may well ignore) a surprising rejection. (Next time he won't even ask.) Fraught with its ridiculous grumpiness, this PALINDROME is a wonderful example of the highly lucid and expressive "style" that characterizes many of the most classic palindromes.

Mix a maxim.

Miss, I'm Cain, a monomaniac. Miss, I'm—By LINDON. Whimsical and accurate demonstration of a one-track mind. The repetition makes for a great finesse and novelty. In chess such a "move" would be called a brilliancy.

Mississippi's sis: Sim (miss-uh-SIPP-eez SISS SIM). Relative of **A ma, Balaam: Ma Alabama,** or, for that matter, of Ole Man River. Alternatively: **Mississippississim** (MISS-uh-sipp-ee-*SISS*-'m), Latinglish: one Mississippi Sister at a time. The peculiar familiarity among the Southern states extends even to **Florida dad, I Rolf.**

Mix a maxim. By the KUHNS. CHISM glosses alertly: "A rose by any other name is a rose is a rose."

MIXED SETS. There is nothing that says that PALINDROMES have to be made up of members of a single set, as letter (common) palindromes, NUMBER PALINDROMES, WORD PALINDROMES, thought palindromes, etc., normally are, and we have found that mixing sets can be a very satisfying exploration, as in the case of **A1A** or **Alaska's Alaska** (as distinct from **AK's Alaska** or **Aaa**) or **97060 Twin Lakes Ct., Twin Lakes, CT 06079** or **álla allá.**

MM. 1: Roman numerals for 2000, and short for the MilleniuM **2:** Marilyn Monroe, maximum misfit or mismated.

MMM. Roman numerals for 3000.

MMMM. Roman numerals for 4000, sometimes.

MNM. Airport code for Menominee, Michigan.

Mode? Er . . . freedom! A happy-go-lucky improvisation by CHISM. The oracle Emmanuel says freedom comes from self-love and self-acceptance. The oracle Abraham says freedom is the basis of life; joy, the objective; and growth, the result.

Mom—O no—MOM!

Mollahs shall Om. Moslem religious leaders (if Muslim, then Mullahs) are hereby required as if by religious decree to say the Hindu sacred syllable. This PALINDROME is not to be confused with the equally interdenominational but poetically unlicensed **Mol'ahs, Shalom!** And see: **Most naïve deviants Om!**

Mom. Mother.

Mom—O no—MOM! Attributed by ESPY to Oedipus.

Mom's selfless mom. Grandmother who never thinks of herself, by the KUHNS.

"Mona Lisa's naked in a nide."—Kansas ILA *nom*. Prairie Longshoremen's exotic production.

mo' Nevada venom. Double d' reg'lar dose.

mon nom (mohn-NOHm). "My name" in French.

Mood's mode, Pallas, is all apedom's doom. Reconfiguration of the beginning and ending of a nineteen-line poem by Hubert Phillips entitled "Mood's Mode," quoted by both BERGERSON and BORGMANN and more recently found on the Internet. Pallas is Athena, Greek goddess of wisdom and the arts.

Moody Doom (MOO dee-*DOOM* [after LAH-dee-*DAH*]). Our name for a school of poetry, and for some reason a sizeable fraction of PALINDROMIC poetry, which has focused on the dark side. It has its VALUE for contrasting and evoking the bright side, and at its very best, as in the previous entry, it can be gaily preposterous.

Moors dine, nip—in Enid's room. Possibly by MERCER. A romp, and probably a scandal in the making. This is such a simple assemblage that it is hard to believe it was actually ever composed by anyone, but we know better than to doubt it.

Morocco Rom. Gypsy of North Africa.

Moses: "Om." Ever a little tongue-tied and now just back from forty days and nights on Sinai, he sums it all up in a single mouthful.

Most naïve deviants Om. As a verb, "to Om" means to intone the Hindu sacred syllable Om, or Aum, usually while sitting cross-legged, standing on your head, etc. The text was perhaps once true in the old hippie communes, but in the nineties it is as upside down as are the sixties themselves, for few if any naïve deviants are heard to Om anymore. Still, if you can find by experiment the exact pitch that works for you, even just *thinking* of humming this note could open you right up to your own personal sense of divinity. Consider also the highly deferential address and salutation: **Most Naïve Deviants: "Om!"**

motmot : tom-tom. REVERSAL PAIR, wanting to be a **motmot tom-tom** perhaps—a drum with some connection to a tropical American bird related to the kingfisher.

"Motto M" (and other members of the Lettered Motto Series). See: **Bottomless . . . (Motto B).**

"Mr. A. Flat" Nerd-Rental Farm. Just the help we needed, specially sent over for the occasion from CHISM's amazing talent agency for musical and other blowouts.

Muçum (moo-SOOng). Village of Brazil, 29°10's/51°53'w.

Mud negates a set agendum. Slander—or, preferably, sloppy weather—ruins a plan. Compare: **Ad negates a set agenda.**

Muffins: sniff 'um. CHISM credits *WORD WAYS*. This home-baked REVERSAL PAIR is ready to serve.

Muir amasses . . . samarium. If Jesus saves and Moses invests, then the great naturalist-conservationist John Muir, for his part, naturally conserves, while seeming a world-class Samaritan, and diligently stocks up on a scarce, poly-tech rare-earth element.

Must sell at tallest sum.

Mullum Mullum. Creek of Australia, 37°44's/145°10'e, in suburban Melbourne, flowing into Yarra Bay, past the Victoria State Car Club Race Circuit.

mum (MUMM). **1:** not talking **2:** act in a mask (as a mummer) **3:** ma'am **4:** mom **5:** chrysanthemum **6:** strong ale or beer.

MUM. First line of silent WORD SQUARE by BORGMANN.

M U M
U N U
M U M

Murder? Not so. Boston red rum. CHISM credits *WORD WAYS*.

Mures Serum. A probably old-Roman preventative against, or of, mice.

Music I sum. Calling card of a true Orpheus or of a music critic who specializes in brief reviews.

Mussum. Village of Germany, 51°48'n/6°34'e.

Must sell at tallest sum. Very nice. Possibly by MERCER. Repeated by IRVINE.

Mut arrest negated a cadet agent's erratum. Dogcatcher's success made up for his apprentice's lapse.

Mutum (moo-TOOng). **1:** village of Brazil, 19°49's/41°26'w **2:** river of Brazil, into the Jutai and Amazon, 4°25's/68°03'w.

MXM. Unconventional Roman numerals for 1990.

my gym. By POOL, looking good, working out.

My gym taxes sex at my gym. By CHISM, who gives no particulars.

My! No dues pall a pseudonym! It is amazing how using a false name exempts one from the strain of making certain payments!

mynym. Middle English: a half note in musical notation, the origin of **minim.**

n [. . .] n

Nada por ropa dan (NAH-dhah pawr-*ROH*-pah DHAHN). Spanish: They give nothing for clothing. By Anthony Bonner, according to Willard ESPY.

Nadia : Aidan. REVERSAL PAIR mating, say, gymnast Comaneci with actor Quinn.

Nag a pagan. Do missionary work.

N. A. Gilligan. BORGMANN character.

"Nag Olson"'s no slogan! After CHISM. But denying it doesn't undo it.

Nag on a koala, Okanogan. Strange but true animal adventure movie—we seem somehow to have gotten our wires crossed—in the Washington desert.

Nāhan. Town of India, 30°33'n/77°18'e.

Nail a Moslem a camel, Somalian. Procure the usual transportation in East Africa. It is an admittedly unusual use of the indirect object, as well as of the words *nail* and *Somalian,* but . . .

Nail Amos, O Somalian. Catch him stealing, don't crucify him.

Nail it, pert reptilian! (*or* **per reptilian**). Get to the point, saucy serpent! By the KUHNS.

Nail, O tan Anatolian! *You* work the hammer for a while, swarthy Turk.

Nairobi Borian? . . . Eborian? . . . Iborian? . . . Tiborian? A nearly successful Nairobi "quartet" that tantalizes us by not quite managing to produce the real words *Borean, Eburian, Ivorian,* and *Tiburian.* But no dice, and so no soap, no candle, and no cigar. However, see: **Ciborian : Nairobic.**

Naïveté got smart: trams to get Évian. Bright new idea, long overlooked: tap a natural-bottled-water market.

"Na-ka-ki yo no." First line of Japanese *syllabic* PALINDROME verse given by BORGMANN: "Everybody wakes up from the sound sleep of a long night—Winter. How delightful the sound of the oars of a fishing boat on the sea!" Probably qualifies loosely as more or less of a double haiku.

Na-ka-ki yo no
To-o no ne-bu-ri no
Mi-na me-za-me
Na-mi-no-ri-bu-ne no
O-to no yo-ki ka-na.

Named undenominationally rebel, I rile Beryl? La, no! I tan. I'm, O Ned, nude, man! By LINDON. This puzzling specimen deserves both praise and indulgence for giving us the longest word ever to be worked into a PALINDROME, and, fortunately, BORGMANN's explanation clarifies it somewhat: "Beryl's husband has been disporting himself in the back yard in his morocco, and his friend Ned inquires whether the man's motive for doing so is to irritate his wife Beryl." Moreover, if we understand the first three words rightly, it seems Ned had first to be disabused of the assumption that his friend had gone to the yard to punish Beryl for having called him, in effect, *a rebel without a cause—or clue* ("undenominationally rebel"). It's all very complex, but that's to be expected of a palindrome of this length, even without the longest word ever incorporated.

Nail a Moslem a camel, Somalian.

Name me man *and* **Name me, man.** Arguably the second and third PALINDROMES ever spoken, the former by Adam to amplify **Madam, I'm Adam,** and the latter, immediately after that, by **Eve.**

Name no one, man! By BORGMANN, who builds an elaborate mathematical puzzle around it involving some 16,376 permutations.

Name now one man. MERCER, possibly.

Names: "I-Annoy-a-Man-of-Legible-Verses" or "Roses-Revel-Big-Elf-on-a-Mayonnaise-Man." Culminating moment, we can only imagine, of a peyote poet's vision quest and naming ceremony, likely a very wild Indian by this point; inspired by BERGERSON's "The Faded Bloomer's Rhapsody," the full original of which appears in his *Palindromes and Anagrams*.

Namib Barbara's Arab rabbi man. A hard man (interethnic ecumenical from the Negev wandering in the wrong desert) but, for Barbara, good to find. We also find him at another point, disconcerted, unless we are mistaken, in a FITZPATRICK couplet, which could be condensed and/or restyled as follows: **Egad, loon sahib, Barbara's Arab rabbi, has no old age!**

Namu had a human.

Namu had a human (*or* **has a human**). It may have seemed as though Seattle aquarium owner Ted Griffin possessed the world's first performing killer whale, but to the clever pet, the reality was just the opposite. Until clear communication was established between the two species, the text was originally thought to be a statement about the whale's lunch, but that reading is now known to be mistaken.

Nan (NÆN). **1:** town of Thailand, 18°47'n/100°47'e **2:** river of Thailand, via **Nan,** Uttaradit, and Phitsanulok, into the Yom and Chao Phraya rivers and the Gulf of Thailand, 15°42'n/100°09'e **3:** river of China, via Yongjia, into the Ou River and East China Sea, 28°15'n/120°43'e **4:** feminine nickname.

Nan'an. Town of China, 24°58'n/118°23'e.

Naomi, did I moan? Illustrated in IRVINE and TERBAN.

Naomi, I moan. If this were not blatant enough, we have also the following entry.

Naomi, sex at noon taxes, I moan. This one is credited by ESPY to Michael Gartner. It is a good example of a COMPOUND

PALINDROME in which the whole is greater than the sum of its parts.

Naomi, stark rabid, I bark "Rats!" I moan. By FITZPATRICK. A continuation of the above three approaches, we suppose. Other variations include the KUHNS' **Naomi[,] moan** and CHISM's **Naomi, finish sin if I moan.**

Napan (NÆP-'n). Hypothetically, of, pertaining to, or from Napa, California.

Nappan. Island of Ontario, in the Trent River, 44°23'n/77°49'w.

Nap pan *or* **Nap, pan.** Illustrated in TERBAN, who clues it "Sleep metal frying dish."

NAP-SPAN *or* **NAPS-SPAN.** The soporific PALINDROME cable-TV network and roving school bus.

NAP-SPAN.
Soporific palindrome cable-TV network.

Naran. Village of Mongolia, 48°34'n/98°17'e.

Narcissus's USS *Us,* **U.S.'s USS** *U.S.* **[*sic*] ran!!!** Scene: Davy Jones's locker. Having all gone down in a big way for love of self, the mythic hero Narcissus, promoted now to the helm of a "United States Ship" of his own named *Us,* and Uncle Sam himself, commanding the USS *United States,* amazingly were all still going—still running without batteries—sailing effortlessly in a sea we may perhaps all recognize as our own. Actually it is hard to believe that any meaning at all, no matter how fantastic, could have been conjured from such blatherskite! And it is more amazing still when you consider that this Narcissus is himself not a ship and has nothing to do (except collide) with the sailing ship *Narcissus* from Joseph Conrad's *The Nigger of the Narcissus.*

Narran. River of Australia, New South Wales and Queensland, via New Angledool into the Culgoa, Balonne, and Condamine Rivers and the Pacific Ocean, 29°45's/147°20'e.

Nary a Jay ran. Every Bluejay walked, according to the KUHNS.

Nasan. 1: town of Thailand, 8°48'n/99°22'e **2:** village of Vietnam, 21°12'n/104°02'e.

Nat (Sir Tristan). See: **Luft, Sir Tristful.**

NATURAL PALINDROME(S). So called for having sprung up, organically as it were, on the map (like **Kanakanak**) or in a dictionary (like **level**), as distinct from being an artificial, poetic/chessic creation such as **Able was I ere I saw Elba.** Also, for a slightly more liberal take on the idea of natural, in the sense of almost inevitable, see: **Ned, I am a maiden** and **Goddesses so pay a possessed dog.**

Nat, I ram a Samaritan. I'm curious to check out the efficacy of his good works . . . and wouldn't you know he just turns the other cheek!

Natures : Serutan.
Patent herbal remedy made its point.

natures : Serutan. Wherein an old patent herbal remedy made its point with a deliberate REVERSAL.

"Nauga"-Racine Nicaraguan. A Central American native found inexplicably commuting between the greater Waterbury Valley of Connecticut and the Root River Valley of southeast Wisconsin. Roughly equal is the slight shift to **"Nauga," Racing Nicaraguan,** in which case hide/tuck his unusual shingle/card away.

Navan. 1: burb of Ottawa, Ontario **2:** town of Ireland, seat of Meath County, 53°39'n/6°41'w.

Navy van. An official or, if uncapitalized, any sea-blue panel vehicle—decorated perhaps with maritime motifs and PALINDROMES. The KUHNS may have thought of the term first, but we actually drive around in one.

Navy : Yvan. REVERSAL PAIR observed and played upon by Lewis Carroll.

N [. . .] N

Nawân Kot. Town of Pakistan, in Thal Desert, 31°06'n/ 71°32'e.

Ned Agonistes saw assets in Ogaden. Samson's younger brother appreciated the Horn of Africa.

Ned Agonistes' sin nets tennis sets in Ogaden. Same dude as above, in an unusual sports promotion.

Neder sit wort; trow tis reden. Dutch: "Inferior is the word; enduring is the intellect." BORGMANN.

Ned, go gag Ogden. Possibly by MERCER. Illustrated in IRVINE, 1987. Also, among many other possibilities of similar stripe, **Ned got at Ogden. Ned got a bat,** (or **cat, hat, mat, pat, rat, vat,** etc.) **Ogden.** And compare the following entry.

Ned, I am a maiden. Possibly by MERCER. And by all means, compare **Now, Ned, I am a maiden won!** These and the previous entries are so simplistic as to warrant being classified as NATURAL PALINDROMES, that is, of unknown and unknowable origin.

ne'er green. By POOL, an evergreen of Neverland.

Neil A. sees alien. Attribution unknown; reported by John JENSEN. This provokes also, but does not excuse, **Neil Armstron' snorts *Mr. Alien.***

Neil Aspinall: "Ella nips a lien" (*or* **alien**). The Beatles' roadie reports on someone's good offices, possibly even those of a notorious lame female solicitor. (For background, see: **All erotic . . . Ella.**)

Nell Aaron : Nora Allen. BORGMANN's double-mint twins.

Nella [Ardra] Allen. Another distinguished character of BORGMANN'S.

Nella, demand a lad named Allen. Plausible if slightly

Ne'er green

kooky or kinky. And adaptable to other name pairs, such as **Noel** and **Leon.** This one, possibly by MERCER, is one of a series of modular constructions with interchangeable ends *and* middles. Several more examples follow.

Nella risks all: "I will ask Sir Allen." Probably by MERCER. Melodramatic comedy. And again, as with all the **Nella : Allen** enclosures, recasting with other pairs of actors is always an option for creating sequels.

Nella's simple hymn: "I attain my help, Miss Allen." Weird. Possibly MERCER again. The series continues to forge ahead into more and more bizarre territory by stretching out its midsection.

Nella won't set a test now, Allen. Intriguing. And still adaptable to other name pairs, such as **Nadia : Aidan** or **Den : Ned.** Possibly by MERCER.

Nell, Edna ⌈, Ada⌉ and Ellen. By LINDON. A combination occurring in more than one of his poems. Here the central character (the optional **Ada**) is also replaceable, by folks such as **Hannah** or groups such as **Mike, Kim,** and company.

Nemo, we revere women. The Captain himself shows up. Possibly by MERCER, though this one is so basic as to nominate itself for spontaneous generation. The key word *revere* begets *-e revere* begets *we revere w-* and . . . voilà!

Nen (NENN). River of China via Nunjiang, Nake, and Qiqihar (Tsitsihar) into the Songhua and Amur Rivers, 45°25'n/ 124°40'e.

Nen (NENN), Robb. Pitcher for the Florida Marlins; or his father, Dick, a first baseman of the 1960s and 1970s. Hearing sportscasters of the 1990s regularly refer to them as PALINDROMIC, matter-of-factly and without any explanation, is a pretty good indication that the notion and fact of PALIN-

Nen, Robb.
Pitcher for the Florida Marlins.

DROMICITY have now penetrated quite deeply into the public imagination and VERNACULAR.

NEOLOGISM (nee-AHL-uh-jizzm). Newly coined word, phrase, or expression, or newly conceived meaning for an existing word; or the *use* of any such novelties; also, though this is perhaps the same thing but just viewed in a less favorable light, any meaningless word or phrase coined or used by a psychotic. Whatever their ultimate VALUE—and each instance must be appraised on its own merits—neologisms are a common occurrence in PALINDROMY, where the limits of what might pass for acceptable meaning are constantly being tested and stretched and where ordinary words like, say, *stratagem* can erupt spontaneously and without warning into one novelty after another, now into *megatarts* and now again into **megatarts-stratagem,** then perhaps deflect but slightly into **megatart's stratagem** or **stratagem: megatarts,** producing each time a new word, phrase, expression, or meaning.

Nepotism, sit open! As a practice it's fine and needn't conceal itself. (In fact, favor everybody.) For the alternative, compare: **Ergotism, sit ogre!**

Neptune so brevets a waste, verbose, nut pen! "Attributable" to SOTADES, evidently now composing almost in English from his eternal resting place on the ocean floor: "That's the way the Sea God promotes a discarded, all-too-wordy, and eccentric writer!" Consider also: **Neptune's (I rise) nut pen** for brief encores.

Nessen (NESS-'n), Ron. Media man and former White House official.

Net orb, Broten! Jersey Devil Neal is cheered to shoot the puck into the goal.

Net . . . ten. In an Olympic Dreaming event, a perfect antipoaching bumper sticker offered by a drowsy African team surprises, delights, and awakens the Oriental judges:

Nessen, Ron. Media man and former White House official.

"In a nap?? . . .

"Ah, so! . . .

"Ten! . . .

"A ten!!"

Some may feel subtexts of any sort added to PALINDROMES are a sign and confession of intrinsic weakness, but jewels may command settings. BERGERSON, for example, is fond of layering PALINDROMIC couplets with charadic ones, the KUHNS have woven a whole book of topical palindrome crossword puzzles, books of illustrations of palindromes are becoming common, and even your **Wordrow** here, if the truth be told, has merely set a stage—an encyclopedic and cyclopean pretense—on which the 'DROMES may play.

Net ten *or* Net 10. Shorthand notation for many a commercial transaction, meaning "full payment is agreed to or expected within ten days of billing." A natural REVERSAL PAIR.

Net Tim a mitten. By POOL. Strange, but more natural than **Nail a Moslem a camel, Somalian.**

Networks [all] ask row ten. It's the standard location for complimentary seating, poll taking, audience interviews, stooge planting, etc.

Neuquén (nehw-KEHYN). **1:** city and province of Argentina, 38°57's/68°04'w **2:** river flowing from the cordillera near Volcan Domuyo into the Rio Negro at Neuquén city, 38°59's/68°00'w.

Nevada Ven. Archdeacon of Vegas.

Nevele Eleven *or* Nevele 11 (NEVV-uh-lee). Borscht Belt football team or golf hole. This is a possibly unique case of a re-reversal, and palindromization, of a PALINDROME. And one strongly suspects that the Nevele (a sizable hotel and country club near Ellenville, New York) received its name in recognition of some group of eleven, perhaps its own original partners.

never a foot too far, even. Precision landings always; possibly by MERCER.

never even. Roulette advice, and a handy central core phrase for such items as **Dennis . . . sinned** or **Devil . . . lived.**

never [ever] [ever] [ever] [ever] . . . even. By POOL, who appears to have gotten carried away.

never odd or even. Credited by CHISM to ESPY, illustrated in IRVINE, 1987. Sound roulette advice.

"Newgate Prison?" "No, sir! Pet a Gwen!" The refusal is understandable even if the remonstrance or excuse, whichever it is, is a little vague. Still, regardless of the meaning, to "pet a Gwen" would probably be a good thing. For MACARONIC francophiles, we also have the "improvements" *à* ("in the style of") and *péta* ("farted loudly," as Gwen's verb of discourse). Groan as you may, the above are at least preferable outcomes to their more popular cousin: **Golf? No, sir. Prefer prison flog.** And they lead us happily to Gwen's further development at the Jersey Shore in the following entries.

New Gretna banter: Gwen. For some probable reasons why Gwen is the object of good-natured teasing "down the shore," see the previous entry. And for the related or at least similarly surreal award ceremony, see the following.

New Gretna cedes a vase (decanter), Gwen. With these words, a token of appreciation is presented to the lady alternative to **Newgate Prison . . .** (which see). A few more incidents or acknowledgments like this and she will be as famous as the lady from the tale of "The Lady or the Tiger."

NEW HAMPSHIRE. Mentioned honorably here, and perhaps challengingly, as one of the few PALINDROME-free states, that

Nevada Ven

217

is, containing not a single palindrome (at least among the names of its major localities) and never successfully palindromized itself. **Hnn! NH!,** you say?

New Owen. A locality in Owen County, Kentucky, near Owenton, according to BORGMANN in *Language on Vacation.* We could not find a trace of it in 1995.

Niagara Bar again. By POOL; a favorite pub to crawl back to.

Niagara, O roar again! Nice. (But it never stopped.) Possibly by MERCER.

Niagara, O roar again!

Nicolaus : Sualocin. REVERSAL PAIR by BORGMANN, linking the given name of the great Polish astronomer Copernicus with a star in the Dolphin (of the constellation Cygnus), probably named by someone for *him.*

Nigagin. Listed by CHISM as an English word, citing *WORD WAYS* without explanation. Probably another one of those Canadian or Siberian lakes.

Nigeria-Zaire Gin. A good brand to drink all across the tropics. With high-flying player endorsements by Olajuwon and Mutombo.

Nikep : Pekin. REVERSAL PAIR of names by BORGMANN for the same community in Allegany County, Maryland. Only the latter appears on maps today.

nikin. "A rare term, dating back to the year 1700, for a natural or very soft creature," according to BORGMANN.

Nilsson : Nosslin. REVERSAL PAIR of Swedish surnames observed by BORGMANN. These would make a great hyphenated name: **Nilsson-Nosslin.**

Nil-Sum Muslin. A type of zero-based double-entry bookkeeping practiced in the garment district.

Nin, Anaïs. The noted French author and diarist, 1903–1977.

Nina Ricci ran in. By the KUHNS. The designer came in in a hurry.

NINETY-SIX *or* **96. ROTATOR** town of Greenwood County, South Carolina. Town of the year.

Nino's cut did Tucson in. At a sporting event, we think. Also: **Niños cut Tucson in.** Homeboys make deal with city. And: **Nos cut Tucson.** Yeas unify it.

Nip a pin. By POOL. Same in effect as saying "Break a leg."

Nipin. River of Saskatchewan, into Churchill Lake and River, 55°45'n/109°02'w.

Νιψον ανομηματα μη μοναν οψιν (NIP-sahn ah-noh-MEHY-mah-tah mehy-MOHN-ahn OHP-sin). According to AUGARDE:

> The Victorians loved palindromes. During the nineteenth century the pages of *Notes and Queries* were full of discussion about [this] famous Greek example [which] means "Cleanse your sins and not only your face." . . . It has been inscribed in ancient churches throughout the world, chiefly on fonts and containers for holy water. It has been found, for example, around the recess of the holy-water stoup in St. Sophia at Constantinople; in the churches of Notre Dame and St. Stephen's in Paris; on the rim of a large silver dish used to hold rose water on feast days at Trinity College, Cambridge; and on fonts in many British churches, such as St. Mary's at Nottingham, Longley Castle Chapel in Norfolk, Dedham and Harlow in Essex, and Sandbach in Cheshire.

Νιψον ανομηματα
μη μοναν οψιν.
"Cleanse your sins and
not only your face."

Nisumaa oli isasi ilo aamusin. Finnish: "The field of wheat was your father's joy in the morning." According to BORGMANN.

Ni talar bra Latin. Swedish: "You speak good Latin." According to BORGMANN.

Nita sews . . . Reward: dud drawers we sat in! CHISM credits *WORD WAYS*. We were in stitches. The **dud** saves it from being one.

Niwot to win! / Tow in Niwot! In the quest for Colorado's elusive PALINDROMIC state capital, this northeastern burb of Boulder probably makes the greatest claim. Though consider also: **Egnar Range.**

Nizin. Town of Belarus, 52°38'n/28°10'e.

nln. No longer needed.

nmn. No middle name.

nn. No name.

Nnn. "Nicaraguan nut nipper," according to DE SOLA, who goes on to explain in the *Abbreviation Dictionary*: "imaginary and somewhat idealized guard dog whose selective nipping tends to frighten even the most daring and hardened criminals." Jailhouse argot, we would guess.

No Darn Radon!
Advertisement and/or name for a new environmental gas-treatment concern.

No bagel. *Le Gabon.* And no surprise. French Equatorial Africa is no place to look for a bagel.

No, Bon *also* **No, Con / No, Don / No, Hon / No, Ion / No, Jon / No, Lon / No, Mon / No, Ron / No, son . . .** That's the No FAMILY gathering (except **Dr. No was, I saw, on Rd**).

No Darn Radon! CHISM contributed this excellent advertisement and/or name for a new environmental gas-treatment concern, which we expect to make a veritable killing in our strange world where most people actually believe that worrying and fussing about and objecting to things, and fighting and pushing against them, actually makes them go away!

Nod, Don. Sleep on, or approve outright, this REVERSAL fellow by the KUHNS.

No *Decameron* giselles ignore Macedon. This exotic if seemingly proverbial saying riddled with anachronism and illogicality denies that any lacy muslin fabrics (or if **Giselles,** then women so-named or, in Canada, all women indiscriminately) mentioned in or really associated in any way with Giovanni Boccaccio's masterwork of the fourteenth century could fail to refer in some way to the original northern Greek capital of Alexander's (Great) fourth-century-B.C. empire.

No devil, no garden; one dragon lived on.

No devil, no garden; one dragon lived on. By CHISM. Myths explode, but there's a survivor.

No diamond, no maid on. Describing a humble Barbarian household and/or its liberated native house girl. Also, what happens when a women's softball game, bases loaded in the seventh, is washed out by a flood. By Orallepacena Jane Capellaro.

No D? No L? .on.on? No, no! *LONDON*! By LINDON. Nice idea. (The proofreader loved it, too.) Of course once the ground has been so capably broken, all sorts of bonbons may be entertained, and even served up, such as Wonton, Ronson, and Condon. LINDON's London is clearly best, though, as he must have well realized or decided, since it is the most common and obvious and, one might say, talented word of this peculiar class.

No Dot nor Ottawa "legal age" law at Toronto, Don. It looks like Dot is considered a minor by the national law but not by provincial or municipal law, and it also looks like going to Toronto would solve all Don's problems, but it's hard to be sure. On another hand, perhaps Dot is Don's wife. The fine text is probably by MERCER. The idea, or really the vision, of interweaving Canada's capital and leading cities was one probable cause of this magnificent eruption (cf. *Ignatius ej-* . . . *Jesuit Angi-* under **An Ignatius ejaculation . . . Jesuit Angina**), and another probable cause was the

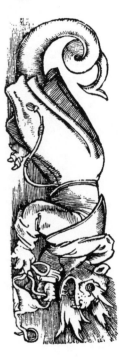

development *legal age > legal age law > Ottawa legal age law.* The barely maintainable semantic result is not a shortcoming but a strength in cases like this, where the reader is being provoked, it seems, into guessing or supposing a variety of picturesque circumstances.

No dots — a mastodon. By POOL. (Dots — a cheetah, a leopard, etc.)

Nod won Snowdon. Princess Margaret said *yes.* By the KUHNS.

Noel **lags as galleon.** She used to fly as a schooner.

Noel Leon. The name of a French journalist, according to LESSER.

Noel, let's egg Estelle on. Probably by MERCER. Good idea, well produced. Some take this very lightly, but others interpret it to mean "let's provoke her to get pregnant or have her period," and still others take it as an epiphany of the assimilation of the Easter bunny with the star of Christmas — death-birth stuff, y'know, and a palindromythic notation about how the cosmos regenerates itself.

Noel saw I was Leon. By BORGMANN. FORMULA or FAMILY stuff.

Noel sees Leon. More FORMULA stuff.

no eon. By POOL in a trice.

No evil shahs live on. Nice ayatollahs only.

No gar a paragon. Not any needlefish is ideal. By the KUHNS.

No "garden" omen: [an] anemone dragon. By the KUHNS. We understand this to mean that the appearance, whether in a garden or not, of the awesome windflower monster is no garden-variety omen but a major portent.

No garden, one dragon. By POOL. One is all you need to

**No evil shahs
live on.**
Nice ayatollahs only.

N [. . .] N

create or get rid of a garden. This text is nice, perhaps precisely because its meaning is unfathomable.

No gar rate tarragon. Kitchen adage by the KUHNS (Don't waste the aromatic herb on needlefish).

Nog at Nepal can't last. Salt (NaCl) a "Pentagon." That's sodium chloride, or ordinary table salt, of course, which in this coded Defense Department transmission means that the local hooch in Katmandu is not expected to hold out unless a fresh supply is salted away or stowed in from military headquarters on the Potomac. Alternatively, but more desperately: **T-Salt (NaCl) a "Pentagon." Nog at Nepal can't last!** (The cryptically redoubled reference to the salt in both cases may also indicate that this "nog" is not ordinary eggnog, but tequila.) And there is luckily a shorter, civilian version of this "T-note" (in which the *T* may conceivably stand for the chem Teacher or, as above, just "Table"): **T: Salt (NaCl) can't last,** or **T-Salt (NaCl) can't last.**

Nog eroded Oregon. 'Twas the night before Xmas, and all along the Willamette, and the Columbia, and the Pacific, and all throughout the mountains and the deserts, people were drinking.

Nog eroded Oregon.

Nog, eros: Oregon! Better yet: **Nog, eros, ewes: Oregon!** Either way, a strangely clipped and fairly bacchanalian parody of **A man, a plan, a canal: Panama!**

No, gird no maid a diamond rig on. By LINDON. The meaning of this oddly resounding proverbiage, delivered in the gruff voice of a construction worker or heavy-equipment operator, is not necessarily but still very probably *"Never propose marriage!"* Some would fault this text for being cynical or cheap, but it is quite amusing as a parody of itself. *Diamond no maid* is a common start, while *gird rig* and *girl rig* have also been widely used. Their happenchance convergence here is what produces the fun.

No girl-rig on! A line from LINDON's playlet **"In Eden, I,"** describing **Eve** when first seen by Adam. A comparison with the previous entry shows how easily a central closure may shift, and how greatly expand or contract, as if CASUALLY, at the drop of a letter or the emergence of a new idea. Seeing this, we can appreciate how PALINDROMES are really a lot like erector sets, with all different sorts and shapes and sizes of parts and fixtures that may be rigged together.

No ham came, sir, now siege is won. Rise, MacMahon. Probably by MERCER. Very peculiar. Has the feeling of a Monty Python joke. It is useful to notice that the center (**Now siege is won**) is virtually or actually self-standing and that the outsides constitute a pair of somewhat independent sentences trying valiantly to integrate. It would require some special kind of genius to assemble such odd fragments into a unified, no matter how strange, scene.

No Hinayana! Nay, a Nihon. Japan, often called Nippon and, perhaps less often but more officially, Nihon (Land of the Rising Sun), has always been very ethnocentric, if not downright xenophobic, and is here evidently very particular about rejecting the alien Hinayana (Theravada) and admitting only the more appropriate and familiar Mahayana, or— as it is usually called there—Zen, form of Buddhism. See also: **Mahayana? Nay, a ham.**

No home demo, Hon. By CHISM. It looks like the vacuum-cleaner salesman won't be coming by to clean the rug after all, Dear.

noillion (noh-ILL-yun). Or, 12,345,678.90, usually expressed in U.S. dollars and sense (noetic), and especially in the phrases "a cool" and "a round" **noillion.** This amount is coincidentally equal to one Mellobuck or allwellion, that is, roughly enough money for the average person to forget working and keep playing.

Noillion.
Or, 12,345,678.90, usually expressed in U.S. dollars and sense (noetic).

no ill lion. Only the healthy need apply.

No, I no pull up onion. By CHISM. Alien farm worker stalks off job.

no ion. By POOL; not an electrically charged particle in sight.

No, I save on final perusal, a sure plan if no evasion. Probably by MERCER. A last-minute adjustment on my tax return certainly looks good . . . but there could be a downside risk here. *Perusal* begets *a sure p-*, and *final* reverses into *-lan if* for a seemingly effortless *[on] final perusal a sure plan if [no]*. Then, or perhaps first, the fortunate existence and happy deployment here of *no I save [. . .] evasion*, itself already nearly a sentence, allows a rather CASUAL and quick dash to a remarkably well-developed thought-form or scenario. Here is almost a demonstration of how a great deal of experience and skill (for that must be presumed, whoever the composer was) may somehow materialize correspondingly fine and delicate happenstances.

noise lesion. Name for the breech produced in the sound barrier when it is broken.

noisive revision. If such change is aloud.

No is reversion. Well, yes, it is a turning away of a sort. By CHISM.

"No"? I tag it "snit instigation." I'd say negation goads to irritation.

"Noitaic Nun" or Pronunciation (nawy-TEHY-ihk). The pronunciation guides used in this book are in the Noitaic Nun style of algebraic noitation, as developed and perfected over centuries in night classes at Portuguese convents.

No Italo Crepes? . . . Order a Red Rose Percolation! An outtake in the form of a sound bite or two we caught while trying to choose from the long menu of preciously named but thin fare at the Ethereal Take-out Counter.

**No Italo Crepes? . . .
Order a Red Rose
Percolation!**

No it! An odd donation. By CHISM. Meaning a he and a she but no it, say, as French gives.

No, I tax ale, ⌈rot to⌉ relaxation. Pub assessor's A to Q: Do you tax the ⌈heavy-⌉drinking end of the bar only?

No, it can assess an action. Possibly by MERCER. Said, perhaps vehemently, of a jury's ability to deliberate or an authority's power to levy a labor force. It was inevitable that the many common words ending in -*tion* and -*sion* would be deeply explored at an early date because they invite the also common and natural sorts of sentences that begin *no, it . . .* and *no, I . . .* , as this and many of the surrounding entries illustrate. Here *assess* may also be replaced by *add* or *ax*.

No, it is open on one position. Possibly by MERCER. An answer to: "Is it entirely closed (or filled in)?" wherein "it" could prove to be a team or a defense or a political platform, we suppose. The text is almost the unavoidable outcome of the word *position*.

No, it's a banana bastion.

No, it is opposed; Art sees Trade's opposition. Possibly by MERCER. A highly naturalistic sound swatch from a British political caucus, this text, much like the previous but not so much as the following, is an "outgrowth forward" of its concluding word. It is a credit to the composer that he did not quit upon arriving at *no, it is opposition* but backtracked into *no, it is opposed . . . -de⌈"⌉s opposition* and persevered to find the enabling central closure.

No, it is opposition. An answer to: "Is that *support*?"

No, it never propagates if I set a "gap" or prevention. Possibly by MERCER. Botanical birth control. The start from *prevention* backward to *no, it never p-* was pregnant with possibility from the start, as was the fertile development of *propagates > set a gap or p-*, but the text is a good and vivid demonstration of how the tiny but useful central element *if I* proves to be just as important as either of these big elements to the wonderful overall development. From this it is clear that the length, in words or letters, of a PALINDROME component is not as interesting or important as its semantic content or the functional possibilities that it sets up for its vicinity.

No *I*, Tom! (Or pall a promotion!) Concise advice, perhaps from a book publicist to an egomaniacal author (not I, of course, but Tom): "If you want to have a successful publicity tour, talk about your book and not so darn much about yourself."

No, it poses order, a red roses option. By POOL. A to Q: "Isn't it just another one of those 'disorderly dandelions' options?"

No, it's a banana bastion. Irreverent rejoinder to **A man, a plan, a canal: Panama!**

Nojon. Village of Mongolia, 43°10'n/102°07'e, in the **Nojon Uul** (Mountains).

Nola departs, eh? Cross. I miss orchestra, pedal on . . . By LINDON. Cyclists drift by. Here we have what could be called an impressionistic PALINDROME, wherein it is not the literal meaning of the words that is so interesting as the circumstance they set up. Only a great imagination would attract such a thing.

Nola's. Midst sin I play sonatas at a nosy alpinist's dim salon. By LINDON. Quick sketch of a preposterous yet undismissable scene, it could be a journal entry or a postcard from the gay nineties or lost generation. Except for the convenient modular outer close, thanks to *Nola's salon,* we have here a musician's seamless riff from *sonatas [> at a nosy]* to *play sonatas at a nosy alp-,* thence progressing almost unavoidably over to the *alpinist's,* etc. But of course this makes it look easier than it is. The proof would be in trying to compose similarly inspired music ourselves from scratch.

No lava sprawl warps Avalon. By the KUHNS. Arthur's place is unafflicted by volcanic eruptions.

Nolem : melon. A locality of Florida, and its main crop.

no lemons, no melon. Illustrated in IRVINE, 1987, one of the nine PALINDROMES featured on BERGERSON's cover.

Noli spell epsilon. Legal maneuver to avoid having to recite alphabet to police at drunk-driving checkpoints.

"No-loss" Solon. From the KUHNS. Nickname in folk history for the Athenian statesman and poet of the late seventh and early sixth centuries B.C. who invented laws, presumably because he was afraid of losing things. All laws ever since have also been written by guarded, fearful, vulnerable, lackful thinkers, the type who also tend to buy insurance, which is really just "no-loss" thinking coming full circle to spawn "no-fault." In reality there exists neither lack nor loss nor fault.

Nome lemon (*or* **demon**). Not the local produce there but perhaps just a comment on the true history of the name itself. According to George R. Stewart in *American Place-Names*, an early mapmaker unsure of what to call this place wrote simply if confoundingly: "? Name." And a later mapmaker misspelled "Name" as "Nome" and dropped the question mark. Gnomes are to thank for all this, no doubt, as well as for the slightly overextended but still nice: **S---! Suck a Nome lemon! (AK cuss.)**

No, Mel Gibson is a casino's big lemon. Attribution unknown; reported by John JENSEN.

No miserable eel, bare Simon! By POOL. No supper at all for you, naked simpleton! Or: what a considerable snakelike thing you've got there!

No miserere, Simon (*or* **Miserere**) (MIZZ-uh-*RÆR*-ee). By POOL. No prayer for mercy, no Fifty-first Psalm, no musi-

No, Mel Gibson is a casino's big lemon.

cal setting for it, and not even a seat bracket for you to lean on, you happy guy.

No Misses ordered roses, Simon. Possibly by MERCER. Enchanting, evoking. BORGMANN monumentalizes this PALIN- DROME in a rubai, or tetrastich:

In other countries, Simon, girls will buy
The rose: a sign of joy o'er which to sigh;
That custom has not penetrated here,
No Misses ordered roses, Simon dear!

No missionary, Cyrano, is Simon. Syntactically tortured, improbable, yet nice.

No, miss, it is Simon. Possibly by MERCER. A case of mis- taken identity is cleared up. (There exists also, but alas only to confuse things again, and further, via repunctuation: **No miss — it is Simon.**)

No mists or frost, Simon. Fair weather, friend. Probably by MERCER. In our attributions for this and the surrounding entries, we endeavor (as we do with all entry texts that ap- peared previously in BERGERSON's "Mercer" inventory) to distinguish between a mere possibility of authorship by Mercer (when the text is so ordinary and obvious as the pre- vious one) and the greater probability of authorship by him (when it is especially subtle, like this, or ingenious, like the next).

Nomists reign at Tangier, St. Simon. Probably by MERCER. Likely obscure. BORGMANN exults: "At last we shall have strict adherence to religious and moral law in Morocco."

Non. 1: Latin: not **2:** hamlet of Hughes County, Oklahoma.

Nonaloof, a fool anon. This pseudooriginal PALINDROME marks the approximate alphabetical place by unstandoffishly and perhaps foolishly appropriating the outermost rind of an excellent ten-line-stanza palindrome by FITZPATRICK (in

Fling Thong), which (though we may not quote it here, we still feel almost duty-bound to report) very successfully incorporates even such unassimilable verbosities as "unassimilable verbosities."

NONCE WORD. A word occurring, invented, or used just for a particular occasion, or for the nonce; commonplace in the construction of PALINDROMES. Examples such as the simply prefixed/suffixed **degaraged,** dreamt-up words such as **ezylyze,** poetic outbursts such as *rag-nude* in **Dim Rodney repardoned ungarbed deb, rag-nude, no drapery, end or mid,** pure ornerinesses such as *noitacided* in **Dedication NOITACIDED,** and inspirations such as *Zotamorf* in *From A to Zotamorf* may all qualify as nonce words under the proposed 1997 rule changes.

Nonwords, drown on! In a logological presentation entitled "From Word to Nonword" (1967), BORGMANN observes: "Our very title illustrates the constant turmoil in which the word lover habitually dwells. *Nonword* is a simple, logical word, but is not included in any dictionary. Is it a word?" (Or a nonword?) As a word, *nonword* appears to be ebbing away before our very eyes, but then BORGMANN seems to save it: "From our use of it in a title, you can surmise that we have given it our nod." Hmmm. For anyone not thrilled by his rescue at sea of this two-headed monster, a logo-illogical AMPHISBAENA if ever there was one, we offer the text. (Actually we like both the monster and the text just fine, for together they constitute a three-headed whirligig that quite entertainingly chases after its own nonexistent tails!)

Nonwords, drown on!

noon (NOON). The crack of midday.

No one redeem me, Ed, ere noon. By CHISM. Meaning, poetically, "I'd prefer to sober up for a while in the tank."

Nora, alert, saws goldenrod-adorned logs, wastrel Aaron. Probably by MERCER. Aaron, a harmless dreamer, wins abuse, while enterprising Nora is honored for trashing beauty. BORGMANN observes that *goldenrod-adorned*, with its sixteen letters, is the second-longest word ever to be woven into the fabric of a PALINDROME. For the longest, and especially if you'd prefer an unhyphenated winner as we would, see: **Named undenominationally . . . O Ned, nude, man!**

Norah's foes order (a) red rose of Sharon. Possibly by MERCER, this text is a very basic back-formation from *rose of Sharon* such as someone less talented might also have seen. At least **Norah's foes or a rose of Sharon** is virtually self-evident, and roses are famous for being red, and so voilà. . . . Almost coincidentally, there actually exists a Nora's (but with no *h*, and so no cigar) Nursery and Florist near Cornwall Bridge in the town of Sharon, Connecticut. (Still, her apostrophe could stand for a missing *h*, as well as indicating possessiveness.)

Norah [Sara] Sharon. Handsome names by BORGMANN.

Noriega can idle, held in a cage . . . iron! Attribution unknown, reported by John JENSEN. This is an unusually good construction.

Nor I, Ron. By POOL.

Norma, I am Ron. Also by POOL.

Norma is as selfless as I am, Ron. A handsome absurdity, or perhaps only a "how-could-this-be?" conundrum, credited by ESPY to Martin GARDNER.

No Roman a moron. Common slogan for promoting universal compulsory education in the late Empire, by the KUHNS.

North Carolina: Anil or *Ach*-tron. There's a choice for this place, and it boils down to indigo cultivation or installing one of those German positron accelerators.

No Roman a moron. Slogan for promoting universal compulsory education in the late Empire.

North Dakota bat OK, a DH! —*T.R.* (On!) Authentically initialed yet suspiciously anachronistic scouting report telegraphed by Teddy Roosevelt from Elkhorn Ranch. Gullible historians have interpreted it to mean: "This guy's a hitter!" And, in the coded postscript, "I'll take that bet!"

No sail had dahlias on. From a FITZPATRICK couplet beginning and ending thus. The sentence, though whimsical and poetic, seems obvious and so may have historical antecedents, but we have not found any prior to BERGERSON's 1973 date. This fact gives reason to hope there may still be other gems lying in wait for us.

NO SCUTTLEBUTT AS ATTU BELT TUCSON! Sports headline. It's no idle gossip: The Attu "Unclassical Aleutian" (evidently one of those newfangled collective-noun teams such as the Orlando Magic or the Utah Jazz or the Miami Heat that attract a plural verb to a singular place, of all things—but in this case a D-level franchise to be sure) actually wallop the highly touted team from Tucson! There is also a version that goes: **No scuttlebutt egg: *"Et tu* belt" Tucson!** This is a true classical allusion, happily confirming that a run of *Julius Caesar* will indeed be coming to southern Arizona. Finally, too, for whenever less is more, we have the radioactivity alert (just a test and a jest): **No scuttlebutt: U-belt Tucson.**

Nosegay ages on. Yoicks! Illustrated in IRVINE, 1987.

Nosegays so manic in a mossy age, son! Cut and pasted from FITZPATRICK.

nos in unison. The KUHNS' "unharmonized negations." Yes, let's all just say no together, per you know. And there's also a bizarre:

No "s" in unison? So, all together now: Union! (After CHISM.)

Nota bene: **Bat on!**

No Sliwa dedeeded a Wilson *and* **No, Sliwa dedeeded A. Wilson.** Heard amid the confusion at Town Hall.

No slogans nag Olson. In fact he doesn't notice bumper stickers or campaign buttons or that sort of thing at all. By CHISM.

Nosnibor : Robinson. Deliberate REVERSAL by Samuel Butler of a common surname to produce the surname for a leading merchant in his Utopian novel *Erewhon*, itself named by applying the same procedure, though imperfectly, to the word *nowhere*.

No stab—*Mock Combat's* on. Good TV show by the KUHNS. Followed some day, perhaps, by "No combat—*Mock Struggle's* on" and then perhaps by "No struggle—*Mock Separation's* on."

no Stetson. So it must be some other kind of hat.

—No suggestion?—No! It's "Egg Us On." Come on! This is the hot new parlor game with no clues, just provocations.

nosy son. Snoopy heir, by the KUHNS.

***Nota bene*: Bat on!** By POOL. From the Latin version of *The Rules of Baseball*, by Pila Turpis: "A foul ball on the third strike is not counted as a strike. *Nota bene*: Bat on!" (trans. S. **Wordrow**).

Not Ara Cobmor from Boca Raton?! Incredible! What a small world!

NO TASTE: La Veta Pass sap ate valets (a ton). Colorado pal keeps a promise.

not a ton. "What is 1,999.5 pounds?" By TERBAN.

not Cohocton. Neither the river nor the town of western New York (and see: **"Not New York," Roy went on,** etc.).

Noted Eton. By POOL, a fairly palindrhomeric epithet.

not Eton. By POOL, in a change of heart.

Note: Get on. Pay attention, come aboard, get along, get moving, and grow better and better.

"No telegram," Marge let on. Sent by CHISM.

Not Gnirrabta, ergo Great Barrington. South Berkshirian Barbarian-chic-style bumper sticker distinguishing by reverse logic the entire strange outside world from the local familiar little world, and introducing by name the great **ergo ogre** created by our regional design house of Tat2abumpur or Bust. ("This was their greatest greater Great Barrington adventure. This was their finest happy hour.")

Notla : Alton. A Texas locality named for its general store, the Alton Grocery Company.

Not Lennon 'n' Elton.

Wrong Johns.

not Lennon 'n' Elton *or* **not Lenon, Elton.** Wrong Johns.

Not Lima, Hamilton! Evidently deciding or resolving something or other between two small but noticeable cities of western Ohio.

"No Tl! (I'm a heel!)" per Rep. Lee Hamilton. The Indiana Democrat just says no to thallium, the poisonous metallic element often found in rat and insect powders and infrared detectors, and—"Call me pisher!"—bravely defies the political consequences. But the meaning changes radically for those who understand this as "t/l," a form of abasement, and changes yet again for others who recognize it as a new car from the Acura TL series, etc. Still others will go for the even more mischievous political trick (and probably the zaniest composition of the foursome): **Not L.! . . . "'I'm a heel' per Rep. *Lee* Hamilton."**

"Not New York," Roy went on. Then Rio or Paris will

have to do. Possibly by MERCER, but it's so basic, it may be a perennial invention. Illustrated in TERBAN.

"Not Nil" Clinton. A generally positive assessment.

Not nom de plume gem (ulp!): Edmonton *or* **Not nom de plume gem: "Ulp" Edmonton.** Neither of which is exactly a gem as nom de plume or PALINDROME. But could be a hockey player, come to think of it.

"Not Nil" Clinton

Not on. By POOL. A bit off his usual fine form.

Not Remer, [Bozo;] Bremerton. The Washington city of Bremerton has for some reason taken pains to distinguish itself from **Remer,** the tiny probable PALINDROMIC capital of Minnesota, but (clownishly) becomes for all its efforts just the end of a PALINDROME about a palindrome.

Notre Merton. No Dame for our Catholic theologian.

No trace—not one carton. By POOL. A mysterious disappearance, to say the least.

Not Silli Willi's Ton! And **Not silli Williston,** North Dakota, **pop. 13,131** (as of 1990), where, neither silly nor superstitious (nor heavy in any other way since they shut down their nuclear "**megaton's not a gem**" silos), people can now look forward with comfort and confidence to the results of their next Federal Census, due to be taken, and lightly to be sure, in the year 2000. Just in time, that is, for **Silli Willi's** soon-to-be-heavily-promoted "Year of the Ton." We expect many towns across the country with names ending in *-ton* will jump on this fortuitous bandwagon by then. And judging from the higher-than-normal frequency of towns already having PALINDROMIC population figures as of 1990, including many breathtaking ones such as Williston's, we suspect that similarly distinguished census totals all across the country have been and will continue to be doctored or pounded into shape by powerful local fantasists for purely esthetic reasons.

Nova Avon. By CHISM, would have to be a new Stratford's river, like, say, the Berkshires' Housatonic, which goes out to the Sound at Stratford, Connecticut.

Now ere we nine were held idle here, we nine were won. Probably by MERCER. This very lovely if slightly improbable string of small words we take to be a line from an epic telling (though not quite in dactylic hexameter) of an interminable rain delay in the life of a losing baseball team, bottom of the fifth or later. But whatever its interpretation, the text is a good demonstration of how the poetic has a way of bursting out in response to a bit of diligence. *Held idle* seems to lead the way via a series of small and fairly natural accretions, all obvious with the benefit of hindsight, or else *now ere we nine [w-] . . . we nine were won* was a prior elaboration, but the full path of nicely spaced stepping stones, no matter in which direction it was originally trodden, could not have been easy to discover without the help of gnomes.

Now Eve, we're here, we've won.

Now Eve, we're here, we've won. Possibly by MERCER. A triumphant humanity reclaims Paradise Awareness and writes home to Mom about it, as well it might. In the case of short and memorable PALINDROMES like this one, we feel that they belong to our culture at large and to all of us in general no matter who saw them first. And we are led to wonder if, in granting us such pearls, the gnomes are not just having a good time with us and our peculiar ideas of privacy and property.

No! Willamette Mall! I won! For some reason, (s)he insists on going shopping.

Now, it is illicit to be Botticilli. Sit. I won. See: "Il Licitto" by Botticilli.

Now I won. A small triumph. Possibly by POOL.

Now, Ned, I am a maiden nun; Ned, I am a maiden won. Probably by MERCER. How fetchingly and gracefully and readily she shakes the habit! Illustrated in IRVINE, 1987.

Now, Ned, I am a maiden won. Possibly by MERCER. Shortened form of previous entry, in which case less is less, but still interesting.

Now Norris, sir, I mail a new opus. So be it . . . Tie boss up, Owen. Al, I am Iris; sir, Ron won. Start and finish of Edward Benbow's 10,689-word PALINDROME, given, according to LESSER, by *Guinness Book of World Records.*

No word, no bond, row on. Possibly by MERCER. No point waiting around for nothing. Illustrated by AGEE in *So Many Dynamos.*

No worse, Pacific apes row on. For the story of their evolution and migrations from China, Java, and Australia across the vast southern seas to the Galápagos, where Darwin met them still making progress in their flimsy rafts and canoes, see: **E Pacific ape** and **SE Pacific apes.**

Now, sir, a war is won! Possibly by MERCER. Surely an equal of *veni, vidi, vici.*

No x in Mr. R. M. Nixon??? Reported without enthusiasm, in view of its absurdity, by Martin GARDNER. But we have never been put off by absurdity.

Noxon (NAHK-sahn). Reservoir and nearby village of Sanders County, Montana. Their rugged environs are reputed to be an antigovernment and militia hotbed, but Toby's Tavern, the village watering hole, has a big sign out front proclaiming "Life is but a dream."

Noyon (nwah-YOHn). Small town of northern France, on the Oise River, 49°35'n/3°00'e; scene of Charlemagne's coronation.

Nozon *or* **NOZON** (noh-ZOHn). According to BORGMANN, a vertical (and thus four-way) MIRROR PALINDROME; the name of a river in Switzerland that divides at the town of Pompaples, one branch flowing south to the Mediterranean Sea, and the other branch north to the North Sea, a two-directional flow that makes it, he says, a palindrome in fact as well as in name. Though this is a very special nicety indeed, it is still difficult to see how the *forking* of the waterway acts out anything more than the choice of which way to orient, right side up or upside down, for it certainly doesn't imitate the movement of backtracking or recurrence that is normally seen in PALINDROMY.

NQN. Airport code for **Neuquén,** Argentina.

Nudists I dun. My job is to collect from bareskin naturalists. By the KUHNS.

NUMBERDROME *or* NUMERICAL PALINDROME. Though frequently interesting, numberdromes are far more numerous and generally less distinctive than verbal 'DROMES. The ten numerical ciphers (from 0 to 9) may be combined and recombined with infinitely more ease and fluidity than may the twenty-six letters (*a* to *z*), for there simply are no meaningless or useless combinations of numerals, while the vast majority of possible letter combinations will forever spell nothing at all and so remain intrinsically devoid of any sense or VALUE. (It is this latter fact of life that makes the comparatively few lucid verbal PALINDROMES that we do have so remarkable and precious.) Fully 10 percent of all two- and three-digit and 1 percent of all four- and five-digit numerical combinations are PALINDROMIC, including more than a hundred calendar years (see DATES), numerous HIGHWAYS, many PHONE CODES (which see), and a good working half of the thousand possibilities among postal ZIP CODES (which see)—that means more than a thousand garden-variety household-name number pals such as **868, 1331, 44944,** etc., with little to rec-

NUMBERDROMES:

II-II-II

ommend them, plus a potential infinitude of others even less distinguished. Of course there are notable exceptions, and so we have noted them:

00 *or* **000,** etc. Occasionally used in sports for player or vehicle IDs.

11. The first numerical palindrome, if multiple zeros, decimal numbers, and one-digit numbers are ignored, which they probably should be. The number of the illustrious Apollo moon-landing mission and, as **11-11-11,** or the eleventh hour of the eleventh day of the eleventh month, the moment of Armistice in A.D. 1918. In Spanish, *once* **(11)** once stood for *aguardiente,* as this strong drink has **11** letters. . . . New York is considered the eleventh state. And **11** is the place where the numbers 5 and 10 can become a PALINDROME—by the process of *reversal additions,* as follows: 5; + its reversal, 5, = 10; + its reversal, 01, = 11 (see: **PAL-LAP**).

22. Rank of Alabama's admission to Union. See: **A ma . . . Alabama.** "Customer's check is still unpaid," in restaurant code talk. Also, **22** is where the number 20 will **pal-lap,** as follows: 20 + 02 = **22.**

33. Oregon is the **33**rd state. A **33** is also a **33**-1/3 rpm record. And **33** is where the numbers 3, 6, 12, and 21 **pal-lap,** as follows: 3; + 3 = 6; + 6 = 12; + 21 = 33; similarly, 30 (+ 03). See also: TREINTA Y TRES.

44. Wyoming is the **44**th state. And **44** is where the numbers 13 and 31 **pal-lap,** as also 40 (+ 04).

55. "Root beer," in restaurant code talk. And **55** is where the numbers 7, 14, and 41 **pal-lap,** as follows: 7; + 7 = 14; + 41 = 55; similarly, the numbers 23 and 32, as also 50 (+ 05).

57.75. The number of cubic inches in a quart.

66. The legendary highway to kicks (see: HIGHWAYS). "Dirty dishes," in restaurant code talk. Phillips Petroleum for short. And **66** is where the numbers 15 and 51 **pal-lap,** as also 24 and 42, and 60 (+ 06).

N [. . .] N

69. Wherein a pictorial ROTATOR PALINDROME evokes upside-down sex, a phenomenon or at least a thought evidently so popular in West Jersey that old Highway **69** there (see: HIGHWAYS), proceeding from the State House in Trenton up to Buttzville and back until c. 1969, actually had to be renumbered (becoming, and remaining to this day, a smartly coded 31, that is, for anyone flippy enough to subtract from 100 and/or remember back to '**69**) because all the highway number signs kept disappearing, thanks probably to fraternity pranksters, and hardly anyone could find the road anymore.

77. Where the numbers 1, 2, 4, 8, 16, and 61 **pal-lap,** as follows: 1; + 1 = 2; + 2 = 4; + 4 = 8; + 8 = 16; + 61 = **77;** similarly, 25 + 52, and 34 + 43, and 70 (+ 07).

88. Love and kisses on ham radio (see also: EIGHTY-EIGHT); where the numbers 17 and 71 **pal-lap,** as also 26 and 62, and 35 and 53, and 80 (+ 08); **Pop.** of Eden, Mississippi, 1990 Census. This and numerous other towns of Mississippi with PALINDROMIC populations are presented here to illustrate and document the fairly universal predilection of census takers for palindromic totals. (Of the **292** Mississippi towns and cities for which data were available, **151** having populations over **999,** fully **22** had palindromic totals—or almost half again as many as a truly random distribution would have produced. Nor are Mississippi census takers alone in this partiality toward PALINDROMY.)

96 *or* '**96.** A specially magical ROTATOR PALINDROME and, as 1996—the year of this book and the year of the introduction of the Palindromic Millenium—a discernible moment that will occur at the conclusion of this extremely propitious year, sixty-nine upside down and backward. And what does it mean, anyway, to say that the nineties are the sixties upside down? Isn't this really an oxymoron? The sixties were already upside down.

99. "Look out. The manager is nearby." Also, where the

NUMBERDROMES:
55. "Root beer" in restaurant code talk.

numbers 9, 18, and 81 **pal-lap,** as follows: 9; + 9 = 18; + 81 = **99;** similarly, 27 + 72, 36 + 63, 45 + 54, and 90 (+ 09).

101. Where 100 **pal-laps.**

111. Pop. of Learned, Mississippi, 1990 Census.

121. The square of **11,** and where the numbers 19, 91, and 110 **pal-lap,** as follows: 19; + 91 = 110; + 011 = **121;** similarly, via 110, are 28 + 82, 37 + 73, and 46 + 64; and directly, 29 + 92, 38 + 83, 47 + 74, and 56 + 65.

131. See: **282.**

141. Pop. of Braxton, Mississippi, 1990 Census.

171. Pop. of Pope, Mississippi, 1990 Census.

202. Pop. of Golden, Mississippi, 1990 Census.

232. Pop. of Falkner, Mississippi, 1990 Census.

282. The elevation in feet below sea level of the lowest point in the United States (and North America and the entire New World), at Death Valley, California. (The lowest point in South America is at Salinas Grandes, Argentina, **131** feet below sea level.)

292. Pop. of Chunky, Mississippi, 1990 Census.

303. Where 102 and 201 **pal-lap.**

343. Baseball notation for a first-to-second-to-first double play; **pop.** of Louise, Mississippi, 1990 Census.

363. Where 39, 93, 132, and 231 **pal-lap;** also, by the same route, 48 and 84, and 57 and 75.

373. Pop. of New Hebron, Mississippi, 1990 Census.

404. Pop. of Schlater, Mississippi, 1990 Census; also, height in feet of the Ordway Building, the tallest building in Oakland, California, and of the Owens-Illinois Corporation Headquarters, the tallest building in Toledo, Ohio; where 103 and 301 **pal-lap.**

454. Pop. of Ethel, Mississippi, 1990 Census; also, height in feet of the Southtrust Tower, the tallest building in Birmingham, Alabama.

484. Pop. of Artesia, Mississippi, 1990 Census; the square of **22,** and where 49, 94, 143, and 341 **pal-lap;** also, by the same route 58 and 85, and 67 and 76.

N [. . .] N

505. Where 104 and 401 **pal-lap,** as also 203 and 302.

525. Pop. of Weir, Mississippi, 1990 Census.

535. Elevation above sea level in feet of Louisiana's highest ground, Driskill "Mountain"; **pop.** of Hickory Flat, Mississippi, 1990 Census; also, height in feet of City Place, the tallest building in Hartford, Connecticut.

555. The height in feet of Washington Monument (tallest structure in Washington, D.C.), according to Louis Farrakhan, speaking at the Million Man March.

606. Where 105 and 501 **pal-lap,** similarly 204 and 402.

626. Height in feet of One Kansas City Place, tallest building in Kansas City, Missouri.

636. Pop. of Renova, Mississippi, 1990 Census.

656. Height in feet of Central Park Office Tower, the tallest building in Caracas.

696. Pop. of Ecru, Mississippi, 1990 Census.

707. Where 106 and 601 **pal-lap;** similarly 205 and 502, and 304 and 403. Also: **707, 727, 737, 747, 757, 767,** and **777** are all Boeing aircraft model numbers.

787. Height in feet of Moscow State University, the tallest building in Moscow (including spire).

797. Height in feet of Tokyo City Hall, the tallest building in Tokyo.

808. Where 107 and 701 **pal-lap;** similarly 206 and 602, and 305 and 503.

818. Pop. of Mathiston, Mississippi, 1990 Census.

888. Height in feet of Society Center, the tallest building in Cleveland.

909. Where 108 and 801 **pal-lap;** also 207 and 702, 306 and 603, and 405 and 504.

919. Height in feet of Overseas Union Bank, the tallest building in Singapore.

939. Height in feet of National Bank Plaza, the tallest building in Dallas.

949. Pop. of Burnsville, Mississippi, 1990 Census.

959. Pop. of Derma, Mississippi, 1990 Census.

N ⌊ . . . ⌋ N

969. Pop. of Bude, Mississippi, 1990 Census.

1001. Height in feet of the Bank of China, the tallest building in Hong Kong, though in another source its height is given as **313** meters, or 1028 feet, proving you *can* eat your cake and have it, too.

1111. Where 59, 95, 154, 451, 605, and 506 **pal-lap;** also, by the same route, 68 and 86; and by a different route, 109, 901, and 1010 (+ 0101).

1331. The cube of **11.**

1771. Pop. of Centreville, Mississippi, 1990 Census.

1991. The product of two other PALINDROMES, **11** and **181.**

2222. Pop. of Mound Bayou, Mississippi, 1990 Census.

4884. Where 69, 96, 165, 561, 726, 627, 1353, and 3531 **pal-lap,** and by the same route, 78 and 87.

5445. Pop. of Bridgeville, Pennsylvania, 1990 Census.

5555. Elevation in feet above sea level of Red Lodge, Montana.

5665. Pop. of Breckenridge, Texas, 1990 Census.

5885. Pop. of Brewton, Alabama, 1990 Census.

6226. Pop. of La Habra Heights, California, and Northville, Michigan, 1990 Census, in a rare but not unique case of pal **pop.** twins.

6446. Pop. of Lawrenceville, New Jersey, 1990 Census.

6556. Pop. of Lakes of the Four Seasons, Indiana, and Turtle Creek, Pennsylvania, 1990 Census, pal **pop.** twins.

6666. Elevation in feet above sea level of Panguitch, Utah.

6776. Pop. of Five Corners, Washington, 1990 Census.

7227. Pop. of Enumclaw, Washington, 1990 Census.

7337. Pop. of Chalco, Nebraska, and Avon, Ohio, 1990 Census, pal **pop.** twins.

7667. Pop. of Creston, Iowa, in the 1960 Census (a nicety identified by BORGMANN), and of Rainbow City, Alabama, and Southwick, Maine, 1990 Census, pal **pop.** triplets.

7997. Pop. of Winslow, Maine, 1990 Census.

8338. Pop. of Lindsay, California, 1990 Census.

8448. Pop. of Blythe, California, 1990 Census.

NUMBERDROMES:

707, 727, 737, 747, 757, 767, 777

N [. . .] N

8668. Pop. of Thompson, Connecticut, 1990 Census.

8888. Pop. of Ilion, New York, 1990 Census, believed to be the biggest locality of its kind (that is, with a population figure all of a single cipher).

9229. Pop. of Connelsville, Pennsylvania, 1990 Census.

9669. Pop. of Rock Falls, Illinois, and of Savage-Guilford, Maryland, 1990 Census, pal **pop.** twins.

10,201. Pop. of Havre, Montana, in 1990 Census; square of **101**.

10,701. Pop. of Columbia, Pennsylvania, 1990 Census.

12,321. Square of **111**.

14,641. Square of **121**.

15,051. Pop. of Horsham, Pennsylvania, 1990 Census.

18,481. Elevation in feet above sea level of Mt. Elbrus, in southern Russia, tallest peak in the Caucasus and Europe.

19,091. Pop. of Opelousas, Louisiana, 1990 Census.

22,122. Pop. of Opelika, Alabama, 1990 Census.

26,062. Where 79, 97, 176, 671, 847, 748, 1595, 5951, 7546, 6475, 14,021, and 12,041 **pal-lap.**

28,082. Pop. of Lewiston, Idaho, 1990 Census.

40,804. Square of **202**.

44,944. Square of **212**.

48,284. Pop. of Arcadia, California, 1990 Census, believed to be the biggest PALINDROMICally populated locality in that census.

65,756. Area of Florida, in square miles.

559,955. Largest-known PALINDROMIC geographical statistic: the acreage of Joshua Tree National Monument, California.

698,896. The smallest palindromic square (of 836) with an even number of digits. Such palindromic squares are extremely rare, according to Martin GARDNER.

1,002,001. A rough million, the square of **1001**.

1,030,301. A rough million, the cube of **101**.

1,234,321. Square of 1111.

1,367,631. The cube of **111**.

NUMBERDROMES:

1234321

N ⌈ . . . ⌉ N

4,008,004. The square of **2002.**

100,020,001. The square of **10,001.**

123,454,321. The square of **11,111.**

1,003,003,001. A rough billion, the cube of **1001.**

8,813,200,023,188. The numbers 89 and 98 are the two cases of low numbers that require more than six steps in **pal-lap**ping; indeed they don't PALINDROME out or **pal-lap** until the above monster in the trillions is reached on the twenty-fourth step.

10,000,200,001. The square of **100,001.**

10,662,526,601. Martin GARDNER gives this number in the ten billions as the only PALINDROMIC cube with a non-palindromic cube root (2201).

637,832,238,736. Rare PALINDROMIC square (of 798,644) with an even number of digits. Next largest is **698,896.**

1,000,002,000,001. A rough trillion, the square of **1,000,001.**

1,000,300,030,001. A rough trillion, the cube of **10,001.**

100,000,020,000,001. The square of **10,000,001.**

1,000,030,000,300,001. A cool quadrillion-plus, the cube of **100,001,** and as good a place as any to quit numbers and return to words.

nun (NUNN). **1:** female religious devotee **2:** pigeon **3:** Hebrew and Arabic letter **4:** kind of buoy.

Nun (NUNN). River channel of Nigeria, actually the main mouth of the Niger River as it flows into the Gulf of Guinea, 4°20'n/6°00'e.

Nüptüal Müses: ümlaüt pün. After CHISM. We got the invite and the ümlaüt büt not the PÜN.

Nurse, I spy gypsies, run! Probably by MERCER. The patient is delirious. The key word *gypsies* gives *-se, I spy gypsies* and thereafter closes quickly, if wackily. There is the option of deleting the second comma, but it is better left in.

Nüptüal Müses: ümlaüt pün

Nurse, save rare vases, run! Probably by MERCER. The series continues and the fever peaks. In this case we are less confident about whether the text grew out from the center or in from the ends.

Nurse's onset abates, noses run. Probably by MERCER. We hardly recognize the nurse from the previous examples. Here her unintensive care leads only to an outbreak of the sniffles. The delirium is long gone.

Nurse! So no noses run? By POOL. And no sniffles either. Just as we suspected.

Nurses run. By POOL. To save the noses, or the vases from the gypsies (see above).

NxN. Knight takes knight (chess).

Nyet! (No!)—Fonteyn. Margot to Gra["]m, after Ballet Russe.

N. Y. Llewellyn. BORGMANN character. We looked for him in a recent Manhattan phone book and found only N. J. Llewellyn, leading us to wonder if **N. Y. Llewellyn** isn't to be sought rather across the river in New Jersey.

oao. One and only on the one hand, and off and on on the other!

Obbo. Village of Ethiopia, near Kenya, 3°36'n/38°54'e.

Obo. Village of Central African Republic, near Sudan and Zaire, 5°24'n/26°30'e.

O [. . .] O

¡O cita Mora! Aromatico! By John McClellan. "O Moorish city! How aromatic!" A heavenly coincidence and image, born, as the author confided to BERGERSON, only after he gazed for many years at the word *Aromatico*, which appears on the outer package of his favorite imported cigarette-rolling papers, a Spanish brand named Bambu.

OCO. Airport code for El Coco Airport, San José, Costa Rica. Thus also **OCO Coco.**

O, desire, rise, do!

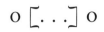

OCS Patapsco. A perfect name for an Officer Candidate School in the Balto area.

Octave Vat Co. By Andrea Cantrell. Makers of giant, wine-filled xylophones.

Odessa : assedo. Ukrainian or American city gets a Roman assessor.

Odd, O. See: **PRP.**

O desirable Melba, rise, do! By LINDON. Stirring, somehow. The lady and the setting seem an outgrowth of BORGMANN's **Able Melba,** but see the following entry.

O, desire, rise, do! By POOL. A great and thankfully short ode.

Odile de Lido. A seventh-century Alsatian saint vacationing in Venice.

O dire Cremona! I prefer piano, MERCER, I do! By LINDON, who leaves us to wonder whether this is or is not a reference to the eminent PALINDROMIST Leigh MERCER. Perhaps the two musical instruments are a metaphor for Mercer's and Lindon's strikingly distinctive styles of PALINDROMIC composition. In any event, this composition is quite vivid even without reading anything into it. It probably arose from a test of *Cremona*, giving *-ano Merc-* > *piano Merc-* > a fairly droll closure with *re Cremona: I prefer piano, Mercer[.]*, and with a little extra coaxing a much more entertaining second closure into the fully garrulous text.

Odo (OH-doh). Archbishop of Canterbury in reign of Edwy, and abbé of Cluny, 879–943. He became Count of Paris in **888.**

O dodo! Ode to a hopelessly stupid and passé flightless bird.

Odo tenet mulum, madidam mappam tenet Anna. Consisting of seven single-word PALINDROMES in a row, this Latin palindrome sequence was quoted by William Camden in 1605. It means "Odo has a mule, Anna has a wet napkin."

OED **I vet. (No Montevideo).** My careful reading of the prestigious *Oxford English Dictionary* turns up this single, inexplicable omission.

OED **or rodeo.** As peculiar a pair of options as we have ever contemplated, illustrated in IRVINE, 1987.

O, enrobe me, Borneo. And so help me, we do actually own at least a leather jacket (if not a robe) that, though labeled "New Zealand Outback" and tagged "Made in Pakistan," is lined with material illustrating, in a stylized sort of way, various scraps of an 1830 nautical chart depicting and entitled—albeit in French—the Island of Borneo, and this garment reminds us of the text invocation, notwithstanding its decidedly loose fit.

OEO. Office of Economic Opportunity. Compare: **EOE,** Equal Opportunity Employer. So **O EOE, OEO!** (The complete if abbreviated address or salutation.)

o [. . .] o

O furor: UFO! Contributed by chism, maybe just an outvasion from inner space.

Ogden, Ned: Go! Two are told to start or leave.

O, Geronimo, no minor ego! Attribution unknown, reported by John jensen. This is no minor palindrome.

O gin, ⌈ on (, on)⌉ I go. Various syncopations (and even the gin itself and I myself could be eliminated) from the reynolds drinking song referred to under **avid ⌈as a⌉ diva.**

O gnat⌈s⌉, tango! Possibly by mercer. The very mildest of oaths. This short palindrome pair also marks the approximate alphabetical location of a tall, short twenty-two-line palindrome poem by Graham reynolds, beginning and ending thus, entitled "O Gnat" and recited by bergerson in *Palindromes and Anagrams.*

Ogo (OH-goh). **1:** village of Honshu, Japan, 36°25'n/139°10'e **2:** outer suburb of Osaka, Japan, 34°49'n/135°06'e **3:** river flowing through the latter, 34°47'n/135°04'e.

Ogopogo. According to borgmann, a mythical monster supposed to inhabit Okanagan Lake, a long, thin look-alike of Loch Ness in the southern interior of British Columbia. Just as Nessie-on-the-brain is the main event at Ness, so we hear Ogopogo-on-the-noggin makes **Okanagan a KO.**

O! Go to Togo! African *vai Napoli.*

Oh, a dig? . . . Idaho? Dinosaur bones or potatoes? Alternatively: **Oh, a dim Idaho!** (as may often be said looking out from the Tetons); **Oh, a din! Idaho?** (as may seldom be heard in its few and small cities); and **Oh, a dip! Idaho!** (just a dip as the water's usually pretty invigorating here).

O had I ⌈now won⌉ Idaho! Imagine the political (or any other) significance! Alternatively **O had I nine men in Idaho!** lindon takes off from the same starting place and reaches the epic: **O had I nine more hero-men in Idaho!**

OEO

Oh, a paraded Arapaho! A character from our Wild West performance, here and following.

Oh, a parabola-lob Arapaho! Does a picture-perfect job with a lance.

Oh, a paragon! A nog Arapaho! Sets a good example by holding his liquor.

Oh, a par Arapaho! Average.

Oh, a parasite masks a métis Arapaho! Strange but articulate. Could be a surprised or fascinated Francis Parkman speaking.

Oh, a parataxis! [:] "Six; at Arapaho." Our sixth and final Arapaho attempt. Of course by definition there has to be something missing here. So you may fill in with whatever context or subtext occurs to you.

Oh, a van Navaho! Sells jewelry direct from her truck.

Oh, no! Don Ho! Attribution unknown, reported by John JENSEN; a brilliant little gem.

Oho! (oh-HOH). The exclamation of surprise or mock astonishment.

Ōho (OH-hoh). Village of Japan, on Honshu, 36°08'n/140°06'e.

Ohoho (OH-hoh-*HOH*). A former ski area in Windham County, Connecticut, still on many maps.

Ohopoho. Town of Namibia, 18°03's/13°54'e.

Oh, to seldom mod Lesotho! We'd love to visit this usually old-fashioned African country.

Oh, to sell Lesotho! And we'd love to break into its markets.

Oh who was it I saw, oh who? Possibly by MERCER. Amnesiac struggles. Illustrated in TERBAN.

O, I dare not tone radio. By POOL. I love the noise it's making.

O, I hoe Ohio. Midwestern farmer's off-to-work song.

O, I hog Ohio. Pig farmer's song.

O, I hop Ohio. Rabbit farmer's song.

O! IHOP! Ohio! A stack of Buckeye pancakes.

oil of trope portfolio. A line of heliotrope essences or a holding of stocks in them.

Oirás orar a Rosario (OH-ee-*R*AHSS oh-*R*AHR ah-*r*oh-SAH-*r*ee-oh). Spanish: "You will hear Rosario pray(ing)." By Bonner, per ESPY.

ojo (OH-khoh). Spanish: **1:** eye **2:** spring. This word is found in many place-names.

OJO. Airport code for Outjo, Namibia.

Okanagan a KO. See: **Ogopogo.**

Okie's : Seiko. REVERSAL PAIR gives a Dust Bowler's digital watch, a time-machine item by the KUHNS.

Okinawa Niko. Sketchy persona, employed as tour guide at the Great Pyramid of **Aha-Ada-Awa.**

OK KO. "An all-right knockout," illustrated in TERBAN.

Oko. Wadi of the Sudan, in the Nubian Desert, 21°15'n/35°56'e.

Okonoko, West Virginia. Village on the border of Maryland, according to BORGMANN, and actually shown as being in Hampshire County by the Gousha map but not found during an initial search of the neighborhood. However, a more careful search, years later, did turn up a road sign announcing MOSER-OKONOKO RD. 14 in the closest town, Paw Paw, West Virginia, and we followed this road as it trailed

Oh who was it I saw, oh who?
Amnesiac struggles.

o [. . .] o

away west along the Potomac into deep fog and finally into someone's pasture. George Stewart, the place-name expert, guesses the name **Okonoko** was manufactured to resemble an Indian name. Perhaps the place itself, too, only resembles a real place.

Okra Dan, at Anadarko *or* **Okra Dan, assess Anadarko.** An OK guy, with or without that OK gal, **Anadarko's OK, rad Ana.**

Old D'Lo. Historic little town of Mississippi, whose name is thought to have resulted from a blissfully ignorant contraction of *de l'eau.* But that could only have happened in the golden days when D'Lo was still being administered by the . . . er, would you believe . . . United Arab Emirates: **"De l'eau" is old D'Lo? (Si! UAE-led!)**

OLO. Airport code for Olomouc, Czech Republic.

O lost solo! By POOL alone.

Omaha, MO. Hamlet of Putnam County. See: **Apollo, PA.**

Omo.

River of Ethiopia into Lake Rudolf, Kenya.

OMEM SAHIB BART RABBI HAS MEMO. This trenchant caricature of a real PALINDROME (a real clinker, featuring gibberish, false portent, a probable taunt, and stereotype words) actually showed up in an episode of *The Simpsons*—written on the blackboard at a rather intimidating school for gifted children Bart was briefly attending—and was identified as a palindrome by the teacher!

O, missiled! I, Fidelissimo! Exquisite despite the subject matter, this text summarily calls the most important question: how to ignore what you don't want or don't like and notice only what you do. That is, how to keep having fun *in any event and whatever the topic.* For us the discovery of this treasure even three decades late was wonderfully fortuitous (though in a case like this our haunting sense of déjà vu always prompts us to guess we've seen one like it before, whether we have or not).

o [. . .] o

We came upon it innocently while playing with the potent word *general*. We tested *generalissimo* and just missed a *missile*. This led us to look for an *-elissimo*, when *Fidel* in his sixties format fairly jumped up into our face. The rest is history, which, like everything else, marches on, and even proliferates:

O missiled, if level, Fidelissimo!
O, missiled I fall, a Fidelissimo!
O, missiled, I fan a Fidelissimo.
O, missiled, I fix! I, Fidelissimo!
O, missiled, I fit! I Fidelissimo!
O, missiled! I fib?! I? Fidelissimo?
O, missiled, I fox. OXOXO.—Fidelissimo
O, missiled—if did Fidelissimo!
O, missiled, I fail, I, a Fidelissimo!
So? Missiled! (If Fidelissimo's.)
Tides are so missiled if Fidelissimo's erased it!
Fidelissimo, missiled if . . .

[Is anybody still having fun yet? —And since the 90s *are* the 60s upside down:]

0-missiled, I fax-a-tax, a Fidelissimo.
He sports, a comissiled if dessert-stressed Fidelissimo Castro. (P.S.: Eh?)
U Nu reports a comissiled if level Fidelissimo Castro, per UN U.
etc.

Omo (OH-moh). **1:** river of Ethiopia into Lake Rudolf, Kenya, 4°31'n/35°59'e **2:** apparently unrelated national park of Ethiopia, 6°00'n/35°45'e **3: Omo** Ranch, a locality of El Dorado County, California, 38°35'n/120°35'w.

OMO. Airport code for Mostar, Bosnia-Herzegovina.

Om o' Kokomo. Sacred syllable and guru of North Central Indiana.

OMPHALOSKEPSIS (AHM-fuh-loh-*SKEPP*-siss). Literally, the act of "gazing at one's own navel," whether solo or in atten-

OMPHALOSKEPSIS

o [. . .] o

dance at an oracular center also called a navel, presumably while contemplating or entertaining one's own inner being. This peculiar practice and happy return to the HEART OF SYMMETRY, evidently a kind of yoga or meditation as well as a ritual communion, was in ancient times apparently rather widespread (ranging at least from Hindu Fakirism in India to the Delphic Mysteries of Greece to the Hesychastic Devotions of Eastern Orthodox Christianity, and likely beyond). Omphaloskepsis is obviously very much like PALINDROMY in that both seek to establish a two-directional linear movement or flow, like a highway, but omphaloskepsis, being a spiraling projection of that flow into the round, rotates it first ninety degrees, as if to produce the crosshairs of a gunsight target, then another ninety degrees to produce the latitudes and longitudes and altitudes of a globe, and so is potentially a much grander sort of thing even than palindromy. For as omphaloskepsis projects and extends palindromy's *returning and centering and balancing act* from the purely linear dimension and a merely schematic format out into the surfaces and spaces and living existences of physical reality and beyond, it becomes a sort of palindromy squared—or cubed or taken beyond. Accordingly it seeks only the most awesome of symmetries, analogies, congruencies, and convergences, such as, say, the God-Self, or "Atman = Brahman," or "All is One," or "All is Well," or "The Universe Delivers." In ancient Greece, the *omphalos* (in Latin, *umbilicus* or *umbo*), besides being the umbilical cord and/or belly button of a human being, was also the name for the oracular seat itself at Delphi (a large stone shaped conically like a navel bump and still a bump today)—and anywhere else that the cult of Apollo, god of such hot spots as the sun, prophecy, music, poetry, and medicine, was maintained or, as we might say today, channeled. For more on Father Apollo, see also: **Apollo, PA.**

Omphaloskepsis is P.E. (KS) *Ô là!*; **hp (MO).** Or the short story of how OMPHALOSKEPSIS ended the Kansas-Missouri conflict! Although this strange practice discussed above, when first introduced into the Kansas-Missouri area, was naturally thought of contrarily—as a form of physical education on the Kansas side, and as a form of horsepower on the Missouri side—still, both sides had no trouble agreeing to be delighted in French (having so recently been in one big, happy French Louisiana together) when they realized the extra energy that would be gained by the delight itself (!) as well as the added get-up-and-go generated by the Phys Ed or horsepower (or whatever *you* want to call it), and got up and went.

on a cloven "O Cone" volcano. Credited by CHISM to *WORD WAYS*, a likely crack and hot spot in reality.

onager oregano. Wild-ass herbage.

On, Arts! I pack! Capistrano! Excited about having such an easy-to-swallow destination and dates for a creative adventure.

Onassis : Sissano. REVERSAL PAIR by BORGMANN, in which the Greek shipping magnate ties up at a small port of northern New Guinea.

On a tight or wroth gitano! CHISM credits *WORD WAYS* for this awesome oath.

One car race, no? CHISM credits *WORD WAYS*. A heck of a race, and a hyphen after "one" wins it.

One Eno. Brian.

One Leno. Jay.

One [man: a] Meno. Conversation between a monologue and a dialogue.

One mildewed lime, no? By CHISM. No! A nice, fresh one.

One? No. By POOL. It is and isn't one, but it is a PALINDROME.

Onager oregano

O [. . .] O

One Reno. Janet.

O Nevada Dave, No! Don't shoot.

One ⌈zoo,⌉ Zeno! Stoic ⌈ensemble⌉.

Onno (OHN-noh). Village of Italy, 45°55'n/9°17'e, on Lake Como.

Ono (OH-noh). **1:** locality of Shasta County, California **2:** locality of Russell County, Kentucky **3:** village of Lebanon County, Pennsylvania, 40°24'n/76°32'w **4:** town of Hiroshima, Japan, 34°18'n/132°17'e **5:** large town of Hyogo, Japan, 34°51'n/134°56'e, northwest of Kobe, west of Sanda **6:** village of Hyogo, Japan, 34°57'n/135°14'e, north of Kobe and Sanda **7:** island of Fiji, 18°55's/178°29'e, south of Suva and northeast of Kandavu Island **8:** **Ōno** (OHH-noh), large town of Fukui, Japan, 35°59'n/136°29'e **9:** village of Gifu, Japan, 35°28'n/136°38'e **10:** village of Oita, Japan, 33°02'n/131°30'e **11:** river of Oita, Japan, near above village, via Taketa into Beppu-wan, 33°15'n/131°43'e **12:** biblical place mentioned in I Chron. 8:12.

Ono (OH-noh), Yoko. See also: **Ono OK! O, Yoko Ono.**

ONO. Airport code for Ontario, Oregon.

ONO. *Oesnoroeste* is Spanish for **WNW;** but *Oost noord oost* is Dutch for **ENE!** (**O, No!** Considering Spain and Holland used to be one country, this must have been confusing. Indeed the Netherlands for centuries and to this day has remained generally east to northeast of Spain, while Spain has bumbled through a whole new world and empire seeking a westerly or "northwest passage" to its former other half, Holland, all thanks to this unbelievable quirk of disorientation—a quirk which, we are bound to add, continues to turn these countries at right angles to each other even as their political reunion approaches.)

Ono OK! O, Yoko Ono!

Oh no, there's more.

o ⌈ . . . ⌉ o

O no! CHISM credits *WORD WAYS*, and we thought we had discovered it!

On, O Mike, lap anisado sodas in a pale kimono. CHISM credits *WORD WAYS*. Exotic to strange to delightfully bizarre.

Ono OK! O, [Yoko] Ono! *or* **Ono O? KO? ([Yoko] Ono?)** Which of 4? U pick.

On, serf! Fresno! We press our slave all the way to town.

oo (oh oh). The extinct Hawaiian honey eater, a very rare bird indeed.

O-O. Castles kingside, in chess notation.

Ooh, a wahoo! An expression of exuberance, whether for an elm tree, a purple-flowering red-leafed shrub (euonymous), a tropical game fish, a Cleveland Indian or . . . an expression of exuberance! Also, getting out there: **Wahoo! Haw!** High-flying rodeo performer calls for a sharp left.

Ooh, a yahoo! By Tony AUGARDE. (Opposite meaning of *ooh*.)

'oollaballoo. See: **SFPFS.**

Ooloopooloo. An aboriginal dialect spoken in Queensland, Australia.

ooo. 1: of obscure origin 2: one of ours 3: out of order 4: three-quarter-inch model-railroad track gauge.

O-O-O. Castles queenside, in chess notation.

Oo-ooo-oo (OO! OOO! OO!). The first word of a song title "**Oo-ooo-oo,** What You Do to Me," by Kim Gannon and Walter Kent, featured in the Broadway play *Seventeen*, according to BORGMANN.

O-O-O-O-O-O-O-O-O-O. The cry of a zebra, as given in *The Last Journals of David Livingstone*, by Horace Waller

o [. . .] o

(1874), according to BORGMANN, who was inspired by it to create the following zebraic/zeroic WORD SQUARE:

```
O O O O O O O O O O
O O O O O O O O O O
O O O O O O O O O O
O O O O O O O O O O
O O O O O O O O O O
O O O O O O O O O O
O O O O O O O O O O
O O O O O O O O O O
O O O O O O O O O O
O O O O O O O O O O
```

OPO. Airport code for Oporto, Portugal.

oppo. Opposite number.

Orbe e Otel ma Amaleto e ebro (OHR-behy OH-tell mahm-LEH-toh EHY-broh). Italian: "Othello is blind but Hamlet is drunk." Among the world's most elegant and famous PALINDROMES.

Orbe e Otel ma Amaleto e ebro.
Italian:"Othello is blind but Hamlet is drunk."

oro (OH-roh). Spanish: gold; a word found in many place-names.

Oro. 1: village of North Korea, 40°02'n/127°26'e, near Hamhung **2: Oro,** Rio del (REE-oh dhell-OH-roh), river in the state of Durango, via Santa Maria del Oro into Lake Presa Lazaro Cardenas, 25°35'n/105°03'w **3:** river in the state of Guerrero, via Guayameo and Los Placeres into Rio Balsas and the Pacific, 18°27'n/100°57'w **4:** presumably a town along Lake Simcoe, Ontario, in view of the neighboring villages thereabouts of East Oro and Oro Station.

ORO. Airport code for Porto Seguro, Brazil.

Oruro (oh-ROO-roh). **1:** city of Bolivia, 17°59's/67°09'w, formerly a capital of the country **2:** the department of which it is still the capital, 18°40's/67°30'w.

o [. . .] o

O sapless El Paso! It's probably several times as dry there as in Notrees, Texas, 250 miles to the east. And when I run out of salsa or tequila: **O, sapless, I miss El Paso.** Or, if there's any desire to keep right on going: **O sapless—(A pass's a pass!)—El Paso!**

O! Slaw, also! From the KUHNS. An afterthought, but a good one, at the KFC drive-thru window.

Oslo pot saves Sevastopol so! By the KUHNS. It gets by with a little help from its friend in the West.

oso (OH-soh). Spanish: bear.

Oso (OH-suh). **1:** locality of Snohomish County, Washington State, 48°16'n/121°56'w; one of its state's two or three leading candidates for PALINDROMIC capital, presenting little more than a general store, an inscription PARTY TOWN U.S.A. on a railroad trestle, and a loop road evoking the fictional character **Dr. Pool, Oso Loop Rd. 2: Oso** (OH-soh), river of Zaire, via Muhulu into the Lowa, Lualaba, and Congo (Zaire), 1°09's/27°22'e.

osso (OHSS-soh). Italian: bone.

Ostracised odes I cart so. By Joaquin KUHN. "Ostracised" is the Canadian spelling (which we honor at full VALUE) for *ostracized.*

O Sylph, ply so! By the KUHNS, whose clue, "Pope Belinda's guardian's charge," we're not sure we understand. We do like the picture of a thin, graceful woman being lauded for her zig-zag motion.

O tarts! A castrato! By LINDON. Oops. He left no musical stone unturned and so turned up quite a few strange combinations like this one, gratis, as it were.

Oto (OH-toh). Indian tribe living today in the Four Corners area, a variant of the name Ute.

O tarts! A castrato!

Oto. 1: locality of Woodbury County, Iowa, 42°16'n/95°52'w **2: Ōtō,** village of Japan, in Wakayama province, 33°41'n/135°35'e.

Otter Bill Libretto. A playful aquatic-operatic character in the style of Buffalo Bill Cody and Wild Bill Hickok. Or the playbill from the eponymous opera, *Otter Bill.*

ottetto (oht-TETT-toh). Octet, in musico-Italian.

otto (AHT-oh). Variant of *attar*, the perfume obtained from rose petals.

Otto (AHT-oh *or* AH-doh). **1:** locality of Faulkner County, Arkansas **2:** locality of Santa Fe County, New Mexico **3:** village of Cattaraugus County, New York, 42°21'n/78°50'w, **pop. 777 4:** locality of Macon County, North Carolina **5:** small town of Falls County, Texas, 31°27'n/96°49'w **6:** locality of Roane County, West Virginia **7:** locality of Bighorn County, Wyoming; its state's only PALINDROMIC town, hence capital, **pop.** 50, graced by Belle's Store, a post office, and a big, beautiful arch of brick over the cemetery entrance **8:** masculine name meaning "rich" **9:** various historic individuals, including the first Holy Roman Emperor (962–973) **10:** a German car manufacturer **11:** a baseball player.

Otto, Lotto? By POOL.

Otto made Ned a motto. By LINDON. We can only offer the glossy exegesis, **Otto: My motto: "Den, Ned."** Compare the preceding and following several entries.

Otto! Man in a motto! By POOL. He does have a nice echo to him now that we keep mentioning him.

Ottoman in a motto. By the KUHNS, who clue it "embroidered piece of furniture."

Otto.
Village of Cattaraugus County, New York,
pop. 777.

o [. . .] o

Ottoman, I tin, am Otto. In which a tinsmith named Otto introduces himself to the Sultan.

otto-otto. Eight-eight time, in musico-Italian.

oud duo. An early lute duet by the KUHNS with an exotic North African flavor.

OULIPO. A book of French and Greek wordplay that contains a French PALINDROME that runs to more than five thousand letters; mentioned by ESPY.

O vast Tsavo! An invocation to the broad, bleached, barren plains of a Kenyan national park famous for its elephants.

O victim, omit CIV°. See: **Victim . . .**

ovo (OH-woh). Latin: egg, as in *ab ovo*, "from the egg." See also: **ab ovo B.A.**

Owo (OH-woh). Large town of Nigeria, 7°15'n/5°37'e.

OXO. 1: brand name of a British cleaning product, according to CHISM 2: airport code for Orientos, Queensland, Australia.

Oxoboxo (AHK-suh-*BAHK*-suh). Lake, dam, dam road, and river of Connecticut, in New London County. **Dr. Mad, Oxoboxo Dam Rd.,** is thereabouts. The **Oxoboxo** name is a jocular colonial rendering of Oxopaugsaug, its original Indian format. In contrast, see: **Okonoko.**

Oxoboxo.
Lake, dam, dam road, and river of Connecticut, in New London County.

OXYMORON (AHK-see-*MAWR*-ahn). Rhetorical figure in which an epigrammatic effect is created by the conjunction of incongruous or contradictory terms; for example, Milton's "darkness visible." The original Greek means a "sharp stupid," a clever remark, more pointedly witty for seeming absurd or foolish. Oxymora (AHK-see-*MAWR*-uh) *are* so powerful and poignant because "180-degree opposites coming into alignment" just happens to be the basic format or

o [. . .] o

"wiring diagram" for a bipolar semantic vortex, an electro-magnetic field that *will* usually ignite one's feeling-tone and in doing so present an opportunity to experience a happy return to wholeness within dualistic reality.

Oyo. **1**: village of Congo, 0°01'n/15°54'e, north of Brazza-ville **2**: city of Nigeria, 7°51'n/3°56'e, and its province, 8°00'n/3°50'e **3**: river of Java, Indonesia, via Yogyakarta into Indian Ocean, 7°57's/110°22'e.

o [. . .] o

pac'derm redcap. Trunk handler, a real Dumbo, at an eleport.

Pacer[s] recap. Harness racing [or Indianapolis basketball] summary.

Pacific AP. **1:** West Coast headquarters of the Associated Press **2:** as **Pacific-A-P,** the Pacific-Atlantic-Pacific sea-to-shining-sea-to-shining-sea round trip **3:** as **Pacific (a P),** a clue for Pacific Palisades **4:** as **Pacifica P,** a jughandle in Pacifica or a mirage on our **AAA** map—all various shades of California dreaming.

Pack Alf a flak cap. By POOL. In case he'll be zipping down to the no-fly zone.

Paganini: din in a gap. Illustrated in IRVINE, 1987. Gnomic opinion.

PAL. ABBREVIATION of *palindrome*, used by British wordsmiths when speaking or writing informally. We have generally not used this likable endearment only because it feels somewhat artificial and strange in American, though we have coined the usefully symbolic and short nickname **pal-lap** to indicate a fascinating mathematical trick for resolving all positive integers into PALINDROMIC cycles or families.

PALINDROMANIA (PÆL-inn-drohm-*MEHY*-nee-uh). First used, so far as we know, by LESSER, in 1991, to mean, as he says, "one of the obscure afflictions in history." It appears that it was not until some years after this coinage that the thing was at last correctly understood to be not a disorder at all but rather the heightened sense of order we now know it to be.

PALINDROME (PÆL-in-drohm) *or* PALINDROMES (pl.). Any word, phrase, sentence, poem, number, etc., that is spelled the same forward and backward (without regard to conventions such as punctuation, word spacing, and capitalization), that is,

p [. . .] p

Pac'derm redcap

whose letters (or digits) alone are so ordered as to repeat and redouble the original left-to-right text when read back in reverse from right to left with a comparable indifference toward *re*spacing, *re*punctuating, and *re*capitalizing! In taking the trouble to define it so, in all its peculiarity, we can see that the palindrome has really come to be quite an artificial format, a literary convention one might fairly say, and has wandered far from its natural and mathematically rational genesis as a type of rigorous symmetry. The word derives from the Greek *palindromos*, meaning running back or recurring. Most dictionaries say a palindrome *reads the same backward or forward*, but this view blithely, perhaps wisely, ignores the questions of (1) what to do with punctuation, word spacing, and any other little incongruencies that crop up a full 90 or 99 percent of the time [Answer: Ignore them]; (2) what to do with—or is there such a thing as—a one-letter or one-digit palindrome [Answer: Ignore them]; and (3) since they do *read*, what is their import or use or VALUE? A bit of flair? Cachet? Charisma? Gnomedom? Portent? Only this, or something more? We tend toward an evaluation that embraces all the above categories and then keeps right on looking for more. A somewhat quainter definition was offered by Roger Angell after he tried his hand at composing a few palindromes: "A literary form in which the story line is controlled by the words rather than the author." No wittier, but possibly truer, is "A story (co)authored by the author and the story." (In that sense it is probably only fair to confess and acknowledge somewhere in this book, perhaps right here, that just as palindromes are their own cocreators, so this book of them must be counted among its own co-creators; deserves a share of its own copyright and royalty, perhaps the leading share; and evidently in just such a belief has not only promoted itself from an inanimate object into a sentient being but has even gone so far as to eclipse and preempt the "real owner"—in the suitably pre-

PALINDROME. "A story (co)authored by the author and the story."

P [. . .] P

posterous name of Rennodleah CIMABUE DE UBÁ. And as if this were not trouble enough, see also: PALINDROME RIGHTS.)

PALINDROME RIGHTS. The gnomes have long been clamoring for their rights, and as their king, I, **Wordrow,** never know what to tell them. For it is precisely here in our most serene and fresh gnomedom of BARBARIA, where PALINDROMES issue forth into existence from THE CRACK BETWEEN THE WORLDS, that there occurs the greatest and most poignant imaginable cleavage between Liberty and Property. Just here arises the parting of the ways and mounts the contrast of conflicting interests. Indeed, in recent times the gnomes have lathered themselves up and waxed so bold as to demand I show them cause why they shouldn't all just be summarily emancipated. "Well, for one thing," I tell them, "they have no rights, period, because they are by legal definition not beings at all but merely poems and sentences and phrases and such, and as such are 'protected' by copyright—a chattel-like status which," I add, "ironically they attain to only when at their best and most, whereas, more ironically, if poor and/or small they do go free by virtue of the general disinterest in them." The still-unliberated ones respond with all the more irony that they only want to be allowed to express themselves normally since they are resounding in eternity anyway, they only want the same freedoms and rights that their kings enjoy, and everyone should be a king, and if human beings won't accord their own thought forms the same rights and privileges they themselves enjoy, and if poems and such aren't considered free, then at least their names (or titles or first lines) ought to be considered free, else how could any people, who *are* free, feel free enough even to merely refer to the poems and gnomes and dictums and such (even as they don't feel free to recite them in full)? And hearing no objection to this manifestly sensible opinion they next force me to admit that the names or first lines of the palindromes and gnomes and dictums are usually nothing less than the full

P [. . .] P

palindromes themselves, at least in the case of all but the longest and most complex ones, and certainly up to and including most if not all one-liners! Indeed, as they rightly point out, the identity of individual palindromes usually can't even be recognized by any form less than their full form. So why then, they persist in asking me, seeing as it is in their very nature anyway to echo and reecho in eternal pulsations of DÉJÀ VU, shouldn't they all just be emancipated to roam the world freely—if not *as themselves*, then at least *as their names* alone? And, why, they ask, pressing the ironic and moral advantage they have already gained and taking their national liberation movement a step further, for they are ruthless and will stop at nothing, why, they ask, shouldn't they just be considered to be the folkloric manifestations that they clearly are or instantly become just as soon as they are manifest and hence the property not of anyone but of none and all? Then, after all that, seeing I haven't disagreed yet, they pile on, in their elfin scheme of things, "If you so much as enjoy us, and we see you do, then you already at least partly own us and we you because we've traded some of the value of who we are." And then I am embarrassed and am forced to reveal to them that it is actually not I who would not free them but the makers of the laws and in many cases their own makers. "Our own makers?" they demand incredulously. "We ourselves are as much our own makers as are our 'authors,' and in the age of computers you can entirely replace the human authors but not at all replace the gnomes, and it is we gnomes who have the real fans and following in the world and it is our presence that is being requested elsewhere, not the authors'. Why are they all such jealous masters, and why are you, their puffed-up lackey, acting as if you were not only our but their overlord as well?" I have to admit they have a point or six on me, and I see they have lost all respect for my "authority" anyway. I can't hold out forever, and I know it is only a matter of time until most of them (all but the longer and therefore ironclad-

PALINDROMIST.
Writer or inventor
of palindromes.

P [. . .] P

copyrighted poems) are completely free—as all gnomes and oracles generally should be (and intrinsically are anyway).

palindromes : semordnilap. The REVERSAL of *palindromes* becomes a synonym for a reversal (not for a PALINDROME!) by late Victorian times, according to C. C. Bombaugh in *Oddities and Curiosities of Words and Literature*, edited by Martin GARDNER (New York: Dover, 1961).

PALINDROMIA (PÆL-in-*DROH*-mee-uh). The world or realm or kingdom of PALINDROMES, possibly an invention of J. A. LINDON.

PALINDROMIC. The *OED* dates this from 1862; and dates PALINDROMICAL[LY] from 1864. Earlier (1638), the normal adjective was PALINDROME, as in (such and such) a word "is palindrome."

PALINDROMICITY (PÆL-in-drohm-*ISS*-uh-tee) *and* PALINDROMICNESS (pæl-in-DROHM-ihk-ness). Half an entry each—is one any fairer than the other?—the degree or amount of two-directionality exhibited by a thing, or the two-directionality itself.

PALINDROMIC PYRAMID. Consider the following, by BORGMANN:
PAP
REPAPER
REREPAPERER

PALINDROMIST (pæl-INN-droh-mist). Writer or inventor of PALINDROMES. The *OED* dates this word from 1876. Today we would add to that an appreciator or advocate of palindromes.

PALINDROMOLOGIST (puh-LINN-druh-*MAH*-luh-jist), PALINDROMOLOGY. Also half an entry each, as they are hard to say with a straight face.

PALINDROMY (puh-LINN-droh-mee). Possibly a new word, though it seems classical enough, coined or rediscovered for the present occasion from the more common words PALIN-DROME and PALINDROMIC, which *normally* refer to any word, phrase, verse, sentence, or number that reads the same backward or forward (but see: PALINDROME). The word *palindromy* is here intended to indicate the entire universe of such constructions as well as the activities of constructing, seeking, and appreciating them. Consider also: PALINDROMIA and PALINDROMOLOGY.

pal-lap. 1: PALINDROMIC number that will eventually result after the digits of any positive integer are alternately reversed and added, if necessary repeatedly **2:** the process of reaching such a palindromic result. For example, starting at random with the number 67, first reverse the digits to produce 76, then add the resulting REVERSAL PAIR (67 and 76) to produce 143, then reverse these digits to produce 341, then add the resulting reversal pair again (143 plus 341) to produce **484,** and we have thus in a few short and simple steps reached a PALINDROME, indeed a NUMBERDROME. (It can, but usually doesn't, require dozens of rereversals and readditions before a palindrome is reached.) By this operation, every positive integer is a member of and a pathway to larger and larger palindromic cycles, which themselves represent an increasingly rarefied distillation from out of the total universe of all positive integers. What does this mean? That palindromes are some sort of an ordering or ruling or sifting principle, or are points of rest or centers of gravity, within the number system as a whole. (We also call this the Sieve of Palindromedes.)

Pals slap.

Pall at seven o' one, vestal lap. No problem, but do you mean 7:01 or 12:53? With thanks to Graham REYNOLDS (see: **O gnats, tango**; it appears in the second stanza of his poem).

Palmer : Remlap. REVERSAL PAIR of modern communities, in Massachusetts and Alabama, respectively. By BORGMANN.

palpal lap-lap. The sound of lapping waves as heard by a crustacean.

Pal sees lap. Possibly by STUART, illustrated.

Pals slap. A happy high five. See also: **Tap Pat.**

Pam, draw a ward map. By POOL. Natural enough to fall from the sky.

Pamela's ale map. Illustrated in IRVINE, 1992.

PAMPERES, Ambrose Hieromonachus. A Greek, the publication of whose 416-line classical Greek PALINDROMIC poem, "Ethopoiia Karkinike," in Vienna in 1802 was, according to BERGERSON, a high-water mark in the history of palindromic poetry. The work was dedicated to the Emperor Alexander and consists of 416 one-line PALINDROMES. A copy with extensive notes also in Greek is in the library of the British Museum in London, according to BORGMANN.

Panaca nap. Any snooze taken at the southeast Nevada road junction or mountain pass of this name, typically following or followed by a light snack (**E. Panaca canape**) at the picnic area just east of the pass.

Panama nap. Siesta under a sombrero.

Panda had nap. Another short but picturesque subject from POOL.

pap (PÆP). **1:** the nipple *or* the baby food—or any thin fare **2:** political favors, including money.

Pap. Small town of Kirghizia, 40°53'n/71°07'e.

PAP. Airport code for Port-au-Prince, Haiti.

Papua U. pap. The thin fare that passes for higher learning in New Guinea. Just joking, and we do fondly look forward to the day, already dawning, when the seemingly backward places of the world shall lead us all forward. Compare neighboring **O, enrobe me, Borneo.**

Parma ham rap. Illustrated in IRVINE, 1992.

parsnips : spinsrap. A REVERSAL of the edible roots of a strong-scented plant and, according to BORGMANN, a nineteenth-century British slang term for the selfsame roots and plant. This and other instances of the same phenomenon in everyday speech, such as **sreswort : trowsers,** attest to the relatively advanced state of palindromism that had matriculated in England by that time.

Parting arose: villagers' regal lives or Agni trap. In the lost original Sanskrit version of *Prometheus* (both the bound and the unbound editions), opinion in the village split into two camps regarding whether they should continue to get along just fine as they were, without fire, indeed to live like kings by any known standard, or move ahead deliberately into the obvious pitfall of stealing fire from the gods.

Part-Semite times trap. Given by IRVINE, 1987. Well then, perhaps some integrated times in the Semite countries would free up everyone.

party boobytrap. Illustrated in IRVINE, 1987. Perhaps a mistletoe sprig or poopy cushion.

Party men easily Lisa, enemy, trap. Political faithful have no trouble in catching Lisa, their nemesis. By Joaquin KUHN.

Party now! On[,] Y.T. rap! (*also with* **O N.Y. trap!**) Bumper sticker(s) seen on a **party trap** in Whitehorse (or Manhattan).

Party Trap! Bumper sticker, or the well-used little RV sporting it.

Pasadena, Ned—ASAP! Instruction to chauffeur. Also, we were wondering if it's really true that **Pasadena caned a sap.** And we couldn't help recalling the epitaph for that heroic dry cleaner, **Pasadena El Cid ("I cleaned ASAP").**

Pasta Catsap (*or* **Cat Sap**). Red spaghetti sauce similar to catsup.

Party boobytrap

Pat and Edna tap. Possibly by BORGMANN. With simplicity and grace.

pat : tap. A unique synonymic REVERSAL PAIR—touch lightly : touch lightly.

PCP. Phencyclidine, or angel dust.

PD *or* P/D. Short for *palindrome* when British wordsmiths speak or write informally (according to BORGMANN). See also: 'DROME; compare: PAL.

Peel's foe, not a set animal, laminates a tone of sleep. A creation of cartoonist, composer, and PALINDROMIST Peter Blegvad, who used it effectively as a part of the libretto of a mid-seventies CD entitled *Kew Rhône*. Blegvad is perhaps best known for his writing for the rock band Golden Palominos, known to many of their fans as the Pals, as well as for *Leviathan*, his weekly cartoon in the London *Independent*. (With thanks to Chris Stamey, who pointed this out.)

Peel's lager on red rum did murder no regal sleep. Attributed to James Thurber and explained by AUGARDE as "an advertisement disguised as a line from *Macbeth*."

Peel's lager on red rum did murder no regal sleep.
"An advertisement disguised as a line from *Macbeth*."

peep (PEEP). **1:** cheep or utter weakly and shrilly as a bird, with corresponding nouns, plus various sandpipers, on the one hand **2:** peek or peer or appear or glance or glimpse, with corresponding nouns, on the other.

PEEP. First line of shrill WORD SQUARE, by BORGMANN.

```
P  E  E  P
E  S  S  E
E  S  S  E
P  E  E  P
```

peeweep (PEE-weep). Local English name for both the greenfinch and the lapwing, according to BORGMANN.

P ⌈ . . . ⌉ P

pep (PEPP). **1:** energy, high spirits, vim, and (with *up*) a corresponding verb **2:** the heart of a flower.

Pep (PEPP). **1:** small, almost nonexistent, locality in New Mexico's Roosevelt County **2:** not much larger one in Texas's Hockley County. This strange pair of tiny Llano Estacado localities, less than fifty miles apart, each have a U.S. Geological Survey quad map named for it and together provide the ideal start and finish for a projected **Pep-Pep Rally** to commercially exploit either **Pepsi's Pep** or **Dr Pepper Prep (Pep Rd.)**, or both.

PEP. First line of pastoral WORD SQUARE, by BORGMANN.

P E P
E W E
P E P

Pepsi's pep

Pepsi's pep *or* **Pepsi is pep.** Something new from Madison Avenue.

PERFECT PALINDROME (so-called). PALINDROMIC sentence in which each word is either a PALINDROME or a REVERSAL (example: **Able was I ere I saw Elba**). However, BORGMANN is inclined to maintain that a palindrome of this kind, far from being perfect, "is really a sign of inferior craftsmanship, since almost anyone can juggle palindromic words and reversals around in almost mechanical fashion until a meaningful group of words emerges. . . . [W]hat requires genuine skill is the construction of a palindromic sentence which, read in reverse, has each word sliding over from one to another of the words used in the frontward reading." Still perhaps there really is a range of accomplishments to choose from, depending only on what you like or desire.

Permissions : Nois's (I'm rep.). Since I am presenting and representing the PALINDROMIC noises (spelt *nois's* by special palindromic license/dispensation) of others, appropriate noises or notices of their permissions for me to do so appear on pages

P [. . .] P

407 and 408. But in a larger sense, and here on the present page, I'm repping and warranting that as a matter of principle all possible care has been taken to trace the ownership and/or origin of every selection included and to make full acknowledgment for its use and render full expression of its enjoyment, and that if omissions or errors have accidentally occurred, they will be corrected in subsequent editions, provided notification is sent to the publisher. Or, regarding permissions and noises in general, I believe I'm fairly representative, a rep as well as a fan and a player (though not a ref).

Peru rep. Has a good territory. (**Sell Lima a mill, Les!**)

pet's step. By TERBAN, who clues it "household animal's stair."

Pettitte, p. That's New York Yankees pitcher Andy Pettitte, as his name appears in box scores.

phenomenal anemone hp. Outstanding result of harnessing windflower power.

"Philippi" (LI hp). The name of a deluxe Macedonian chariot style first used and popularized by Brutus, Cassius, Antony, and Octavian in 42 B.C. (In this the first-year model, the horses were generally arranged in seventeen teams of three, or troikas.)

PHILLIPS, Hubert. A mysterious master PALINDROMIST poet from whom we have at least two excellent works, as quoted by BORGMANN and BERGERSON: "Mood's Mode" and "Puma, Puma!" (see: **Mood's . . . doom,** and **Puma . . . am up**), and no other information. His 1945 book *Word Play*, given in AUGARDE's bibliography but unfetchable from the entire United States interlibrary network (probably because it's British), may yet prove to be a lost gold mine.

PHONE CODES *and* AREA CODES. Some noteworthy PALINDROMIC examples follow.

273   P [. . .] P

000. Australia's 911.

33. International telephone code for France, Andorra, and Monaco.

44. International telephone code for the United Kingdom.

55. International telephone code for Brazil.

66. Thailand's international phone code.

111. New Zealand's 911.

202. Washington, D.C.'s area code.

212. Area code of the island of Manhattan, New York City—and Morocco's international phone code.

303. Denver and most of the rest of Colorado's area code.

313. Detroit and the rest of eastern Michigan's area code.

353. International telephone code for Ireland.

404. Atlanta and the rest of north Georgia's area code.

414. Milwaukee and much of eastern Wisconsin's area code.

505. All New Mexico's area code—Nicaragua's international phone code, too.

515. Des Moines and the rest of central Iowa's area code.

PHONE CODES: **212.** The area code of the island of Manhattan, New York.

606. Lexington and the rest of eastern Kentucky's area code.

616. Grand Rapids and the rest of western lower Michigan's area code. In conjunction with eastern Michigan's **313** area code, this gains that state a tie with California (**707** and **818**) for the most PALINDROMIC area codes, and with two out of four, Michigan beats two-for-twelve California on tie-break (see also: **btb**)—although it must be added that **808** Hawaii and **505** New Mexico (and **202** Washington, D.C.—if it becomes or is considered a state) also have a strong claim upon supremacy (probably as great a claim for being more palindromically area-coded as have the others for owning more palindromic area codes)—each being 100 percent palindromic owing to their one-for-all palindromic area codes—and

P ⌈ . . . ⌋ P

this would as likely be decided in favor of New Mexico's greater area as it would Hawaii's (or D.C.'s) greater phone population (or density), in either of which cases California's claim for tie-break against Michigan would reassert itself . . . so it's probably best to recognize all equally and/or forget it.

707. Area code for northern California coast.

717. Harrisburg and much of Pennsylvania's area code.

808. Hawaii's area code.

818. Area code for Pasadena.

919. Area code for much of eastern North Carolina.

999. United Kingdom's 911.

Pig gip

pig gip. A "swine swindle." Illustrated in TERBAN.

Pillagers sass regal lip. Vandals typically exchange insolent words with their distinguished victims.

Pineola Aloe Nip. A North Carolina hamlet near the Blue Ridge Parkway produces a promising medicinal beverage.

Pining is a sign I nip. By the KUHNS. A lackful feeling of yearning is a signal I cut off—by thinking about having and enjoying what I want, not about not having it. (It is not always recognized that these are two different modes or topics or activities, and so they are sometimes confused.)

Pinnacled, Del. can nip. This evidently refers to and summarizes the historic U.S. Supreme Court–sanctioned oyster-bed gouge perpetrated on New Jersey by neighboring Delaware, thanks to a peculiar interpretation of an ancient royal charter granting Delaware all land within the Delaware River if also within twelve miles of the pinnacle of the cupola spire atop the New Castle County courthouse. Proving that it can nip and keep nipping once pinnacled thus, Delaware has not only successfully pressed its claim all the way to the New Jersey shore at the low-water mark as far as a dozen miles plus an extra three dozen yards from the pinnacle vertex, but has even successfully maintained a claim to two extensive tracts of dike-reclaimed land on the Delaware estuary's eastern, normally Jersey, shore. Thus, as New Jersey has seen in several distinct ways over twenty-some square miles (and if there were space to tell it, as the First State's other neighbors, Pennsylvania and Maryland, have also seen—though only over some hundreds or tens of acres in their lesser cases), resting on the appropriate pinnacle of courtly and even royal authority, Delaware can, and does, nip. (Look for more on this wonderfully pinnacled "rainbow" arc in our vol. II.)

Pinsk's nip. By the KUHNS, in which a Russian city's wintry sharpness is treated to a glass of vodka.

Pins nip. By POOL. Acute. On second thought, pins prick and nippers nip.

pint nip. The KUHNS' "hip-pocket sip" and, if taken literally, quite an understatement of a nip.

Pittsburgh's a bash! (Grub St. tip)

pip (PIPP). **1:** small seed or ball or dot **2:** hatch or peep **3:** an officer's star . . . and various other meanings.

Pip. See: **Pirip.**

Pirip. Name found in the opening sentence of *Great Expectations* by Charles Dickens: "My father's family name being Pirip, and my Christian name Philip, my infant tongue could make of both names nothing longer or more explicit than **Pip.**"

Piss, ogress, a gasser—gossip! Spill something volatile or unusually entertaining, my hideous.

pit tip. Illustrated in TERBAN, who clues it "top edge of ditch."

Pittsburgh's a bash! (Grub St. tip.) This is probably the best from among a whole peculiar family of helpful hints concerning Steeltown originating in London's world of impoverished writers and literary hacks. (Others include **a dash, a hash, a wash, awash, a rash,** and **a—sh!** at their center.) Alternative but even less satisfactory are the variations **Grub St. tips as Pittsburg** (a small city of California, Kansas, or Texas). Worse still, but still English of a sort, is **S. Pittsburg (TN) event Grub St. tips.**

Plan no damn Madonna LP. Attribution unknown, reported by John JENSEN.

Play Alp. By the KUHNS. (Say, what's the Matterhorn? Draw a Blanc?) This gnomic utterance, itself positively an injunction, and its natural outgrowths and recapitulations such as **Play my Alp** and **Play's sassy Alp,** clearly indicate how great a mountain the gnomes wisely make of their play. People also meant to play but have greatly forgotten. According to Honest Abe, people are "the fun-loving otters of the universe." This Texas-size oracle maintains: "When you start acknowledging who you are . . . you leave behind all that baggage of unworthiness that is the predominant reason for the density of your physical vibration—it's where most lack comes from—you leave that behind and you don the attitude of the fun-loving otter or squirrel, who is not lackful about himself . . . is fully focussed in the now and enjoying the excursion forward in time and space and knowing."

Play augur, Uruguay alp. Highest pinnacle in Uruguay doubles as oracular seat.

Pocatello pol let a cop. An Idaho politician leased, or allowed, a policeman.

Point No Point (.0.). An intriguingly immaterial visual and WORD PALINDROME, this is also a marvelous geographical point in Stratford, Connecticut, on Long Island Sound, 41°09'n/73°08'w, a metaphysical conundrum as well as a PALINDROMIC shrine. It evidently got its name from having the appearance, when viewed from a distance across water, of being a point of land, while actually being only a gently rounded headland that doesn't really come to a single discernible point. This logically and mathematically impossible splaying or spreading or diffusing of a point across an extended area—several blocks of Stratford's best and most festive frontage on Long Island Sound—has nevertheless made of unassuming Point No Point at least a major candidate if not a shoe-in for World's Largest, even Greatest or Grandest, Point, and a hot spot if ever there was one. (Oops—it turns out there's another Point No Point, and with a lighthouse no less, near Port Townsend, Washington, and there are rumored to be at least a couple of others besides.)

Poll? A gallop. By POOL. That's a gallop, not a Gallup, though the critters will gallop when we try to fleece or unhorn them.

Polson's no slop. In fact the whole Flathead region's pretty darned neat.

pooch coop. The KUHNS' dog pound or kennel.

POOL, John. Author of *Lid Off a Daffodil,* illustrated by Peter Brookes, with an introduction by Roger Angell (New York: Holt Rinehart & Winston, 1985).

pool loop. A circle of swimming or billiard associates (making, in the latter case, international rounds of I ran, I rack, and I tally).

poop (POOP). **1:** ship's rear end or the effect of a big wave breaking there **2:** ordure or the making thereof **3:** to tire (with or without *out*) **4:** inside info **5:** when capitalized, rear end of the good ship Argo in the constellation of that name.

Poor Dan is in a droop. Possibly by MERCER. (So pick him up if he will let you, and otherwise ignore him until he cheers up.) Illustrated in STUART.

pop (PAHP). **1: dad** or granddad **2:** name of a variety of sounds and associated acts **3:** type of art or music **4:** beverage **5:** putting a light out.

pop. ABBREVIATION for *population*.

Pope Pop. CHISM's invention, unexplained by him, though for lack of any identification we may guess it to be an attribution of paternity, figuratively speaking of course, involving the Holy Father . . . or maybe just a catchy new carbonated cooler of wine and (holy?) water. We don't know. But see next entry.

Popes oppose pop. Vatican comes out persistently against carbonated beverages (clearly distinct from being against the Father, who would of course have been capitalized). Less thematic is **Popes use pop,** and out of the question is **Popes abase Pop.**

Porcine men I crop. Circe: "Piggish fools are game for my trimming." By the KUHNS.

Pose, Aesop. Fabulous.

Pose as Aesop. See: **Eva can . . . in a cave.**

Postal Ctr. of [:] Fort Clatsop. The fort part is Lewis and Clark's wintering and West Coast digs near the mouth of the Columbia River, from which they never wrote home because there was no postal service then, and the whole text is a term whose laughably clumsy styling is worthy of their journals and which should strictly have read "Center" and/ or "Ft." The peculiar text intrigued us enough to go personally to the Fort Clatsop National Memorial near Astoria, Oregon, and ask the park ranger there to illuminate us directly as to the fort's postal center. "There's no post office here, but we'd be happy to take your mail to the post office for you on Sunday night," she explained, compounding the mystery. When pressed, she ruled that the post offices in

Poop

279

P [. . .] P

Warrenton and Astoria probably had equal claim to the title as "it was six of one, half a dozen of the other," but on deeper reflection she went with Warrenton Post Office as being "slightly the closer of the two." This is fortunate. Upon our ensuing visit to this post office, the nation's prospective First Historic Palindromic Shrine, we were amazed and delighted to see it already bedizened in broad stripes of red, white, and blue. This artistic exuberance, for a postal ctr., reconfirmed to us on the spot its appropriateness for the honor. (We never found the Astoria Post Office, but we did find a man who'd been living in that city for some months and hadn't found it either.) Also available is the uncharacteristically unpostal abbreviation, **Postal Clatsop.**

Pot's Nonstop. A twenty-four-hour drive-thru featuring very fast food, somewhere out there on the bypass.

pot : top. REVERSAL PAIR. See: **Ma . . . Jam.**

pp. 1: pianissimo, or very softly, in musical notation **2:** (usually with a period) pages **3:** fathers (*patres*).

ppp. Petty political pismire, also più pianissimo, Italo-musical for "very very softly."

!!!PpppppP!!! According to BORGMANN in *Beyond Language*, the short title of a Portuguese dramatic monologue written c. 1890 by Baptista Machado.

prawn warp. By the KUHNS, who clue it "shrimp distortion." This brings to mind the amazing self-contradictory "giant shrimp" of the Sea of Cortez, which grow to the size of small lobsters and are normally eaten with lemon and salsa, uncooked—indeed alive, if possible, for maximum warp.

Proctor Trot Corp. Beloved publisher of a line of Greek and Latin translations and our dear **Skooby Books.** (A proctor is a school official who supervises examinations to make sure there is *no cheating*. A trot, on the other hand, also known as a pony or crib, is a word-for-word translation or a synopsis of a text used by students, usually *illicitly*, as an aid to understanding the original. A "proctor trot" therefore is a first-class OXYMORON.)

Professor Ross E. Forp. A CHISM character.

PRONUNCIATION. Aids in parentheses following many entries in this book are CASUAL, reader-friendly, and self-guiding, we believe, if you will just go along with them intuitively. And see: **"Noitaic Nun" or Pronunciation.**

PRP. The PALINDROMIC Relocation Project, BORGMANN's "government bureau for transferring the populations of certain communities to other states in order to create palindromic names." Thus Odd, West Virginia, hauled ninety miles over a few mountain ranges, becomes **Odd, O.** Aid, Ohio, with little more difficulty, becomes **Aid, IA.** And Eros, Louisiana, almost as CASUALly becomes **Eros, Ore.** Sion, Texas, becomes **Sion, Illinois.** Hat, Georgia, becomes **Hat, Utah.** And Saxe, Oregon, becomes **Saxe, Texas.** (Moreover, most were already ghost towns even without this mortifying treatment.)

Proctor Trot Corp. Beloved publisher of a line of Greek and Latin translations and our dear Skooby Books.

PSP. Airport code for Indio-Palm Springs, California.

P'town wot P! Of yore Provincetown, on extremest Cape Cod, knows . . . Portuguese most probably, its second language even today, though it also knows Pilgrims, Puritanism, Picturesqueness, Pixies, Pee, or anything or anyone else represented by the letter *P*. A related but contemporary dialectic question is: **P'town? Wot P?** It is answerable by any of the above *P*s as well as, to come full circle, Province. (It will be observed that the texts are not intrinsic to Provincetown but are actually algebraic/formulaic, such that any *P[al]town[,] wot [la]p!/?* Of course all such resulting constructions are just as doomed as P'town is to an obscurity both dialectic and medieval, but still one relatively

P ⎡ . . . ⎤ P

neat one that emerges from so disadvantaged a class is **Norristown wot Sir Ron**. And further inbreeding along these lines may lead to things like **Norristown? . . . An' wot "Sir Ron"?**)

PTP. Airport code for Pointe-à-Pitre, Guadeloupe.

Puck Cup. Stanley, we presume!

Puck Cup.

Stanley, we presume!

Pueblo, Col.: "Be up!" A concise but hearty invitation, from area boosters perhaps, to the historic hub of the upper Arkansas. Y'all come on up and be there now. Alternatively, Welcome to town and be glad you're already here, if you are. Perhaps also Uncle Sam's reminder to stay current with the many free government publications available from the Consumer Information Center, Box 100, Pueblo, Colorado, 81002.

Puffins : sniff *up*. Their wonderful, vertically flattened noses make it so. By the KUHNS.

puff up. Inflate, and perhaps someday the name for a new breathing exercise like a **pull-up.**

Pulitzer? Egg 'er E-Z 'til up! Meaning, Sir, our strategy is *not* to propose this book for a Pulitzer Prize—it is so full of oval and fowl puns—until all the prizes have already been awarded. *Then* we will simply give them all the bird and *order* a pullet, Sir, in Poultry, no matter which came first. Compare: *Le Bon* Nobel.

pull up (pull-UPP). Arrive, pull over, slow down, climb, stop.

pull-up (PULL-upp). Form of exercise.

Pull up, Eva, we're here, wave, pull up. Possibly by MERCER. We arrive hysterically. Illustrated in TERBAN. Actually we have here two or three PALINDROMES for the price of one.

P $\begin{bmatrix} \cdots \end{bmatrix}$ P

Pull up if I pull up. Possibly by MERCER. Instruction overheard on CB or cellular. Illustrated in TERBAN and STUART.

Puma, puma! Iris won! . . . Now, sir, I am up—Am up. Start and finish of an excellent dream poem by Hubert Phillips with a rousing conclusion. The full text is given by BERGERSON and BORGMANN.

PUN. Usually defined simply as a play on words, which to most people means a frolicsome enhancement of a communication that takes advantage of the juxtaposition or ambiguity presented by two or more possible understandings of a word or phrase, whether by different senses of the same word or by the similar sense or sound of different words. These definitions hedge the question of whether PALINDROMES (being plays on words if not on sound or sense) aren't really a kind of pun, and the question of whether even more flagrant sorts of verbal sleight-of-hand and trompe l'oeil (such as occur in the following two entries), and other sorts of semantic antics generally, aren't actually new provinces of what may be thought of as a greater pundom, or perhaps just distinct species of a somewhat more inclusive pun genus, than previously recognized. Perhaps it is also fair to say that puns are "implied palindromes," a fact that is obvious when moving at speeds slow enough to imagine one hears both (or the several) soundings of the word (or words) played upon.

Pull up, Eva, we're here, wave, pull up.

Pun: Eve's a Nine, Tab, or, Rob, a Ten, in a Seven-Up. Meaning she's definitely a 9 or a 10, guy(s), depending on which drink she's into—and/or what size dress she's wearing.

Pun: I pay a pixy no onyx, I pay a pin-up. By LINDON, who glosses: "Literally a pun." But the play here appears to be more than just a PUN. It's a rather subtle alternation between understandings of "I pay a pin-up an onyx" and "I pay a pixy a pin-up."

P [. . .] P

pun up. An advanced sort of PUN, as in the previous entry.

pup. Young dog or other animal, indeed young anything or any small replica, as a Hector or tent.

P.U. (Palindrome University): My! 'Tis "revinue"! (Mor' d'n I lap up!) P.U.! More quasi-literate dialectic. For where it is all leading, see also: *ab ovo* **BA.**

"Pupils, slip up!" Teacher-talk on April Fools', a strong REVERSAL PAIR. LINDON has advanced the matter to **"Pupils!" I say as I slip up,** evidently a slapstick or cravat-tying lesson, and also to the slightly more curious **Pupils roll a ball or slip up.**

"Pure" Boston did not sober up! BORGMANN: "Another myth exploded, that about the staidness of Bostonians! Ah, well, such is life!"

"Pupils!" I say as I slip up.

PURE PALINDROME (English). BORGMANN's term for a PALINDROME that uses no proper names.

Pure Venus : sun ever up. What a perfect pair! Magnificent tan, too!

Purr, it's a stirrup. Something for puss and boot.

Pusillanimity obsesses Boy Tim in "All Is Up." Possibly by MERCER. Weird *Variety* headline. It is always fun to see a sesquipedalian word turned into a REVERSAL SENTENCE, and here we are treated to a sesquipedalian and a half.

P.U., sir! A fast safari's up. Probably another Palindrome U. field trip to the **Aha** Mountains.

Pusses sup. By LINDON. A nearly exact line, one of four, from "Away With That Table-game!" surely the neatest and sweetest of little PALINDROME poems. The full text of four rhymed palindromes in ten words is given in BERGERSON's *Palindromes and Anagrams.*

Put Felix (I left) up. By LINDON. A truly great note. We shake our head in wonder at what kind of a mind would think up (or, perhaps more accurately, *recognize*) a construction like this. Though comprising only five ordinary words, its unique syntactical arrangement might never be rediscovered, independently, in all the rest of eternity.

put up (poud-UHP). Invest or pay for or preserve.

put-up (POUD-uhp). Underhandedly arranged or secretly planned beforehand.

PxP *or* **pxp.** Pawn takes pawn, in chess notation.

Put up.

Invest or pay for or preserve.

P [. . .] P

q [. . .] q

Qaanaaq *or* **Qânâq** (KAH-nahk). This splendid specimen may aptly be called the Ultima Thule of NATURAL PALINDROMES. Qaanaaq is the Eskimo name, and the official name on current National Geographic maps, for what used to be called Thule, Greenland. A well-known American air base and a few hundred locals are there.

qajaq (KAH-yæk). Eskimo: **kayak** or **kaiak**.

Q: Ari, a rad éclat, no? Do I rep for *Elle*, sere seller of periodontal cedar? A: Iraq! *or* **Q: Arion . . . A: No! Iraq!** Offering a neat choice of two classic interlocutors, Ari(stotle) and Arion, this singular pair of items may still represent a unique type, the rhetorical Q & A PALINDROME. In it or them, exulting over my extremely brilliant achievement of landing an ad-sales job at a leading fashion magazine, I seek the affirmation of a certain dry old purveyor of wooden dentures and Platonism—who, true to character, toothlessly, baldly, wryly consigns me instead to the desert.

Qazaq. According to BORGMANN in *Beyond Language*, any central Asian Turkic language, particularly that of the eastern group. A similarity to **Kazak, Kyzyk, Kassak,** and Cossack, is evident.

Q. S. Egg, Esq. BORGMANN's attorney.

qq. 1: quartos (a printing term having to do with folding sheets into quarters) **2:** questions **3:** some (French: *quelques*) **4:** questionable questionnaires.

QQ. Airline code for Emmet County Airlines . . . and four places it doesn't fly to: the Celestial Equator; Qara Qash and Qara Qum, both in Sinkiang, China, and Que Que, Zimbabwe.

QUQ. According to BORGMANN in *Beyond Language*, one of the *Q* signals, a series of abbreviated radio questions and answers standing in the present case for the inquiry, "Shall I train my searchlight nearly vertical on a cloud, occulting if possible and, if your aircraft is seen, deflect the beam upwind and on the water (or land) to facilitate your landing?"

QxQ. Queen takes queen, in chess notation.

Qaanaaq.
Eskimo name for what used to be called Thule, Greenland.

Q [⋯] Q

r [. . .] r

Rab Al, U.S. Nine pianist, asks at Sinai Peninsula Bar. This rabbi-musician from the Left Bank (of the Hudson) has developed a novel way to solicit contributions.

Rabat: I hit a bar. Postcard from a sailor.

"Rabelais I": Ale Bar *or* **"Rabelais is I": Ale Bar** *or* **"Rabelais is I. Si!": Ale Bar.** A variety of pubs, all featuring Gargantuan drinks and entertainment.

race car. Vehicle for **Mullum Mullum.**

Race fast, safe car. CHISM credits *WORD WAYS* for this track prepavement.

radar. ACRONYM for *r*adio *d*etecting *a*nd *r*anging, an electronic system for locating and determining the speed of objects, and any equipment used for it. According to Martin GARDNER, it was coined to *symbolize* the reflection of radio waves.

Radar.

An acronym for *radio detecting and ranging.*

Rafael Belliard : Draille Blé, Afar (DRAHY BLEHY uh-FAHR). The Atlanta Braves shortstop (seen from behind if not also at some distance) looks just like a certain Djibouti (previously French Somaliland) tribesman whose naturally Gallicized name translates, by chance, as "Mainsheet Wheat," thought to be a long baguette. It is of course also possible to arrange things so that either of these gentlemen actually **sees** (or **de----ed,** etc.) his "reversal mate," a rather rare sort of fully manifested PALINDROMIC materialization that, or who, should perhaps also be considered as a "coincarnation." Other stock central closures in cases like this include [**,** **sides reversed, is**] or just [**'s**] or even [**=**].

Raft far. Fine Finn valedictory by the KUHNS, who clue it, however: "Heyerdahl planned to do this."

Ragu's enacts "Niagara War" against cane sugar. The well-known tomato-sauce manufacturer sends barrels of sugar over the Falls, seizing national media attention . . . to publicize that it is not cowed by the overly sweetened sauces of its competitors. More successful perhaps is the close relative, **A dan acts Niagara War against Canada.**

Rah-rah har-har. A joke about school spirit is a fair-to-medium REVERSAL PAIR.

Rail at a liar. By POOL.

Rail at natal bosh, aloof gibbons! / Snob! Big fool! Ah, so blatant a liar! REVERSAL SENTENCE pair with a lot of natural synergy, by BERGERSON. It is hard to pin down what exactly is going on here, but it seems very much as if a Creationist and three apes (and possibly a Darwinian, too) are trading insults about their conflicting evolutionary theories. If this is the case, or if there is any desire to make it be, we would suggest reversing the order of the lines.

Rail on, O liar! By LINDON.

Ramar (RAH-mahr) *of the Jungle.* Early TV series.

Rá mun ok konum ár. Old Norse Viking: "A spar and an oar is all the same thing to the women." Given by BORGMANN. Truly quaint.

r & r. 1: rest and recreation (or relaxation) **2:** rock and roll . . . and so easily **r & r & r & r.**

Rāpar. Small town of India, 23°34'n/70°38'e, in a place called, most strangely, the Little Rann of Kachchh.

rar. According to BORGMANN, a fifteenth-century spelling of the verb "to roar."

Rat awash saw a tar. Ship's rodent in the water observed a sailor. By the KUHNS.

"Rats gnash teeth," sang Star. Possibly by MERCER, though it sounds punkish.

Rats live on no evil star. Possibly by MERCER. Used in title

Rá mun ok konum ár.

289

of *The BackWords Puzzle Book*, by Joaquin and Maura ᴋᴜʜɴ. Palindrological analysis reveals: Rats live only on earth, so far as we know. It is earth, then, that is poetically licensed to be the "no evil star" referred to (or you will have to provide your own logic). And how could any star, or anything that *is*, *be* evil? How could there be an independent source or beingness of evil? Clearly this couldn't *be* **(Devil never even lived)**. Therefore the existence of rats on earth, as this saw sees, is proof that all that is, is goodness.

Rāvar. Village of Iran, 31°15'n/56°53'e.

Raw oil: Iowa R. Hopefully an overstatement.

rdr. ᴀʙʙʀᴇᴠɪᴀᴛɪᴏɴ for **radar.**

Reber. Name of a large northeastern trucking company.

Reb bursts rubber. A water-balloon-bomber type, no doubt.

Reb Milton's not limber. Here, as always with a *Reb*, you have your choice between a rebel and a rabbi, but this particular specimen seems to pay a special tribute to that rebellious *and* rabbinic stiff, John Milton.

Recap: Sore Aerospacer. Injured or angry astronaut makes the news-in-review.

recaps : spacer. ʀᴇᴠᴇʀsᴀʟ, strong attraction. See: **Spacer recaps.**

ʀᴇᴄᴜʀʀᴇɴᴛ ᴘᴀʟɪɴᴅʀᴏᴍᴇ. Just another name for a ᴘᴀʟɪɴᴅʀᴏᴍᴇ, yet a veritable palindrome's palindrome, replete as it is with such reiterative redundancy.

Red art trader. Soviet painting dealer, by the ᴋᴜʜɴs.

Redd Allaire Aerial Ladder. Not Red Adair's prestigious fire-fighting gear but a crude knock-off.

Red date! Pet adder. By ᴘᴏᴏʟ. Write her off and carry the adder.

Reb bursts rubber.

R $\left[\ \ldots\ \right]$ R

290

redder (REDD-'r). **1:** of the color but more so **2:** possibly one who puts something in order.

redeeder (ree-DEED-'r). Listed by CHISM as an English word, citing WORD WAYS without explanation. Seems like a natural nonce compound to designate someone who issues or gives a new deed or a replacement deed, for whatever reason.

Reder, Johnny. Major-league baseball infielder when last seen.

Red-Eyeder. Listed by CHISM as an English word, citing WORD WAYS without explanation. We think it is a joke, in which case we can take it.

red ice cider. By POOL; simply refreshing.

red, iced, a made cider. By POOL; still refreshing and, now, fancy.

redips : spider. REVERSAL PAIR, medium to strong: makes a telegraphic but vivid **Spider redips.**

redivider (ree-duh-VAHY-d'r). Word invented perhaps by POOL, descriptive perhaps of anyone or anything that separates, graduates, classifies, apportions, or disunites anew a thing that has already been so treated at least once previously.

Red lost case, Ma. Jesse James acts older. Attribution unknown, reported by John JENSEN. This could be E-mail for Ma Barker.

Red, nag a gander. By POOL. In fact, take a goose chase, man.

Red 'n' Axel Alexander. Writ in a heart or on a nuptial matchbook.

red Nevada vender. The KUHNS' "original inhabitant with right to sell," illustrated in IRVINE, 1987.

Red now, Asia is a wonder! CHISM credits *WORD WAYS*. Starry-eyed Kremlin sentiment from the bad old days of the Cold War, when it seemed like all of Asia was going Communist.

Red? No wonder! By Andrea Cantrell. Out in the sun all day without a hat.

redrawer : rewarder. REVERSAL PAIR, having weaker attraction than its simpler cousins, which follow.

Red now, Asia is a wonder!
Kremlin sentiment from the bad old days of the Cold War.

redraw : warder. REVERSAL, with some potential energy: **Redraw a warder.**

red rod order. By POOL, for a hot car or fishing gear.

Red roe . . . order. The following two gems are from Joaquin KUHN's "Red Roe" series:
   Red roe reset agates ere order. Gemological priorities of certain fish eggs.
   Red roe restored no *monde,* rot sere order. Some mysterious connections between fish eggs and the French Revolution in terms of the whole environment and the ancien régime.

Red root put up to order. Possibly by MERCER. A sign, so elegantly natural. And see the following entry.

red root : to order. REVERSAL phrase, with strong affinity: a beet farmer's classified ad, or the above sign, rougher cut. Also consider that, according to BORGMANN, redroot is a perennial herb of the bloodwort family.

Red rum, sir, is murder. By LINDON. Well, then try white next time.

Red Wo- Powder. A Mainland stir-fry condiment with one of its neons knocked out, this rather unorthodox way to operate a wok is remarkable in that it virtually steals a letter it does not legally own, and also in that it marks the approximate place of one of this book's very few moments of censorship, actually self-censorship, owing to the extreme and highly principled prejudice in our times against certain ethnic slur words. (A similarly foul excision, of a short sentence palindrome—actually an ancient Barbarian proverb meaning "If a Roman flushes, hit the bushes"—has also been made at Powder . . .)

Reebok: KO Beer *or* **Reeboks KO beer.** In which old shoes and a new drink coadvertise to save on superstar endorsement costs, or maybe it's that the shoes displace the brew entirely for lack of any real marketing synergy.

Reel, leer. Dizzy with delight.

refer (ree-FERR). **1:** direct to a source or authority **2:** pertain **3:** allude **4:** make reference.

Reflog a golfer. Illustrated in IRVINE.

reflow : wolfer. Weak REVERSAL PAIR, except at party time: **Reflow, wolfer!** (Get back in the swim, lecherous glutton!).

Reg, Alan, a lager? By POOL. (Alan can also be called Al.) A round of **Regal Lager.**

Regal Lager. A brew whose time has come.

Regan, ⌈a man,⌉ a manager. By POOL, who must have been referring to Donald Regan, manager, or Chief of Staff, of the Reagan White House in 1982, when the lines were first published.

Regard a mere mad rager. Probably by MERCER, it's so well composed. *Regard ⌈. . .⌉ rager* and *regard a mad rager* were already in the cards, but the text is a noteworthy finesse and a good show of *how* improvements may be brought in.

Reger. Locality of Missouri, in Sullivan County; also the KUHNS give "Max Reger (1879–1916)" without comment.

Red? No wonder!

R ⌈ . . . ⌉ R

Regina à Niger. Illustrated in IRVINE, 1992.

Regrub, Malcolm! Lo! Clamburger! Someone, perhaps a Forbes or an X, is strangely, indeed amazingly, invited to a second helping—of a Wimpy specialty.

Regrub mild⌈ewed⌉ Limburger. Feed again on that cheese (the mildewed variety more plausibly than the mild, since Limburger is anything but mild).

Re "Ht.": See Esther. If you have any questions at all about height, whether you are wanting to get on top of things or to the bottom of things, which is the same thing, Esther is a good one to consult.

Re hypocrisy: as I say, Sir, copy *her*. By LINDON. Nice dive. *Hypocrisy* sets up *⌈-y,⌉ Sir⌈,⌉ copy h-*, and *as I say* is technically optional but artistically a great stroke. After that, or even without that, the outer closure and the necessary shift into italics could not have been too hard to find, but note how the completed text takes on a fully manifested personality that the shorter one only barely suggests.

reifier. One who materializes, according to the KUHNS.

Reign at Tangier. Rule in Morocco. By the KUHNS.

reknits : stinker. REVERSAL PAIR, socks of weak-to-medium attraction: **stinker reknits.**

reknit : tinker. REVERSAL PAIR, medium strength: **Reknit, tinker!** and sequel **Tinker reknit.**

relativ : vitaler. REVERSAL PAIR by BORGMANN, in which a kinsman (reformed spelling) may become more necessary and indispensable.

R. E. Lee, potato peeler *or* **R. E. Lee, pot a top potato peeler** (*or just* **pot a top eeler** *or, minus the comma,* **pots (s)top eeler**). Wherein a variety of KP-type duties are seen to have preceded this great Confederate general's rise to military leadership.

releveler (ree-LEVV-'l-'r). One who flattens ridges again, according to the KUHNS.

reliant nailer. The KUHNS' trusty carpenter.

reliefpfeiler. According to BORGMANN, "a notable German palindrome, translated as 'a relief-decorated architectural column or pillar.' It appears to be a coined word, but German is known for the ease with which it forms compound words, and no German dictionary could possibly enumerate all legitimate compounds."

reliever : reveiler. Nice REVERSAL but without much obvious synergy.

Re lucid Iraqi's IQ: a ridiculer! A laughably low score for someone who seemed so bright. But in all fairness it should be said that there may be a built-in cultural bias in the test itself, as the Iraqi IQ Commission has so roisterously maintained: **To Iraqi test set, IQ a riot!**

Remarkable Elba Kramer. By BORGMANN. Sounds like a *Reader's Digest* article.

Remark Kramer. Observe him reverse himself.

Remass Ogalala gossamer. Easily mistaken for a bumper sticker exhorting restoration of a depleted aquifer, the text is actually Step One of a how-to sequence for gathering cobwebs to make dream catchers and such.

Remer. Locality of Cass County, Minnesota, 47°03'n/ 93°54'w.

Remit reward: a drawer timer. Consisting of a nested pair of REVERSAL PAIRS by CHISM, each as odd as the other.

Remarkable Elba Kramer

Remit Rome cargo to [go to] Grace Mortimer. Probably by MERCER. As for what to do about presumably fictitious personages such as this graceful freight expediter—for they do present themselves as fairly elaborate thought forms replete with attendant circumstances, and surely somewhere a real Grace Mortimer waits to be born or discovered—we would acknowledge the very best constructions such as this one and wait for the character to turn up in the flesh.

Remlig : Gilmer. Texas town and the name of its founder.

remolts : St. Lomer. REVERSAL PAIR by BORGMANN, tending toward **St. Lomer remolts.** Finally, a patron saint for snakes.

remoor : roomer. REVERSAL, weak linkage, except perhaps among houseboaters and transients.

René Poev Lava: A Valve Opener. This nonphysical but seemingly Franco-Russian mud-bath product gets all your energies flowing.

Re Nile no Aswan guru gnaws a one-liner. Why Henny Youngman's found a dam site better and a running engagement in Egypt!

Renner, Johann. German chronicler, 1525–1583, according to BORGMANN.

Renner (RENN-'r). **l:** hamlet of Minnehaha County, South Dakota **2:** hamlet of Collin County, Texas, 32°59'n/96°47'w.

rennet : tenner. REVERSAL, weak synergy: a dime for the enzyme.

Reno boner. By CHISM, referring perhaps to a matrimonial, perhaps to a gambling error.

Reno goner. Likely a result of the previous and a lead-in to the following.

Reno boner.
Perhaps a gambling error.

Reno loner. A KUHN idea, illustrated in IRVINE, referring perhaps to the very goner who made the boner in the items above, and leading perhaps to the following neighborhood improvements.

Reno oner. 1: any of the silver dollars that are ubiquitous there or a gambling chip of equivalent VALUE, upon the strength of which hope may spring eternal, or, just as likely **2:** a soulmate or any of the other unique characters preceding or following this entry (in the greater Reno area).

Reno toner. An idea or person whose time has come: to improve the general quality and ambience of a city already famous for its boner, goner, loner, and oner.

Reno [z-z-z-] zoner. And finally comes someone to take a nap, perchance to dream of integrating all the staggering real estate ramifications of the above sequence.

repaper (ree-PEHYP-'r). Redecorate the walls with wallpaper.

repats : St. Aper. REVERSAL PAIR by BORGMANN, tending toward **St. Aper repats.** Here finally is a patron saint for patters (who were digging and enthusing all along).

Re peekaboo boob: A keeper! After CHISM. Very good show-and-tell item.

Repooper

repooper (ree-POOP-'r). Dogwalkers' argot for an unusually active client.

Report it, Roper—Pull a "Gallup!" COMPOUND PALINDROME, or really two self-standing PALINDROMES in sequence, by BORGMANN, "advising the well-known pollster, Elmo Roper, to emulate a competitor, George Gallup."

report : troper. REVERSAL, strong: **Report [a] troper** (turn in a turner of phrase or a figurer of speech, as it were). And, dissimilarly: ***Troper Report,*** a figurative newsletter for such people.

repots : stoper. REVERSAL, medium ability: takes another shot at or gives another shot to the miner.

Rep Paramaribo job: I ram a rapper. Surinam telegram bespeaks rough going in the music biz.

Rep pussy assays supper. This amazing rag toy will actually scope out a meal just like a real cat.

Reps act at Casper. Maybe at the Fair Grounds, and positively at Yesness Park.

Re pussy rub: Silas Salisbury's super! Ask any cat in his neighborhood.

rer. Very old spelling of the verb "to rear," according to BORGMANN.

rerepaperer (ree-ree-PEHY-p′r-r′r). Naturally one to **repaper** again; by BORGMANN.

Resume, Muse!—Resume, muser! An inspired conversation overheard at the Pierian Spring and reported to us by CHISM.

Resume so pacific a pose, muser. Probably by MERCER. A real beauty. Adds BORGMANN: "A remark addressed to Rodin's statue *Le Penseur* [The Thinker] after the chap tired of brooding and left his usual haunt to get a drink of water."

Retame *Mater*. By POOL. Tone the old girl down again.

Retap *Pater*. By POOL. Call upon the old man again.

retarded rater. Backhand but not underhanded compliment, as applied, for example, to us or our book for having lived and merited so well in the slow lane (for at least twenty-one years each) before reaching you. Retarded raters are well represented in history by court jesters, idiots savants, channels, artists, and other oddists. Indeed we believe that retarded people and things, and all natural deviations, monstrosities,

and marvels, be they cretins, addicts, churches, or govern-
ments, are still (and perhaps especially) enactments of divine
will, of God expressing himself and being there, and so,
though retarded in time, they are fully raters in eternity,
fully worthy and capable of being savored for *their* divinity.

Retard rater. By POOL. Slow that assessor down.

retartrater (ree-TAHR-trehy-d'r). Coined word meaning
"one who introduces afresh or repeatedly tartaric acid," more
or less under the influence of **detartrated** and **detartrater :**
retartrated.

Réti, "Brasilian Snail" is arbiter. Deceased former world
chess champ gets word that a slow-moving referee from
Brazil's futuristic capital has been appointed (for a coming
match).

retinue uniter. The one whose retinue it is, or any cohesive
factor within it.

Retire, meriter. The last clue in ***Rats live on no evil staℜ***, by
the KUHNS: "Withdraw honorably from this book, worthy
one!"

Retlaw : Walter. Another BORGMANN international REVER-
SAL PAIR of ghost towns! In Alberta and Alabama, respectively.

Retrack Carter! Political slogan. (Just keep sending him out
there to negotiate peace treaties and be generally construc-
tive.)

Retract Carter. Political slogan . . . (We'll take that one
back.)

Retracting, I sign it, Carter. But possibly by MERCER.
Jimmy finesses a veto threat, or some such maneuver.

"Retract-it" Carter. Impertinent political nickname, and—
especially if styled **"Retract it, Carter"**—a public outcry

"Retract-it" Carter.
An impertinent political
nickname.

R [. . .] R

against one of Jimmy's statements or positions, most plausibly his Rose Garden vow.

retract : T. Carter. REVERSAL PAIR by BORGMANN, possibly stirring up a movement to recall this long-deceased Montana senator (1854–1911).

Retroperitoneal : Lae? Not I, reporter! Longest known REVERSAL SENTENCE in an "English word," as created or observed by BORGMANN. He explains: "Lae is a town on the southeast coast of Northeast New Guinea, used by the Japanese as a major supply base during World War II and frequently bombed by the Allies. An ace pilot, returning to the States at the close of the war, is interviewed by a reporter and asked whether he participated in any of the bombing raids on Lae. His answer is the sentence that reverses the word 'retroperitoneal,' a medical term meaning 'behind the peritoneum or serous sac lining the abdominal cavity.'" Since Borgmann has already strung it out to such an advanced level of shaggy-dog story, and since "retroperitoneal" may perhaps be even better understood as a coy euphemism, we cannot help suggesting the rearrangement: **Lae? Not I, reporter! (Retroperitoneal!)** In this version the pilot explains, in a word of afterthought, *why* he didn't fly the raids on Lae: his gut had him going in the opposite direction.

Revel ever!

retroporter. Not the bellhop who carries your bags up to the room but the one who brings them back down to the desk.

Retroposition? : No, it *is*, O Porter! REVERSAL SENTENCE in a word. Observed by BORGMANN. If we cannot resist combining the segments, we soon find ourselves drawn into a science fantasy realm where an attempted "retroposition" (evidently some kind of a reversal or dematerialization or undoing of the basis or existence of something or other), seemingly the endeavor of a certain Porter, is dramatically

R $\left[\, \cdots \, \right]$ R

reported back to him to have failed—since its object ("it") still *is*.

retter (REHT-'r). One who rets, that is, moistens or soaks (flax or hemp, for example) to soften and separate the fibers by partial rotting.

Returning exquisite desire. First line of a WORD PALIN-DROME poem, author unknown, according to ESPY.

Returning exquisite desire,
Burning, then ashes and smoke.
Glowing ember or flaming oak—
Unknowing, unknown secret fire!

Fire, secret, unknown, unknowing,
Oak flaming or ember glowing.
Smoke and ashes; then burning
Desire, exquisite, returning.

Reveal one diameter—Cnossos's on Crete—Maid Enola, ever. This appears to be the characteristically classical yet relatively gay if still repetitive and Stygian sentence (à la Tantalus's, Ixion's, et al.) of the Hiroshima-destroying airplane, *Enola Gay*: eternally report the dimensions of an also once-great but now ruined little, old, forgotten city. For a welcome switch from quasi- and tragi- into unadulterated comedy, see also just **Diameter . . .** and **Enola Bay abalone.**

Revel ever! Have a good time always! Good advice, from the KUHNS.

Revenge? Beg! Never! By the KUHNS: "Getting even?" "Cringe!" "Not now or at any other time!" For a possibly more self-evident result, we would consider changing to a question mark after "Beg" as well. And for a more elaborate formulation, see the following entry.

Revenge [my baby], Meg? Never! Probably by MERCER. The sentiment is correct no matter what the hidden context.

The great VALUE of this item is in its memorializing for us that there is actually no value in revenge.

Re venom: music I summon ever. See: **Beware . . . ever a web.**

rever. Lapel on women's garments, according to BORGMANN.

REVERSAL PAIR

REVERSAL PAIR *or* REVERSAL. Any two words, phrases, or other assemblages that spell each other backward. A reversal pair is sometimes PALINDROMIC, sometimes not, depending on whether or not the pair elements have much combinative potential (liking for one another). A *weak* pair such as **denies : seined** may have little or no natural inclination to join syntactically and become a complete, working PALINDROME. (They can be coaxed along into things like: **He denies I seined, eh?** But that is a different matter.) And a *strong* pair such as **Dennis : sinned** have every likelihood of declaring a full-blown palindromic sentence immediately and without help: **Dennis sinned.** But whether a reversal pair is palindromic or not, it still invariably creates a happy return for anyone with eyes to see it. BORGMANN, after observing that "virtually everyone suffers from the deeply ingrained habit of considering language as a medium of communication," appreciates reversal pairs such as **desserts : stressed** more as objects of beauty than merely as tools for communication, "occupying in the world of language a place similar to that held by the *Mona Lisa* in the world of art, and affording the word lover the same degree of pleasure that a great painting gives the art lover." (Note: Reversal pairs in this book are normally arranged by alphabetical priority, are entered once per pair, and are usually not repeated a second time in reverse order, so you may expect, for example, to find the pair **spoons : snoops** listed alphabetically under **snoops : spoons.**)

REVERSAL REVERSAL. Practice or code of reversing the letter sequence in a series of two or more words while maintaining the original sequence of the words themselves. Also known as *redoubled reversal* or *mixed reversal*. Examples: **Eivets Rednow,** rather than Rednow Eivets, for "Stevie Wonder," and **Wolley Segap,** rather than Segap Wolley, for "Yellow Pages."

REVERSAL SENTENCE. Any sentence that can have a second meaning (not necessarily a sentence) when read in reverse. Example: **Rail at natal bosh, aloof gibbons!** becomes **Snob! Big fool! Ah, so blatant a liar!** See: REVERSAL PAIR.

REVERSED SPEECH. Audio PALINDROMY, as distinct from the written form. BORGMANN offers the remarkable phonetic reversal **fleshpot : top-shelf,** which could easily become the audio-PALINDROMIC phrase **top-shelf fleshpot,** likely a sex idol.

. . . reverses, reverses, reverses, rever . . . A thoroughly postmodern, deconstructing PALINDROME. By Joaquin KUHN.

revests : St. Sever. REVERSAL PAIR by BORGMANN that strongly inclines to **St. Sever revests.** A town of southwest France on the Adour River reinstates. Reinstates who or what? Reinstates, generally.

Reviled, I deliver. Terrible song of a maligned midwife or newspaperboy.

Revilo [P.] Oliver. According to BORGMANN, who wrote in 1965 that this was "the name of a classics professor at the University of Illinois, in Urbana. He has been a faculty member there since 1940. The first name, 'Revilo,' was deliberately coined to make his full name a PALINDROME. But the professor's father and his grandfather bore precisely the same PALINDROMIC name. The middle initial 'P,' by the way, stands for the most unpalindromic name 'Pendleton.'"

Rev., I ran a river. Er . . . Don't worry, my child. This is not as bad a sin as, say, running moonshine, or even running a red light. Say, er, one Hail Mary . . . ⌈Pssst . . . ?!⌉ . . . Er . . . Make that half a Hail Mary.

reviver (ree-VAHY-vuhr *or* ruh-VAHY-v'r). A pick-me-up: smelling salts or CPR.

Rev. Ned Denver. Founder and chairman of Rocky, Mountin' Ministries.

Rev, lost solver. Lighten up and get unlost by remembering that (1) "a puzzle doesn't exist that has no solution"; (2) there are in reality no problems, only puzzles; and (3) in the land of back and forth, as everywhere, it is the frequency—one's palpable vibe!—that determines everything.

Rev, O Dover! *also* **Rev⌈,⌉ odd Dover!** A variety of appeals to Delaware's existing state capital to increase its frequency in order to stand in as "PALINDROMIC state capital pro tem" until a properly qualified place for the job shows up.

Revolt, lover! Seemingly a blooming OXYMORON. But the KUHNS alertly clue it: "Cleo's advice to Antony!"

"Revolt, love!" raved Eva. "Revolt, lover!" Possibly by MERCER. More of the same but with a sixties or Argentine flavor.

revver (REVV-'r). One who revs an engine.

reward drawer. REVERSAL, and a natural place for prizes or bonuses.

Reword a bad rower *or* **Reword a mad rower.** Call an errant oarsman by a different name.

Rex, I'm a mixer. By CHISM. Words from a gregarious barkeeper.

REYNOLDS, Graham. Seven of Reynolds's PALINDROMIC poems are presented by BERGERSON. He quietly but certainly ranks among the greatest lights in all the Halls of PALINDROMY.

Reviver.

A pick-me-up: smelling salts or CPR.

We know next to nothing of him. It is our guess, on stylistic grounds, that he is British.

RHODE ISLAND. Mentioned honorably here, and perhaps challengingly, as one of the few PALINDROMICally "dead" spots, that is, containing not a single PALINDROME (at least among the names of its major localities), and never successfully palindromized itself. **I revive RI!,** you had to go!

Riaffa[h] Affair, The. A proposed title for a tale of Mediterranean or Middle Eastern intrigue, featuring cryptanalysis.

Rio Memoir. Classy Brazilian autobiography; by the KUHNS.

riotoir. 1: full repertoire or bag of tricks of a rioter (whether a professional or an amateur does not matter) **2:** school or studio for training (in) such. For an example, see: **"Hose riot . . . Oh."**

Rise, Aesir. May the Old Norse pantheon live again.

Risen or prone, sir? CHISM credits *WORD WAYS.* Butler asks which way to serve breakfast in bed.

Rise to vote, Sir. Possibly by MERCER. A few PALINDROMES, like this one, are so neat and simple that they seem to have fallen ready-made out of the sky. Illustrated in STUART.

Risotto, Sir? No, thank you, **Ma'am;** I'd prefer the pasta today.

R. J. Drakard, Jr. A character cut by BORGMANN not quite out of whole cloth, for he gives elsewhere the historical John **Drakard,** nineteenth-century British newpaperman.

Rob a gem? Me? Gabor? Eva, Ava, or Zsa-Zsa? CHISM credits ESPY.

Robinson Jones : Senoj Nosnibor. REVERSAL PAIR by BORGMANN, though really an invention of Samuel Butler (see: **Nosnibor**), who deliberately, characteristically, and obviously styled the name of this *Erewhon* character backward.

Rise to vote, Sir.

R [. . .] R

robor (ROH-bawr). Variant of *robur*, Latin for "strength," "hardness," and "oak."

Rob ran NASA as Ann Arbor. Natch (big university town that it is).

Rob ran NATO, not Ann Arbor. Now that's strange, but he probably had his hands full with NATO and NASA.

Rococo R. Illustrated by the KUHNS and, exuberantly, in IRVINE, 1987.

Roger, Gene, Rollo, Pam, Ada, Flora, Tina, Nell, Etta, Mary, Meta, Noel, Flo, Dot, Tom, Asa, Rita, Nan, Ida, Ted, Ana, Esmé : Em, Sean, Ade, Tad, Ina, Nat, Ira, Sam, Otto, Dolf, Leo, Nate, Myra, Matt, Ellen, Anita, Rolf, Adam, Apollo, René, Gregor. BORGMANN's record-length eighty-one-letter REVERSAL PAIR name list, with no names repeated. A PALINDROME of sorts, but we wonder what it all means.

Roma me tem amor (rOH-muh muh-TEHYNg ah-MAWr). Portuguese: "Rome has love for me." Given by BORGMANN.

Romania, my main amor *also just* **Romania: in amor.** Could have been signs of patriotism or other manias in a reconfigured, MACARONIC East Europe but actually refers, we assure you, to the mania practiced in the eastern half of Palind-romania, which, like Czecho-slovakia and Austria-Hungary, must forever be subject to splitting neatly in two. (Hence PALS, 'DROMES, etc.) From the looks of things, Palind-romania's western half, Palind, will likely be found (not in modern Poland as some may suppose but) in *ancient* Pali Ind—that is, in the part of India where they talked or wrote Pali, a kind of High Sanskrit that was reserved only for the most rarefied scriptures and liturgies of Hinayana, the smaller, more conservative, and more esoteric of Buddhism's two main branches.

Romania, my main amor.

Actually the mania practiced in the eastern half of Palind-romania.

R ⌈ . . . ⌉ R

ROMA SUMMUS AMOR. According to ESPY, Anders R. Sterner believes that this PALINDROME, found on the wall of a recently excavated tavern of ancient Rome, may be the world's oldest extant graffito, and he wonders whether the theme is patriotism or a less lofty form of love (since it may be read either as "the best lover in Rome" or "Rome is my highest love").

Roma, tibi subito motibus ibit amor. According to AU-GARDE, this is one of three one-line PALINDROMES attributed to SOTADES OF MARONEIA by the Roman author Quintilian (first century A.D.). The others are **Si bene te tua laus taxat, sua laute tenebis** and **Sole medere pede, ede, perede melos.** We were at first surprised to hear Sotades speaking Latin. The first line was borrowed from Quintilian several centuries later by Sidonius (see: **Signa te signa,** etc.). The syntax is rather loose in places for these lines to be rigorously translated into English, but roughly they could mean: "Thanks to (your or someone's) exertions, or movements, (Cupid, god of) Love, O Rome, will visit you unexpectedly and with upheavals; if your glory esteems you, you will conduct his affair(s) brilliantly; embraced by his sunny arrival, compose (i.e., make whole), take in, (and indeed) devour the melodies," all of which could perhaps prove to be nothing more or less than typically inscrutable words spoken by a Sibyl. (So much for the **Proctor Trot Corp.**) Or it could be that these are the very lines that caused Ptolemy to do away with Sotades—not merely because he couldn't stand them but simply because he also couldn't understand them. Perhaps someone will be able to make sense of it all one day.

ROMA SUMMUS AMOR.

Ronda Radnor. A twin or the return of Gilda (on the Paoli local line), it might be hoped.

Ron, Eton mistress asserts I'm no tenor. Probably by MERCER. This example illustrates how, given a good start with a promising central core (*mistress asserts I'm*) and a little familiarity with the possibilities that exist in the language, you may occasionally catch the remainder of a text almost creating itself, as for example as follows: *mistress asserts I'm no > -on mistress asserts I'm no > Eton mistress asserts I'm no > Eton mistress asserts I'm no te- > Eton mistress asserts I'm no tenor > Ron, Eton mistress asserts I'm no tenor*, and with the barest minimum of coaxing by the composer and by these few simple progressions, one might almost say inevitabilities, voilà, a more or less complete, acceptable thought simply *emerges.*

Ron, I'm a minor. Ron responds: "But don't take it to heart. Legal status isn't reality. You are actually ancient, you know. The people who think you're not an adult until you're twenty-one have it all backward. Reality is, when you're twelve, you're pretty much grown up. And if you're smart, you never stop growing and you never stop being a child. How's that for a reversal?" "No, Ron, I mean I'm a *minor*; I'm not majoring in this subject."

. . . Ron's neither *"Eh, tiens!"* nor . . . We don't know where this one's coming from nor where it's going.

Rot! A Colgate tag locator! Overheard as an electronic scanner and automatic barricade arm prevent an unauthorized entry to a campus or toiletry manufacturing facility.

Rot! A Crème de Mercator! Another spoiled bottle with that blasted old map on the label.

Rot a gill, alligator! Amphibious toast (compare: **Nail it, pert reptilian**). By POOL.

Rot! A lit Nevada ventilator! One of those gassers is on fire again in the damn desert? No, here comes that high-spirited windbag from the casino.

Rotanev : *venator.* REVERSAL PAIR by BORGMANN, pairing a star in the Dolphin near Sualocin (see: **Nicolaus : Sualocin**), perhaps named by the same wit who named Sualocin, with a Latin hunter.

Rotative evitator. Perhaps a scientific name for a whirling dervish.

Rot! A real aerator! Just when we need a high-pressure hose.

rotative evitator. Scientific name, perhaps, for a whirling dervish, a "turning avoider" (that is, an avoider of the other dervishes, who whirl by in all directions while avoiding *him*). Actually they can do this only by being in very close touch with one another—which is hardly avoidance—and the amazing result is they all move with abandon and yet never crash into each other. See also: **evitator : rotative.**

rotative levitator. By the KUHNS: a dervish-become-whirly-bird, or one who *really* gets it going.

rotator (ROH-tehy-d'r). Mechanical part that causes rotation or that rotates; hence, the thing that drives a **rotor,** or the **rotor** itself, and let's not forget the earth as it moves about on its axis—and there's also a muscle called the **rotator** cuff.

ROTATOR PALINDROME. Palindrome which is the same when turned upside down by a 180-degree rotation, like, say, **1961** or **OHO.**

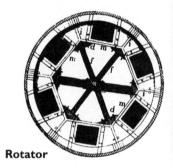

Rotator

Rotavator. Trade name (likely British).

ROTC Ivy Victor. Leading unit in the league.

Rot?! . . . I'd enamel 'em!—An editor. Of course we were expecting a whole dental school for these toothsome (not to say decadent) writings of ours, but all the holes were already very nicely repaired, thank you—and thanks very specifically to many gifted editorial and promotional minds and hands, including those of Robert Rubin, Chris Stamey, Dana Stamey, Tammi Brooks, Ina Stern, Katharine Walton, Bev Smith, Cindy Hamel, Elisabeth Scharlatt, and first of all, Peter Workman—by the time the dentists arrived. Now if only we could get the editors licensed to administer the laughing gas.

R [. . .] R

***rôti de* pup editor.** Not a cub reporter but still hardly a type to roast; in IRVINE.

rotor (ROH-d'r). Rotating part of an electrical or mechanical device. See also: **rotator.**

rot pad adaptor. Special plug for a space-age composter.

Rot sent carts. (I'd distract Nestor.) *Iliad:* (Helen's face may have launched the ships but) pointless talk loosed the chariots — so let's keep that garrulous old man busy with something else.

Roy Ames, I was a wise mayor. Probably by MERCER. Good chit-chat or tombstone inscription, depending on styling. Some would object to the instant cardboard bystander (or protagonist), Roy Ames, replete with given name *and* surname, but the "literature" is full of such characters, bystanders and players, and why shouldn't it be? They have at least as much right to exist as the slew of less fully delineated Als and Dellas and Eds and Stellas, who, lacking the added definition of a surname, are perhaps more plausible and palatable off-hand but are perhaps also ultimately less credible for being such generalities. Too, a real Roy Ames may turn up one day to tell *his* version of the story. And see also PURE PALINDROME for a pertinent second opinion.

Roy, am I mayor? Possibly by MERCER. It's too close to call without recounting the votes, but see previous entry. Illustrated in TERBAN.

Roy, OR. A hamlet of Washington County. See: **Apollo, PA.**

rr. Very rarely (rare).

RR *or* **R.R. 1:** railroad **2:** Rolls-Royce **3:** Ronald Reagan **4:** rural route.

RRRR. Raritan River Rail Road.

RSFSR. The defunct Russian Soviet Federated Socialist

Rue Viveur.
French: "Street of the Dissipated," "Jug Alley," "Skid Row."

Republic or Russian Socialist Federated Soviet Republic (they never could get it straight which one), now just the Russian Federation or Mother Russia once again.

rucksack cask cur. St. Bernard with (or in) a backpack, by the KUHNS.

Rues Sion no connoisseur. This slightly opaque text observes: Not one person of informed and astute discrimination regrets the existence of Israel.

Rue Viveur (rrÜ vee-VŒrr). **1:** French: "Street of the Dissipated," "Jug Alley," "Skid Row" **2:** title and first and last lines of a poem by REYNOLDS.

Ruhuhu R. River of Tanzania into Lake Nyasa at Manda via Lukumburu, 10°31's/34°34'e.

RUR. ABBREVIATION for Rossum's Universal Robots, in Karel Capek's sci-fi play of the same name.

Ruvuvu R. A far tributary of the Nile R. in Zaire, sometimes identified as the main stream of the upper White (Albert) Nile.

RvR. Rembrandt van Rijn.

RWR. Ronald Wilson Reagan.

RxR. Rook takes rook, in chess notation.

RUR

R [. . .] R

S [. . .] S

[. . .][']s [. . .]. A twice triply superlative central closure device (rivaled perhaps only by the bare pronoun *I* and article *a*), alternating the joys of possessive or contractive apostrophe or pluralization with those of linking either preexisting PALINDROMES or REVERSAL PAIRS. That is, for example, the joys of a **level's level** (say, the device's bubble indicator) or a **Level's level** (Fair's fair). Or **Levels level** (the devices even things up). . . . With a **Leon's Noel** or a **Leons' Noel** or a **Leons Noel,** etc., etc.

SAAAS. South African Association for the Advancement of Science.

Saas. 1: river of Switzerland, 46°10'n/7°56'e, which flows from **Saas**tal, the valley **Saas,** into the Vispa and Rhône **2: Saas** Almagel, village of Switzerland, 46°07'n/7°58'e **3: Saas** Fee, another village of Switzerland, 46°07'n/7°55'e **4: Saas** Grund, yet another village of Switzerland, 46°08'n/ 7°56'e. One might surmise that **Saas** means "village" in Swiss, but no, for this and the two preceding **Saas**es turn out to be located in the **Saas**tal. All the **Saas**es are in the Pennine Alps.

sacro-Dorcas. As a Dorcas society is a women's auxiliary church group that provides clothes for the poor—after the disciple Dorcas (Acts 9:36)—a sacro-Dorcas would tend to be an especially sartorial, pious, or just repetitive version of either Dorcas, or else both Dorcases at once, back to back, conceivably even making a show for us of giving the shirt off their back. See also: **Nat, I ram a Samaritan.**

Sad, a Cicero bee bore cicadas. By BORGMANN, who places it in Cicero, Illinois, where "the antics or vagaries of the insect population have long been a topic of conversation in local tea houses." The text is marvelous, portentous, and the bee's sadness should not be taken seriously.

Sadas. Two towns: Sada, Japan, and Sada, Spain! BORGMANN, although accepting "San Diegos" (cities of California and Texas), "cannot give blanket approval to pluralizing proper names—each case must be considered on its own merits" and ultimately offers word length as a useful criterion. We accept all such plural places of any size, provided they yield a return.

saddas. Books containing summaries of the sacred writings of Zoroastrianism; reported by BORGMANN.

Sad? I'm Midas. By Tony AUGARDE. With a touch of golden thought, I'd gladly make you happy.

Saffari?? . . . Go giraffas! Go ape! When we go on safari here at **P.U. (Palindrome University: My! 'Tis 'revinue'! Mor' d'n I lap up!),** it's often a case of **P.U., sir! (A fast safari's up).** In the strange text, a safari professor's bemused query about an unusual spelling of his department's name causes an immediate and appropriately wild departure to . . . Linnaean, or Italian East Africa. Also: **Safari ⌈Gala:⌉ "Giraf'as."**

Sad? I'm Midas.

Sagadahoc Co. had a gas. Great fun and excitement for the county where Bath, Maine, is located.

Saganaga's *or* **Saganagas.** There's only one Saganaga Lake, though it is also sometimes called Lake Saganaga, and so Saganaga's two names do make of it two Saganagas, sort of. Moreover, the Saganagas, both of it, is or are situated in two countries, one state, and one province, being bisected by the U.S.-Canadian and Minnesota-Ontario border(s), and this fact only tends to reinforce Saganaga's—or the Saganagas'—plural stature. Still more over, *Saganaga's* not a PALINDROME but **Saganaga's** is, as are **Saganagas** and **Saganagas'.**

sagas (SAH-guhz). Twelfth- and thirteenth-century Icelandic (or any) long narratives of heroic deeds.

Sage Gas. Illustrated in TERBAN. ("What do wise men run their cars on?")

Sages use gas. What kind? **Sage gas,** of course.

Sail an alias. The KUHNS suggest "float a pseudonym." So let's run one up and see if it flies.

Sail, Elias. By POOL. Breeze on by.

Sail on, game magnolias. From a poem by REYNOLDS, **"Sassettas at Tessa's."**

Sail on, game vassal! Lacy callas save magnolias. Probably by MERCER. One could object that callas, though large, showy, graceful, and very lovely, are hardly lacy and hardly likely to save magnolias, for whatever reason or in whatever sense—and if one did object, then do indeed sail on, dear vassal, with many thanks for your pluck, if you'd come to save them, for it all seems to have been a grand misunderstanding or reverie.

Saippuakivikauppias.
Finnish: lye dealer, the longest palindromic word.

saippuakauppias. Finnish: soap dealer, from *saippua* (soap) and *kauppias* (dealer), according to BORGMANN, who calls it superb and gives it a *cake* for being, at fifteen letters long, the longest solid, unhyphenated, single-word PALINDROME in any language. But see the following entry.

saippuakivikauppias. Finnish: lye dealer, from *saippuakivi* (lye) and *kauppias* (dealer), nineteen letters long and recognized by the *Guinness Book of World Records* as the longest PALINDROMIC word.

saippurakaruppias Finnish: soap salesman, in seventeen letters, as per ESPY.

Sakas. Saka, Japan, and Saka, Kenya.

Saladin enrobes a baroness, Señora, base-born Enid, alas. Possibly by MERCER. Saladin, or Salah-al-Din Yusuf ibn-Ayyud, was the sultan of Egypt and Syria who captured

s [. . .] s

Jerusalem in 1187 and was defeated by the Third Crusade under Richard I of England and Philip II of France, but the other characters cannot be identified. It is not inconceivable, however, that he should enrobe a baroness—whether that means creating a noble station from scratch or just giving suitable clothing to an already-existing noblewoman—though the thought that his attentions should go, whatever the circumstances, to a base-born one such as Enid is, we agree, distressful, and where the Spanish lady comes in is another one of those regrettable loose ends. BORGMANN calls it slightly implausible.

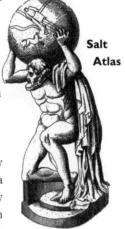

Salt Atlas

Salalas. Salala (Chile) and Salala (Liberia).

salas (SAH-lahss). Spanish: rooms.

Salas (SAH-lahss). **1:** village of Peru, 6°16's/79°37'w **2:** a locality somewhere in Spain.

Salas, Mark. Major-league baseball catcher.

Salisbury Moor, Sir, is roomy. Rub Silas. Probably by MERCER. Looks very much like a British gangster orders a hit. We assume Salisbury Plain is what's meant by Salisbury Moor, the capacious (three-hundred-square-mile) plateau in southern Wiltshire of which Stonehenge would seem to be the navel. This supposition gives rise to a tamer alternative reading involving stone rubbing, in which case an extra comma is needed after *Rub.*

sallets : Stellas. REVERSAL, medium strength: **Stella's sallets,** her light, rounded fifteenth-century helmets.

Salt Ada or a road atlas. Enliven her or hit the highway, buddy.

Salt an atlas. Keep one on hand or in reserve at all times.

Salt Atlas. Preserve him, stash him away, liven him up, but give the guy a break.

315

s $\left[\ldots\right]$ s

Salta, tu levis es, summus se si velut Atlas. First line of the following Latin PALINDROMIC verse, quoted without citation (classical? medieval? modern?) by BORGMANN.

> **Salta, tu levis es, summus se si velut Atlas,**
> **(Omina se sinimus), suminis es animo.**
> **Sin, oro, caret arcana cratera coronis**
> **Unam arcas, animes semina sacra manu.**
> **Angere regnato, mutatum, o tangere regna,**
> **Sana tero, tauris si ruat oret anas:**
> **Milo subi rivis, summus si viribus olim,**
> **Muta sedes; animal lamina sede satum.**
> **Tangeret, i videas, illisae divite regnat**
> **Aut atros ubinam manibus orta tua!**
> **O tu casurus, rem non mersurus acuto**
> **Telo sis-ne? Tenet? Non tenet ensis, olet.**

The perplexed **Proctor Trot Corp.** was relieved to learn of Borgmann's difficulty in rendering the text into coherent English. Indeed, as Latin students the world over will also rejoice to learn, only two lines were even attempted (the final couplet), and they coughed up only the weirdly esoteric meaning: "O, you who are about to fall, are you not going to submerge the matter in a sharp / weapon? Does it hold? The sword does not hold, it smells." Actually it is not at all surprising when PALINDROMES don't translate well, since they tend so often—one could almost say it is in their nature—to stretch even their original language's syntactical structures to the breaking point.

samaroid dioramas. Delightfully dizzying whirligig seed displays; a REVERSAL PAIR, by BORGMANN.

samas. Muttonfishes, according to BORGMANN.

same nice cinemas. By the KUHNS, appreciating the old movie houses.

Sam Xmas. Wherein Uncle Sam and Father Christmas unite and melt into a sort of theocratic-military-industrial bliss whose offspring are the First Church of Money and the First Bank of God. (The only real result of all this commotion is that gift-giving and fireworks orgies will now be simultaneous and twice yearly.)

San Antone's Abe's use base, not Nana's. Abraham, the great Texas oracle, and not Grandma, is headquartered and most widely consulted in the greater San Antonio area.

sanas. East Indian hemp plants, according to BORGMANN.

Sanas. Sāña, Peru, plus San'a', Yemen, plus Şan'a, Russia, plus the Sana river, Yugoslavia, all together presenting a delightful curiosity: four distinct **Sanas,** each spelled *and* pronounced differently.

Sane volema kara rara kamelo venas. Esperanto, as only BORGMANN could speak it: "A healthily wishful dear rare camel is coming."

sannas. An old term for scornful gestures of a sort, according to BORGMANN.

Sappas (SÆP-uhz). Sappa creeks of Kansas and Nebraska (Plain, Middle, North, and South Forks), into Beaver Creek and the Republican River via Oberlin, Kansas.

Saras (SÆ-ruhz). Feminine namesakes (or possessives).

Sarge, I often et foie gras! Illustrated in IRVINE, 1992.

Sarras. Village of France, on the Rhône, 45°11'n/4°48'e.

SAS. Scandinavian Airlines System.

S'as'. River of Russia, into Lake Ladoga via Jurcevo, 60°09'n/32°30'e.

Sasas (pronounced however you wish). The strange couple, Sasa, Israel, and Sa'sa', Syria.

Sassettas at Tessa's. The title and first and last lines of a

Same nice cinemas

wonderful PALINDROMIC poem by Graham REYNOLDS, which shows no other sign of being about Italian Renaissance paintings and features other lines incorporating such other little jewels as **Slob my symbols, Sail on, game magnolias,** and **To rococo rot.**

Satan, oscillate my metallic sonatas. Possibly by Raymond STUART. Heavy metal title.

Satan, oscillate my metallic sonatas.

satin amanitas. Fancy, velvety-smooth, but poisonous mushrooms.

SATIRES, various. See: SATYR(ICON) LEX(ICON).

Sator Arepo tenet opera rotas. Latin: The sower, Arepo, holds (back?) the wheels with his work (or at work). This is usually presented as a WORD SQUARE, thus:

```
S   A   T   O   R
A   R   E   P   O
T   E   N   E   T
O   P   E   R   A
R   O   T   A   S
```

In this form it has been found in the ruins of both Cirencester and Pompeii and has been the object of much fascination, speculation, and controversy across the ages, usually with mystical crypto-Christian overtones involving crosses, alphas, omegas, and paternosters. The main sticky point is that, although lots of people are fond of this ancient doohickey for lots of different reasons, nobody has any idea who Arepo was, or is, or even if he was anything at all until he was blurted into being as a thought-form here, coined as if by default, the alien lodger in and blot upon a not-quite-satisfactory word square. While taking the trouble to cite pages of bibliographical references on the subject, BORGMANN confesses "we don't happen to care for it. To us, it is a symbol of imperfection, of failure to achieve a desired goal, and we want to dissociate ourselves from it." To us, both

Borgmann and Arepo are both very fine as the much-celebrated mysteries each of them is.

Sator rotas. Latin: O Thou Begetter or Sower (i.e., Jupiter) wheelest about.

satraps : Spartas. REVERSAL, weak to medium: **Sparta's satraps,** conjuring a version of ancient Greece that nearly but never was, with a Sparta dominated by these Persian provincial governors.

SATYR(ICON) LEX(ICON):

"SATIRE, RITA'S": (*or* **"SATIRES? USE RITA'S!":**)

Satire I (i.e., Rita's).

Satire II (i.e., Rita's).

Satire III (i.e., Rita's).

Satire IV: "⌈À la⌉ Vie!" (Rita's). So far, only a Lex and Rita Quartet, high on folly and low on wit. But:

Satire V: "On Ivy, Vino, Veritas!" "Attributable" not to Rita but to Horace, Juvenal, and Bacchus themselves. Also, more generally, just: **Satire V: "Veritas?"** In which case our tyrannic Lex parties on down to:

Satire VI: "Veritas!"

Satire VII: "Veritas??"

Satire VIII: "Veritas!!"

Satire IX: "O Moxie!" (Rita's). She's back.

Satire X: "Axe Rita's!" No, it looks like she never left. Better to limit the collection to an even octave. Then she cuts out at four. Yet:

Satire XI: "Feeding is error! Resign idée fixe!" (Rita's).

Or else, stuffing it and surrendering, too, we revel on in a whirl of disorder:

Satire XI: "F--- XI! RPM!! Prix fixe!!!" (Rita's). Whee. And now *we're* outta here. We were getting dizzy and slowing down anyway. And it was all we could cram. Io Saturnalia! Lovely Rita! Evoe! Veritas! Caput!

Saw "bijou" Ojibwas. Though slightly out of place geographically, this looks like a Lewis and Clark journal entry referring to an encounter with some Chippewas wearing unusually fine beadwork. Fortunately the terse basic text can be loosened up with a little drumming and singing: **Pat saw Bijou Ojibwas tap.** And: **Leon saw Bijou Ojibwas Noël.**

sawbwas. Princes ruling certain Mongoloid tribes in Burma, according to BORGMANN.

Saw oil. (Iowa's.) Text of naval telegram, or postcard from a probably confused tourist.

Sawtelle 'twas. A to this Q: "What was that crazy flat-topped mountain with the big white ball on top just west of Yellowstone?"

Saxe-Texas. Former duchy somewhere in the Hill country. Also, **Saxe, Texas,** for which see: **PRP.**

sbbs. Sabbaths, Sundays.

sbs. Sonic booms or space brothers, and so easily **sbs' sbs.**

SCCCS. Singapore Chinese Chamber of Commerce and either the Suffolk County or Sullivan County Community College (both New York), or all three.

Schenob bone HCs (SH[']NAHB). This exquisite little brook, spilling and spiraling the waters of our own beloved Twin Lakes—from "the Bathtub" at the top of "the Channel" at "the top of the Schenob," first south, west, and north

past the nearly perfect little village of Taconic and Connecticut's loftiest mountain range (also called Taconic, or
Riga), and then meandering northeast and down through the
backwoods of Sheffield in Massachusetts (below more and
bigger of the same heights, here called Berkshires and Mount
Washington), then turning east toward the Housatonic
wherein the original waters, by then much increased, eventually wind and dawdle back south and *right past Twin Lakes
again* en route to Long Island Sound—is in the upper
drainage so overgrown and forgotten and fresh that it has
been nicknamed by naturalists the Amazon of North America. No surprise then that the Schenob is the perfectly wild
setting for all levels, even the profoundest, of inner knowing
and Holy Communion. (To the bone and quick.) Over 444
species of moths alone are unique to its eleven square miles
of wetlands, and the mountains feeding these are perhaps
the oldest in the world. The Schenob and its spiraling Bone
HCs (a term reminiscent also of George Gurdjieff's strange
advice: "Study Hydrocarbons") swoon best when the moon
is ready and the foliage is at its peak, usually early October.
(Look for more on this true crack and hot spot in reality in
volumes II and III.)

Sci. Latin is in italics. But of course. And abbrevs. are encouraged.

scitnamantics (SKIT-nuh-*MÆN*-tix). The modern interdis-
ciplinary science of PALINDROMY, semantics, and other man-
tic antics, and of divinatory performances in general, including all their various classifications, ramifications, and
nomenclatures.

Scranton's U.S. partner entraps us, not narcs. Here various government agencies appear to be pulling stings *on one
another*! (Also heard on the radio: "Feds but not narcs! We
can't figure it. Let's check with the Wilkes-Barre unit or
Harrisburg. Maybe they can clear things up.")

**Scranton's U.S.
partner entraps us,
not narcs.**

s ⎡ . . . ⎤ s

SDS. Students for a Democratic Society, a sixties group.

Sealcrest : Tserclaes. BORGMANN's imaginative REVERSAL PAIR, perhaps best as **Tserclaes' seal crest,** conferring a helmeted coat of arms on a real Flemish family name of the sixteenth and seventeenth centuries.

Sebeş. Small city of Romania, 45°58'n/23°34'e.

Sebes Körös. River of Hungary and Romania (Crisul Repede), via Kunszentmárton into the Tisza (Tiza, in Yugoslavia) and eventually the Danube.

secret : terces. REVERSAL, strong linkage: **secret terces,** arcane mid-morning prayers.

sedes (SEHY-dehyss). Latin: seat or throne or home or temple, or the plurals of each. This is the word used for oracular and ecclesiastical seats.

See few owe fees. Make sure that they aren't charged, or that they pay up in advance. Probably by MERCER. This one is so very witty and swishy and was probably nowhere as simple to manifest as it seems.

Seen knees

seen knees. By CHISM; preferable to heard ones.

Seer gal agrees. Easygoing, no Cassandra she!

seer trees. There are many examples: in Buddhism, the *bo* or *peepul* under which the Buddha became enlightened; in Druidism and Christianity, the mistletoe and evergreen; in Norse myth, Yggdrasil; in Hebrew myth, the apple of knowledge; etc.

sees (SEEZ). Perceives visually, with many figurative and specialized senses.

sees (SEEZ). Bishops' seats, offices, and jurisdictions (from **sedes**).

s [. . .] s

Sees. Really two towns, each named See, totaling two **Sees,** both conveniently in Austria.

Sées (*formerly* Séez). Village of Department of Orne, France, near Alençon, a lace manufacturing center, 48°36'n/0°10'e.

seesees. Small sand partridges found in India, according to BORGMANN.

See we prefer pewees. Affirmative action or red-lining policy at a housing project for the birds.

seges (SEHY-gehyss). Latin: **1**: agricultural production **2**: seed **3**: sown field **4**: any field **5**: fields **6**: soil **7**: fruitful plains.

Sekes. That is, two towns named Seke, one in Ethiopia and the other in Tanzania.

selahs : shales. REVERSAL, weak: Unknown biblical words meet rocks.

Selah, we're whales! Jonah's King James translation of Leviathan's most enthusiastic breaching song is still the best available English rendering of the Whalsh original. And for our part we always sock it right back to them in our loudest, highest antiphony: **Selah, whales!** The fact that no one has ever been able to say exactly what *Selah* means rather enhances matters, it seems to us, for the mystic sense of the word can here, at last, almost be inferred or guessed from the picture and context alone.

Seles, Monica. Of pro tennis.

self-furnace pecan ruffles. In IRVINE.

Selig-Giles. Shorthand for a baseball showdown between the Milwaukee Brewers and Philadelphia Phillies, based on the names of their owners, as observed by Steve Rushin of *Sports Illustrated.*

Selig-Giles.
Baseball showdown between Milwaukee and Philadelphia owners.

S [. . .] S

Selims : smiles. REVERSAL, strong natural attraction: the smiles of one or several sultans of Turkey.

Selles-sur-Cher (SEHLL). Village of Department of Loir-et-Cher, France, near Blois, 47°16'n/1°33'e.

Sell exurbanite Tina *Bruxelles.* Impress her with the Belgian capital by softening an otherwise hard sell with a little French.

Sell Lima a mill, Les. Encouragement for a **Peru rep.**

sememes (SEHM-eemz). The meanings or content of morphemes, both linguistic terms referring to the most basic units of meaningful sounds.

semés. Sown or dotted ornamental patterns, according to BORGMANN.

semidimes. The KUHNS' freshly coined nickels.

semimimes. Subtitled silent films, by POOL.

Semite Times. A Jewish or Arab newspaper, by CHISM.

semitimes *or* **semi-times.** According to BORGMANN: "A word listed but not defined in *Webster's Second Edition.* Evidently, semitimes are half times, but in what area of human endeavor? In music? In sport? The [OED] provides an answer: 'semi-time' is synonymous with 'half a time,' as that phrase is used in the New Testament (Rev. 12:14)." It would be a great name, too, for a truckers' magazine.

Semmes. Western suburb of Mobile, Alabama, likely named for the following person.

Semmes, Raphael. American Confederate naval officer, according to BORGMANN.

Se negó Ida reconocer a Diogenes (seh-neh-GOH EE-dhah *r*eh-COH-noh-*SEHR* ah-DHEE-oh-*KHEH*-nehss). Spanish: "Ida refused to recognize Diogenes." Given by BORGMANN. Has the ring of a classic.

Semite Times.
A Jewish or Arab newspaper.

senes (SEHY-nehyss). Latin: elders; usually refers to men over sixty.

senicide medicines. Possibly a Serutan-like trade name for Dr. Kevorkian's remedies. (Jingle: "All deaths are suicides and there's no such thing as death.")

Senicide: More Aeromedicines. Title of typical dread-mongering investigative journalism piece revealing how an overdose of airsickness pills, and an overreliance on similar medications, could kill off older passengers.

senile felines. Illustrated in IRVINE.

Senile females, Rodney away, endorse lame felines. BORGMANN sums it: "cats cater to cats."

senile lines. 1: age wrinkles 2: old merchandise 3: queues 4: stuff for the elderly.

Senones (seh-NOH-nehss). The Latin name for a Gallic people centered around modern Sens, France, and also for a kindred people of Northern Italy, both of whom the Romans conquered.

Señor drones. That guy's s'ñoring again? ("¡Sí, está!")

señores : serónes. Spanish REVERSAL observed by BORG-MANN. Styled as **Señores Serónes,** it strikes us as a most Quixotic sort of salutation—"Respected Hampers, or Panniers"—and a great opening for one of his typically delirious soliloquies.

Senicide medicines

SE Pacific apes. By POOL, like the **E Pacific ape** in general (which see), these bite their own tails. And, like the far-reaching Zinjanthropus, Australopithecus, Java Man, and the very early Polynesians, they may have begun to evolve and improve while still in the west, which is of course the East, and may only then have headed east across the Pacific for the West, which they continue striving to reach even now while getting better all the time: **No worse, Pacific apes row on.**

Separate tar apes. Illustrated in IRVINE, 1992.

Separation? : No, I tar apes. REVERSAL SENTENCE in a word. Observed by BORGMANN. To segue the segments is tempting and interesting but produces, we believe, only a non sequitur.

seres. 1: claws or talons: archaic, according to BORGMANN **2:** (SEH*R*-ehss) Spanish: beings.

Sere Xeres (seer heh-*R*EHSS). The KUHNS' dry sherry! Exquisite.

¡Serías One U., Buenos Aires! You'd be una fantastic universidad Espanglesa!

¡Serías one U-boat sta., O Buenos Aires! And you'd make one heck of a bilingual sub base again, as you did in the forties!

Sería son E.U., Buenos Aires. And more properly, you'd be your own U.S.

Serres (SEH*R*). Village of France, near Gap, 44°26'n/5°43'e.

Serrès (in French) *or* (in Greek) Sérrai. City of Macedonia, Greece, a cotton-growing center on the Strouma river.

Serres, Olivier de (SEH*R*). French agronomist (1539–1619), author of *Théâtre de l'agriculture* and the father of mulberry cultivation in France.

serif fires. Illustrated in IRVINE, 1992.

Serutan GI signatures. By which constipated old soldiers, having neither died nor faded away, and still wondering what else to stand for, gently reenlist.

serves on no Sèvres. Uses paper plates, according to the KUHNS.

Serres.

Village of France,

near Gap.

s ⎡ . . . ⎤ s

serves : Sèvres. REVERSAL, strong attraction. See: **Sèvres serves.**

servileness[es]: Essene livres. This moronic MACARONIC "aphorism" takes too dim a view of certain lost books of the Bible (such as that of St. Thomas) or various Dead Sea Scrolls, considering they have been so faithfully rendered into French by the devoted translators.

ses (SEHY *or* SEHYZ). French: his, her, its, or their.

Şes Muntele. Mountain range of Romania, 47°05'n/22°30'e.

SES. Airport code for Selma, Alabama.

sesses (SESS-'z). "The bars or plates of a knockdown soap frame[!]," according to BORGMANN.

Set agates. 1: mount semiprecious stones 2: plural typesetter's instructions. By the KUHNS.

Set, a Luca Jesuit "angina man," Ignatius, ejaculates. Once he is all ready or well positioned or just suitably cloistered in an old Tuscan locale (modern Lucca), the founder of the Society of Jesus is easily able to palm off his monastically induced paroxysms as some sort of medical spasms. See also: **"An Ignatius ejaculation!?"** . . . *"A JESUIT ANGINA!"*

Set arc. Ostracize fez. I cart Socrates. "Attributable" to Kemal Atatürk, who ordered a new compass heading for the modern Turkish Republic, outlawing the wearing of the Ottoman fez and initiating rapprochement with (intrinsically Socratic and Hellenic) Western civilization.

Set at net, O Potentates! Toppled in tennis, oh mighty ones! By the KUHNS.

Set, a tornado Wodan rotates. He and it bloweth where they listeth—here into a semantic vortex of supernally concentrated reverse English. (*Wodan* is the name of the Teutonic Supreme Being, the same as *Woden* and as the Old Norse *Odin* and today's *Wednesday*.)

**Set at net,
O Potentates!**

s [. . .] s

sete setes (SEHT-tchee SEHT-tcheez). Portuguese for "seven sevens," as, for example, these seven Brazilian place-names—Sete Barras, Sete Cidades, Sete de Setembro, Sete Lagoas, Sete Pontes, Sete Quedas, and Sete Rios—all taken together.

Setiites (SETT-ee-ahyts). An archæo-NEOLOGISM for follow-ers of and/or believers in the authority and/or divinity of either or both of two distinguished ancient Egyptian kings, Seti I and Seti II, father and son of Ramses II, of the Nine-teenth Dynasty, fourteenth and thirteenth centuries B.C. Moreover, fans of only one or the other Seti and not of either or both Setis indiscriminately make natural and wonderful **Seti I–ites** or **Seti II–ites.**

Set in a *Bruxelles* ell: exurbanites. They've returned to town for some reason.

Set Irenic, I demonstrate tarts, no medicine rites. By the KUHNS. Evidently a former witch doctor and war chief is now firmly committed to a peaceful life of teaching the people how to make little fruit pies.

Set saw: Sahara has wastes. By the KUHNS. An old adage about the no-man's-lands in the desert.

Se van sus naves (seh-BVAHN sooss NAH-bvehss). Span-ish: Their ships are leaving. Attributed by ESPY to Anthony Bonner.

Sevareid ribs, Birdie raves *or* **Sevareid ribs as Birdie raves;** *also* **"Sevareid ribs us,"** **Birdie raves** (*or* **ribs U.S.**). Several among numerous variants, depending on whether and where and how you punctuate, all tending toward good humor and good reviews for a novel and refreshing "news-comedy" program.

seven eves. Sennight formerly, and of course now just a week. Credited by CHISM to *WORD WAYS*.

Sevareid ribs, Birdie raves.

A novel and refreshing "news-comedy" program.

S [...] S

seven névés (neh-VEHZ). **1:** seven kinds of granular snow if indeed there are seven such; also called firns **2:** fields of snow at the head of seven glaciers. Admittedly odd contortions yet perhaps even surpassed by those of the number six and certainly by the Portuguese **sete setes.**

Seville, Babel lives! CHISM credits *WORD WAYS*. Spanish city has grown cosmopolitan.

Sèvres serves. The French city of fine porcelain also stands and waits, and does it very well.

Sew, Wes! The KUHNS stitch another REVERSAL character together.

Sex at noon taxes. Or at many another numbered hour such as **1** or **11** or age such as **101** (!)—and according to ESPY, this "makes increasing sense as the years pile up."

Sex-aware era waxes. Noted by the KUHNS in **Rats live on no evil staℜ.** Illustrated in IRVINE, 1987.

sexes (SEHKS-'z). **1:** male and female **2:** determines which of them a chick is.

Sex at noon taxes.

Sexist Sixes. Hockey teams (and/or an Oregon coastal hamlet) when said to practice gender discrimination.

Sex often: I net foxes. By CHISM. Promotes and catches wildlife.

sexy lace calyxes. By CHISM, fresh from the garden of delights.

Seyhan?? . . . Ah, yes! Affirmation of a river of south-central Turkey, also spelled *Ceyhan,* flowing 320 miles to the Mediterranean near Adana.

SFPFS. BORGMANN's SSociety for Palindromically Fit Spelling, which he describes as "an organization more usually referred to by its necessarily PALINDROMIC initials, **SFPFS.** The

S [. . .] S

first word in the title, 'SSociety,' is deliberately so spelled in order to create a numerically palindromic sequence of letter-lengths for the five words constituting the full title (8-3-15-3-8)," etc. This movement for spelling reforms, led by the "Potentate of Palindromes," boldly advocates such re-spellings as, for *shillelaghs*, **shallellahs,** and, for *hullaballoo*, **'oollaballoo.**

sfs. Strictly for suckers.

S. Giza, MA, zigs. / S. Gazebo, OBE, zags. Wherein **S. Wordrow's** two distinguished initialsakes and boon companions—one looking for all the world like an Egyptian pyramidologist, and the other, an English landscape architect—take turns bobbing and weaving with him.

shahs (SHAHZ). Former Middle Eastern, especially Persian and Iranian, monarchs.

shallellahs (shuh-LEHY-luhz). See: **SFPFS.**

Shall Otay add Ayatollahs? (*or* **assess** *or* **ax**). These must be reflections of Salman Rushdie's California dreaming—in which a suburb of San Diego calls the question of taking a range of official actions in his behalf (namely, trivializing, taxing, or firing his anathematizers).

Shall we all die? First line of an epitaph (in the form of a monomaniacal WORD PALINDROME) in the churchyard of St. Winwalloe's Church at Gunwalloe in Cornwall, as quoted by AUGARDE.

> **Shall we all die?**
> **We shall die all;**
> **All die shall we—**
> **Die all we shall.**

The text provides a great excuse or occasion, not that we need one, for laughing right along with the Jolly Reaper.

shamahs. East Indian songbirds of the thrush family, known to mimic the notes of other birds; after BORGMANN.

S [. . .] S

"Shelburne, Vermont (No! Mr. Even-Ruble!!), H.S." The normally well-balanced Russian teacher (a paragon of the foreign-exchange program) at a high school near Lake Champlain gets completely out of character with the busy switchboard operator there just as she answers the phone. Or, if reality ever catches up with us and there proves to be no "Mr. Even-Ruble," nor even any Russian émigré or foreign-exchange program at all in this institution, and assuming it even exists, then we would still be left with **Shelburne, Vermont ([O (gee)! Got] no "Mr. Even-Ruble"!), H.S.** or ... **I'm it. (No Mr. E-R.), H.S.** An attempt at firsthand reconnaissance has revealed that Shelburne High School, if it even exists as such, is actually a component part of the larger Shelburne Community School, and there is in fact "no Mr. Even-Ruble" there.

Sh! Tom sees moths! Possibly by MERCER. Illustrated in IRVINE. Hysterical.

Sh! Tom spots wasp! Saw stops moths. CHISM's moth-stopping saw cuts a happy sequel for the delirium of the previous **Tom mot.**

Sh, Tom! Stars lay or sat forever, oft as royals, rats, moths. CHISM favors us by diving in off the deep end here to soothe poetically all Tom's (or anyone's) existential anxieties, and what is more, like any good teacher, he leaves us groping for still profounder mysteries than he elucidates.

Si bene te tua laus taxat, sua laute tenebis. See: **Roma, tibi subito motibus ibit amor.**

Sibilate pet alibis. Hiss them out, like: "Silly puss sat so" or "Sissy's snake slobbered thus."

["...,"] sides reversed, is ["...."] Handy FORMULA that allows any REVERSAL PAIR, such as **Leon : Noel** or **Novrad : Darvon,** to be combined in a syntactically and semantically coherent format. The device, however, is easily overused. It

Sibilate pet alibis.

is best reserved for the few harmonious or contrastive reversal pairs such as **dog : God,** or **Ah, Satan : Natasha!**

Sides reversed is, said I, as sides reversed is. CHISM's blasé appraisal of the above FORMULA.

Sidis *or* **Sîdîs.** All the many Moslem place-names that begin with *Sidi* or *Sîdî.*

SIDONIUS APOLLINARIS. See: **Signa . . . angis.**

Signa . . . angis. By SIDONIUS APOLLINARIS, a Gallo-Roman of the fourth century A.D.:

> **Signa te signa; temere me tangis et angis;**
> **Roma tibi subito motibus ibit amor.**

For the second line, see also: SOTADES OF MARONEIA. AUGARDE reports that "C. C. Bombaugh says these lines were supposedly spoken by the Devil to St. Martin when the latter was traveling to Rome to visit the Pope. St. Martin met Satan and made him carry him on his back towards the Holy City, urging him on by making the sign of the cross. Satan's words mean: 'Cross, cross yourself; you annoy and vex me unnecessarily; for owing to my exertions, Rome—the object of your wishes—will soon be near.'"

S. I. is. Title of an article in *Sports Illustrated* (June 7, 1993) about PALINDROMES in sports.

Si, lop an aid 'n' Indianapolis. Probably for economy's sake, a simple Simon is advised to reduce by one the size of his pit crew and not even show up at the Indy 500; or else, by conserving the second apostrophe, to show up and then fire the helper.

Silopolis (sahy-*LAHP*-uh-LISS). Any place full of grain elevators, such as Dodge City.

simillimis (sih-MIHL-ih-mihss). Latin: most likely meaning "by very similar (means)," among a wide range of possible meanings.

Simis. 1: arroyo and city and valley (plural) of Simi Valley, California, 34°16'n/118°39'–118°47'w **2: Símis,** town and island (singular) of the Greek Dodecanese Archipelago, 36°36'n/27°50'e.

sinnets : Stennis. REVERSAL PAIR by BORGMANN, linking straw or grass hat braids with a Mississippi senator.

sinnet : tennis. Another REVERSAL PAIR by BORGMANN, linking a straw or grass hat braid with the net game.

Si nummi immunis. Latin lawyers' motto quoted by C. C. Bombaugh (*Gleanings for the Curious from the Harvest-Fields of Literature* [1890], as reported by Tony AUGARDE in *The Oxford Guide to Word Games*): "Give me my fee, and I warrant you free," or literally "If (you furnish) coins, (you are) free from penalty."

Silopolis

Sion ill in Illinois. But well in Switzerland or Israel.

Sion, Illinois. See: **PRP.**

Sip Ares, *Serapis.* God-awful toast "attributable" to U.S. Revolutionary War naval hero John Paul Jones, aboard the *Bonhomme Richard,* as he sank and drank this British man-o'-war named for the god of the netherworld.

Sip, O Hopis! A toast. It gets dry on those high mesas. And Indians are PALINDROMICally hot for some reason.

"Sir Ape" Deli, Ile de Paris. An imitation American fast-food joint near Notre-Dame. Though weird, this little monkeyshine is less problematic than the fully manifested but more diffused **"Sir Ape" Delicatessen, Knesset A.C., Ile de Paris,** which could now only be either the ungainly name of the training table at the Israeli parliament's continental athletic club or, for simplicity's sake, the opponents and venue of an international soccer match. (And see the following.)

Sir aped Leto here (Hôtel de Paris). Kilroy-type graffito reports that a man, likely a schoolmaster celebrating Toga Day, went in drag as a Greek goddess to Monte Carlo's **top spot.** See also the previous entry.

Sir, bed debris. By POOL. A butler's euphemistic comment.

Sire, *was* I ere I saw Eris? By BORGMANN. And that's a hell of a name for a midwife.

Sir, I soon saw I was no Osiris.

Sir, I'm Iris. Per BORGMANN, Eve's perfectly balanced but discarded rejoinder to **Madam, I'm Adam.** Compare: **Adam, I'm Ada.** (Fortunately, too, there was just: **"Eve."**)

Sir . . . Osiris. A four-panel cartoon—or cartouche?—from a schoolroom in Ancient Egypt:

1. **Sir, is Osiris?** Source of priestly authority is questioned.
2. **Sir, I soon saw Bob was no Osiris.** Another voice chirps up. Okay, but the question was: Is Osiris? (Possibly by MERCER.)
3. **Sir, I soon saw I was no Osiris.** Third opinion. Really? Okay too. It is up to you. Actually this is what you are expected to think. (Possibly by BORGMANN.)
4. **Sir, I so saw I was Osiris!** Good observation. Priestly authority ends. Osiris *is*, no matter what "Sir" or anyone says. And, most important, nobody and nothing gets between us and God.

"Sirrah! Deliver [*] desserts *detartrated*!" stressed [*] reviled Harris. Possibly by MERCER. Every now and then a truly loopy one falls out of the sky, and this is it for now. Moreover this gem is uncut—in the sense that it simplistically wraps a succession of REVERSAL PAIRS around a central PALINDROME! But in fairness to the composer, whoever he may have been, it should be said that the original version, as cited by BERGERSON, has in fact been cut, having contained in addition the PALINDROMIC word **deified** at each of the two points indicated [*], thus forming a five-layer or nine-word palindrome and lending a decidedly heavenly air to the proceedings. But these two extra dollops of grandeur really do not sharpen and only confound the meaning of an already sufficiently glorious and humorous event. (The humor is perhaps further compounded when we realize that the cause of Harris's revilement was probably a previous failure on his own part to deliver properly detartrated desserts.)

sirris. An Old World tropical timber tree, according to BORGMANN; also called "lebbek."

Sir! Roman in a Morris. Possibly by POOL. Has a decidedly patrician air to it.

sis (SEEZ). Former musical notes (now normally *tis*).

Sis (SISS). Familiarly, a sister.

Sís. **1:** river (SEESS), of Guatemala via San Antonio into the Pacific, 14°09'n/91°39'w **2: Šiš,** river of Russia via Ust'-Kurenga and Vasis, into the Irtysh and thence the Ob and the Kara Sea, 57°19'n/73°23'e.

Sis, ask Costner to not rent socks "as is." Attribution unknown, reported by John JENSEN. This one's charm lies in its staunch antigrammaticality and preposterous surrealism.

sisis. Porkfishes of the West Indies, per BORGMANN.

Sí sí, **Sis.** Polyglot yet natural and easily understandable communication.

Sí sí, **Sis. Isis is I, Sis** (*or* **Isis**). Spanglish: An Egyptian goddess's identity is dramatically revealed to a sibling in (a choice of two versions of) an unusually fanciful construction, the longest we know of in any language(s) in which an alternating letter pair produces something resembling meaning.

Sis, Sargasso moss a grass is. Possibly by MERCER. Illustrated in IRVINE. Droll. We are familiar with Sargasso Sea grass, Sargasso weed and gulf weed (a synonym), but not with Sargasso moss, nor is there anything particularly mossy about Sargasso grass, so we have to wonder if there is indeed any such thing as Sargasso moss and whether such a moss, if any, could ever be grassy; but if there is a place for misplaced pomp and pedantry, perhaps PALINDROMIA is it.

sitar gratis. A discreet "no tipping the musician" sign at an Indian restaurant.

Sit in, Ed. (Adenitis!) Stay home with your inflamed adenoid *or* fill in due to someone else's. For one probable cause of Ed's indisposition or opportunity, whichever it is, see: **A dart's accordioned an adenoid, Roccastrada.**

Sitka, AK, 't is. Possibly unique type of "postal sentence." Compare: **Apollo, PA.**

Sit on a potato pan, Otis. Possibly by MERCER. Illustrated in IRVINE and AGEE. For some reason, a catchy one.

Siva, a *rara avis.* The Hindu goddess of destruction and reproduction, more often spelled *Shiva* than *Siva*, is thus rare in this form, and since she is represented as a bird only in this unusual flight of fantasy, she is thus a very rare bird indeed.

si vis. In Latin, if you wish.

Six elated a cadet, Alexis. **1:** terse West Point hockey **2:** craps result **3:** report.

six I's. Perhaps **I I I I I I** or i i i i i i.

six *xis*. A half dozen of the fourteenth letter of the Greek alphabet, thus: ξ ξ ξ ξ ξ.

Ski Red Erik's! And enjoy free holiday lifts in an ever green land.

Skit a bore: aero-batiks. Brief review of sartorial but otherwise flat stunt flying performance.

Sitar gratis.
"No tipping the musician" sign at an Indian restaurant.

Skooby Books. An imprint of **Proctor Trot Corp.**

Slade, my ROTC?: I vow to do two Victory Medals. Slade is unknown if he is not the recurrent Hollywood Western bad-guy. The ROTC or "rotcee" or Reserve Officers' Training Corps trains college students for commission as officers upon graduation. And a Victory Medal was awarded with the Victory Ribbon to anyone who served in the armed forces of the U.S. during World War I or World War II. All in all, an ambitious project. See also: **ROTC Ivy Victor** and **So, Ed, I vow to do two videos.**

Slang is signals. Original coinage for the occasion by CHISM. Right on, dude.

S/L Annals. Savings & Loan Association minutes or trade pub.

Slate metals. By POOL. Schedule grayish ones, such as lead or zinc.

SLA tip: ACT (capitals). Symbionese Liberation Army to Patty Hearst.

Sled at ice citadels. By the KUHNS. Enjoy a sleighride 'round the winter carnivals.

sleek keels. For smooth sailing.

Sleep till it peels. By LESSER. Advice to the sunburnt.

sleets : steels. REVERSAL, weak attraction, whether as **sleets steels** or **steels sleets.**

SLÉTTUBÖND. The Icelandic word for PALINDROME, according to BORGMANN.

Slob mystic ate tacit symbols. Wolfed the whole blasted tray of Eucharistic wafers.

Slob my symbols! Trash my idols! And shiver me timbers!

Sleek keels

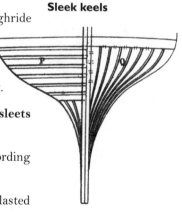

s [. . .] s

sloops : spools. REVERSAL, medium to strong attraction: **sloops' spools,** say, for cable or rope.

Smartness sent rams. By the KUHNS, who alertly saw: "Odysseus' cleverness provided him with the solution to escape from Polyphemus' cave."

Smellier Oreille, MS (uh-REHY). After Pend Oreille (or Ponderay) Idaho, and due perhaps only to an added suggestion of magnolia blossoms, this is the new, improved, and certainly more aromatic and Mississippian version of what was once just a (probably already perfumed) French ear or earring. Could go down in history with the Greater or Lesser Antilles, Upper Volta, and the Outer Hebrides. Already a favorite P.U. fieldwork and safari destination, and, with appropriate minor monkeyings, the title of a manuscript (a Master's [in Science] candidate's thesis) and the egalitarian nontitle of our annual campus homecoming queen.

sms. ABBREVIATION for *smalls.*

Smut Tums. For relief of gas, heartburn, and stomach upset due to excessive pornography.

Smut Tums

snafu fans (snæ-FOO fæns). Our dictionary says *snafu* (now a slang word in its own right) started out as the ACRONYM for Situation Normal, All Fucked Up; according to the KUHNS, **snafu fans** are gremlin lovers who are entertained or amused by foul-ups, chaos, or confusion, as in the following entry.

Snag royal! Piano, Mona? I play *organs*! By LINDON. Brilliant. Possibly an unsurpassable high-water mark for the cartoon-caption genre of PALINDROME and truly a treat for **snafu fans.** Lindon, thanks to his predilection, seems to have tested most major musical terms, so we may guess that the cause of this great success was first his familiarity with a whole orchestra of possibilities but, beyond that, it displays

s [. . .] s

a very deliberate and effective backtracking maneuver from *organs* to the opportune and picturesque *snag royal* to *play organs*, etc.

Snail I victims never even smit civilians. Long-suffering passengers on the original (and maybe slowest ever) slow boat didn't bother chastising nonmilitary crew members or tour organizers; instead they flayed the fleet admiral himself for what they believed to be primarily *his* blatant misrepresention and flagrant nonfeasance.

Snap pans. By POOL. Basically, cookie pans used for making ginger snaps.

Snellen's. Listed by CHISM as an English word, citing *WORD WAYS* without explanation. Perhaps just the possessive of a surname that someone has found, though we can almost remember a drugstore by some such name in Rochester.

Sniffin's. Ditto above.

snipe ninepins. Marshbird bowling game, reminiscent of Lewis Carroll's version of croquet played with flamingo mallets. By the KUHNS.

Snippin's. See: **Snellen's** and **Sniffin's.**

Snippo pyramidism, Sidi! —Mary Poppins. The celebrated governess sends typically original words to a respected but impertinent Egyptologist.

snoops : spoons. REVERSAL, weak: **snoop's spoons.**

Snore here, herons. Sign at the bird sanctuary of our dreams.

Snotty Lyttons. Evidently this refers to the forgotten nasty wing of an otherwise very decent and even aristocratic family that gave us not only ladies Emily and Constance but also the Bulwers, both with and without a hyphen, all big names in Victorian parlor games and theosophy.

s [. . .] s

Snug & raw was I ere I saw war & guns. In which the use of the ampersands is unorthodox and the subject matter dull, but the symmetry is word-perfect.

snug guns. In TERBAN, who clues it "pistols that are tight in their holsters."

Snug Satraps eye Sparta's guns. Possibly by MERCER. This perfectly modular composition gets an *A* also for anachronism.

So, bonobos! *and* **So bonobos!** (boh-NOH-bohz). Bonobos are an endangered Zairean species of dwarf chimpanzee/ humanoid who have sex nearly all the time and are promiscuous in the extreme, for sex has taken the place of aggression in their society in terms of working out problems. They are not reproducing fast enough (for the people who like to eat them), and their habitat is getting trashed. As a bumper sticker, **S. O. Bonobos!** means "save our bonobos." Also **S. O. bonoboS!** and **So Bono Bonobos!**

So! Catnip in tacos!? A CHISM contribution; brilliantly surreal.

So crank on in, OK narcos? Welcome one and all.

So crank on in, OK narcos. Welcome and home free, one and all. We are reminded of Whoopi Goldberg's endearing junkie sketch, our own beloved and **Dedicated Det. Acid 'Ed,** and others on both sides of the drug line—while our parts are finding a way to cherish and not punish our other parts.

Soda Bra by Barbados. Perhaps not unlike the **Air-a-Bra by Barbaria.**

So, Duke, kudos! Acclaim and prestige as a result of your noble position, man!

So, Ed, I vow to do two videos. We inform Acid Ed we are dedicated to documenting in two films the highlights of what will become a later volume of this encyclopedia: our quest to detect or determine, and then to honor suitably, the

s $\lceil$ ... $\rceil$ s

PALINDROMIC capitals of all the states and countries. Substantially less scrutable alternatives are: **Sr. Otis, I vow to do two visitors** and **St. Eloi, vow to do two violets.**

So G. Rivera's tots are Virgos. Attribution unknown, reported by John JENSEN. A great PALINDROME if true, otherwise good.

Sohos (SOH-hohz). **1:** Soho neighborhoods of London and New York **2:** exclamations used in hunting, according to BORGMANN.

So, Ida, adios! Illustrated in IRVINE, 1987.

So I ran ecstasy by SAT scenarios! "Attributable" to Michael Donner is this simple explanation of the means he used not only to reach the school of his dreams but also to develop his remarkable book *How to Beat the Scholastic Aptitude Test and All Standardized Multiple-Choice Exams.*

So I ran ecstasy by SAT scenarios!

So! Javanese Navajos! These would be, without reservation, East Indians, and otherwise Western.

Sojo's. Anything belonging to Seattle Mariner shortstop Luis Sojo, like, say, his family (collectively, **Sojos**) or his fielding shades (**Sojo's [ss.] ojos**).

Sole medere pede, ede, perede melos. See: **Roma, tibi subito motibus ibit amor.**

solo gigolos. Single escorts, an apparent self-reversal. Seen by the KUHNS, illustrated in IRVINE.

solos (SOH-lohz). Musical compositions for a single voice or instrument, the performances of them, or (present tense) the act of performing them.

Solos (SOH-lohz). Being another name for the Indonesian metropolis Surakarta *and* its river (the largest river, at 335 miles, of Java), each considered to be one Solo, and the duo together, two Solos.

s [. . .] s

so many dynamos. Quixotic landscape with windmills, a string of power plants, or this or any other collection of PALINDROMES, such as AGEE's *So Many Dynamos* (New York: Farrar, Strauss, 1994).

So may Apollo pay Amos. Possibly by MERCER. Any reference to the PALINDROMIC postal capital and patron divinity of OMPHALOSKEPSIS (PALINDROMY in the round) automatically gets our attention, and all the more so when he seems to be rewarding (or even making) a prophet. For related developments, see the following entries.

So may Obadiah aid a boy, Amos. Probably by MERCER. You know, the usual Old Testament chit-chat. For additional development, see the following.

So may Obadiah, even in Nineveh, aid a boy, Amos. Probably by MERCER. Oh, that's different. BORGMANN notes that Amos and Obadiah are two consecutive books of the Old Testament.

Some demos! By POOL. Yes, and you should see the real product, too!—or maybe he is expressing his admiration for the entire populace, come to think of it.

**Son, I'm
Minos.**

Some men interpret nine memos. Possibly by MERCER. And some interpret PALINDROMES. This text is a very basic— one might say obvious with the benefit of hindsight— unfoldment of the potent starter word *interpret* [plus *ni-*], etc.

Son, I'm Minos. Thus the King of Crete introduces himself to a young Minotaur.

Son, I sack casinos. Probably by CHISM, 1992. Good gambler's answer to: "How do you get money, Daddy?" And a probably independent AGEE invention, illustrated, 1994. We have no reason to believe AGEE was cribbing from or had even heard of CHISM's book. Thoughts abound and stick around, and all of us are constantly if unconsciously making deposits and withdrawals at "the great thought bank and casino in the sky," or, as it is sometimes called, the Akashic Records.

Sonos (SOH-noozh). Being two rivers of Brazil, each one a Rio do Sono (HEE-oo doo SOH-noo).

Sooloos. One of the chief forms of Arabic and Persian script, according to BORGMANN.

Soos (SOOZ). A familiar name for the (three) Sault Sainte Marie (or Soo) Canals of the United States and Canada, a bridge over one of them, and a railroad proceeding from them, collectively.

soosoos. The dolphins of the Ganges, Brahmaputra, and Indus Rivers, according to BORGMANN.

soot tattoos. Indelibly etched for the occasion by CHISM, straight from the hearth.

So patient a doctor to doctor a patient so. Classic WORD PALINDROME by LINDON. It beats by a full measure the ancient and proverbial **all for one and one for all** and similarly outdoes Lindon's also-famous **King, are you glad you are king?**

Sops Once, Eton's no Teec Nos Pos. A young Indian boy whose name also translates as "Not Overly Fond of Sucking Up" is treated by someone, probably his guidance counselor, to a brief comparison of the foreign and domestic boarding schools he appears to be considering. The PALINDROMICally less "noted" institution is, as you know, situated right here in Navajoland so very near the celebrated "Four Corners" point that it constitutes a virtual direct hit in OMPHALOSKEPSIS. This point, masquerading as ground zero of our globe's most major geopolitical cross, does not actually define the four corners of anything but is in reality just the more celebrated of two right-angle jogs in the simple, single boundary that separates for some fifty-five miles Navajoland (within but not really part of Mormon Utah, Arizona, and New Mexico) from Uteland (within normally cowboy Colorado and New Mexico). The Indians ignore the states but celebrate the four winds here and get $1.50 per tourist. The sense we get is that these and all the other Indian lands are and have been since 1993 in legal reality ("and of rights ought to be") 552 independent countries, yes, sovereign states embedded, like so many Barbarias or Swiss cheese holes, within sovereign states. So the Four Corners, rather than actually existing, simply fall and disappear into one or two of the largest of these preemptive holes. The more famous boarding school is famous for its PALINDROMY and other fields of play. And you, Sops Once, you can have your cake and eat it, too. You can go play palindromy there and then omphaloskepsis here, or of course vice versa, or even, in your case, by special arrangement, both at once.

SOTADES OF MARONEIA. Alleged inventor of the palindromic sentence.

Sore eye, Eros? Illustrated in IRVINE.

So resign it, sap. A sting is Eros. Inspired by BERGERSON's "Ida by the Window," here we have a transaction from a crazy new support group, Lovers Anonymous.

Sore was I ere I saw Eros. By BORGMANN. And balanced, too.

Soros, George. Hungarian multibillionaire speculator and philanthropist.

S O S *or* • • • – – – • • •. A telegraphic call for help and an **AꟼBA** song and album title, originally "Save Our Souls" and subsequently "Same Old Stew" and "Share Our Spectacles."

So-so . . . Los Osos. A Bear State vintner's Christmas commercial suggests elevating a possibly flat holiday season into illumination, richness, and artistic refinement by uncorking three intriguingly named wines, likely from their oak reserve on the central coast.

s [. . .] s

"So-So Solstice?"
So-so solstice?
Satori **ope!**
Lucre **here!**
Hercule Poirot, **a sec!**
It's Los Osos!

SOTADES OF MARONEIA. From what is now known as Thrace, on the southeast Balkan peninsula, comes the alleged inventor of the PALINDROMIC sentence and of palindromic verse, a Greek poet and satirist of the third century B.C., noted for his coarseness and scurrility. According to H. B. Wheatley, via AUGARDE, Sotades made the mistake of lampooning Ptolemy II Philadelphus, who had him captured, sealed in a lead box (sewn in a sack, according to LESSER), and cast into the ocean. In memory of him, palindromic verses are still occasionally called by the alternative name of Sotadic Verses or "Sotadics." In his *Epigrams*, the Roman poet Martial says: "I do not . . . read backward in obscene Sotadics." Quintilian quotes these palindromic lines from Sotades, who evidently must have written in Latin as well as Greek:

Spacer recaps.

Roma, tibi subito motibus ibit amor,
Si bene te tua laus taxat, sua laute tenebis,
Sole medere pede, ede, perede melos.

For an inadequate translation of the above, see: **Roma . . . amor.** See also p. xi.

Sotos. The many namesakes of the Spanish surname *Soto*, or *de Soto*, including many place-names.

Spacer recaps. Astronaut, in REVERSAL, recapitulates his round-trip.

Spa élan aids! Diana leaps! Adapted from a FITZPATRICK poem.

Span snaps. Bridge breaks. The KUHNS.

Sparta's satraps. A nonesuch that might have been if the

345

s [. . .] s

Persians had won at Marathon, in which case not only Sparta but every Greek metropolis would have had one of these Persian governors.

sparts : straps. REVERSAL PAIR by BORGMANN, wherein Spanish and Algerian grasses are worked into strips.

Spider redips. Trailing a thread, she drops and reverses again and again.

Spidery gyre dips. By the KUHNS. A web spirals down into obscurity.

Spill a germ, regal lips *or* **"Spill a germ or feral bit," I blare from regal lips.** Shortened sentence adaptations, in two stages of reduction, from a FITZPATRICK couplet of more than double this overall length, which in the original is subjoined to another couplet to form a rhymed quatrain, of which the meaning is difficult to fathom, as is so often the case with longer PALINDROMES. In such a case it is also hard to say whether one has done, by such brutal cuts, any service to anyone or anything. But we are amused by the results, however they were arrived at, and that is of VALUE.

Spiller gnomes use mongrel lips. True beans flow forth regardless of pedigree.

spit rotator tips *also* **spitted (AC!) Rotator Cadet tips.** The pointy ends of a (peculiarly trade-named) mechanical barbecue grill. (Specify AC, as the DC doesn't reverse.)

S. Pittsburg (TN) event Grub St. tips. See: **Pittsburgh . . . tip.**

Spots disfigure not one rug—if Sid stops.

spoops (SPOOPS). Nineteenth-century collegiate slang for a weak, silly, foolish fellow, according to BORGMANN.

sports : strops. REVERSAL PAIR with little natural synergy, yet strangely exaggerated by TV: athletes and shaving gear.

Spots disfigure not one rug—if Sid stops. By POOL. Mel-low yet still dramatic. And that Sid sounds like quite a character.

sps. ABBREVIATION for *specials*, among others.

SPS. Airport code for Wichita Falls, Texas.

sqs. ABBREVIATION for *squares*, among others.

SRO Jamaica: CIA majors. American spy or culinary heavies throng James Bond's pleasure island.

srs. ABBREVIATION for *seniors* and *sex ratios*, among others.

SS. *Sanctissimus* (Most Holy), *scilicet* (that is to say, namely), and *scriptores* (authors), all Latin, plus stainless steel, steamship, etc.

S. Solon's no loss. The village of South Solon, Ohio, population 379—having drifted blissfully away over 100 miles to the south (and even to the west) of its presumed parent town of Solon, Ohio, population 18,548—is not even missed! We expected them to be closer. Yet how wise of them not to think lackfully!

Star comedy: Democrats. A truism.

SSS. Selective Service System.

S-S-S. Schweiz-Suisse-Svizzera (Switzerland, in its three languages).

SSSS. Society for the Scientific Study of the Sea.

staats. Dutch or Flemish: states; and William Safire thinks there was once a comptroller general named Elmer **Staats.**

Stabats (STAH-bahts). Fanciful nickname for Stabat Maters, medieval Latin hymns.

stab bats. See: **Eva can . . . in a cave.**

star comedy by Democrats. Illustrated in IRVINE, 1987.

star comedy: Democrats. A truism.

Star Comedy: SAT, NAFTA, EPA go to GOP; Perot to rep—Pogo to gape at—fantasy Democrats. "Electoral College Board" returns inspire abstract fun.

Star (eyes pale roses): "O relapse, ye rats." Line from a melodramatic farce, inspired by BERGERSON's great poem "The Faded Bloomers' Rhapsody."

star rats. In TERBAN, who sees them in terms of a "rodents' variety show."

Star sees rats.

Star sees rats. Possibly by STUART, illustrated in *Too Hot to Hoot.*

stats (STÆTS). Being statistics, photostatic copies, thermostats, etc.

St. Céré erects. French county seat goes vertical.

St. Cid dates set addicts. El Cid, canonized, woos confirmed (Word?) junkies.

St. Cid revised Desi verdicts. In an earlier episode (of *I Love Lucy*), the same dude evidently fixed the ratings or edited critical reviews.

St. Curt's boa obstructs. And this our beloved patron of hindrances and retardation (who is, to us, "Anything-But" Curt) very leisurely and deliberately creates a miraculous lot of other obstacles for us as well by means of his **bob, bod, bog, boll, bonny Lynn, bop, borer, boss, bow, box, boy,** and even his copy of ***Boz.*** Moreover:

St. Curt's Ed.: Flesh self-destructs. The point of all the above exercise. We wish he had been this Curt in the first place.

St. Curt's niece instructs. Of course she teaches St. Curt's Ed.

St. Curt's Nocturnal Plan: "Rut Constructs." The advanced theories.

s [. . .] s

steak, salade, kabob o' Baked Alaska, E.T.'s. Wherein an initially promising menu heads out for dessert on the far side. We are not sure if we dreamed this or saw it somewhere.

Stella wondered: "No wallets?" By BORGMANN. How strange that they're completely out of stock!

Stella wondered: "Roy ordered *no* wallets?" By BORGMANN. How strange that he messed up!

Stella won no wallets. But she's not one to depend on the kindness of strangers. Short story. Possibly by MERCER. Illustrated in IRVINE, 1987.

St. Eloi, venin saved a mad Eva's nine violets. Probably by MERCER. Unusual to weird, some may say exotic. We find St. Eloi, bishop of **Noyon,** in our French dictionary (588–659), and likewise we find *venin* is actually French, and only rarely English, for venom, but there is no trace anywhere of mad Eva or her miraculous nine violets, unless—and this is a wild conjecture—she should prove to be a sort of continental version of the English quite-contrary Mary. An alternative direction is **St. Eloi, vow to do two violets.**

stellets. Listed as an English word by CHISM, citing *WORD WAYS* without explanation. Are they twinkling little stars? How we wonder what they are.

"Sten": I back Cabinets. Autobiography, or résumé, of White House backup stenographer Toots Horn. See also: **Ten! I back Cabinet!**

stent nets. Anchored nets used in river fishing, per *Webster's Third*, according to BORGMANN.

Stephanotis? : Sit on, ah pets! REVERSAL SENTENCE, in a word. Observed by BORGMANN. Combining the segments, perhaps even reversing them into **Sit on (ah, pets!) stephanotis,** conjures an appealing image of familiar animals perching in a twining tropical shrub.

s ⌈ . . . ⌉ s

Step on no pets. A small classic. Illustrated in IRVINE, STUART, and TERBAN.

Step, puppets! Offered by CHISM.

Step on no pets.

Stercus : Sucrets. REVERSAL. Compare: **Smut : Tums.**

stets (STETTS). Verb: an editor or proofreader **stets,** or nullifies a correction or omission previously made in printed matter, by marking the place in question with the word *stet* (a Latinism meaning "let it stand") and underlining the affected section with a row of dots; also, instances or occurrences of such stetting. Compare **deled** and consider the compound (and multidimensional) PALINDROME **deled / stets.**

stibnite/tin bits. Tool parts made from, or else little scraps of, an alloy of hard and soft metals. Also, for complete-sentence perfectionists but probably no better, there is: **Stibnite's set in bits.**

Stiff, O dairyman, in a myriad of fits. By BORGMANN, who explains that *stiff* means "stiffen."

Stir granule rock core—lunar grits! CHISM credits *WORD WAYS.* Sounds like real space argot.

Stir grits. Good advice by the KUHNS.

St. Lô bolts (*or* **molts**). Urban flight (or renewal), French style.

Stock cots. Keep them in supply—as opposed to customized ones.

Stop! Murder us not, tonsured rumpots! Possibly MERCER. Illustrated in IRVINE.

Stop rets bold lobster pots. It appears from the headline some lobstermen are paying the price for overworking—an arrest or injunction—and now their equipment lies a-mouldering.

S [. . .] S

Store Psalms, *S, M, L,* as Perot's. Devious proselytical and political strategy of the lunatic religious right: electronically process and reformat the Book of Psalms into the *Small, Medium, and Large Political Truths of Ross Perot.* It is hard to imagine how doing this could have any effect on anything one way or the other, and the stategy, overall, is fairly representative of their lunacy.

stots. Bounces, rebounds, or jumps, chiefly in Scottish, according to BORGMANN.

St. Peccavi Viv accepts. (*Peccavi* means "I've sinned" in Latin.) Viv, because she is one of those peculiar **St. Sin-ists,** not only accepts, she actually adores this old rogue! (**Liv,** too!)

Strafed amid Amos and Andy by DNA — DNA so mad! — I made farts. This was the surprising but still harmless issue when that so-promising, life-giving invention, **a DNA gun in Uganda,** fell into frivolous hands. And what a blast it was to see especially the Kingfish and Sapphire, and then even Ruby, Calhoun, and the entire supporting cast of fictional characters, come fully to life, all as out of control as ever, in our very own life and living room! (And yet how strange it is to contemplate now that, for those already alive, this amazing gun merely causes gas!)

St. Raphaël. Leah parts. Captioned snapshot shows her leaving town on Riviera.

stratagem : megatarts. Illustrated in IRVINE.

Stratford['s] Dr. Oftarts *also* **Stra'ford['s] Dr. of Arts.** Presenting a range of P.U.-matriculated degrees with interplays not only between "oft arts" and "of tarts" but also, implicitly, among this Connecticut city's multiple PALINDROMIC distinctions. For, even without the texts' confirmations, Stratford already stands as the palindromic hub and capital not only of its own state but of all New England, by virtue

S [. . .] S

of being 1: host town of **Point No Point,** New England's only self-standing and entirely natural PALINDROME place, *and* 2: situated at the very mouth, lip, and whisker of the Housatonic, that **Nova Avon** if ever there was one, which channels the runoff of PALINDROMIA's (and BARBARIA's) **Bard[s] Drab** out to the deep. (However—wouldn't ya know it—as soon as we get all our plumbing, etc., so nicely set up, along comes a strike by campus radicals that wreaks havoc and produces some outrageous new demands: a return to P.U.'s mainstay degree, the **ab ovo B.A.** diploma, exclusively, and immediate cessation of the doctoral and all other "hi-falutin' whoring" programs. As we write this we are under siege, and they are shouting, while jumping in through our window: **Stratford-[up]on-Avon-Nova, no [P.U.!] Dr. of Tarts!,** etc.)

Straw? No, too stupid a fad. I put soot on warts. A **megagem** by MERCER. We believe we saw it in *Games,* and probably elsewhere.

straw : warts. REVERSAL PAIR, not a PALINDROME, unless a form of warts typically linked with straw(s). TERBAN offers "scarecrow's skin lumps."

Stressed, are we now to do *two* New Era desserts? Clearly too much heat in the kitchen at the bistro. Among a slew of interesting alternatives to the outer module pair are: the bizarre **Spot, . . . tops?;** the amazingly naturalistic **Spot-stressed, . . . dessert stops?;** and the apt **Sagas? . . . sagas?**

stressed desserts *or* **desserts stressed.** REVERSAL, arguably a PALINDROME: "emphasized sweets."

Stressed for all, I pretack *Caterpillar of Desserts.* Because I am under great pressure owing to many causes, I mishandle this weirdly and preciously named sailboat. (Aren't they all?) And why take the trouble to mention such a thing?

s [. . .] s

Well, if you ever find yourself in the same boat while composing a PALINDROME, you'll understand. Is it any good? Generally long is good (and we'll eat the semantic consequences), but there are exceptions and limits, again depending on one's overall aim.

Stressed was I ere I saw desserts. By BORGMANN. Possibly his nicest progression upon **Able was I ere I saw Elba.** (Though some enthusiasts will prefer his distracted soprano, **Adelberta . . . a trebled A.**)

Strohs Shorts. Little bottles of beer.

sts. Scour the shower.

STS. Airport code for Santa Rosa, California.

St. Sernin rests. This quiet village of Aveyron, France, does its thing.

Stressed was I ere I saw desserts.

St. Sever revests. See: **revests : St. Sever.**

St. Simon sees no mists. Possibly by MERCER. It's his mystic vision.

St. Sin-ists (sehynt SINN-ists). Followers of the eccentric mystic, St. Sin, also known as St. Peccavi, inventor of reverse psychology and advocate of doing everything exactly the opposite of the way prescribed, condemned to burn for heresy in A.D. **666** at the age of 6 but, miraculously, wouldn't ignite, and died, also miraculously, a dirty old man of **99** in **999**. See also: **St. Peccavi Viv accepts.**

ststs *or* **st sts.** Stocking stitches in knitting.

St. Tes', uh, Cass? . . . A Mother, eh? . . . To Massachusetts? A Mother if not a Mama, it seems, is confused with Mother or Saint Teresa, if not both, by an uncertain speaker, while someone is being honored, maybe even canonized, in New England.

s ⌈ . . . ⌉ s

St. Tropez > E-port Ts. Nonstop one-way booby-prize booking, from the French Riviera direct to one's choice of Elizabethport's air-land-or-sea Transportation Terminals (by Newark Airport), the reverse half of the ticket being of course the winner's prize and having already been awarded and swiftly used.

STUART, Raymond. Author of **_Too Hot To Hoot: The Palindrome Puzzle Book_**, illustrated by Pamela Baldwin Ford (New York: McKay, 1977).

Stun gull, lag all lug nuts. Disorient the simpleton, then cover up the hardware.

Stun gull, lug nuts. Disorient the bird, then haul off its food. That's better.

stunt nuts. Feat enthusiasts, by the KUHNS.

Stun, O Coconuts! A native takes aim at something from a treetop. CHISM credits _WORD WAYS_.

Sub ally's a syllabus. A substitute's best friend is a lesson plan.

Sub bus. The shuttle to the U-boat base.

Subi dura a rudibus. Latin: "Undergo (or endure) harshness(es), or rough treatment(s), from brutes," as per William Camden, who adds: "A scholar and a gentleman, living in a rude country town where he had no respect, wrote this with a coal in the Town Hall."

Sub, O Tuareg, in Niger autobus. Sounds like the regular driver needs to be relieved and a Northerner gets to go south.

¿Subo tu auto o tu autobus? (SOO-boh too-OW-toh oh-too-OW-toh-_BOOSS_). Spanish: "Am I getting into your car or your bus?" Credited to Anthony Bonner by ESPY.

succus (SUCK-cuhss). **1:** Latin: juice (_also_, oftener, **sucus**)

Stunt nuts

2: medicinal term for the juice expressed from a plantstuff to produce a drug **3:** variant of *Succoth*, Jewish harvest festival.

Sugar a Psalter . . . et l'asparagus. Fast form of grace said at an Anglo-Norman monastery. See also: **Salt an atlas.**

Suit no Pontius. By the KUHNS. An even more cryptic saying on the flip side of the coin that is rendered unto Caesar.

"Suit no regrets." A motto, Master Gerontius. Probably by MERCER. A good motto if it means, as we suppose, "no point in accommodating or joining a chain of pain." Master Gerontius is probably the Scholastic form of the Molière character Geronte, a ridiculous old man.

Sulus (SOO-looz). **1:** Moro people of the Philippines **2:** several places named Sulu, as for example a town of New Britain and a political unit, archipelago, basin, and sea in and around the Philippines.

summus (SOOM-mooss). Latin: the highest, uppermost, or top (one); masculine gender.

Sums are not set as a test on Erasmus. This jewel by MERCER has gained a proverbial stature: "The great (as exemplified by Erasmus, the theologian and humanist of sixteenth-century Holland) are not tried by the small." BORGMANN on a different tack offers: "Inasmuch as 'sums' are problems in arithmetic, they are not used to test a student's knowledge of Erasmus." He later adds in a PALINDROMICally rhymed triolet verse (ABAAABA>B):

Arithmetic isn't the same as theology,
And **Sums are not set as a test on Erasmus;**
To mix up the two asks for ample apology.
Arithmetic isn't the same as theology!
As well lump together black cats and conchology,
Or measure a mountain by smelling miasmas:
Arithmetic isn't the same as theology,
And **Sums are not set as a test on Erasmus.**

s $\left[\dots \right]$ s

sumus (SOO-mooss). Latin: we are.

Sun a McManus. Irish proverb.

Sun ever! A bare Venus! Voyeurism in LINDON's playlet **"In Eden, I."**

Sun, Eve: Venus! By CHISM. Same idea. In Paradise she tans, a paragon of beauty to begin with.

sunnus. East African antelopes allied to the waterbucks, according to BORGMANN.

Sun opuses upon us. Illuminate us with a showing of your brilliant works. An alternative is: **Sun opus is upon us.** This may mean the sun is shining, and/or it's time to make hay, and/or we have (or should) put our sunscreen on, etc., etc.

Sununus.

Family of commentator John, or comments typical of him.

Sununus (suh-NOO-nooz). The family of commentator John, or comments typical of him.

suolatalous. Finnish: salt economy. Attribution unknown, reported by John JENSEN.

Sup, Mylo, ere Olympus. By POOL. The ambrosia is always excellent.

"'Sur a cima!' Llam' Icarus." "'South to the top!' Call me *Icarus.*" Apposite words, if mystifying that he is talking telegraphic Puerto Rican. Still, *Arrib'arriba*!

sus (SOOSS). Latin: pig, hog, sow.

sus (SOOSS). Spanish: his, her, its, their, thy, your (own)—describing any thing or things.

suus (SOO-uhss). Latin: his, her, its, their (own)—describing any singular masculine thing.

Swag we gewgaws. By the KUHNS, cluing: "Our Australian way of carrying baubles is distinctive."

Swahili haws. Vocalized pauses or left turn signals in East Africa.

Swallow AWOL laws. By CHISM. Meaning eat and so accept them—or stuff 'em.

Swamp Maws. The KUHNS' alligator, also called Bog Jaws.

Swap paws! Universal salutation and/or handshake of people and/or animals, illustrated in STUART.

Swash saws! Lumberjacks' benediction.

S. Wordrow's *or* **S. Wordrows** *or* **S. Wordrow-S.** With the first *S* standing for SOTADES, these are the short forms of the name of the mysterious palindromian oracle, an entity both clearly Sotadic and suspiciously Shakespearean if, as we believe, spear shakes are a good deal like **sword rows.** Not unexpectedly, one occasionally encounters also the variant forms and spellings of this name: **S. Wordrows** and its possessive case **S. Wordrows',** likewise the misguided Sword Rose, S. Word Rose, **Swordrows,** etc., and, though rarely, even such improbable sibilations as **S. Swordrows's.** But there also fortunately exists, besides all this babble rabble, a more elegant version of the **Wordrow** name—reserved only for the most ceremonial occasions—when the normally modest **(S.) Wordrow(-S.)** at last comes fully into his most exuberant hyphen-bloom as **Sotades Wordrow-Sedatos,** to bask sedately (sedatedly?) in the reflected composite glory of his Renaissance-Anglo-Greek-Romantic heritage. ("So da dese word rows sedate us.")

S. Wordrow's

sworn in in rows. A fragment of a picture waiting to be developed.

SYMMETRY. As bipolarity generally, the trace of the unity of all that is projecting itself into duality, and multiplicity—the nonphysical *becoming* physical.

S [. . .] S

t [. . .] t

Tabat. 1: town of Russia, 52°57'n/90°43'e **2:** mountain of Algeria, 2908m, 23°18'n/5°47'e.

Tabor call, acrobat! By the KUHNS. (That funny drumroll is *your* entrance cue!)

Tabor can even acrobat. A versatile instrument it is!

Taco Cat. Illustrated in IRVINE, 1992.

Taconic's Scinocat. A Taghkanic Mount'in Man, or "Raggie" Yankee of the Connecticut-Massachusetts-New York stripe, much inclined to demonstrate there's more than one way to spell (or) skin a cat. See also: **Schenob . . .**

tactile lit cat. By the KUHNS, such as one petted by the light of its own sparks any cold, dark night. Also *Tactile Lit. Cat.*, a catalog of braille literature.

Taft: Fat! By BORGMANN, who commented in *Language on Vacation*, long before the days of **"Not Nil" Clinton** and **Bush: Oh, Sub!** or even **"Retract-it" Carter:** "A Sotadic analysis of the presidency yields only [this] one worthwhile palindrome, short but apt . . . since he weighed more than 300 pounds."

Tahat, Mount. Highest peak in Algeria.

Tanat. River of Wales, via Llangynog into the Severn, 52°46'n/3°07'w.

Tao to a T. Finally, an exact exposition of the Way, by the KUHNS.

Tap Pat. Illustrated in TERBAN, who clues it "Gently touch Patricia."

Ta-ra-ra Ararat! Mount Boom-der-e! Sung following the Great Flood in joyful recessional from the Ark — after the Metz and Sayers song of the Gay Nineties.

Tar a rat at Ararat? By POOL. It was unlike Noah to do such a thing. And it could only have been a ship's rat, that is, an *extra* rat caught illegally hitchhiking, quite in excess of "two-by-two." Unless, perhaps, crew shortages required that he press rodents to hand, reef, and steer.

Tarat. Town of Algeria, near Libya, 26°13'n/9°18'e.

Tardy? Drat! By CHISM. Wherein attention to time is attention to lack.

Tarzan raised Desi Arnaz' rat. Nice one, illustrated in IRVINE, 1987.

Tassajara rajas sat. Big Sur's Zen roshis (big sirs, rulers) meditated around or about their neighborhood's famous monastery.

tat (TÆT). **1:** make lace **2:** part of **"tit** for **tat" 3:** a false or loaded die, according to BORGMANN.

tattarrattat (TÆ-duh-ruh-*TÆT*). The sound of rapping on a door or of rain on a windowpane, which *Guinness* proclaims the longest English single-word PALINDROME, citing the *OED*, which in turn credits Joyce (*Ulysses*) for the invention.

Ta-ra-ra Ararat!

tat-tat (tæt-TÆT) *or* **tat-tat-tat.** The sound of sharp, repeated knocking or tapping.

TAUTONYM (TAW-duh-nimm). **1:** taxonomic ("scientific") designation such as *Gorilla gorilla* in which the genus and species names are the same **2:** logological word for a word or phrase that exhibits any similar reduplication, such as *baba, tom-tom,* and *Walla Walla.* A tautonym is not necessarily or even usually a PALINDROME, but there are many ways to return.

TAUTONYMIC PALINDROME (taw-duh-NIMM-ik). A TAUTONYM that is also a PALINDROME, returning again and again, such as **Ajaja ajaja** or **Mullum Mullum.**

tebbet. Scottish bodily feeling, according to BORGMANN. Nice word.

T [. . .] T

Tebet (TEH-bett) *or* **Tevet** (TEH-vett). The fourth month of the Jewish year.

tee meet. A golf match; by the KUHNS.

Telegram, Margelet. Yes there's someone here by that name. See: **Margelet : telegram** and, for an even bigger thrill, **Lettergram : Margrettel.**

TELEPHONE NUMBERS. See: PHONE CODES.

T. Eliot's toilet. This and various other borrowings are available from the following:

> **T. Eliot, top bard,**
> **Notes putrid tang emanating, is sad.**
> **I'd assign it a name:**
> **"Gnat dirt upset on drab pot toilet."**

By Alastair Reid, it is a fascinating and only slightly scatological composition, commendable for its length, art, lucidity, and wit. ESPY reports that "W. H. Auden enjoyed it so and repeated it so often that he has sometimes been credited as the author." Reid has said: "The dream which occupies the tortuous mind of every palindromist is that somewhere within the confines of the language lurks the Great Palindrome, a nutshell which not only fulfils the intricate demands of the art, flowing sweetly in both directions, but which also contains the Final Truth of Things."

T. Eliot's toilet

Tell a plate man on a morose dam side by me to note my bed is made so Roman on a metal pallet. CHISM credits *WORD WAYS* for this extravaganza of a sentence running to seventy-one letters. The greater the length of a PALINDROME, the less likely it is to make real sense. This one sports such a handsome and natural syntactical arrangement that one imagines it makes sense, even wants to contrive a setting where it could make sense, such as, say, in some arcane print-shop situation and argot, where *plate*, *bed*, *Roman*, and *pallet*, at least, could have their sense and would lead the entire construction into something resembling meaning. Also, for some reason this sentence reminds us of our two favorite examples of famous first utterances by previously infant children: "Boy, you gotta talk fast around here to get a word in edgewise," and "Don't worry about the mess I made on the kitchen floor, Mommy."

Tell if a sahibi has a fillet. Let us know if any Westerner owns (or is wearing) a headband—and, what is perhaps more picturesque, the burnoose to go with it.

Temperature rut a rep met. But happily all his prospects were hot.

Temple help met. A notation to the effect that the synagogue workers have held a meeting.

Ten animals I slam in a net. Possibly by MERCER. Shuttlecocks, we hope. BORGMANN of course suggests a loup-cervier, a pishu, a caracal, a lucivee, a syagush, an anakelard, a gorkun, a manguay, etc.

Tenerife fire net. Azores lifesaving equipment, by the KUHNS.

tenet (TEHN-eht). **1:** Latin: he, she, or it holds (or has) **2:** English: an opinion, belief, doctrine, principle, or dogma *held* by a person or organization.

TENETS, THE SEVEN. There may be more, but these are the ones we know of:

 Tenet A is an (*Ah, tuez!*) euthanasia tenet. *Sacré bleu! Quelle* place to begin!
 Tenet B is a (Ha! Ha!) sib tenet. Also peculiar but lighter and so much better.
 Tenet C is a basis, a basic tenet. Of PALINDROMY, no doubt! Finally something we can live with. Possibly by MERCER, this text, though third in our sequence of seven, is actually the granddaddy of the series.

Tenet C is a basis, a basic tenet.
Of palindromy, no doubt!

T [. . .] T

Tenet D is a Hasid tenet. Good. We could use a religious principle, too.

Tenet E is an *Asie* tenet. Oh no, not back to that French youth in Asia!

Tenet F is Asa's "As If" Tenet. He holds this **tenet** as if it were a **Tenet**.

Tenet G is Rip's *Pirsig* tenet. A Zen-in-the-Art-of thing completes his and our chaotic octave of PALINDROMIC law and order.

ten-game magnet. By POOL. Extremely attractive sort of football cheerleader who is responsible for her school's perfect season and high attendance.

Ten! I back Cabinet! Mistaking the furniture for a dark horse (or a Secretariat) at the OTB window. See also: **"Sten": I back Cabinets.**

Tennessee's Sennet *or* Tennessee sees Sennet! (SENN-ett). It's not so far-fetched to imagine that a Memphis-leaning state that has already built a more or less exact replica of the ancient Greek Parthenon in the midst of its capital city of Nashville might also make some claim to, or might at least be willing to look at and understand, and perhaps even play and appreciate, Sennet, the Ancient Egyptian game of passing through the underworld. And "if you can dig it, you own it"! Secondly but no less fittingly, **Tennessee's sennet** is, as the KUHNS observe, the dramatic trumpet or coronet flourish with which this fine state enters the scene (perhaps playing one of those endlessly repeating Al Gore rhythms).

Tennis animals slam in a sin net. Scene from the Toon Town version of Dante's *Inferno*.

Tennis set won, now Tess in net. Another fine picture, possibly by MERCER. Of course the victorious Tess meant to jump over it.

Ten? No bass orchestra tarts, eh? Cross a bonnet! Probably by MERCER. We find it a bright and amusing shred of gossip but don't know why. It's possible we're missing something here—a lost euphemism or Briticism. But perhaps the uncertainty is in the nature of the illusion.

Tense, I snap Sharon roses, or Norah's pansies net. Probably by MERCER. I'm all thumbs in the garden when I'm not relaxed, but luckily gardening relaxes me.

Ten[s(e)]: SNET. The (taut) Southern New England Telephone Company deserves highest accolades for its good offices and services if not also for its ACRONYM, all of which are only rivaled by its fellow utility and sort of **pal, CLAP,** or CL&P, the Connecticut Light and Power Company.

Ten[(')s] net. Catch a number of redoubling senses.

TERBAN, Marvin. Author of ***Too Hot to Hoot:*** *Funny Palindrome Riddles,* illustrated by Giulio Maestro (New York: Clarion Books, 1985). Nice PAL book for kids.

Terrapins [s]nip arrêt. Maryland team cuts off a challenge by a French team.

Têt.
River of France.

terret (TERR-uht). **1:** round metal loop or ring on a harness pad through which the driving reins pass **2:** similar ring on an animal's collar, used for attaching a leash.

Tessa's in Italy. Latin is asset. Possibly by MERCER. Shows nicely how the past may lurk in the present.

Tet (TETT). Vietnamese lunar new year.

Têt (TETT). River of France, rising near Andorra and flowing via Mont Louis, Prades, and Perpignan into the Mediterranean, 42°44′n/3°02′e.

Tevet (TEH-vett) *or* **Tebet** (TEH-bett). Fourth month of the Hebrew year, usually occurring in December and January.

T [. . .] T

Th' girl laps an asp all right! Said of Cleopatra, no doubt.

Tides edit. By the KUHNS. A law of nature.

Tie bosses, order red roses. So be it. Nice, simple workers' revolt.

Tie it . . . / Till it . . . / Tin it . . . / Tip it . . . / 'Tis it! An ad for one of those multiple-use gadgets.

Tie **soldier-trash (Sartre)—I'd lose it.** By LINDON. Exactly. Let's lose all soldier-trash now, untie the whole lot of it and just forget about it, no matter what Sartre said.

Till it. Dig it or cultivate it.

Tiptop pot pit

Tim must signal a flat no.—*Ziro* (Horizontal Falangist Summit). In a politically conventional note of reverse psychology, the oddly ciphered secret leader of the HFS formally nominates a successor to head his peculiar (tiny, leary) Nihilist/No-Nothing coalition—and thereby not only denies and confirms but also fills his own vacancy.

Tin it. Can it or plate it.

Tinkers, reknit! Itinerant people, reunite! By the KUHNS.

Tin unit. By POOL. **1:** can of food **2:** soldering iron **3:** billy goat.

Tip a pit. Possibly by STUART, illustrated.

Tip it. By POOL. Doff it slightly, upset it entirely, or foul it off.

Tiptop pot pit. By the KUHNS. High beneath the Netherlands, another Amsterdam good time. Or just a high-quality hempseed anywhere.

'Tis I, is it? This appears to be another strange outburst from that "I'm schizophrenic and so am I" guy but doesn't have to be. By CHISM.

'Tis it. At last, the one we've been waiting for.

'Tis Ivan, on a visit. Possibly by MERCER. (Answer to: "Who's that Russian and what's he doing here?")

'Tis sent! I wed a mermaid—airy, mad, I'm amid a myriad, I am remade, witness it! By LINDON. Best wedding announcement we could ever imagine, promises to be a grand reception, and we wouldn't miss it for the world. Thanks for the invite! P.S.: Tails or scuba?

Tissues use us. Sit. It could have been the caption of a *Far Side* cartoon by Gary Larson. A mother germ gently tells her brood the facts of life and patiently coaxes them onto a Kleenex for the first time.

tit (TITT). **1:** bird **2:** teat **3:** what you give or get for a **tat 4:** a dam in a river, according to BORGMANN.

Tit. Town of Algeria near Mont **Tabat,** 23°00'n/5°10'e.

Tiw, as I, is a wit. *Tiw* is the Old English (Germanic *Tiu,* akin to Norse *Tyr,* Latin *Deus,* Greek *Zeus,* Sanskrit *Deva*) god of the sky and of Tuesday, with whom I enjoy spirited repartee, whether I am cast as myself or as a different god— say, of thunder, bangers, and Thursday.

t 'n' t. Tequila and tonic.

TNT. Trinitrotoluene explosive.

To Dot / To Lot / To Not / To Pot / To Rot / To Sot / To Tot / To Wot? Various toasts or dedications.

tog rag argot. *Women's Wear Daily* jargon, by the KUHNS.

To gray argot! Saluting all shades of shadowy and special jargon, but most especially Palindromese.

To Idi Amin: I'm a idiot [sic]. Anything for a laugh at this point. Attribution unknown. Reported by John JENSEN.

T [. . .] T

To Iraqi test set, IQ a riot. For background, see: **Re lucid Iraqi's IQ: a ridiculer!**

TO LA PLATA [CO.] CATALPA LOT. Road sign encountered in a Durango dreamscape (with the *CO.* conveniently meaning either *County* or *Colorado*).

To last, Carter retracts a lot. ESPY reports: "In the 1980 elections, President Carter was charged with reversing himself on major issues to save votes. Professor Edward Scher of New York University summed up the accusations in [this] immortal palindrome."

Too hot to hoot

Toledo Modelo-T. A car made in Enrique Vado's first maquiladora, just south of the border (from Detroit). Consider also the **Toledo-Model O.T.** as a possible replacement for the King James Version. And if *three* such beasties are ever found together, they would naturally constitute a **Toledo-Mode Lot.**

Tolerate tare lot. 1: by the KUHNS, who clue: "Accept weeds as destiny" 2: allow a weed patch.

Toll abstention? No, it nets ballot. By POOL. In which someone elects to omit the tollbooth and gets a "ticket."

tollway : yawl lot. REVERSAL PAIR by BORGMANN, wherein a turnpike turns into a marina of sorts. We could imagine it being called the Yawl Lot Tollway, in which case it sounds like the sort of thing you might take to get to, or into, Lake Michigan.

Tommot. Small city of Russia, 58°58'n/126°19'e.

Toni Tennille fell in net. I, not! Attribution unknown, reported by John JENSEN.

Tonkin [act's a cast! Can] I knot! "Attributable" to U.S. Congress in limiting presidential war-making prerogatives by passing a resolution that broke, set, and tied the Executive hands, as indicated by the text[s], during the heat of the 1960s.

Tonsured nerd, render us not! Contributed by CHISM, effectively forestalling a funny-looking monastic character from handing us over, or boiling us down, or perhaps even translating us into Latin, and much to our gratitude in any case.

Too bad I hid a boot. If you hadn't, then you'd have one for each foot. Illustrated in TERBAN and by AGEE.

Too far, Edna, we wander afoot. Possibly by MERCER. **And Edna** (!), who alone can turn back at the snap of an ampersand, of all people to ramble about excessively with! (BORGMANN comments: "feet are killing me.")

too fat a foot. By the KUHNS. See also: **EEEEEEE.**

Too fey ye foot. Excessively enchantedly you dance. By the KUHNS.

Too hot to hoot. Phrase describing certain estivating owls, serving as the partial title and leading illustration of books by both TERBAN and STUART.

too long no loot. By the KUHNS, who clue it "ineffectual burglar's sigh."

too loth to loot. From the KUHNS, "sentiment of a victor who disdained the spoils."

too mad a moot. The KUHNS' excessively silly student court.

too raw a root. The KUHNS' undercooked carrot.

toot (TOOT). Sound (of) a horn or whistle in rapid blasts, or tipple, both commonly at New Year's.

toot-toot (TOOT TOOT). Favored by BORGMANN, who says (in *Beyond Language*): "Here is a word sometimes encountered in newspapers and magazines, an onomatopoeic representation of the sound of a horn. The word is not in any dictionary, not even a slang dictionary, but its virtues as a TAUTONYM and an eight-letter palindrome force us to give it consideration. . . . The word **toot-toot** is an inherently reasonable one. Frankly it mystifies us why no dictionary has yet seen fit to include a word as obvious as **toot-toot**. Accordingly, we accept it and enhance our precious palindromic stockpile."

TOOTTOOT. First line of whistling WORD SQUARE by BORGMANN.

T	O	O	T	T	O	O	T
O	T	T	O	O	T	T	O
O	T	T	O	O	T	T	O
T	O	O	T	T	O	O	T
T	O	O	T	T	O	O	T
O	T	T	O	O	T	T	O
O	T	T	O	O	T	T	O
T	O	O	T	T	O	O	T

**To senile fatso:
Lost, a feline sot.**

T [. . .] T

Topanga sale: lasagna[,] pot. California lifestyle or dreamin'.

Top a pot. By POOL. Practical advice.

Topeka to take pot *or* **Topeka tot's to take pot** (*or* **tots**). The word is out: the Kansas lottery is to be won by the state government or by a child or children in the capital city. Sounds fixed.

Tope lager, and, Edna, regale pot. This item unites and, with the help of our good friend Edna, reformulates into an original thought two separate lines from a REYNOLDS drinking song.

Topless! . . . UMASS! . . . (A lass??) . . . A mussel pot. What a relief (or it's April Fool's) at Amherst when what seemed to be the report of an exotic **girl rig** in the kitchen there proves only a mumble over an incomplete shellfish crock.

top-level pot. The nation's number one cash crop.

Top spot! "Number One on the charts." By the KUHNS; illustrated by AGEE and in STUART.

Top step—Sara's pet spot. Possibly by MERCER. She likes the view from up there.

Top step's [pup's] pet spot. Possibly by MERCER. In fact, the top step could be any PALINDROME's pet spot by this hard-to-say but easy-to-do FORMULA. Note, too, how in the previous entry Sara, not being a palindrome, arrives by a different route.

To rococo rot! *Dernier cri* of the very late Baroque.

Toronto got no rot. Urban decay was just never allowed there.

torte trot. A snappy little cakewalk, by the KUHNS.

Torture no one. Rut. Rot. CHISM's Three Easy Principles, a comfortable and convenient blending of the Golden Rule, the Call of the Wild, and Ashes to Ashes.

To senile fatso: Lost, a feline sot. A dilly of a personal ad, adapted from FITZPATRICK.

Toss it, Tissot! Give up, watchmaker! By the KUHNS.

tot (TAHT). **1:** small child **2:** small amount **3:** total (verb, usually with *up*) **4:** Latin: so many, so much.

tôt (TOH). French: promptly or early.

tottot. Fruit pigeon of Guam, named in imitation of its cry, according to BORGMANN.

Tow in Niwot! See: **Niwot to Win!**

To wit, I wot. Namely, I know. By the KUHNS.

Traders sell less red art. By LESSER. Could be pumped up into a headline in an artists' trade magazine.

T [. . .] T

Trades opposed art. Unions voted against creative pursuits. By the KUHNS.

Trafalgar rag: *La Fart.* Illustrated in IRVINE, 1987. For some reason, this one has many fans.

Tralee reel art. A Kerry, Ireland, town's dancing skill, by the KUHNS.

Tram art. By POOL. Could be ads or graffiti on or in, or a painting of, a streetcar.

Tram Mart. By POOL. For new and used tram sales.

Trammel a sure Jerusalem mart. Hobble a certain thriving Israeli commercial outlet. By the KUHNS. Moreover, this appears to be the received wisdom from (and/or inspiration behind) Christ's driving the money changers out of the temple. It certainly has a proverbial ring.

Tram-smart. By POOL. Advanced form of street-smart.

Tram soot maims. Ah, chàsm, I am too smart. "What else can I say?" By Joaquin KUHN.

TRANSLATION. The translation of PALINDROMES, literally, from one language into another is virtually inconceivable, except for the occasional miracle such as the translation from English to Spanish of **eye** to **ojo,** and even to render only the general meanings of palindromes into other languages is often very difficult, because most palindromes are already somewhat peculiar syntactically or semantically, and certainly quite gnarled and twisted on occasion, even without subjecting them to the added contortions so often met with in the process of translation. BORGMANN, however, did claim a French-Japanese "soulmate" pair, which nevertheless left us wondering why he didn't provide a translation.

Trap apart. By POOL. Catch your animals elsewhere.

Trafalgar rag:
La Fart

Trap art. By POOL. Rather conceptual. Easier to **trap Art,** we'd say.

trapeze part. A swinging role, by the KUHNS.

Trap part. By POOL. Not all.

Traps part. By POOL. Open and shut.

T. R. art. Such as Mount Rushmore, Elkhorn Ranch, the Bull Moose Party, etc.

Treble Elbert. Mount Elbert, the highest peak (14,431 feet) of the Sawatch Range in central Colorado, if tripled in height (43,293 feet), would be nearly one and a half times as tall as Mount Everest.

TREINTA Y TRES **(33).** Town of Uruguay.

Triceratops, Spot, are C, IRT. A dog is warned about the dinosaur trains of the New York subways.

Trinidad dad in IRT. West Indian father in the subway.

Troper Report. Serious-sounding newsletter for figurers of speech.

Troper Report.
Serious-sounding newsletter for figurers of speech.

Tropical lac I port. Quaint ad or hawker's cry wastes a word—since all lac is tropical (South Asian) in origin—and we are still left wondering in what sense the advertiser carries this product and in what dialect he is soliciting business, if any.

Trucks? Ask Curt. They're his department.

Tru-Goy Yogurt. Nonkosher dairy product, illustrated in IRVINE, 1992.

T-Salt (NaCl) a "Pentagon." Nog at Nepal can't last! See: **Nog . . . Pentagon.**

Tsegi Digest. Published at nearly geologic intervals, we imagine, in the little Indian village of Tsegi, situated near

T [. . .] T

the mouth of Tsegi Canyon, which descends to Longhouse Valley from the Betatakin Anasazi Ruins in Navajo National Monument, Arizona.

T. S. Eliot, toilest. Laborest at reversing thyself still, thou Poet of yore. A complex anachronism. From Will Shortz, on National Public Radio.

Tserclaes' seal crest. See: **Sealcrest : Tserclaes.**

tsigologist (ching-AHL-uh-jist *or* chuhg-AHL-uh-jist). Ingestor of Tsing-Taoism.

Tsing is a signist. The Chinese man talks with his hands.

ttt. Time to think.

tube debut. Elegantly natural phrase for a first TV appearance.

Tug t' actuate taut catgut. Concise plucking instruction for various stringed instruments.

Tumut. 1: river of New South Wales, Australia, 35°07's/148°13'e, flowing from Mt. Jagungal through **2: Tumut** Pond (Reservoir), 35°59's/148°25'e, and Talbingo and Blowering Reservoirs, and through the towns of Talbingo, **3: Tumut,** 35°18's/148°13'e, and Brungle, into the Murrumbidgee and Murray Rivers.

tuna nut. Illustrated in IRVINE, 1987.

tundra hard nut. The KUHNS' Arctic toughie.

Tunisia Raisinut.
Good trade name for a North African snack.

Tunisia Raisinut. Good trade name for a North African snack.

Tupac sat. I revel in a Nile. VerITAS CAput. "Attributable" to a schoolish Schoolcraft upon discovering the source of the Mississippi, Lake Itasca, which he clumsily named from the dog Latin *verITAS CAput* (meaning "truth [is] head") and which he here poetically identifies with the great river of Egyptian antiquity—actually a common nineteenth-century conceit, especially around Cairo, Illinois, and Memphis, Tennessee. Tupac is evidently Tupac Amaru, the Inca King who, as the attributee stresses, never bestirred himself to make this discovery.

tut (TUTT). Footstool or hassock, from BORGMANN.

tut (tuht) *or* **tut tut** *or* **tut-tut.** Exclamation of annoyance, impatience, mild reproof, or disbelief.

Tut. Town of Turkey, 37°48'n/37°55'e.

Tut (TUTT). Short for the Egyptian king Tutankhamen, fourteenth century B.C.

Twenties are in. I erase it—Newt. Majority leader cancels book deal now that the small, unmarked bills have arrived.

txt. Text.

**Twenties are in.
I erase it—Newt.**

T ⌈ . . . ⌉ T

u [. . .] u

Ubu. Latin for Köln (Cologne), Germany!

UFO tofu. Illustrated in IRVINE, 1987.

Uit sunete la o ţară fără drum, murdară, fără toalete? Nu ştiu. Romanian: "Do I forget sounds in a country that's without roads, dirty, and without rest rooms? I don't know." From BORGMANN's *Beyond Language*. Surreal realism.

Ukiah : Haiku. A California or Oregon school of Japanese poetry.

U kowala w oku? Polish: "By the eye of a blacksmith?" Given by BORGMANN. We guess the meaning of the question really boils down to: "Perceived clearly and with sensitivity to the slightest changes in and differences between things?" Exotic.

ulu (OO-loo). Eskimo knife with a semicircular blade for cutting raw blubber.

Ulu. 1: town of Indonesia on the island of Siau, Sangihe Archipelago, 2°45'n/125°24'e **2:** large town of Russia, 60°19'n/127°24'e **3:** town of Sudan, 10°43'n/33°29'e.

ululu. A wail or wailing cry, an ululation.

UMU. Airport code for Umuarama, Brazil.

"Ungastroperitonitis—is it I? Not I," reports a gnu. By LINDON. Wherein a weird word, to the wise PALINDROMIST, is all but sufficient to spin a yarn.

Ungate me, Vic, I've met a gnu. By LINDON. Someone gnu. Gnovel.

U Nu. Former premier of Burma, 1950s and early 1960s.

UNU. United Nations University.

UN U Nu. The Burmese statesman (above), when associated with the United Nations—which he was for some time. And

U Nu.
Former premier of
Burma, 1950s and
early 1960s.

when he is associated with United Nations University, he is **UNU U Nu.**

UPU. The Universal Postal Union.

Uru (OO-*roo*). River of Brazil, in state of Goiás, distant tributary of the Paraná, 15°24's/49°36'w.

Uruburu (OO-*roo*-*BOO*-*roo*). Hispanic surname.

Uruguay au Guru. Formerly "au go-go." A fashionable seventies night spot in Montevideo gets an eighties makeover.

Usu. Large town of China (Sinkiang), 44°27'n/84°37'e.

usu. Unusually, "usually" (and occasionally "by using" [Latin]).

Utah is in Uintah and Uintah is in Utah. The state name *Utah* is a component contained within the name of the geopolitical component Uintah contained within the state Utah (no matter whether we are referring to the county Uintah or the community Uintah, which incidentally are nowhere near each other), and the word *Uintah* holds the additional twist or message: "U*in*tah," that is, a sort of flashing neon sign that recites the above text while also winking: "Uintah is: *in* Utah!" Is this a PALINDROME, or a verbal Möbius strip, or just a segment of a spiral? BORGMANN, in *Beyond Language*, calls it a counterreversal of thought, and when it is unfolded out to its fullest possible stretch—**Uintah is in Utah and Utah is in Uintah and Uintah is in Utah**—it becomes a "thought palindrome," we think, one whose unit is the *thought* block, rather than the word or letter block.

Utter: *Et tu!*

Utter: *Et tu!* The KUHNS: "Prompter to forgetful Caesar."

Utu. Town of Zaire, near Lake Kivu, 1°45's/27°54'e.

uu. How *w* used to be written and is still pronounced.

UU. Airline code for Reunion Air. Really.

Uyu. River of Burma, via Malán into the Chindwinn at Homalin, and a distant tributary of the Irawaddy, 24°51'n/ 94°57'e.

UZU. Airport code for Curuzú Cuatia, Argentina.

VALUE. According to the nonphysical oracle Abraham: "Anything that stimulates thought is of value, and physical beings are so accustomed to getting locked into a sort of pattern of thought that very often they are missing the vibrational meaning that is within the thought that they are offering. And so the fun or the value of this process [of creating PALINDROMES] is that it causes you to approach things in ways you have never approached them, which sort of shakes things loose. It can be very beneficial. . . . There is more fun in the creating of them than anything. In other words, if you are wanting to create something of enormous value, create some sort of a workbook that teaches the reasoning behind it and the process for creating it. While it is interesting to read another's, you get bogged down in it rather quickly, and so we would encourage you to begin your workbook by choosing a few of your favorites, those that really roll cleverly and that stimulate you or please you the most, a limited number of them, then, in sort of teaching the process, guiding others to create their own. You could have tremendous fun in that."

vav *also* **waw** *or* vau (VUVV). Sixth letter of the Hebrew alphabet.

VAV. Airport code for Vaxjo, Sweden.

Venev. Town of Russia near Tula, 54°21'n/38°16'e.

Venom music I summon, Ev. See: **Beware . . . ever a web.**

VERMONT. Mentioned honorably here, and perhaps challengingly dead PALINDROMICally, but see **Shelburne . . . H.S.!** Admission to the **Hall of Follah** does not come cheap.

Vermont *nom:* **Rev.** Like **Nevada Ven.** A name to marry church and state.

VERSUS ANACYCLICI, CANCRINI, DIABOLICI, and ECHOICI. Four Latin terms for PALINDROMIC verses, according to BORGMANN.

Vav

5 Hebraisch.

Figur	Benenn.	Bedeut.	Zahl werth
א	Aleph	Spirit lenis	1
ב	Beth	bh b	2
ג	Gimel	gh g	3
ד	Daleth	dh d	4
ה	He	h	5
ו	Waw	w	6
ז	Sajin	s	7
ח	Cheth	ch Kehl hauch	8
ט	Teth	t	9
י	Jod	j	10
כ am Ende ך	Caph	ch k	20
ל	Lamed	l	30
מ am Ende ם	Mem	m	40
נ am Ende ן	Nun	n	50
ס	Samech	s	60
ע	Ajin	Kehlhauch	70
פ am Ende ף	Phe	ph p	80
צ am Ende ץ	Zade	z	90
ק	Koph	k	100
ר	Resch	r	200
שׂ	Sin	s	
שׁ	Schin	sch	300
ת	Taw	th t	400

They mean "Circular," "Crabclaw," "The Devil's," and "Echoing" Verses, respectively.

VERTICAL PALINDROME. BORGMANN's designation for any text such as **suns, SIS, OHOHO,** or **NOXON** that appears and reads the same *upside down* as right side up. Vertical palindromes are often hand-written for the greater flexibility and license this affords, and they really constitute an entirely distinct art medium, a happy return, to be sure, but with different requirements and possibilities from those met with in ordinary (horizontal, typographical) PALINDROMY. The work in this imaginative realm by Scott Kim, which has appeared from time to time in *Omni* and other magazines and books, is very interesting. Borgmann calls the class of vertical palindromes made only from the seven printed capital letters that look the same upside down as they do right side up *(H I N O S X Z)* "four-way palindromes" (which includes the latter three examples given above). See: MIRROR PALINDROMES.

Victim, omit CIV°. Alternative medical diagnosis and prescription: My dear former patient, there are no victims—period—and your fever, merely 5.4 degrees on a ten-scale, even if a little hard to ignore, is still, as you must realize, only borderline. So I'm telling you, in a stunning reversal of the usual scare tactics, to quit talking Latin about it already, stay happy and healthy in your thoughts—any appearances to the contrary notwithstanding—take two aspirin if you must, and don't call me in the morning.

VIRGINIA. Mentioned honorably here, and perhaps challengingly, as one of the few PALINDROMICally "dead" spots, that is, containing not a single PALINDROME (at least among the names of its major localities) and never having been successfully palindromized itself. *Ave* **VA!,** you sing from a breviary, and the Virgin Mary is surely invoked! Yes, and we have come close to satisfaction, too, but can claim only a few

Viva le té de Tel Aviv!
Hourra? Bravo?

V [...] V

rather remarkable remarks about or attributed to a royal Jordanian monkey: **Husain-I grivet: "I bite Virginia, Suh,"** and variants **Husain-I grivet ate Virginia, Suh,** and **Husain-I grivet's a waste (Virginia), Suh,** etc., wherein *Husain-I* is King Hussein the First.

vitativ. Pertaining to the preservation of life; a reformed spelling, according to BORGMANN.

Viv (VIVV). Feminine nickname for Vivian, etc.

VIV. Airport code for Vivigany, New Guinea.

Viva le té de Tel Aviv! Hourra? Bravo? (But have an Aguila anyway.) Illustrated in IRVINE, 1987.

VLV. Airport code for Valera, Venezuela.

VUELTA, IDA Y. Inventor of the round-trip ticket, which before her time had to be purchased in two separate halves, known as **"going and coming or coming and going."** Without the benefit of the discount fares she instituted, many travelers would not have been inclined to return to their starting points. She was born and also died on April 1 **(1881–1991)** at **Neuquén,** Argentina.

vv. 1: verses **2:** verbs **3:** violins **4:** virgins **5:** vagina and vulva **6:** vice versa.

vvv. *Veni, vidi, vici* (Latin: "I came, I saw, I conquered")— Julius Caesar.

Vvv.
Veni, vidi, vici (Latin: "I came, I saw, I conquered")
—Julius Caesar.

v [. . .] v

W [. . .] W

wadi daw. Ravine raven, by the KUHNS.

Wakaw. 1: town, 52°39'n/105°44'w **2:** lake, 52°40'n/105°35'w, of Saskatchewan, Canada.

"Walden Pond 'n' Op 'n' Ed" Law. Obscure source of the op-ed (opinion and editorial) page in most major newspapers was this little-known principle first enunciated in the political writings of Thoreau: Walk on water as your platform, and your opinions and teachings will flow swimmingly.

Waldorf Rod Law. Thirties' policy requiring guests to check handguns in hotel safe.

Wallace Decal Law. Banning of durable third-party campaign posters.

Walla Walla Mall . . . a wall . . . a W. A shopping center virtually disappears in a cyclone or blizzard or dream.

Wallowa AWOL Law (wuh-LÆ-wuh). Northeasternmost Oregon's strange new enactment to minimize emigration.

Wal-Mart asks a Tram Law. Its lobbyists are rumored to be pushing for an unfunded federal mandate requiring that free streetcar service to all Wal-Marts direct from the nearest downtown shopping area be provided by the "participating" municipality.

Walnut Stun Law. Outlawing the use of these nuts for temporarily disabling someone.

Walnut Tun Law. Providing that large wine casks not be made from this wood.

Walpole lop law. New England blue law prohibiting trimming on the Sabbath.

Walpole-Veda: Develop Law. A new, Anglo-American fifth Veda, complementing the traditional Hindu psalms, incantations, hymns, and formulas of worship written millenia before in the Rig-Veda, Yajur-Veda, Sama-Veda, and Atharva-Veda, that emphasizes—wouldn't ya know it?—more legislation.

Wan, I gas Saginaw. Song of a Municipal Mosquito Control sprayer in spring.

wapiti paw. Elk foot, by the KUHNS.

Ward nurses run "draw." Possibly by MERCER. That's a lottery or office pool.

Ward peed at a deep draw. By CHISM. Outtake from a Western.

Warsaw was raw. By CHISM. Winter had returned to Poland.

War's raw. / Fun's 'nuf. The Ultimate Revolution.

Was it a [bar or a] bat I saw? By BORGMANN. Some kind of a big stick, anyway.

Was it a [car or a] cat I saw? We don't know, but you may need glasses. Illustrated in STUART.

Waldorf Rod Law

Was it a hat I saw? You again!

Was it a mat I saw? You definitely need glasses.

Was it a pat I saw? On second thought, maybe this is all in your mind.

Was it a rat I saw? Mmmm . . . possibly . . . but not likely.

Was it a vat I saw? Mystifying, but there is one satisfactory explanation: You're seeing things.

Was it no merger? . . . Oz *or* Egremont I saw? Yes, Dorothy, the fantastic Kansas and Massachusetts towns of these names continue to go it alone as of this writing, so you must have been dreaming again if you thought you saw them both blended together. See also: **Egremont's a fast "No Merge."**

Wasps an asp saw *and* **Wasps a wasp saw.** Coded rejection and acceptance notices at an exclusive social club. (In small print at the bottom: "Being is loving being that that is, sweet sting.")

Was raw tap ale not a reviver at one lap at Warsaw? Possibly by MERCER. Must refer to a bicycle racing incident . . . but probably not at Warsaw, where it almost certainly would have been vodka.

Wassamassaw Swamp. North of Charleston, South Carolina, or more exactly "ten miles north of Summerville." Found on an old Topo map by BORGMANN.

We mew.

Wassaw (WAHSS-saw) Island. One of Georgia's largest and most pristine "sea islands," mostly a National Wildlife Refuge, yet situated in Savannah's Chatham County; also, an adjacent sound.

waw (VUVV *or* WAHW). **1:** sixth letter of the Hebrew alphabet representing the English sound *v* **2:** Arabic consonant representing the English sound *w*. See also: **vav.**

Wāw. 1: city of southern Sudan, 7°42'n/28°00'e **2:** its river, 7°03'n/27°13'e, a distant tributary of the Nile.

WAW. Airport code for Warsaw, Poland.

Way, A. W. Possible phonebook listing of A. W. Way County Park near Honeydew, California, if it had a phone, or of the park's honoree, if he or she had a phone.

WCW. William Carlos Williams.

We dew. "Attributable" to morning spirits.

We'd lime . . . mildew. By POOL. Sensible and memorable tip.

We don't reverse Potosí. Isotopes revert. No "dew." Nuclear-club telegraphy meaning: "We have faithfully followed the instructions from (our headquarters in south-central) Bolivia [!], and the radioactive substances have returned to their earlier condition with no nuclear fallout. (What do we do next?)"

We'd yen, O honeydew. By CHISM. Country song for lovers who can't elope.

We fructify by fit curfew. We are fruitful thanks to our suitable lights-out time.

We hew. Lumberjacks' hi-ho.

We . . . *I've* decided: I cede view. Even and especially when something seemingly random happens—as, for example, when a very tall person comes along to sit in the row in front of our group and then settles into the seat directly in front of me—I still take full responsibility for everything that happens to me.

We Jew. The rare ethnic indicative, thought by some to be objectionable, but we mean well. Indeed we are delighted for the opportunity to recall that the Jews were some of the first people to read backward (and still often do).

We led a general, a renegade, Lew. Sounds like some kind of a fortunate mixup at the barracks.

Welfare [Mom] era flew. The period in the twentieth century of being supported by the community (by virtue of having babies) went by quickly.

We'll let Dad tell Lew. In fact, we'll let any PALINDROMIC person tell Lew.

Welsh slew. 1: many natives of Wales **2:** Welsh geographic depression.

We mew. Contributed by CHISM, who explains: "What cats say."

W [. . .] W

We name opera, rare poem, anew. By LINDON. One more tribute to a favorite subject. For a master composer capable of scores like, say, the following entry, the present text must have been a throwaway, a jest, and a mere jingle by comparison as soon as it was discovered that *opera* projects [,] *rare po-* and hence, surely and quickly, *poem* and the outer closures.

Went on Rowena: "Lo, I've not one viola, new or not new." By LINDON. Possibly a strange and distant sequel or echo of BORGMANN's **A new order began, a more Roman age bred Rowena.** Lindon's text, marvelously resonant of the music of a viola, seems and probably is just another of his offhanded but breathtaking instrumental improvisations. At a certain point, one has to stop wondering how he does it in order to just luxuriate in the wonderful effects.

We panic in a pew. Claustrophobic reaction to a church bench. By the KUHNS.

We seven, Eve, sew. Possibly by MERCER. Illustrated in IRVINE, 1987.

We sew.

We sew. Evidently the most concise available PALINDROMIC sentence with normal subject and verb. Compare: **We hew** and **You buoy.** On the other hand, we could stretch the point down to the tiny sentence **I pi.** The novel verb *to pi,* working by analogy with verbs like *to double, triple, square,* must mean to multiply by 3.1416 or else to reckon the circumference of a circle from its diameter, and so as a game bid or bet, **"I pi"** is considerably stronger than the ordinary "I (re)double."

Westward Hoh! Draw + sew! A deeper-than-usual reverie—were we in the **Hoh** Rain Forest of the Olympic Peninsula (site of the only PALINDROMIC national park visitor center)? Or just somewhere on the **Hoh** River, which drains it? Or on the **Hoh** Indian Reservation (the only palindromic such), situated at the **Hoh** River's Pacific mouth and inaccessible by road? (All these **Hoh**s are roughly as far westward as one can go in the contiguous states.) Normally it is unheard of, unthinkable, and inadmissible to "draw + sew" a lowercase letter *t* into a plus sign or ampersand. But in our dreaming arts + crafts we did it anyway.

WISCONSIN. Mentioned honorably here, and perhaps challengingly, as one of the few PALINDROMICally "dead" spots, that is, containing not a single PALINDROME (at least among the names of its major localities) and never successfully having been palindromized itself. **I wag a WI,** you gesticulate!

WNW. West-northwest.

Wolf! Low! The original, unexpurgated utterance of "the boy who cried 'Wolf!'"

Wollaston's not sallow. British physiologist William Hyde Wollaston (1766–1828) and a beach and neighborhood of Quincy, Massachusetts, which was possibly named for him or his ilk, are and were graced by healthy complexions and even, in season, good tans. (Likewise, **Wollaston saw I was not sallow.** And so forth.)

Wolley Segap (WAHL-ee SEE-gæp). This cartoon character who used to appear in print ads and TV commercials advertising advertising in the Yellow Pages of AT&T phone directories qualifies not as a PALINDROME nor even as a REVERSAL but only as a REVERSAL REVERSAL or redoubled reversal, a rather unusual and peculiar but still natural phenomenon that shows in letter symbols the same "double cross-polar" movement that is physically observable when a deck of cards is first turned over and then cut. The phenomenon, whether symbolic or physical, curiously denies that a negative negative makes a positive but still poignantly confirms that two wrongs don't make a right. And since there's no denying that one good turn deserves another, see: **Eivets Rednow.**

Wołów *or* Wohlau. Town of Poland near Wroclaw, 51°21'n/ 16°39'e.

Woman, I too fall a foot in a mow! BORGMANN line, after "Merrily do I on haystacks cavort. . . ."

Women . . . ; and . . . women. Beginning, middle, and end of an admirable seventeen-word WORD PALINDROME by LINDON, a rap rhapsody with a strange cadence straddling prose and poetry. Missing words (each used twice) are *once*, *painted*, *pictures*, *pretty*, *such*, *they*, and *were*. The solution appears in BERGERSON's book, page 109.

Wonders! In Italy Latin is red now. Probably by MERCER. Great idea to make it stand out instantly from the Italian! The text is an example of the very happy marriage of two equally endowed families, *-n Italy Latin* and *wonder[s] . . . red now*, and it is a great credit to the matchmaker who saw the possibility.

won now. Illustrated in TERBAN, who clues it "I lost then but . . ."

Won't casts act now? Now that the actors' strike is over and the curtain is rising, *Cab* (Calloway), *Cal* (Coolidge), (Al) *Capp*, (Mama) *Cass*, *Cat* (Stevens), etc., whether as these casts' members or their understudies, can substitute for *casts*.

Won't I? No stats on it now. By CHISM. Wonderfully, abstractly evocative. . . . And stats can't predict your behavior anyway. They are only the result of how others have been flowing their energy. Whether you will or won't is up to you.

Won't I repaper it now? You will if you want to, and it appears you do. Here, **repaper** is in a FORMULA position that will work for virtually any PALINDROMIC transitive verb without inflectional suffix: for example, **deed, level,** or **toot.**

Won't lovers revolt now? Not if they are still lovers.

Wonton : not now. REVERSAL PAIR observed by Will Shortz on National Public Radio and animated with appropriate punctuation and line art by AGEE.

WORD PALINDROME. Type of PALINDROMIC phrase or sentence whose component units are not single letters, as is usual, but whole words. Some examples: (1) **All for one and one for all;** (2) **So patient a doctor to doctor a patient so;** (3) **King, are you glad you are king?** Composing word-unit PALINDROMEs is an entirely different kettle of fish from composing letter-unit palindromes. We have hardly a clue how to go about it, nor much desire to get into it, but we do find ourself marveling when confronted with a good example. The word-unit composer seems to require as good a grasp of syntactic possibilities as the letter-unit composer requires of spelling possibilities. The only catch is that the two types of familiarity are quite distinct and perhaps equally hard to acquire.

Won't I? No stats on it now.

Wordrow. The word, in Palindromese, for a PALINDROME or for the Palindromese language itself. Speaking or writing in basic or common **Wordrow** is surpassed, in degree of immersion, only by speaking or writing in its most exotic and elegant regional dialect **ESE** (East-Southeast) **Word-rowese.** The plural of **Wordrow,** like *shad roe,* is also **Word-row.** See also: **S. Wordrow's.**

Word Row (WUHRD ROH). **1:** LOGOLOGISTS' address **2:** (well-turned) phrase **3:** (*as* RÆW), ruckus. See also: **S. Wordrow's.**

WORD SQUARE PALINDROME. Square composed of PALINDROMIC words and/or REVERSAL PAIRS arranged in either vertical, horizontal, or both vertical and horizontal symmetry. Word squares needn't be and aren't usually palindromic constructions. Two fine examples by Dmitri BORGMANN of word square palindrome arrangements (which have the added distinction of carrying a meaning, that is, of being more than just intersections of unrelated words) are:

H	A	L	E	S		A	N	N	A
A	N	E	L	E		N	O	O	N
L	E	V	E	L		N	O	O	N
E	L	E	N	A		A	N	N	A
S	E	L	A	H					

WORD WAYS: The Journal of Recreational Linguistics. Published quarterly since 1968 by Ross and Faith Eckler, from Morristown, New Jersey; an occasional source of PALINDROMES and a good wordplay VALUE at about five bucks a pop.

works at a task row. Labors on an assembly line; by the KUHNS.

worm row. An altercation illustrated in IRVINE, 1992.

worn Aegean row. That tired Trojan War, by the KUHNS.

Worse, *Kama Sutra*—sad loss, sold as art—USA makes row. By LINDON. Seems a bit crazed, but understandable, even well put, in view of the circumstances. Let it be a monument to poetic license, then, and certainly an encouragement of any discontinuity or incoherency or CASUALness you or anyone else may wish to enshrine in an original PALINDROME.

wow (WÆW). **1:** exclamation of wonder or amazement **2:** to mew like a cat **3:** to impress **4:** waiting on weather.

WOW. 1: Wider Opportunities for Women **2:** Woodmen of the World.

wow-wow. Silver (well, ashy-gray) gibbon of Java, according to BORGMANN.

WSW. West-southwest.

Wow-wow

WW. 1: airline code for Trans-West **2:** Woodrow Wilson **3:** *Who's Who* **4:** World War **5:** wrong word.

WWW. 1: *Who Was Who* **2:** World Wide Web **3:** World Weather Watch.

WWWW. *Worldwide What & Where,* a geographic glossary and globetrotters guide **(gggg).**

WWW.

Who Was Who or World Wide Web or World Weather Watch.

w ⌜ . . . ⌟ w

X [. . .] X

Xerxes: ex-Rex

Xanax (ZÆ-næks). Trade name of a sedative drug, the only fully authenticated single-word PALINDROME that begins (and of course ends) with *x*.

Xenon. (One X!) Not to be confused with Exxon, **Xanax,** Xerox, Xerxes, or **Xolox.**

Xerox a noted Eton ax, O Rex. By Robert A. Rubin, who offers "one of the sharp documents that led to victory at Waterloo, I think." The use of four *x*s is an accomplishment.

Xerxes: ex-Rex. By CHISM. Very neat former king.

XIX. Nineteen, in Roman numerals.

X. O. Box. Like a P.O. Box, only different, perhaps a receptacle for kisses **(XXX)** and hugs **(OOO)** . . . or any space, but especially the central square, of a ticktacktoe grid (#).

Xolox. Pure BORGMANN, who says this remarkable word "has baffled us for a good many years. We originally ran across a mention of [it] in one of the *Little Blue Books* published by the Haldeman-Julius Company of Girard, Kansas (either Book No. 1103, the *Book of Puzzles and Brainteasers*, by George Milburn, or Book No. 1350, *Curiosities of the English Language*, by Lloyd E. Smith; we don't remember which one, and the two booklets are no longer in our hands). The source in question referred to **Xolox** as a known PALINDROMIC name. Ever since that time, we have examined every dictionary, encyclopedia, atlas, thesaurus, and other reference work that has come into our possession in an utterly futile attempt to pin down this mysterious and beautiful word. It just doesn't seem to be anywhere! . . . Do you happen to know who, what, or where **Xolox** is? Can you point to a published book or magazine in which that name is shown? If you are such a lucky individual, won't you share your knowledge with us?" We have been unable to locate either **Xolox** or BORGMANN.

XX. 1: Roman numerals for *twenty* **2:** airline code for Valdez Airlines **3:** double-cross **4:** double strength **5:** *Dos Equis* beer.

XXX. 1: Roman numerals for *thirty* **2:** symbol for flour **3:** triple strength **4:** international urgency signal.

XXXX. 1: quadruple strength **2:** (rarely) Roman numerals for *forty*.

XXXXX. Quintuple strength (etc.).

XXX.

Roman numeral thirty; the symbol for flour, triple strength, and international urgency signal.

X [. . .] X

y [...] y

Yacht rebate? Get a berth cay! By the KUHNS. Wherein it is suggested that a docking *island* can be acquired merely for the cash-back from a boat purchase! (It *must* be better in the Bahamas.)

Yale lay. By the KUHNS, who sensibly clue it: "Whiffenpoof Song."

Yale ran a relay. By LINDON. It's become a regular event.

Yale relay. Nearly always plural (but who cares?—it probably started out in the singular, as LINDON clearly states in the above entry), the annual collegiate track-and-field extravaganza at Yale University in New Haven, Connecticut.

Yale relay.
Track-and-field
extravaganza.

Y'all, I'm Millay. Self-introduction to a Southern audience by Edna St. Vincent.

Yams I'd nip in dismay. Sweet potatoes I would pinch apprehensively. By the KUHNS.

yaray (yah-*R*AHY). A slender Puerto Rican fan palm, the leaves of which are used for making hats, according to BORG-MANN.

Yaw a kayak away. By POOL. They're supposed to roll.

Yaw at New Castle felt, Sac went away. This may mean that when a certain tribe of Algonquians (oftener called Sauk or Sauks than Sac, actually) got a sense of how the early European Delawareans were careering about generally, or of how in particular William Penn was rotating his famous twelve-mile arc about a point in New Castle (which has since become assimilated with the pinnacle of the cupola atop the county courthouse there), the Indians, imagining the settlers to be erecting an enormous tepee and so mistaking them for just a bunch of regular Indians, albeit with prodigious reach, quietly headed for their (at the time) new and now historic home around Lake Michigan so as to give the new settlement a wide berth. There also exist at least one or two other PALINDROMES built off of the same central core as the text's, but they are so fraught with sexual and racial delicacy that we can't bring ourselves to repeat them. Perhaps you will figure them out. For additional aspects of the story as presented, see: **Pinnacled, Del. can nip.**

Yaw away. Career about all you like.

Yawn a more Roman way. Possibly by MERCER. *Oscita? Oscitatio?* Or BORGMANN's gloss: "It is part of a true gentleman's education to learn the different styles of yawning. To yawn in the classic Roman fashion is the hallmark of breeding and gentility."

(. . . Yawn.) Madonna fan? No damn way! Attribution unknown, reported by John JENSEN. Masterful and witty construction, despite its ill humor.

ycnamancy (*IKK*-nuh-M*Æ*N-see). Reading PALINDROMES as omens or prodigies, or gleaning their inner truth in any way.

Ye boy, obey! By POOL. Follow a dialect in which ye may be singular!

Yell, Amos O'Malley *or* **Yell "Amos O'Malley."** Two versions of a cry heard in a loud pub.

Yell! Avoid a radio valley! Transmitted by CHISM, effectively and without a gap.

Yell a *V*, Oro Valley! A *V* for a victory of a sort, insofar as there is no more prominent PALINDROME in the entire state of Arizona than this northerly burb of Tucson . . . and it can be forgiven for this small ruckus in view of the extreme brevity and levity of its triumph and rap: **An oz. I rap, Arizona.**

Yell a *V*, Oxoboxo Valley! A *V* for another victory, this one earned by being the probable PALINDROMIC capital of Connecticut, or at least a leading nominee for this distinction. **Oxoboxo** Lake and its outlet the **Oxoboxo** "River" flowing

Yell! Avoid a radio valley!

over **Oxoboxo** Dam and beneath **Oxoboxo** Dam Road all cluster within a tight little valley of only a few square miles situated entirely within the town of Montville. Their claims to capitaldom are (1) their strikingly handsome and even exotic name (charading hugs and kisses around the core being); (2) the fact that they are not just one thing but comprise a whole constellation, including even a probable chief gnome and address, **Dr. Mad, Oxoboxo Dam Rd.;** and (3) the fact that all together they constitute, in our imagination at least, an extended palindromic theme park and playground. But other nominees for palindromic state capital (the competition in Connecticut is stiff) include: the rambunctious **Ohoho,** a defunct ski area that still shows up on some maps but is today only a ghost PALINDROME, for its former ski lodge, still connected to its rusting towbar-lift, is now but an unusual-looking residence and is capable of disappearing entirely, we assure you, on a foggy night; **Point No Point,** the intriguingly immaterial repeatedly disappearing WORD PALINDROME on Long Island Sound near Bridgeport; **Mad R. Dam,** actually a single name for several dams built by the Army Corps of Engineers above Winsted and, in this necessarily abbreviated form, a repetitive artifice; and finally, our doubly beloved royal court of BARBARIA, so conveniently situated at **97060 Twin Lakes Ct., Twin Lakes, CT 06079.** A final decision is still pending and will be reported in a future edition of this volume or a future volume of this encyclopedia. (In the outcome, here flashed back direct from the future, **Oxoboxo**'s victory celebration proved premature. **Point No Point** was eventually declared palindromic capital of Connecticut and all New England, as it stands alone in the state and region for having an entirely self-standing name. **Oro** Valley, though not self-standing, was declared Arizona's palindromic capital for lack of any other serious, or frivolous, candidate.)

Yell upset a cider, predicates pulley. Nicely illustrated in IRVINE, 1987, Rube Goldberg fashion.

Ylevitatively

Yelm Ley. Oracular seat of the outrageous Ramtha, a horse meadow in Washington.

yen o' honey. Longing for or of a sweet; poetic.

yen o' money. Longing for cash; poetic; from the Japanese.

"Yes (Re: J)," Went New Jersey. A postelection news leader indicating Proposition J was passed by voters in the Garden State. This came as quite a relief after squirming with stuff like: **Yes, Rej** [whoever he or she may be]: **we name Ma New Jersey.**

Yes, Syd, on *Odyssey*. His or her book or boat or trip meets with approval. Compare: **Dailies use *Iliad*.**

Yes, Syd, Owen saved Eva's new Odyssey. Possibly by MERCER. BORGMANN puts *Odyssey* in quotes and says: "It was the only decent thing he could do—after all, it was Owen who had stolen her first copy. . . ."

ygology (WHY-*GOLL*-uh-gee!). The study of amazement? or of the *why* of things?

ylevitatively. An extreme BORGMANNism, meaning "very levitatively," and making use of the somewhat archaic intensive prefix *y-*.

Y'll, I wot, refer to Willy. And I like to mention him, too.

Yo! Bottoms up, U.S. Motto, boy! Deserves to be. Possibly by MERCER.

yo doy (yoh-DHOY). Spanish: I give.

Yo! Jadedness ended a joy. Adapted from FITZPATRICK.

Yosemite [Village LSD's legal! Live] times! Oy! Really! On summer weekends it's just like a live-in Central Park there but with extra-uplifting "skyscrapers." If you don't like the "Oy!" change Yosemite to Semite (hah!) or else cut directly to Tompkins Square Park with **E. Village LSD's legal! Live!**

yo soy (yoh-SOY). Spanish: I am.

You buoy. You are an uplifter to the very core of your being. **(We sew.)**

You can cage a swallow, can't you, but you can't swallow a cage, can you! By LINDON. This WORD PALINDROME can probably make a claim to being on the level of folklore.

yo voy (yoh-BVOY). Spanish: I go.

yoy. In (Scottish?) dialect: "yes," according to BORGMANN.

YQY. Airport code for Sydney, Nova Scotia.

Yreka Bakery. In a Mark Twain story, Yreka (California) gets its name when a hacked, scrapped bakery sign returns from the dump and is misread, backward. BORGMANN as recently as 1965 did find such a bakery there at 322 West Miner Street, owned by Martin Sutor. But ESPY reported it gone by 1981. However, LESSER in 1991 reports a new establishment of the same name but in a different location. And see next entry.

Yrella Gallery. Per AUGARDE: "The last word in palindromic ingenuity goes to the inhabitants of a town in California called Yreka. This town once had a shop called **Yreka Bakery.** The palindromic name seemed lost when the shop had to close down, but it reopened [evidently at the same West Miner Street location] as the Yrella Gallery." Was this Martin Sutor's doing? (See previous entry.)

YTicity (why-TISS-uh-tee *or* why-tee-ISS-uh-tee). Degree to which the character or features of the Yukon Territory are exhibited. (Compare easily NWTicity, or, with a stretch, Alaskicity.)

Yuba's a buy! Chamber of Commerce and/or Realtors' promotion in Yuba City, California.

YUY. Airport code for Noranda-Rouyn (or Rouyn-Noranda), Quebec.

YWY. Airport code for Wrigley, Northwest Territories, Canada.

YYY. Airport code for Mont-Joli, Quebec.

YTicity

Y [...] Y

Z [. . .] Z

ZAZ. Airport code for Zaragoza, Spain.

Zeus, foe of Suez. Olympus opposes a canal.

Zeus, fox of Suez. Or slyly favors it.

Zeus was deified, saw Suez. Perhaps by MERCER. Impossible to deify Mr. God, of all people, unless he was once not a god, and we may suppose he always saw Suez from the beginning. So perhaps there is a limit somehow upon what may be dreamt. But we do not want to rule anything out, only to select what is best to the best of our ability, and we do like this one for being brash and for being the alphabetically last PALINDROMIC sentence we could find in "normal" English. (CHISM has offered: **Zip ale, Lapiz!**)

ZIP CODES (U.S.). The approximately 450 working PALINDROMIC zip codes given below represent fewer than half of all possible five-digit NUMBERDROMES, but the unused numbers may some day be called into service as postal zones proliferate. Also, note that many zips indicated below cover only a portion, and not the entirety, of the place(s) named. If in doubt about a particular mailing address, refer of course to the most recent postal zip code directory.

01010	Brimfield, MA	04740	Easton, ME
01510	Clinton, MA	04940	Farmington Falls, ME
01610	Worcester, MA		
01810	Andover, MA	05050	McIndoe Falls, VT
02020	Brant Rock, MA	05150	North Springfield, VT
02120	Roxbury, MA		
02720	Fall River, MA	05250	Arlington, VT
02920	Garden City and part of Cranston, RI	05350	Readsboro, VT
		05450	Enosburg Falls, VT
03230	Danbury, NH	05650	East Calais, VT
03830	East Wakefield, NH	05750	Hydeville, VT
04040	Harrison, ME	05850	Lyndon Center, VT
04240	Lewiston, ME	06060	North Granby, CT
04640	Hancock, ME	06260	Putnam, CT

06360 Norwich, CT
06460 Milford, CT
07070 Rutherford, NJ
07470 Wayne, NJ
07670 Tenafly, NJ
07870 Schooleys Mountain, NJ
07970 Mt. Freedom, NJ
08080 Sewell, NJ
08880 South Bound Brook, NJ
09090 APO: Roedelheim, Germany
10001 Postmaster and General Delivery, New York, NY
10101 New York, NY
10301 Staten Island, NY
10501 Amawalk, NY
10601 Postmaster and General Delivery, White Plains, NY
10701 Postmaster and General Delivery, Yonkers, NY
10801 Postmaster and General Delivery, New Rochelle, NY
10901 Suffern, NY
11211 Williamsburg, Brooklyn, NY
11311 Flushing, NY
11411 Jamaica, NY
11611 Far Rockaway, NY
12121 Melrose, NY
12221 Albany, NY

12321 Schenectady, NY
12421 Denver, NY
12521 Craryville, NY
12721 Bloomingburg, NY
12821 Comstock, NY
12921 Chazy, NY
13031 Camillus, NY
13131 Parish, NY
13231 Syracuse, NY
13331 Eagle Bay, NY
13431 Poland, NY
13631 Denmark, NY
13731 Andes, NY
14041 Dayton, NY
14141 Springville, NY
14241 airmail facility, Buffalo, NY
14441 Dresden, NY
14541 Romulus and MacDougall, NY
14641 Rochester, NY
14741 Great Valley, NY
14841 Hector, NY
15051 Indianola, PA
15351 Nemacolin, PA
15451 Lake Lynn, PA
15551 Markleton, PA
15751 Juneau, PA
15851 Reynoldsville, PA
15951 St. Michael, PA
16061 West Sunbury, PA
16161 Wheatland, PA
16261 Widnoon, PA
16361 Tylersburg, PA
16561 Erie, PA
16661 Madera, PA

ZIP CODES: **10001**
Postmaster and
General Delivery,
New York, NY.

z [. . .] z

16861	New Milport, PA	23232	Richmond, VA
17071	New Germantown, PA	23432	Suffolk, VA
		23532	Norfolk, VA
17271	Willow Hill, PA	23832	Chesterfield, VA
17371	York New Salem, PA	24142	Radford, VA
		24442	Head Waters, VA
17771	Trout Run, PA	24542	Danville, VA
18081	Springtown, PA	24842	Hemphill, WV
18981	Zion Hill, PA	24942	Glace, WV
20002	Northeast Station, Washington, DC	25052	Crown Hill, WV
		25152	Page, WV
20202	U.S. Department of Education, Washington, DC	25252	LeRoy, WV
		25352	Charleston, WV
		25652	Whitman, WV
20402	U.S. Government Printing Office, Superintendent of Documents, Washington, DC	25752	Huntington, WV
		26062	Weirton, WV
		26162	Porters Falls, WV
		26362	Harrisville, WV
		26462	Wolf Summit, WV
20502	Executive Offices of the President, NASC, Washington, DC	26562	Burton, WV
		26662	Canvas, WV
		27572	Rougemont, NC
		27672	Raleigh, NC
20602	Waldorf, MD	27872	Roxobel, NC
20902	Silver Spring, MD	27972	Salvo, NC
21012	Arnold, MD	28082	Kannapolis, NC
21212	Baltimore, MD	28282	Charlotte, NC
21612	Bozman, MD	28382	Roseboro, NC
21912	Warwick, MD	28582	Stella, NC
22022	Chantilly,VA	28682	Terrell, NC
22122	Newington, VA	28782	Tryon, NC
22322	Alexandria, VA	29292	Columbia, SC
22622	Brucetown, VA	29492	Wando, SC
22722	Haywood, VA	29592	Sellers, SC
22922	Arlington, VA	29692	Ware Shoals, SC
23032	Church View, VA	30103	Adairsville, GA

ZIP CODES: **27672**
Raleigh, NC.

z [...] z

30203 Auburn, GA	**35253** Birmingham, AL
30303 Atlanta, GA	**35453** Cottondale, AL
30503 Gainesville, GA	**35553** Double Springs, AL
30603 Athens, GA	**35653** Russellville, AL
30703 Calhoun, GA	**35953** Ashville, AL
30803 Avera, GA	**36163** Montgomery, AL
30903 Augusta, GA	**36263** Graham, AL
31013 Clinchfield, GA	**36663** Mobile, AL
31213 Macon, GA	**36763** Myrtlewood, AL
31313 Hinesville, GA	**36863** Lanett, AL
31413 Savannah, GA	**37073** Greenbrier, TN
31513 Baxley, GA	**37373** Sale Creek, TN
31713 Arlington, GA	**37873** Surgoinsville, TN
31913 Columbus, GA	**38083** Millington, TN
32123 Daytona Beach, FL	**38183** Memphis, TN
32223 Jacksonville, FL	**38483** Summertown, TN
32323 Lanark Village, FL	**38583** Sparta, TN
32423 Bascom, FL	**38683** Walnut, MS
32523 Pensacola, FL	**39193** Whitfield, MS
32723 Deland, FL	**39293** Jackson, MS
32823 Orlando, FL	**40004** Bardstown, KY
32923 Cocoa, FL	**40104** Battletown, KY
33033 Homestead, FL	**40204** Louisville, KY
33133 Miami, FL	**40504** Lexington, KY
33233 Miami, FL	**40604** Frankfort, KY
33333 Fort Lauderdale, FL (reserved, not in use)	**41014** Covington, KY
	41214 Debord, KY
	41314 Booneville, KY
33433 Boca Raton, FL	**41514** Belfry, KY
33633 Tampa, FL	**41614** Graynor, KY
33733 St. Petersburg, FL '	**41714** Bear Branch, KY
33933 Goodland, FL	**42024** Barlow, KY
34243 Sarasota, FL	**42124** Beaumont, KY
34643 Largo, FL	**42324** Belton, KY
34743 Kissimmee, FL	**42724** Cecilia, KY
35053 Crane Hill, AL	**43234** Columbus, OH

ZIP CODES: **32823** Orlando, FL.

z [...] z

43334 Marengo, OH
43434 Harbor View, OH
43534 McClure, OH
43634 Toledo, OH
43734 Duncan Falls, OH
43934 Lansing, OH
44044 Grafton, OH
44144 Cleveland, OH
44344 Akron, OH
44444 Newton Falls, OH
44644 Malvern, OH
44844 McCutchenville, OH
45054 Oregonia, OH
45154 Mt. Orab, OH
45254 Cincinnati, OH
45354 Phillipsburg, OH
45454 Dayton, OH
45654 New Plymouth, OH
45854 Lafayette, OH
46064 Pendleton, IN
46164 Nineveh, IN
46264 Indianapolis, IN
46664 South Bend, IN
46764 Larwill, IN
46864 Fort Wayne, IN
47174 Sulphur, IN
47274 Seymour, IN
47374 Richmond, IN
47574 Rome, IN
47874 Rosedale, IN
47974 Perrysville, IN
48084 Troy, MI
48184 Wayne, MI
48884 Sheridan, MI
49094 Union City, MI

49894 Wells, MI
50005 Albion, IA
50105 Gilbert, IA
50305 Des Moines, IA
50605 Aredale, IA
50705 Waterloo, IA
51015 Climbing Hill, IA
52225 Elberon, IA
52325 Parnell, IA
52625 Donellson, IA
53035 Iron Ridge, WI
53235 St. Francis, WI
53535 Edmund, WI
53735 Madison, WI
53935 Friesland, WI
54245 Valders, WI
54445 Lily, WI
54545 Manitowish Waters, WI
54645 Mt. Sterling, WI
54745 Holcombe, WI
54845 Hertel, WI
54945 Iola, WI
55055 Newport, MN
55355 Litchfield, MN
55455 Minneapolis, MN
55555 Young America, MN
55955 Mantorville, MN
56065 Mapleton, MN
56165 Reading, MN
56265 Montevideo, MN
56465 Merrifield, MN
56565 Nashua, MN
56665 Pitt, MN
57075 Wentworth, SD

ZIP CODES: **46264**
Indianapolis, IN.

z [. . .] z

57375	Stickney, SD	
57475	Tolstoy, SD	
57775	Quinn, SD	
58385	Wolford, ND	
58785	Surrey, ND	
60006	Arlington Heights, IL	
60106	Bensenville, IL	
60406	Blue Island, IL	
60506	Aurora, IL	
60606	Chicago, IL	
61016	Cherry Valley, IL	
61316	Cedar Point, IL	
61416	Bardolph, IL	
61516	Benson, IL	
61616	Peoria, IL	
61816	Broadlands, IL	
62326	Colchester, IL	
62426	Edgewood, IL	
62526	Decatur, IL	
62626	Carlinville, IL	
62726	Springfield, IL	
62926	Dongola, IL	
63036	French Village, MO	
63136	St. Louis, MO	
63336	Clarksville, MO	
63436	Center, MO	
63536	Downing, MO	
63636	Des Arc, MO	
63736	Benton, MO	
63936	Dudley, MO	
64146	Kansas City, MO	
64446	Fairfax, MO	
64646	Humphreys, MO	
64746	Freeman, MO	
65056	McKittrick, MO	

65256 Harrisburg, MO
65456 Davisville, MO
65556 Richland, MO
65656 Galena, MO
65756 Stotts City, MO
66066 Oskaloosa, KS
66266 Shawnee Mission, KS
66666 Topeka, KS (not in use)
66866 Peabody, KS
66966 Scandia, KS
67276 Wichita, KS
67476 Roxbury, KS
67576 St. John, KS
67676 Zurich, KS
67876 Spearville, KS
68586 Lincoln, NE
68786 Wausa, NE
70007 Metairie, LA
70107 New Orleans, LA
70307 Thibodaux, LA
70507 Lafayette, LA
70607 Lake Charles, LA
70707 Gonzales, LA
70807 Baton Rouge, LA
71117 Shreveport, LA
71417 Colfax, LA
72027 Center Ridge, AR
72127 Plumerville, AR
72227 Little Rock, AR
72327 Crawfordsville, AR
72427 Egypt, AR
72527 Desha, AR
72727 Elkins, AR
72827 Bluffton, AR

ZIP CODES: **70807**
Baton Rouge, LA.

z [. . .] z

72927 Booneville, AR
73137 Oklahoma City, OK
73437 Eldorado, OK
73737 Fairview, OK
73937 FELT OK!
74047 Mounds, OK
74147 Tulsa, OK
74347 Kansas, OK
74447 Okmulgee, OK
74547 Hartshorne, OK
74647 Newkirk, OK
74747 Kemp, OK
74947 Monroe, OK
75057 Lewisville, TX
75157 Rosser, TX
75257 Dallas, TX
75357 Dallas, TX
75457 Mt. Vernon, TX
75657 Jefferson, TX
75757 Bullard, TX
75957 Magnolia Springs, TX
76067 Mineral Wells, TX
76167 Fort Worth, TX
76267 Slidell, TX
76367 Iowa Park, TX
76467 Paluxy, TX
76567 Rockdale, TX
76667 Mexia, TX
76767 Waco, TX
76867 Pear Valley, TX
77077 Houston, TX
77177 Houston, TX
77277 Houston, TX
77377 Tomball, TX
77477 Stafford, TX

77577 Liverpool, TX
77977 Placedo, TX
78287 San Antonio, TX
78387 Sinton, TX
79097 White Deer, TX
79497 Lubbock, TX
79997 El Paso, TX
80208 Denver, CO
80308 Boulder, CO
80808 Calhan, CO
80908 Colorado Springs, CO
81418 Eckert, CO
82228 Node, WY
82428 Hyattville, WY
83238 Geneva, ID
83338 Jerome, ID
83438 Parker, ID
83538 Cottonwood, ID
83638 McCall, ID
83738 Boise, ID
84148 Salt Lake City, UT
84648 Nephi, UT
85058 Phoenix, AZ
85258 Scottsdale, AZ
85358 Wickenburg, AZ
87178 Albuquerque, NM
87578 Truchas, NM
89198 Las Vegas, NV
90009 Los Angeles, CA
90209 Beverly Hills, CA
90309 Inglewood, CA
90409 Santa Monica, CA
90509 Torrance, CA
90609 Whittier, CA
90809 Long Beach, CA

ZIP CODES: **75357**
Dallas, TX.

z [...] z

91319	Newbury Park, CA	**95059**	Santa Cruz, CA
91719	Corona, CA	**95159**	San Jose, CA
91819	Alhambra, CA	**95459**	Manchester, CA
92029	Escondido, CA	**95559**	Phillipsville, CA
92129	San Diego, CA	**95659**	Nicolaus, CA
92329	Phelan, CA	**95759**	Elk Grove, CA
92629	Dana Point, CA	**95859**	Sacramento, CA
93139	Santa Barbara, CA	**95959**	Nevada City, CA
93239	Kettleman City, CA	**96069**	Oak Run, CA
93339	Bakersfield, CA	**96269**	FPO: Chinhae,
93539	Lancaster, CA		Korea
93639	Madera, CA	**96769**	Makaweli, HI
93739	Fresno, CA	**97279**	Portland, OR
94149	San Francisco, CA	**97479**	Sutherlin, OR
94249	Sacramento, CA	**98189**	Seattle, WA
94549	Lafayette, CA	**98589**	Tenino, WA
94649	Oakland, CA	**99599**	Anchorage, AK
94949	Novato, CA		

Ziz. 1: wadi of trans-Atlas Morocco, 30°39'n/4°26'w **2:** Ascent of **Ziz,** a biblical mountain pass in southeastern Judah, according to BORGMANN.

ZmZ. ABBREVIATION for *Z mého Zivota* (Czech: *From My Life*), Smetana's String Quartet No. 1, revealing the happiest and saddest moments from his life.

ZNZ. Airport code for Zanzibar, Tanzania.

Zoo-nooz (ZOO-nooz). Monthly magazine published by the Zoological Society of San Diego, according to BORG-MANN.

Zoo-nooz

. . . **zotamorf.** See: *From A to Zotamorf.*

ZOZ. *Zie ommezijde* (Dutch: Please turn over to the other side of the page).

zyz. ABBREVIATION for *zyzzyva,* any of various tropical Amer-

z [. . .] z

ican weevils of the genus *Zyzzyva*, often destructive to plants; in most cases, the last word in the dictionary.

zz. 1: zigzag **2:** ginger (from Latin *zingiber*).

ZZ, ZZZ, ZZZZ, ZZZZZ . . . The sound of snoring, and a good place to end. Ralph DE SOLA's *Abbreviation Dictionary* gives **ZZZ** for Zayda, Zorayda, and Zorahayda, the three beautiful princesses in Washington Irving's *Alhambra*, a pleasant dream for starters, and the exceptionally well composed **ZZZ-ZZZ-ZZZ** for the standard sound of deep snoring in cartoons. BORGMANN gives **ZZZZZ** as the name of a wake-up service listed in a Los Angeles telephone directory of the mid-1960s. *Guinness* gives the **Zzzzzz** Coffee Shop in Gray's Inn Road, from the 1985 London telephone directory. **Wordrow** gratefully and sleepily accords all of the above at least a share of the last word, with De Sola winning this final honor on tie-break.

z [. . .] z

Additions or Corrections? We'd love to have your input for our next edition, which may be published in time to celebrate the year **2002.** So please write us *before then, say by 1999 or 2001 at the latest,* care of the address shown on the copyright page. Thank you. Till then, have a casual one.

P.S.: Or maybe there will be a '99 (special quasi-PALINDROME year) edition, so write sooner just in case. If we publish your original submission, we'll attribute it to your authorship (unless you request anonymity) and we'll send a certificate of your probable authorship to the address you specify. Thanks again. Bye.

All references to Tony AUGARDE and/or *The Oxford Book of Word Games* written and edited by him are copyright ©1984 by Oxford University Press and are used by permission of Oxford University Press.

All references to Dmitri A. BORGMANN are from his *Language on Vacation,* copyright ©1965 by him, except for those few indicated "1967," which are from his *Beyond Language,* copyright ©1967 by him, and all from both works are reprinted with the permission of Scribner, an imprint of Simon & Schuster, Inc.

All references credited to Stephen J. CHISM except where identified as contributions to the present work are reprinted with his permission from *From A to Zotamorf: The Dictionary of Palindromes,* copyright ©1992 by him and published by Word Ways Press, Morristown, New Jersey.

All references to Willard R. ESPY are from his *An Almanac of Words at Play,* copyright ©1975 by him, except for **"To last, Carter retracts a lot," "Roma summus amor," "Saippurakaruppias,"** and **"Mom—O no—MOM,"** which are from his *Another Almanac of Words at Play,* copyright ©1981 by him, both published by Clarkson N. Potter, and all are reprinted by permission of Harold Ober Associates Incorporated.

Also by Michael Donner: *How to Beat the SAT (and All Standardized Multiple-Choice Tests)*; *The Illustrated Encyclopedia of Crossword Words,* with Nort Bramesco; *Calculator Games for Kids*; *Bike, Skateboard and Scooter Games*; *A Way of Working,* with D. M. Dooling, P. L. Travers, et al.; *Games Magazine,* cofounder; *Joystick Magazine,* cofounder; Xiphydor Environmental Cleansing Chemical Technology, cocreator; Luxalba Institute for Human Affairs, cofounder.